# The Invention of Art

# The Invention of Art

A Cultural History

Larry Shiner

The University of Chicago Press
CHICAGO AND LONDON

The University of Chicago Press, Chicago 60637
The University of Chicago Press, Ltd., London

Printed in the United States of America

17 16 15 14 13 12 11 10 4 5 6 7
ISBN-13: 978-0-226-75342-3 (cloth)
ISBN-10: 0-226-75342-5 (cloth)
ISBN-13: 978-0-226-75343-0 (paper)
ISBN-10: 0-226-75343-3 (paper)

Library of Congress Cataloging-in-Publication Data

Shiner, L. E. (Larry E.), 1934–
The invention of art : a cultural history / Larry Shiner.
p. cm.
Includes bibliographical references and index.
ISBN 0-226-75342-5 (alk. paper)
1. Arts—History. 2. Arts—Philosophy. I. Title.
NX440 .S5 2001
700′.9—dc21 00-053247

⊗ The paper used in this publication meets the minimum requirements of the American National Standard for Information Sciences—Permanence of Paper for Printed Library Materials, ANSI Z39.48-1992.

*To the memory of my mother,*
*whose love of music, art, and literature*
*was the beginning of this book*

# Contents

# Illustrations

# Preface

IN THIS TIME of confusion over what art is and what its role ought to be, I have often wished I could recommend a brief history of the idea of art to students and friends. Not finding what I wanted, I wrote this one. Although it has a strong point of view, I believe that is the best way to throw contemporary issues into relief. I tell a story of art divided in the eighteenth century and our seeking in vain to overcome that division ever since. My aim in telling this story is not to produce a new theory of art but to put the question of art in a historical context that can help people make better sense of it. There are other stories that could be told, but I believe this one does justice to the evidence in a way that even readers who disagree with its perspective may find useful.

That perspective has been shaped by a series of experiences that go back to an incident that occurred many years ago. When I was about fifteen, my parents took us on a vacation trip from Kansas to Chicago to hear the Chicago Symphony and to visit the Art Institute and other museums. Although I was excited by the symphony and by paintings like Seurat's *La Grande Jatte* at the Art Institute, I was equally fascinated by another museum a few blocks away, the Field Museum of Natural History, with its endless cases full of African, Oceanic, and Native American artifacts: bowls and tools, shields and spears, chieftain's chairs and staffs, some scary-looking power figures, many masks, and costumes. A few years later, when I transferred to the Chicago area to complete my senior year of college, I went back to the Art Institute and discovered that some of those African figures and masks (minus the costumes) seemed to have miraculously migrated up the street from the Field Museum to enter the Art Institute. I didn't see any problem with their transformation into "art" until one day in an anthropology class Melville Herskovits pointed out that not only was there no category of "art" in most African languages, but, in addition, once masks and power figures were used in religious rituals, they were typically wrapped up and stored away until needed again. Suddenly, the very idea of "art" seemed problematic.

It wasn't until many years later that I discovered an important clue to understanding what happens when we turn ritual works into "art." I came across Paul Oskar Kristeller's article arguing that the modern concept of art only dates from the eighteenth century when an older functional idea of art was definitively split into the categories of fine art and craft. I now saw what had happened when those African masks escaped the dusty company of bowls and spears at the Field Museum to go live with the Rembrandts and Seurats at the Art Institute. In the Field Museum, African ritual and utilitarian objects were indeed art, but in the older sense of things made for a purpose, and so they served as exemplars of a way of life. Once transferred to the Art Institute they became (fine) art, or things meant for aesthetic looking: tokens of art itself.

One of the lessons I learned in my struggle to understand what happens when African or Native American ritual objects are transformed into art in the modern sense is that institutions such as the museum, the concert hall, and the literature curriculum have been central to constituting things as art. I soon came to the conclusion that we could no longer do either aesthetics or the history and criticism of music, art, and literature in traditional ways. I became something of a pest, constantly taking my fellow academics to task for not prefacing their eager praise of African or Native American or Chinese "art" with some sort of disclaimer. These colleagues were understandably irritated since they sincerely believed they were engaged in a worthy, even complimentary, pursuit and wanted to get on with their aesthetic appreciation and analysis. Although most of them were prepared to admit that the meaning of "art" might differ from culture to culture or that it had changed some in our own culture since the eighteenth century, they didn't view cultural and historical differences as having significant consequences in the way I did.

Meanwhile, something equally important had been taking place in the arts themselves. By the time I finished graduate school and settled into my first teaching job in the early 1960s, abstract expressionism was already being challenged by neodada and pop art. Over the next two decades, new art movements and approaches succeeded each other at a dizzying pace: pop, op, minimal, conceptual, neorealism, land art, video, performance, installation, and so on. Soon it seemed as if artists in every medium were trying to overthrow the boundaries of art and overcome the separation of "art" and "life." By the 1980s, when I began gathering material for this book, I realized that any history of the ideas of art, artist, and the aesthetic not only would have to give an important place to social and institutional changes but would also need to bring the story from the eighteenth century down to the present and pay particular attention to efforts to overcome the polarities of the modern fine art system.

Moreover, for such a history to be useful as a background source for students and general readers, it could not be based on one of the arts alone, or even the visual arts as a group, but it would need to include both literature and music as well. The book's usefulness also required that, despite covering so many topics and periods, it had to be brief and written in a nontechnical style. With those aims in mind, I have obviously had to sacrifice much in the way of qualifiers and nuances and keep footnotes and references to a minimum. Even so, I have used many quotations from artists and thinkers of the past to give something of the force and flavor of their views, and I have chosen illustrations that sometimes convey aspects of thought and behavior better than words would. I owe an enormous intellectual debt to the authors of articles, monographs, and surveys of the history of the various arts and aesthetics, only some of which are listed in the references. But there are also many particular debts I want to acknowledge specifically.

Present and former colleagues at the University of Illinois at Springfield have read parts of the manuscript or listened to its themes and offered valuable advice and encouragement: Harry Berman, Piotr Boltuc, Ed Cell, Cecilia Cornell, Razak Dahmane, Cullom Davis, Anne Devaney, Judy Everson, Mauri Formigoni, Ron Havens, Mark Heyman, Linda King, J. Michael Lennon, Ethan Lewis, Deborah McGregor, Robert McGregor, Christine Nelson, Margaret Rossiter, Marsha Salner, Karl Scroggin, Judy Shereikis, Richard Shereikis, Mark Siebert, Bill Siles, Larry Smith, Don Stanhope, and Charles B. Strozier. I am especially grateful to Peter Wenz, who read and commented on many chapters. I am also grateful to the many students in my philosophy of art and history of literary theory courses over the years who read and responded to versions of the manuscript. I thank friends from the Central Illinois Philosophy Group: George Agich, José Arce, Meredith Cargill, Bernd Estabrook, Royce Jones, Robert Kunath, and Richard Palmer. I am grateful to the many colleagues in the American Society for Aesthetics who have listened to and critiqued papers related to the book as it developed over the years and made a number of helpful suggestions: Sondra Bacharach, Joyce Brodsky, Anthony J. Cascardi, Ted Cohen, Arthur Danto, Mary Devereux, Dennis Dutton, Jo Ellen Jacobs, Michael Kelly, Carolyn Korsmeyer, Estella Lauter, Tom Leddy, Paul Mattick, Joan Pearlman, Yuriko Saito, Barbara Sandrisser, Gary Schapiro, Catherine Soussloff, Kevin Sweeney, and Mary Wiseman. Carolyn Korsmeyer also read several chapters and gave good advice as always. My special thanks to Micheline Guiton, Bill and Vivian Heywood, Shigeo and Louise Kanda, Mike and Donna Lennon, Thomas Mikelson and Patricia Sheppard, Bob and Nona Richardson, Richard and Judy Shereikis, Kevin Sweeney and Elizabeth Winston, and Étienne and Ann Trocmé for their patience, encouragement and suggestions over the years in many settings.

The book is richer because of three National Endowment for the Humanities Summer Seminars at which I worked on pieces of it. My thanks to my summer colleagues and to the seminar directors: Frances Ferguson and Ronald Paulson on eighteenth century art and aesthetics at Johns Hopkins, Jules Brody for the seminar on seventeenth-century French literature at Harvard, and particularly to Alvin Kernan, whose stimulating ideas and warm encouragement during his seminar on literature and society at Princeton meant a great deal. I am also grateful to the University of Illinois at Springfield for two sabbatical leaves that were crucial to the book's inception and completion and to Dean William Bloemer, Provost Wayne Penn, and Chancellor Naomi Lynn for their assistance and encouragement. Over the years I have incurred an enormous debt of gratitude to the staff of Brookens Library at the University of Illinois at Springfield, especially to Beverly Frailey, Denise Green, John Holz, Dick Kipp, Linda Kopecky, Mary Jane MacDonald, Nancy Stump, Ned Wass, and the late Florence Lewis. Other libraries and institutions that have been important are the one at the University of Illinois at Urbana-Champaign, in particular Nancy Romero of the Rare Book and Special Collections division, and the Bibliothèque National in Paris, especially the staff of the Cabinet des Estampes. I am also grateful to Kent Smith and Jan Wass of the Illinois State Museum in Springfield for their advice and encouragement. James Clifford and Hayden White were generous with their time and ideas during a sabbatical I spent at the University of California, Santa Cruz. I received valuable counsel from Annie Becq, now retired from the Université de Caen in France, whose history of French aesthetics remains indispensable. Robin Briggs of Oxford University and Martha Woodmansee of Case Western Reserve University also gave useful advice. At a crucial point in the late stages of gestation, an invitation from Christopher Breiseth and J. Michael Lennon to give a public lecture at Wilkes University helped me find the right voice for the audience I sought. I am grateful to Deborah Roese for her editorial reading, Margie Towery for the index, Lula Lester for the careful work on the reference section, and Julie Atwell for secretarial help. I also want to thank Doug Mitchell, Executive Editor at the University of Chicago Press, for his faith in the manuscript and his suggestions along the way, Robert Devens for his special help in preparing the manuscript and illustrations, and Yvonne Zipter for her many cogent editorial suggestions. I want to remember Gene Swenson, a friend of my youth in Topeka, Kansas, gone many years now, who first opened my eyes to the importance of pop art when we were both in the New York area in the late 1950s and who was one of the first critics to champion it. Recently, I had a chance to spend time with another classmate from Topeka, Dr. Douglas Sheafor, and his wife Bo, whose conversation around their glass kiln deepened my appreciation of the dignity and artistry of the craft arts. Finally, I thank my sisters Kay Klausmeier and Carol Wilson and their husbands for offering me shelter and encouragement during two sabbaticals and several summer writing stints. Special thanks to my daughter, Suzanna, for help with the illustrations and for solving computer conundrums and my son Larry for memorable meals along the way. But my deepest debt is to my wife, Catherine Walters, who put up with this paper rival for over ten years with uncommon generosity and patience and offered good advice as always.

# The Invention of Art

# Introduction

TODAY YOU can call virtually anything "art" and get away with it. One reason for the explosion in what counts as art is that the art world itself has taken up the old theme of getting "art" and "life" back together. Gestures of this kind have lurched between the innocent and the outrageous, from taking quilts into fine art museums or pulp fiction into literature courses, to playing street noises in symphony halls or undergoing plastic surgery on satellite video. The entry of so many eccentric artifacts, writings, noises, and performances into fine art has led some to talk darkly of a "death" of art, or literature, or classical music. Others, wrapped in the banner of postmodernism, agree that the modern fine art system is dead but invite us to dance on its grave in celebration of yet another liberation.

I am less interested in whether we ought to dance or weep than in understanding how we have come to this place. If we want to make sense of the explosion in what counts as art and the yearning to reunite art and life, we need to understand where the modern ideas and institutions of fine art came from. The modern system of art is not an essence or a fate but something we have made. Art as we have generally understood it is a European invention barely two hundred years old. It was preceded by a broader, more utilitarian system of art that lasted over two thousand years, and it is likely to be followed by a third system of the arts. What some critics fear or applaud as the death of art or literature or serious music may only be the end of a particular social institution constructed in the course of the eighteenth century.

Yet, like so much else that emerged from the Enlightenment, the European idea of fine art was believed to be universal, and European and American armies, missionaries, entrepreneurs, and intellectuals have been doing their best to make it so ever since. Scholars and critics ascribed it to the ancient Chinese and Egyptians, and once the European colonial grip was firmly established, Western artists and critics discovered that the conquered peoples of Africa, the Americas, and the Pacific had all along possessed something called "primitive art." This assimilation of the activities and artifacts of all peoples and

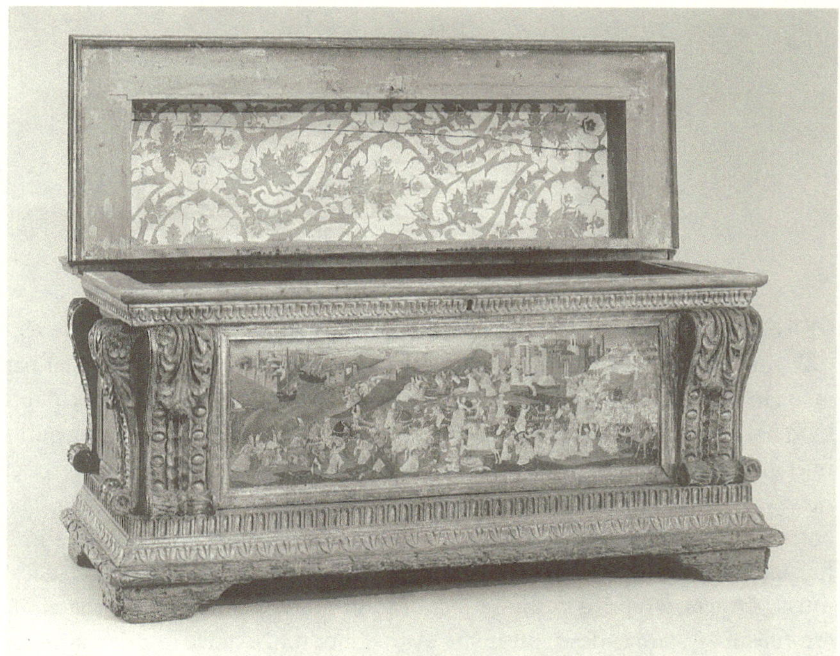

Figure 1. Florentine cassone with panel showing the conquest of Trebizond (fifteenth century), made by Marco de Buono Giamberti and Appollonio di Giovanni de Tomaso. Courtesy Metropolitan Museum of Art, John Steward Kennedy Fund, 1913. (14.39.) All Rights Reserved.

all past epochs to our notions has now been around for so long that the universality of the European idea of art is taken for granted.

Unfortunately, popular histories, museum displays, symphony programs, and literary anthologies encourage our natural bent to focus on whatever in the past seems most like the present and to pass over differences. For example, Renaissance paintings are almost always presented framed on museum walls or isolated on lecture hall screens or art book pages with little to remind us that almost all were originally made for a specific purpose and place—parts of altars or wedding chests, built into bedroom walls or council hall ceilings (fig. 1). Similarly, Shakespeare's plays were written not as fixed and timeless "works" to be read as masterpieces of literature but as changeable scripts for popular performance. Viewing Renaissance paintings in isolation, like reading Shakespeare's plays out of literature anthologies or listening to Bach passions in a symphony hall, reinforces the false impression that the people of the past shared our notion of art as a realm of autonomous works meant for aesthetic contemplation. Only by a deliberate effort can we break the trance induced by our culture and see that the category of fine art is a recent historical construction that could disappear in its turn.

## The Great Division

The illusion that the modern ideals and practices of art are universal and eternal or at least go back to ancient Greece or the Renaissance has been easier to swallow thanks to an ambiguity in the word "art" itself. The English word "art" is derived from the Latin *ars* and Greek *techne*, which meant any human skill whether horse breaking, verse writing, shoemaking, vase painting, or governing. The opposite of human art in that older way of thinking was not craft but nature. Some of the older sense of "art" lingers on in our use of the phrase "an art" for things such as medicine or cooking. But in the eighteenth century a fateful division occurred in the traditional concept of art. After over two thousand years of signifying any human activity performed with skill and grace, the concept of art was split apart, generating the new category fine arts (poetry, painting, sculpture, architecture, music) as opposed to crafts and popular arts (shoemaking, embroidery, storytelling, popular songs, etc.). The fine arts, it was now said, are a matter of inspiration and genius and meant to be enjoyed for themselves in moments of refined pleasure, whereas the crafts and popular arts require only skill and rules and are meant for mere use or entertainment. But this historic change of meaning became difficult to remember after nineteenth-century usage dropped the adjective "fine" and spoke only of art versus craft or art versus entertainment or art versus society. Today, when we ask, "Is it really art?" we no longer mean, "Is it a human rather than a natural product?" but "Does it belong in the prestigious category of (fine) art?"

What has been effaced in ordinary usage is not only the fracturing of the older idea of art/craft into art *versus* craft, but a parallel division that separated the artist from the craftsperson and aesthetic concerns from utility and ordinary pleasures. Before the eighteenth century, the terms "artist" and "artisan" were used interchangeably, and the word "artist" could be applied not only to painters and composers but also to shoemakers and wheelwrights, to alchemists and liberal arts students. There were neither artists nor artisans, in the modern meaning of those terms, but only the artisan/artists who constructed their poems and paintings, watches and boots according to a *techne* or *ars*, an art/craft. But by the end of the eighteenth century, "artist" and "artisan" had become opposites; "artist" now meant the creator of works of fine art whereas "artisan" or "craftsman" meant the mere maker of something useful or entertaining.

A third and equally fateful division occurred in the eighteenth century: pleasure in the arts was divided into a special, refined pleasure appropriate to the fine arts and the ordinary pleasures that we take in the useful or entertaining. The refined or contemplative pleasure came to be called by the new name "aesthetic." The older and broader view of art as construction was compatible with enjoyment in a functional context; the new idea of art as creation called for a contemplative attitude and a separation from context. M. H. Abrams has called this change a "Copernican revolution" in the concept of art: "In the course of a single century . . . the construction model . . . was replaced by the contemplation model, which treated the products of all the fine arts as . . . objects of rapt attention" (1989, 140). By the early nineteenth century the older idea of function in the arts was also divided, with the fine arts given a transcendent spiritual role of revealing higher truth or healing the soul. Heretofore, the idea of disinterested contemplation had been applied primarily to God; now art, for many of the cultured elite, was about to become a new arena of spiritual investment.

Because this conceptual revolution along with its related institutions still governs our cultural practices, it takes some effort to appreciate the depth of the rupture that had occurred. It was not merely the substitution of one definition of art for another, as if the word "art" designated a neutral and unchanging substrate, but the substitution of one entire system of concepts, practices, and institutions for another. In the older art system, the idea of art as any kind of object or performance for use or diversion went hand in hand with institutions that joined together what we separate as arts, crafts, and sciences. Instead of the modern art museum, for example, the sixteenth and seventeenth century had the "cabinet of curiosities," which displayed seashells, clocks, sculptures, and precious stones as a visual table of knowledge. Instead of separate concert halls, most music accompanied religious worship, political ceremony, or social recreation. Most artisan/artists worked on commissions from patrons whose contracts often specified content, form, and materials and envisaged a specific place and purpose for the finished piece. Even Leonardo da Vinci signed a contract for *Virgin of the Rocks* that specified the contents, the color of the Virgin's robe, the date of delivery, and a guarantee of repairs. Similarly, professional writers spent much of their time copying, note taking, and letter writing for their employers or churning out birthday poems, encomiums, and satirical attacks as required. Moreover, making art was usually a cooperative affair, with many minds and hands involved, whether in painting frescoes (Raphael), in the multiple authorship of theater productions (Shakespeare), or in the free borrowing of melodies and harmonies among composers (Bach). How different the dominant norms of the modern system of (fine) art are, where the ideal is not inventive collaboration but individual creation, where works are seldom meant for a specific place or purpose but exist for themselves, where the separation of art works from a functional context leads to the ideal of silent and reverential attention in concert halls, art museums, theaters, and reading rooms.

But the new system of fine arts not only was tied to behaviors and institutions, it was also part of more general relations of power and gender. The key factor in splitting apart the old art system was the replacement of patronage by an art market and a middle-class art public. When Friedrich Schiller and other eighteenth-century German writers championed the new ideas of the self-contained work of art and the need for a special aesthetic response to it, they were specifically reacting to their own frustrations with the art market and the new public. Of course, a central belief of the modern system of art has always been that money and class are irrelevant to the creation and appreciation of art. But to elevate some genres to the spiritual status of fine art and their producers to heroic creators while relegating other genres to the status of mere utility and their producers to fabricators is more than a conceptual transformation. And when the genres and activities chosen for elevation and those chosen for demotion reinforce race, class, and gender lines, what once looked like a purely conceptual change begins to look like an underwriting of power relations as well. If women's needlework has been rescued from the dungeon of "domestic art" to enter the main floor of our art museums, it is partly because pressure from the women's movement finally overcame a long-standing gender bias of the fine art system. So long as the modern system of art remains the established norm, feminist insistence on getting women into art institutions is certainly the order of the day. Yet women should not be satisfied with just getting "into" art but should recognize that fine art assumptions themselves have been gendered from the beginning and need to be fundamentally reshaped. Similarly, the multiculturalist movement is right to want the genres and works of excluded minorities to enter the literary, art, and music curricula, yet the very success of this effort could end up reinforcing the imperial claims of the Euro-American system of the fine arts unless we critique its underlying divisions. Instead of simply assimilating the arts of traditional African or Native American cultures to European norms in the patronizing belief that we pay them a compliment, we need to learn from their very different understanding of the arts and their place in society.

Although the modern system of fine arts has dominated European and American culture since the early nineteenth century, some artists and critics have resisted its basic polarities of art versus craft, artist versus artisan, aesthetic versus purpose. In later chapters I will explore a few instances of this resistance since one task of history is to give voice to those possibilities and ideals defeated, marginalized, or forgotten. For example, people like Hogarth, Rousseau, and Wollstonecraft rejected the splitting apart of artist and artisan and of the aesthetic and instrumental even as these divisions were taking place, and equally radical challenges came from Emerson, Ruskin, and Morris, who struck at the underlying art-versus-craft and art-versus-life dichotomies. Then there have been the twentieth-century mockers, doubters, and ironists of art, from the dadaists and Duchamp, to the leading figures of pop and conceptual art. Despite this long tradition of resistance, the works of most of the resisters and apostates from the norms of fine art have been quickly absorbed back into the Church of Art and are now ensconced in the very art museums and literary and musical canons they meant to mock. But even as the fine art world was recapturing acts of resistance, it was also expanding its own limits, first by assimilating new types of art, such as photography, film, or jazz, then by appropriating works of "primitive" and folk art, and finally by seemingly dissolving its own boundaries completely by embracing everything from self-mutilation to the noises of John Cage.

Despite all these assimilations, the modern system of art has retained its most general features even in the gestures and writings of those who challenge it. When critics like Rosalind Krauss expose the "myth of the avant-garde" or artists like Sherrie Levine exhibit photographic copies of Walker Evans's works as a parody of "originality," they pay tribute to the norms of the modern system of art even as they challenge them. One reason I emphasize that art is not just an "idea" but is, instead, a system of ideals, practices, and institutions is to show that much of the current rhetoric about the death of art or literature or serious music—whether alarmist or celebratory—underestimates the staying power of the established art system.

So far, I have not touched on what may be the most important dimension of art: feeling. To talk of art as a "system of concepts, practices, and institutions" hardly does justice to the powerful emotions people experience through literature, music, dance, theater, film, painting, sculpture, and architecture. Art is not just a set of concepts and institutions but also something people believe in, a source of comfort, an object of love. To those who love art, my claim that the idea of fine art is a recent and parochial construction, marked by class and gender interests, will seem part of a hostile conspiracy to undermine one of our highest values. In the acrimonious debates over literary theory during recent decades, traditionalists have often accused their opponents of "hostility to literature." A few years ago, one prominent literary theorist beat his breast in public, declaring that he no longer taught his students literary theory but the love of literature (Lentricchia 1996). The traditionalists' and the repentents' anger at skeptical theories and histories is understandable. If one loves literature, why try to expose its questionable paternity? As an artist friend of mine exclaimed after I described the thesis of this book one day, "Don't do it! Don't we artists have enough trouble already?" I confess that I too am a lover of the arts. But one need not belong to the party of "hostility" to literature, art, or music to explore the historical roots of one's beliefs as a prelude to rethinking existing ideals and institutions.

My history of art's fateful division asks: What would the story of the ideas and institutions of the fine arts look like if we no longer wrote it as the inevitable triumph of Art over craft, Artist over artisan, Aesthetic over function and ordinary pleasure? What if we wrote our history from a perspective more sympathetic to a system of art that tried to hold together imagination and skill, pleasure and use, freedom and service? From that vantage point, the construction of the modern system of art would look less like a great liberation than a fracture we have been trying to heal ever since.

Part I, "Before Fine Art and Craft," explores some striking cases from the more than two-thousand-year period when "art" still meant human making or performance of any kind dedicated to a purpose and when the distinction between artist and artisan was not yet normative. I argue against the widely held belief that the Renaissance established the modern ideals of art, artist, and aesthetic and show, that despite important steps in that direction, the older system that united art and craft, artisan and artist was still the norm in both Michelangelo's Italy and Shakespeare's England. Part II, "Art Divided," describes the great fracture in the older system of art that occurred in the course of the eighteenth century, finally severing fine art from craft, artist from artisan, the aesthetic from the instrumental and establishing such institutions as the art museum, the secular concert, and copyright. These central chapters also explore the social, economic, and gender aspects of that rupture. Part III, "Counter Currents," looks at three cases of resistance to a disinterested aesthetic (Hogarth, Rousseau, and Wollstonecraft) and then examines the audacious attempts of the French Revolution to revitalize the old system of art for a purpose only to end up accelerating the arrival of the new system of art for itself. Part IV, "The Apotheosis of Art," completes the story of the construction of the fine art system by showing how the nineteenth century raised Art to the level of the highest values, made the artist's vocation a unique spiritual calling, and spread the institutions of fine art over Europe and the Americas, inculcating the proper aesthetic behavior along the way. Yet there have also been many new arts added to the category of fine art over the past 150 years, even as there have been many new forms of resistance to it. Part V, "Beyond Fine Art and Craft," examines a few examples of these expansions and challenges, in the late nineteenth and early twentieth centuries, to show how the modern system of art has been able to assimilate both new arts (photography) and new forms of resistance (arts and crafts, Russian constructivism) without altering its basic polarities. The final chapter of part V looks at some twentieth-century examples of the continuing force of the fine art–versus-craft division and its use to assimilate new areas of the arts by division (primitive art), as well as some of the vigorous signs of resistance (community-based art). Together the processes of assimilation and resistance have seriously undermined the polarities of the fine art system, raising the question of whether we are moving toward a third system of art.

For the sake of clarity in exposition, most chapters are organized around three central concepts and their allied institutions: the category of art, the ideal of the artist, and the experience of the aesthetic. Although it is possible to understand the later chapters of the book by beginning with part II, the chapters of part I provide insights into the world that was lost in the great division and can help us understand why some people have been trying to overcome the separation of art and craft, art and life ever since. Those interested in the difficulties created by the multiple meanings of words like "art," "craft," "artist," "artisan," and "aesthetic," or wonder why I use "system" of art rather than the more familiar "art world," or how there could be a "revolution" rather than merely an evolution in the concept of art may wish to read the next section before proceeding.

## Words and Institutions

This book was inspired by Paul Oskar Kristeller's essays of fifty years ago showing that the category of fine art did not exist before the eighteenth century ([1950] 1990). Although some recent surveys in the history of the arts now give a passing nod to Kristeller's thesis, I have long felt that students and general readers could benefit from a brief account that integrated the history of the idea of fine art and the aesthetic with social and institutional changes, expanded it to include the concept of the artist, and brought the whole down to the present, showing its relevance to current debates.[1] Since I began this project over a decade ago, several others have also begun to flesh out Kristeller's description by connecting the concept of art to practices, institutions, and social changes (Becq 1994a; Woodmansee 1994; Mortensen 1997). In writing a cultural rather than a purely intellectual history, I have tried to capture this wider social and institutional component by combining the idea that certain concepts and ideals "regulate" artistic practice with the notion that artistic practices and institutions form a social "subsystem" (Kernan 1989; Goehr 1992). Regulative concepts and ideals of art and social systems of art are reciprocal: concepts and ideals cannot exist without a system of practices and institutions (composing and symphony orchestras, collecting and art museums, canons and copyright) any more than the institutions can function without a network of normative concepts and ideals (artist and work, creation and masterpiece).[2] I thought of calling this book a "social history of ideas" but that might have suggested its theme was the social determination of ideas rather than the mutual dependence of ideals and social changes. I have chosen the more general term "cultural history" since it suggests a meeting of the social and intellectual, the point of intersection for which I take to be the art institutions established in the eighteenth century. The important role of institutions in mediating between ideas and general social and economic forces is further examined in the overview to part II, "Art Divided."

I have chosen "system of art" over the more familiar "art world" because an art system has a larger scope that includes the various art worlds and subworlds of literature, music, dance, theater, film, and visual arts. Art worlds are networks of artists, critics, audiences, and others who share a common field of interest along with a commitment to certain values, practices, and institutions. An art system embraces the underlying concepts and ideals shared by various art worlds and by the culture at large, including those who only participate marginally in one of the art worlds. For example, the ideal of the "artist" in the modern system of fine art has many common features (freedom, imagination, originality), which underlie the specific ideals of the author and the composer in literature and music, respectively. Obviously, there has been much historical variation in the interpretation of such norms, but some assumptions and practices are sufficiently general to permit a contrast between an older system of art and the modern system of fine arts.[3] I use the term "modern" in "modern system of art" simply as a marker to contrast the "old" system of art with the "new" system of (fine) art and do not intend thereby any claim about when the "modern era" as a whole began or whether we are now living in a "postmodern" era. The "eighteenth century" designates the center of a period stretching from around 1680 to 1830, during which time the various elements that make up the modern system of art came together and were consolidated.

Of course, the linguistic, intellectual, and institutional evidence for a decisive turn in the course of the long eighteenth century does not form itself into a neat array of facts marching in lockstep to a magical date when the modern system of art became regulative. The transformation in each of the component concepts of fine art and the emergence of new art institutions varied in timing, as well as by geography and by genre. The prestige and role of the poet, for example, had a very different development from that of the painter, and the separation of imaginative literature from literature in general did not coincide perfectly with the split of the visual arts into fine art versus craft. It is also clear that painting, sculpture, and architecture and their makers achieved "liberal arts" status in Italy well before they did in the rest of Europe, and in Florence before the rest of Italy, and that the term "aesthetic" was regulative in German discourse on art decades before it was the norm in France or England.

In ordinary usage, the term "art" can designate either the visual arts alone or the fine arts as a group; I include all genres of fine art, although I will focus on painting, literature, music, architecture, theater, and photography. But how should we mark the difference between the older, broader understanding of "art" and the narrower modern sense of (fine) "art"? Given the ambiguity of the simple word "art" in the lower case, the two senses are often held apart by capitalization: art in general versus Art. But capitalization creates its own problems. Consider the opening paragraph of one of the most widely read popular histories of the visual arts, E. H. Gombrich's *The Story of Art:*

> There really is no such thing as Art. There are only artists. Once these were men who took colored earth and roughed out the forms of a bison on the wall of a cave. . . . There is no harm in calling all these activities art as long as we keep in mind that such a word may mean very different things in different times and places, and as long as we realize that Art with a capital A has no existence. For Art with a capital A has come to be something of a bogey and a fetish. (1984, 4)

Yet Gombrich, no more than the rest of us, can escape the fact that the capital "A" of fine art nearly always lurks within the small "a" of art in our twentieth-century usage. Nor can we escape the modern idea of fine art by saying "there is no such thing as Art . . . only artists" since the modern concept of the artist as independent creator was itself part of the establishment of the fine art–versus-craft polarity in the eighteenth century.

The drawback of a strategy like Gombrich's is that the resulting histories often conceal the sharp differences that separate the old system of art from the modern system of (fine) art. Since I want to write the history of those differences and foreground the very break that most histories of literature, music, and art pass over as quickly as possible, I have adopted three terminological expedients: I will usually contrast an "older" system of art to the "modern" system of art, or for shorthand, "art" and "fine art," and sometimes even "art" and "Art." Obviously, none of these pairs is completely satisfactory since the word "art" today, although it usually conveys the meanings associated with "fine art," still bears the sedimented weight of older meanings.

Similar problems attach to the term "craft." It is sometimes said that the older, broader idea of art was closer to our concept of craft than to the modern idea of fine art. Yet we must not forget that the old system of art/craft also included many ideals that were split off in the eighteenth century and ascribed exclusively to fine art and the artist. For example, after the eighteenth-century break, all the nobler aspects of the older image of the artisan/artist, such as grace, invention, and imagination, were ascribed solely to the artist, whereas the artisan or craftsperson was said to possess only skill, to work by rule, and to care primarily for money. Thus, while it is true that the traditional idea of art was closer to craft than to our idea of fine art, that is partly because the older idea of art contained characteristics of both fine art and craft. Moreover, "craft," like "art," has both wider and more specific meanings. In its more specific sense, "craft" refers not only to skill and technique (the craft of the novel) but also to categories of objects and practices of varied status, for example, studio crafts (ceramics), building crafts (carpentry), home crafts (sewing), and hobby crafts (papier-mâché). Yet in its widest sense, which I will use, "craft" also serves as a general marker for the opposite of fine art, embracing such overlapping categories as applied art, minor art, folk art, popular art, commercial art, and entertainment arts. Once the modern system of fine arts was firmly in place in the nineteenth century and "art" had come to designate an autonomous realm within society, the art-versus-craft polarity was absorbed into the more general polarities of art versus society or art versus life. The latter polarities emphasize art's autonomy and, like the art-versus-craft pair that they incorporate, suggest fine art's independence from the purposes and pleasures of everyday life.

The terms "craftsman," "artisan," and "artist" also have a complex history. In order to respect the rules for gender neutrality, I often use "craftsperson" rather than "craftsman," but not rigidly. William Morris spoke eloquently of the term "handicraftsman" as conveying a dignity and honor absent from "artisan." Rather than pairing the cumbersome "craftsperson" with "artist," I have generally preferred "artisan" despite its modern associations with ordinary labor, especially in British usage. Under the old system of art, of course, there were neither artisans nor artists in the current meaning of those terms but artisan/artists who united qualities that were only definitively pulled apart in the eighteenth century.

By foregrounding the break that split art into fine art versus craft and artisan/artist into artist versus artisan, I believe I can offer a clearer view of what was gained and lost in the "Copernican revolution" of the eighteenth century. But such cultural revolutions seldom occur out of the blue, and a favorite employment of historians is to search out signs, portents, and origins. But emphasizing anticipations of modern ideals and practices leaves the nonspecialist reader with the impression that modern ideas of literature, art, or serious music are the outcome of a destined development. My survey is designed to avoid such comforting implications by refusing to treat the modern system of art as the outcome of an inevitable evolution and to see it instead as the result of an eighteenth-century invention.

By invention, I do not mean that the modern system of art appeared all at once as if cooked up by a handful of philosophes one afternoon in the salon of Madame du Deffand. To insist that there was a break between the premodern system of art and the modern system of fine art is not to deny the existence of continuities, especially since the elements of both fine art and craft were united under the old system. One can indeed find singular aspects of the modern ideals of fine art, the artist, and the aesthetic scattered among ancient Greek writers, Renaissance painters, and seventeenth-century philosophers, but those ideas only coalesced into a regulative discourse and institutional system at the end of the eighteenth century. As Roger Chartier has remarked, gradual development does not preclude radical disjunctures: "The passage from one system . . . to another can be understood at the same time as a profound break . . . and as a process made of hesitations, steps backward and obstacles" (1988, 36; see also Burke 1997).[4]

The modern system of art resulted from the conjunction of many factors, some of general scope and gradual development, others more restricted and immediate, some primarily intellectual and cultural, others social, political, and economic. That conjunction was gradual, uneven, and contested, but this much is certain: prior to the eighteenth century neither the modern ideas of fine art, artist, and aesthetic nor the set of practices and institutions we associate with them were integrated into a normative system, whereas after the eighteenth century, the major conceptual polarities and institutions of the modern system of art were largely taken for granted and have been regulative ever since. Only after the modern system of art was established as an autonomous realm could one ask, "Is it really art?" or, "What is the relation of 'art' to 'society'?" Obviously, the ideas and practices of the fine arts have continued to evolve, but the art system established in the course of the eighteenth century has remained the framework within which most of those changes have taken place.

In a book that challenges the universalist claims of the European system of fine art, a comparison with the art practices and conceptions of China, Japan,

India, and Africa would have been useful. In the past, few popular surveys with titles like "Japanese Art" or "Chinese Art" have bothered to discuss the profound differences between those cultures' basic assumptions about the arts and the mainstream assumptions of Europe and the Americas. Yet the Japanese language had no collective noun for "art" in our sense until the nineteenth century, and as Craig Clunas points out, the phrase "Chinese Art" is a "quite recent invention . . . no one in China before the nineteenth century" grouped painting, sculpture, ceramics, and calligraphy together as objects "constituting part of the same field of inquiry" (1997, 9). No doubt China and Japan, like most cultures, had a notion of "art" in the older and broader sense, and since our term "aesthetic" can also be used generically for any sort of theory or attitude about beauty one can legitimately speak of Japanese or Indian "aesthetics" (Saito 1998). But we should not be too quick to collapse those rich and complex traditions into European notions of fine art and the aesthetic. To sort out the actual similarities between the specifically European and the varied Asian concepts and practices would require another book. In a later chapter, I briefly discuss some of the distortions and paradoxes that have resulted from trying to assimilate the so-called primitive or tribal arts of traditional African or Native American cultures into the polarized European system. But before we can adequately understand the art ideals and institutions of other cultures, we need a better understanding of the particularity of Western concepts, practices, and institutions.

By focusing my essay on the discontinuities between the old European system of art and the more recent system of fine art, I believe I have told a story more faithful to the evidence and more illuminating for the present than traditional narratives of continuity and inevitability.[5] It is up to those who believe in the universality or the ancient origins of the ideals and institutions of fine art to do the same and a few are now attempting it (Marino 1996). In a book intended for the general reader it would be out of place to debate scholars who defend an essentialist or continuity view, but it may be helpful to offer a brief comparison of my approach with Arthur Danto's recent *After the End of Art* (1997), which makes a strong case for the story of an inevitable emergence.

Although Danto writes as a philosopher not a historian, he audaciously combines an essentialist's conviction that "art is eternally the same" with a historicist's conviction that the essence of art has gradually revealed itself through history (95). One of the surprises in Danto's story is that he does not consider the aesthetic to be part of art's essence but merely a contingent (and mistaken) view arising in the eighteenth century. Yet Danto as an essentialist is equally convinced that the art-versus-craft polarity *is* eternal and universal, although he grants that Western culture did not become fully aware of the essential difference between fine art and craft until after the Renaissance (114).

Danto can even admit that there was an eighteenth-century "revolution" in the concept of art, but he is equally convinced that "there must be some extrahistorical concept of art for there to be historical revolutions in" (187). Reduced to its barest outline, Danto's historical scenario is this: art and craft are eternally separate, yet were not originally distinguished but were united under the concept of imitation. When people first became conscious of their essential difference in the eighteenth century, they not only treated fine art as a higher form of imitation but also primarily (and erroneously) separated it from craft in terms of the aesthetic. Yet art continued to be viewed as imitation until the advent of modernism, after which artists themselves embarked on a quest for the essence of art that ended in 1965 when pop and conceptual art proved that there was no "right" way for art to look. Art had finally revealed its true nature: something that makes a statement and self-consciously embodies it. After the revelation that the essence of art is "embodied meaning," the true form of the art-versus-craft polarity was also apparent: embodied meaning versus mere utility and genius versus mere skill.

I agree with Danto that there was a concept of art prior to the eighteenth century "for their to be revolutions in," but it was art in the older sense that united meaning with use and genius with skill. Whereas my history tries to put together many contingent factors (intellectual, institutional, social), Danto looks beyond such contingencies to follow the destined emergence of the essence of art through the internal history of the visual arts. For Danto, the essence of art was always going to be what it has become and now that the essence is revealed, its historical phase is over: art no longer has a "narrative direction" (2000, 430). This is the meaning of Danto's controversial phrase "the end of art," which, provocative as it sounds, simply means the end of the art's own quest for its essence. For me, the question of whether there might be a third system of art, beyond both the older system, to which we cannot return, and the modern system, which many are struggling to overcome, is a question that is both possible and urgent.[6]

PART I

# BEFORE FINE ART AND CRAFT

## Overview

IT IS COMFORTING to think that people in the past were "just like us" and to treat Homer's *Iliad,* Michelangelo's Sistine ceiling, or Bach's *St. Matthew Passion* as if they were art in the modern sense. The next few chapters will show how misleading this practice can be—even though it is often reinforced by popular surveys and anthologies. Although I want to expose the bias of modernizing narratives and displays, I also want to do justice to the aspect of truth they contain. What is true in them is that one can indeed find scattered similarities in the past for the modern ideals and practices of fine art. What is false is to let these reassuring familiarities blind us to the enormous differences and create the illusion that the modern idea of art has always been with us. Obviously, the past leads to the present by many small steps, but there are points at which gradual changes finally coalesce to produce a rapid shift over a couple of generations. The issue is not whether we can find comments of Plato or gestures of Donatello that sound modern but, rather, how and when an older system of art/craft—an integrated complex of ideals, practices, and institutions—was replaced by a new system of fine art *versus* craft.

To show how decisive the break of the eighteenth century was, the following chapters will focus on the radical differences between our assumptions and the dominant conception and organization of the arts from ancient Greece to the mid-seventeenth century. Chapters 1 and 2 show that for over two thousand years Western culture had no word or concept of fine art, viewed the artisan/artist as a maker rather than creator, and generally treated statues, poems, and musical works as serving particular purposes rather than as existing primarily for themselves. There was neither fine art nor craft in the ancient world or the

Middle Ages but only arts, just as there were neither "artists" nor "artisans" but only artisan/artists who gave equal honor to skill and imagination, tradition and invention. Nor was there was as sharp a break between the Middle Ages and the Renaissance as once believed. In chapter 3, I explore some early signs of the modern idea of fine art in the Renaissance such as the rise in the status and image of painters and sculptors or the new emphasis on the ideal of the permanent literary "work." But I also show that the arts and their makers in the Renaissance still operated within a patronage/commission system that destined most things for particular audiences, places, or functions, whether the paintings of Raphael or the plays of Shakespeare. The sixteenth century did see the beginning of several new practices (artist's biographies, self-portraits), some new institutions (art academies), and some hints at new relations of production (a few collectors and art markets), yet the older way of conceiving and organizing the arts remained dominant. Chapter 4 explores the crucial period of transition toward the modern system of art in the seventeenth century. Although the status of painters and sculptors was still debated in most of Europe during the seventeenth century, a new prestige was conferred on writers by the monarchist states, and something like the modern category of literature began to emerge. At the same time, the rise of science and the further development of a market economy were undermining the intellectual and social basis of the old system of art, rendering the liberal arts/mechanical arts scheme obsolete and giving the idea of taste a larger role in the experience of the arts. Although the old system of art was beginning to break up, seventeenth-century societies still managed to hold together art and craft, artist and artisan, pleasure and purpose. We cannot resurrect the old system of art—it was tied to a hierarchical society of orders that will never return—but we might still have something to learn from it.

CHAPTER 1

# The Greeks Had No Word for It

FOR MOST of us, going to a performance of *Antigone* is an "art" experience like going to the symphony or ballet on a Saturday night. But when the ancient Athenians first witnessed *Antigone,* they did so as part of a religious-political festival, the annual "City Dionysia." Citizens received the price of a ticket from their township council and sat with their respective political "tribes" as they did at civic assemblies held in the same amphitheater. The priests of Dionysus, who performed sacrifices at an altar on the floor of the great amphitheater, sat in specially carved seats in the front row (fig. 2). The five-day festival opened with a great religious procession and ceremonies honoring the war dead, introducing war orphans raised at state expense, and recognizing Athen's allies and their tribute money. Only then did the contests begin, featuring nine tragedies, three satyr plays, five comedies, and twenty choral hymns to Dionysus. The Roman theater was equally embedded in a religious-political context, and plays often accompanied civic games as "adjuncts to ceremonies that honored the gods and expressed communal solidarity and elation"(Gruen 1992, 221). In such contexts, as Winkler and Zeitlin say of Greek drama, "it seems wrong even to call them plays in the modern sense of the word" (1990, 4). It would be equally wrong to call them "fine art" in the modern sense.

## Art, *techne, ars*

In fact, the ancient Greeks, who had precise distinctions for so many things, had no word for what we call fine art. The word we often translate as "art" was *techne* which, like the Roman *ars,* included many things we would call "craft." *Techne/ars* embraced things as diverse as carpentry and poetry, shoemaking and medicine, sculpture and horse breaking. In fact, *techne* and *ars* referred less to a class of objects than to the human ability to make and perform. Even so, generations of philosophers and historians have claimed that Greek and Roman society embraced a concept of fine art like ours even if they lacked the word. Yet the issue is not about the presence or absence of a word but about the

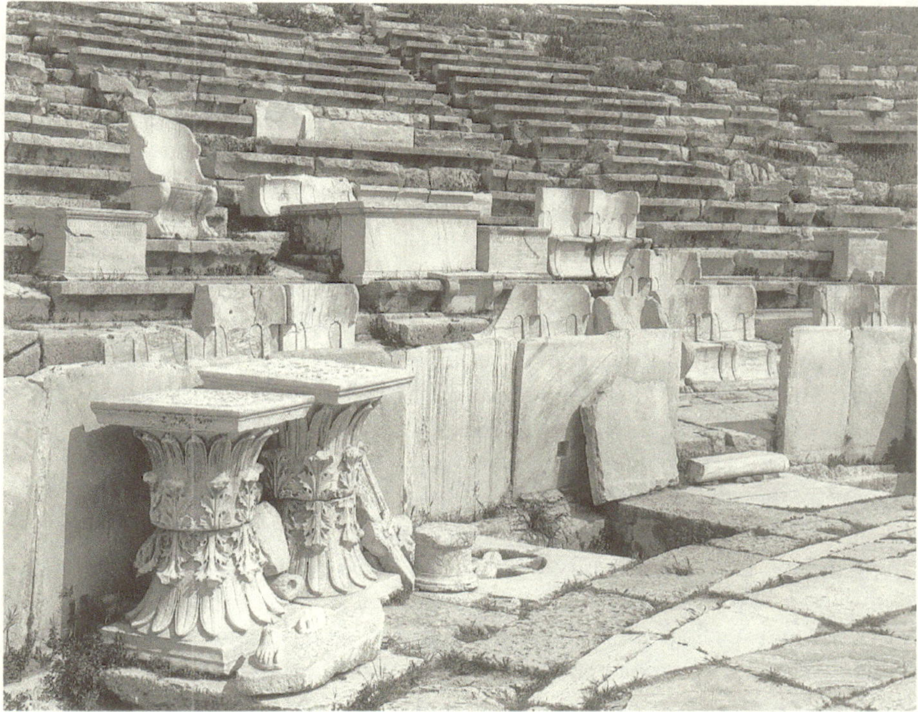

Figure 2. View of benches, Theater of Dionysus, Athens. Courtesy Alinari/Art Resource, New York.

interpretation of a body of evidence, and I believe there is massive evidence that the ancient Greeks and Romans had no category of fine art. Even the scattered statements or practices that seem similar to our own often turn out to have a different meaning when examined in context. However comforting the quest for precedents and origins, we have far more to learn from the profound differences between ancient attitudes and our own.

Since many philosophers and historians persist in anachronistically talking of Plato's or Aristotle's idea of fine art, we might begin by noting that neither Plato nor Aristotle—nor Greek society generally—treated painting, sculpture, architecture, poetry, and music as belonging to a single, distinct category. Of course, there were many attempts to conceptually organize the human arts into subgroups, but none of them corresponded to our modern division into fine art versus craft (Tatarkiewicz 1970). The ancient practice, always cited as foreshadowing our idea of fine art, is the treatment of painting, epic, and tragedy as arts of imitation *(mimesis)*. But in identifying a common property of imitation for some arts, Plato and Aristotle did not spin them off as a fixed group; "mimetic arts" in Aristotle does not equal "fine arts" in the modern sense. For Aristotle, what painting and tragedy have in common as imitations does not separate them in their *procedures* from arts like shoemaking or medicine. As offensive as it may be to our postromantic sensibilities, Aristotle believed that the artisan/artist takes a particular raw material (human character/leather) and uses a particular set of ideas and procedures (plot/shoe form) to produce a product (tragedy/shoes). As J. J. Pollitt puts it, "In the mimetic arts the final forms, it is true, are images as well as objects, and this fact distinguishes them as a particular group; but Aristotle nowhere indicates that he thought of their modus operandi as different from that of other arts. . . . If he had felt that there was a special group of fine arts, it seems likely that Aristotle would have said so in a straightforward manner" (1974, 98). Although Plato's famous attack on imitation in book 10 of the *Republic* treats poetry and painting together as imitative arts, Plato elsewhere classifies sophistry, magic tricks, and the miming of animal voices as imitative arts as well. Of course, neither Plato nor Aristotle simply equated everything that was the product of human art *(techne),* as if tragedies were situated no higher than farm tools or statues were no better than sandals (Roochnik 1996). But a hierarchy is not a polarity. After reviewing the arguments of scholars who keep trying to find a theory of fine art in Plato, Eric Havelock concluded that they do so "in defiance of the fact that neither 'art' nor 'artist,' *as we use the words,* is translatable into archaic or high-classical Greek" (1963, 33).[1]

If our modern category of fine art had no equivalent in the ancient world, neither did such components of it as "literature" or "music." Although in late antiquity the term *litteratura* could occasionally be used to refer to a body of writings, "literature" certainly did not have the modern sense of a canon of creative writing. Rather, it connoted grammar or written learning in general. Erich Auerbach has argued that in imperial Rome there was a distinct "literary" or "high" language spoken and written by the small stratum of educated classes who were also the principal reciters/readers of texts. Yet those texts included not only poetry but also legal and ceremonial writings, and if the speakers and writers of this "High Latin" were often preoccupied with style, their cultivated "literary" writing was much broader than modern notions of a special realm of imaginative literature (Auerbach 1993).

Among the ancients the closest equivalent to our idea of literature was the category of poetry. Certainly, poetry held a much higher rank than any of the visual arts, partly because it was associated with upper-class education. As a result, ancient ideas of poetry do more closely resemble ours. Scholars who stress the continuities between ancient and modern views of poetry have a number of favorite texts, such as Aristotle's *Poetics,* which distinguished tragic poetry as the imitation of an action from versified science and contrasted the universality of poetry with the particularity of history. But we should not exaggerate the parallel between Aristotle's distinctions and our own. The verb form for poetizing *(poein),* for example, means simply "to make" with none of our overtones of romantic creativity.

The only general classification of the arts in the ancient world that significantly resembled modern ideas was the late Hellenistic and Roman division of the arts into the liberal and vulgar (or "servile"). The vulgar arts were those that involved physical labor and/or payment, whereas the liberal or free arts were intellectual and appropriate to the highborn and educated. Although the category of free arts was not a rigid one, the core included the verbal arts of grammar, rhetoric, and dialectic and the mathematical arts of arithmetic, geometry, astronomy, and music. Poetry was generally treated as a subdivision of grammar or rhetoric and music was included because of its educational function and its mathematical nature, as expounded by the Pythagorean tradition of the harmony of octave, soul, and cosmos. Yet the "music" envisaged as a liberal art was primarily the *science* of music, which explored theories of harmony; the skill of singing or playing an instrument was only considered a liberal art when it was part of upper-class education or recreation. Singing and playing at banquets for pay was part of the vulgar arts (Shapiro 1992). Some writers in antiquity added other arts to the core of seven, most frequently medicine, agriculture, mechanics, navigation, and gymnastics, although occasionally architecture or painting were added as well. More often, these additional arts were placed in a third category of "mixed arts," seen as combining liberal and servile elements. Thus, the liberal arts schemes of antiquity generally grouped poetry with grammar and rhetoric, music (theory) with mathematics and astronomy, and either consigned the visual arts and musical practice to the "servile" realm or joined them with things like agriculture and navigation as intermediate arts (Whitney 1990).

## The Artisan/Artist

If we turn to the ancient view of the "artist," we find that it was much closer to our idea of the craftsperson than to modern ideals of independence and originality. In painting and sculpture, as in carpentry and sailing, the Greek or Roman artisan/artist had to combine an intellectual grasp of principles with practical understanding, skill, and grace. In the ancient world, calling an activity "an art" carried the kind of prestige that calling something "a science" does today. Hence, there were numerous treatises on the question, "Is X an art?" Writers from Hippocrates to Cicero distinguished between productive arts, like shipbuilding or sculpture, where a maker could guarantee a satisfactory product, and performance arts like medicine or rhetoric, where both knowledge and outcome were less certain. But these treatises did not develop a distinction between fine art and craft in our sense (Roochnik 1996).

Aristotle's influential contrast of productive art (*techne*) and ethical wisdom *(phronesis)* exaggerated the calculating rationality of the artisan/artist with unfortunate effects on later theories of craft. In the *Nicomachean Ethics*, for example, Aristotle defined productive *techne* as the "trained ability of making something under the guidance of rational thought" (1140.9–10). Yet the general meaning of *techne* for Greek culture was not so narrowly rationalist or "technical" as Aristotle's formula suggests but included a dimension of spontaneous tact. This wider sense of *techne* as involving supple understanding had a parallel in the Greek notion of *metis*, the "cunning intelligence" of the hunter or of Homer's Odysseus.[2] The ancient practitioners of various arts from medicine and military strategy to pottery making and poetry were neither "artisans" nor "artists" in the modern sense but artisan/artists: skilled and tactful practitioners.

What is strikingly absent in the ancient Greek view of the artisan/artist is our modern emphasis on imagination, originality, and autonomy. In a general way, imagination and innovation were appreciated as part of the craftsmanship of commissioned production for a purpose, but not in their emphatic modern sense.[3] Although the achievements of Greek naturalism in painting and sculpture of the fifth and fourth centuries B.C.E. were much admired, for the most part painters and sculptors were still viewed as manual workers, and Plutarch said that no talented young aristocrat upon seeing and admiring the famous Zeus of Phidias would want to *be* Phidias (Burford 1972, 12). The broader Greek population did not always share this aristocratic disdain for artisan/artists and later on the status of (dead) Greek sculptors and painters was very high in some Roman circles, although what most ancients admired in sculptors and painters was their skill in producing convincing likenesses. Despite passages in Pliny or Cicero that show a greater respect for painters and sculptors, there remained a strong aristocratic prejudice against all manual production or performance for pay no matter how intelligent, skilled, or inspired it might be.

Of course, the preceding remarks about the somewhat low status of the makers of paintings or sculptures do not apply to the makers of speeches or poetry. The concept and figure of the poet was a complex one and went through many permutations in the course of the nearly eight hundred years that separate Homer from Plutarch (Nagy 1989). At the beginning of this period, the notions of poet and prophet were not yet fully distinguished, although even when the two became separate, poets continued to receive commissions for festival hymns or victory odes (Pindar). Some philosophers and literary theorists have claimed that Plato's statement in the *Ion* that poetry is not rational production but irrational inspiration (not meant as a compliment) shows that the Greeks made an implicit distinction between a fine art of inspired genius and a mere craft of rules. This claim not only projects a modern depreciation of craft skill onto the past but also overlooks the fact that the formulas for invoking the Muses summon the divinities as much to infuse the writer with information, wisdom, and effective technique as with what we call inspiration (Gentili 1988). Late Greek and Roman allusions to the freedom of the poet should not be read as claims to independence or "romantic conceptions of creative imagination" (Halliwell 1989, 153). Nor should the revival of the Roman figure of the *vates* (priest-poet) by Virgil and Horace be seen through the haze of romantic ideas; Virgil and Horace used the *vates* notion in part to cover their role as patronized writers, in part as a stand-in for the idea of talent as the complement of technique. Yet technique *(ars)* remained absolutely central; Horace's *Art of Poetry* codified for subsequent centuries the doctrines of unity and appropriateness (decorum) and the need to polish incessantly.

In fact, the typical Roman writer of poetry was either an aristocratic amateur or a dependent who lived from patronage and rarely had complete freedom to chose themes or styles (Gold 1982). Roman patrons generally "expected poets, like house philosophers, to keep them company and provide distraction" (Fantham 1996, 78). Some poets provided distinguished distraction indeed, and Augustus's patronage manager, Maecenas, knew how to foster gratitude in writers like Virgil and Horace whose celebrations of the Emperor were tastefully indirect. Clearly, the figure of the poet stood far above that of the painters and sculptors who worked with their hands, yet the poet was also a figure quite different in both conception and practice from modern notions of the artist.[4]

## Beauty and Function

If the Greeks and Romans did not have our categories of fine art or the artist, did they perhaps look upon sculpture, poetry, or music with the kind of contemplative detachment we call aesthetic? There are two reasons to think not. First, most of the things we classify as Greek or Roman fine art were thoroughly embedded in social, political, religious, and practical contexts, such as the competitive performance of tragedies at the Athenian festival to Dionysius. The Panathenaia festival, for example, included not only processions and rituals accompanied by music but also competitive recitations from Homer's epics and athletic contests for which the prizes were finely decorated jars of olive oil. A special feature of the Panathenaia was the presentation to Athena of a peplos woven by selected upper-class girls, a rectangular cloth, probably draped around a statue's shoulders, which depicted Athena leading the Olympians to victory over the giants (Neils 1992). Roman epic and lyric poetry were also tied to social contexts as a means of communication, persuasion, instruction, or recreation. The *Aeneid* was memorized and recited primarily not as a work of imaginative fine art in our sense but was used to teach correct grammar and fine style, to inculcate examples of civic virtue, and to show one's membership in the "educated" classes. Similarly, "music," in its broad ancient meaning (which included drama and the dance), was not something to listen to in a silent, aesthetic frame of mind but something to march to, to drink to, and, above all, to sing and play as an aid in memorization, communication, and religious ritual.

Apart from the many social functions of the Greek arts, a second reason there was little of the modern "aesthetic" attitude is that most Greeks and Romans admired sculptures or poetic recitals as they would have admired well-made political speeches—for their union of moral use with felicitous execution. As Martha Nussbaum puts it, "Poetry, visual art and music were all taken to have an ethical role, in virtue of their form as well as in virtue of their content" (1996, 1:175). The most famous example is Plato's argument in *The Republic* against certain meters in poetry and certain rhythms in music because of their effects on the soul. When Aristotle in the *Poetics* spoke of the pleasure derived from represented suffering he might seem to come closer to modern notions of the aesthetic. Yet Aristotle's focus was on the way tragedy combined pleasure with edification, and his famous comment about pity and fear leading to a catharsis seems to mean not only purgation and purification but also, above all, a "clarification," a clearing of the soul and deepening of moral understanding (Nussbaum 1986). Halliwell concludes simply that Aristotle had "no doctrine of an autonomous aesthetic pleasure" (1989, 162).

The visual arts were even more firmly embedded in functional contexts. Architecture, according to Vitruvius, depends equally on solidity, utility, and beauty. As for sculpture and painting, most of what we contemplate in our museums today were things of everyday or cult use: storage jars, drinking cups, votive statuary, funerary markers, parts of temples, fragments of house decoration. Even the free-standing statuary of ancient Greece that we contemplate aesthetically was made not to be admired as fine art but to serve various religious, political, and social purposes (Barber 1990; Spivey 1996). John Boardman bluntly says of Greek attitudes toward the visual arts before the Hellenistic period: "'Art for Art's sake' was virtually an unknown concept; there was neither a real Art Market nor Collectors; all art had a function and artists were suppliers of a commodity on a par with shoemakers" (1996, 16).

But what about beauty? The idea of beauty in the ancient world usually combined what our aesthetic theories have typically separated. "Beauty" *(kalon)* was a general term of commendation that applied to mind and character, customs and political systems as much as to form or physical appearance. Both the Greek *kalon* and the Latin *pulchrum* were often used simply to mean "morally good." Despite the emergence of a somewhat narrower idea of beauty as sensuous appearance among the Sophists, the broader sense of beauty remained dominant.[5] At the end of antiquity, Plotinus, and later Augustine, who did include sculpture, architecture, and music in their discussions of beauty, still placed these arts far below moral, intellectual, and spiritual beauty. Even in Plotinus's influential treatise we are far from any notion of a set of fine arts united by a common internal principle and as sharply opposed to the crafts. Nor does Plotinus recommend a disinterested contemplation of art works as ends in themselves.[6] Although the ancients were "confronted with excellent works of art and quite susceptible to their charm, [they] were neither able nor eager to detach the aesthetic quality of these works of art from their intellectual, moral, religious and practical functioning or content, or to use such an aesthetic quality for grouping the fine arts together" (Kristeller 1990, 174).

But in the long Hellentistic period from the death of Alexander in 323 B.C.E. to the beginning of the Roman Empire with Augustus's victory of 31 B.C.E., there is evidence that attitudes and behaviors more like ours began to appear among the upper classes and here and there even survived the triumph of Christianity. Some Alexandrine writers like Callimachus, for example, focused on poetic technique to the exclusion of moral purpose. And one can cite the claim of the Roman aristocrat Ovid (hoping to reverse Augustus's decree of banishment) that poetry aims only at innocent pleasures. Quite apart from the fact that the pleasure alluded to here is not likely to have been the specifically disinterested pleasure of modern aesthetic theory, the views of writers like Callimachus and Ovid were hardly the norm. Instead, the mixture of "instruct and please" *(prodesse . . . delectare)* or "use and delight" *(utile dulci)* of Horace's *Art of Poetry* remained the more typical attitude and was handed on to the Middle Ages and the Renaissance.

There were also some striking anticipations of modern ideas and practices with respect to the visual arts. When Roman armies had finished plundering statuary and gold vessels from Greece, many prominent Romans began collecting and ordering copies of Greek works. Some historians have argued that this collecting and the art and antiquities market it produced, along with the Roman copying of statues or paintings by well-known Greek artisan/artists, implies that such works were now enjoyed for themselves as fine art.[7] The Emperor Hadrian, for example, was a passionate admirer and collector of Greek sculpture and an inspired patron of architecture, as the Tivoli gardens and the Pantheon attest. And one can certainly find in Cicero, Pliny, and other writers comments about painting and sculpture that have a modern ring. Yet much of the collecting and copying that occurred at this time had more to do with enrichment and prestige than with an interest in art for itself. And even in the late Hellenistic and Roman imperial era a good deal of Roman visual art was still produced as sociopolitical cult imagery, and the emergent mystery religions also subordinated images to religious purposes (Elsner 1995). The official recognition of Christianity in the fourth century and the subsequent destruction of the Roman Empire further reinforced the functionality of poetry, music, and visual images so that Europe would require another fifteen hundred years before the modern system of fine art and the aesthetic could be established.

CHAPTER 2

# Aquinas's Saw

IN THE MEDIEVAL period, many arts that the modern world has relegated to the status of crafts were as admired as painting or sculpture. Medieval and early Renaissance embroiderers, for example, produced works of astonishing pictorial and decorative accomplishment, using silk and metal threads, jewels, pearls, and beaten gold (fig. 3). Nor were embroiderers merely skilled laborers who sewed the designs of others; Henry III's commission to the respected embroiderer Mabel of Bury St. Edmunds asked for the Virgin and Saint John but left the design up to her (Parker 1984). Medieval people made no division like ours between fine arts and "mere" crafts. Lists of the arts from Augustine in the fifth century to Aquinas in the thirteenth mixed painting, sculpture, and architecture with cooking, navigation, horsemanship, shoemaking, and juggling.

## From "Servile" to "Mechanical" Arts

Early Medieval writers did continue the late Greco-Roman division of the arts into "liberal" versus the "vulgar" or "servile" and, for educational purposes, divided the liberal arts into the trivium (logic, grammar, rhetoric) and quadrivium (arithmetic, geometry, astronomy, and music theory). As Elspeth Whitney has shown, by the twelfth century an incisive change occurred in the way of conceiving the traditional opposition between the "liberal" and "vulgar" arts (1990). Hugh of St. Victor made an influential argument for replacing the pejorative terms "vulgar" or "servile" with the term "mechanical arts," claiming that since there were seven liberal arts there should be seven mechanical arts. In the ancient world, mechanics had been a discipline of applied mathematics for moving heavy objects, but by the ninth century, its meaning had broadened to include all the manual arts. Of itself, the new name and the parallel with the liberal arts gave the mechanical arts greater dignity, but Hugh went much further, making the mechanical arts an equal partner with the theoretical arts (philosophy, physics) and practical arts (politics, ethics) in the restoration of fallen humanity. Just as the theoretical arts were given by God as a remedy for our igno-

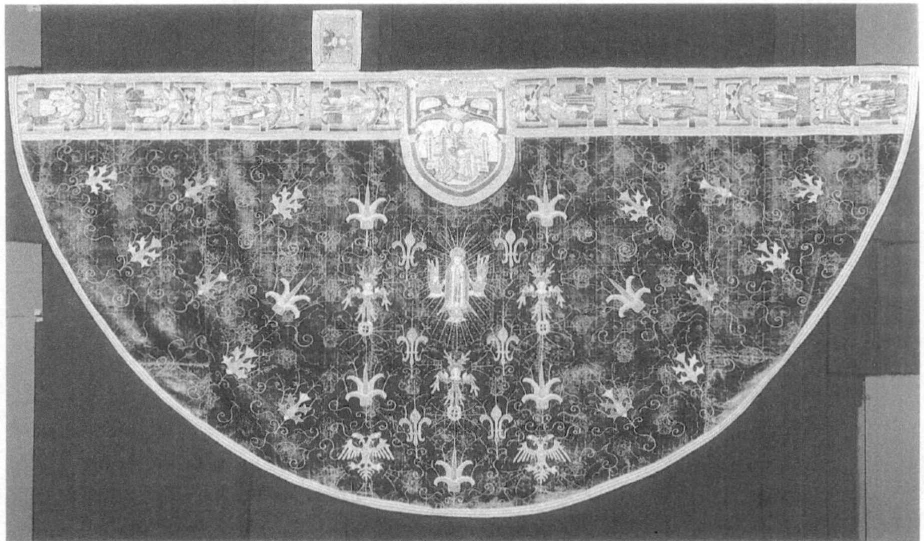

Figure 3. British cope (late fifteenth century): silk, broken-warp chevron twill weave-cut voided velvet; appliquéd with linen, plain weave; couching; embroidered with silk and gilt-strip-wrapped silk and satin and split stitches; laid work, couching and padded couching; spangles, 114 × 291.1 centimeters. Grace R. Smith Textile Endowment, 1971.312a. Photograph © 2000, Art Institute Chicago. All Rights Reserved.

rance and the practical arts as a remedy for our vices, according to Hugh, so the mechanical arts remedy our physical weakness.

> Now there are three works—the work of God, the work of nature, and the work of the artificer, who imitates nature. The work of God is to create . . . the work of nature is to bring forth into actuality . . . the work of the artificer is to put together things disjoined. Man alone is brought forth naked and unarmed . . . man's reason shines forth much more brilliantly in inventing things than . . . had man naturally possessed them. From this the infinite varieties of painting, weaving, carving, and founding have arisen, so that we look with wonder not at nature alone but at the artificer as well. (Whitney 1990, 91)

Hugh's seven mechanical arts—weaving, armament, commerce, agriculture, hunting, medicine, and theatrics—were actually general categories with many subdivisions.[1] Architecture was mentioned as a subdivision of *armatura* or "constructed coverings," and "theatrics" included entertainments of any kind, including wrestling, racing, and dances (table 1). By the end of the twelfth century, the term "mechanical arts" had become standard in the West, although Hugh's particular list was often modified.

Yet Hugh's attempt to give the mechanical arts a higher status was soon challenged by the arrival of Arabic philosophy and the complete corpus of

TABLE 1
Medieval Classifications of the Arts

| | Disciplines |
|---|---|
| Liberal arts (vs. "servile arts"): | |
| Trivium | Grammar, rhetoric, logic |
| Quadrivium | Arithmetic, geometry, astronomy, music |
| Mechanical arts (Hugh of St. Victor) | Weaving, armament,* commerce, agriculture, hunting, medicine, theatrics† |

* Includes arms, forging, architecture, and so on.
† Includes wrestling, racing, dances, epic recitals, puppet plays, and so forth.

Aristotle's preserved writings. Thomas Aquinas, for example, accepted Aristotle's disjuncture between the theoretical sciences and the productive arts, as well as Aristotle's tendency to look upon utility and paid work as degrading. As a result, Aquinas could write that "those arts that are ordered to some utility through performing an action are called mechanical, or servile" (Whitney 1990, 140). Thus, already in the thirteenth century, the "Victorine moment," when all arts/crafts were granted a place of dignity, was challenged by a powerful resurgence of the ancient depreciation of utility and handwork as "vulgar" and "servile." Even so, many medieval writers continued to respect all the arts, embroidery as well as painting, pottery as well as sculpture, forging as well as architecture and, like Hugh of St. Victor, gave them a place of dignity in the scheme of creation and the system of knowledge.

## Artificers

In the medieval period, the term *artista* was usually reserved for those who studied the liberal arts, whereas a person engaged in the production or performance of one of the many mechanical arts was often called an *artifex.* Even terms that are more specific, such as "painter," "sculptor," and "architect," did not have the sense they do today. The medieval painter was primarily a "decorative" artificer, covering the walls of churches, public buildings, and the houses of the wealthy and painting furniture, banners, shields, and signs on commission. There were seldom any separate guilds for the individual arts; painters often belonged to the druggists guild (since they ground their own pigments), sculptors to the goldsmiths guild, and architects to the stone masons guild, although there is evidence some architects had a more gentlemanly status.[2] Most medieval artificers, whether stone carvers, ceramists, or painters, worked for patrons who often specified content, general design, and materials. Further, the medieval artificer generally responded to commissions not as an individual but, rather, as a member of a workshop in which various aspects of the job were shared out. Yet even though artificers often held the lower status associated with manual labor, most of the mechanical arts required intelligent planning, imaginative conception, and sound judgment, as well as manual dexterity. But the artificer, as Bonaventura said, was a maker, not a creator. God creates nature out of nothing, nature in turn brings potential being to actuality; the artificer simply modifies what nature has made actual. This attitude remained the norm in the medieval period despite occasional hints at something more modern (Eco 1986).

Yet the desire to project our modern ideals onto the past dies hard. For several decades now, historians of medieval art have been attacking the old stereotype of the anonymous medieval artisan. According to a popular myth, the sculptors and stained-glass makers of the great cathedrals worked only for the glory of God and never signed their works. Thanks to a massive sleuthing job, medieval specialists have uncovered a number of signatures and evidence that many carvers and painters developed regional reputations. Although this work is a welcome corrective, some interpreters have jumped to the conclusion that it is evidence of "individualism" and the modern idea of the "artist." Such a conclusion is only possible if one ignores the workshop context of most production, the central role of the patron and client, and the fact that the pride expressed by the signature was more likely to have been in craft skill and innovation than in something akin to modern notions of creativity and originality. But the revisionists are right to reject the idea that the medieval sculptor or painter was a "mere" craftsman who simply followed pattern books and workshop routines. Both the wielders of the old stereotype of anonymity and the modernizing revisionists are trapped in the same binary polarities of the modern system of art. The medieval artisan/artist was neither the anonymous craftsman of the romantics nor the modern individualist of the revisionists.[3]

Just as there was no invidious categorical division of artist from artisan in the Middle Ages, there was no sharp gender division in the production of the arts. Few trades or arts were practiced exclusively by either men or women. One reason was that a good deal of production came from religious orders. Fine illuminated manuscripts and elaborate embroidery as well as religious poetry and musical settings issued from both female and male religious houses. As for secular production, women painted, wove, carved and stitched alongside men in the family workshops. This is not to suggest some idyllic equality since women were discriminated against in law, status, and pay as much then as later. But there was not yet the general separation of public and private that contributed to the domestication of women in later centuries. Not only were medieval women master shoemakers, bakers, armorers, goldsmiths, painters, and embroiderers, but they also often belonged to guilds, usually through their husbands but sometimes on their own *(femmes soles)*. Widowed craftswomen had the right to continue the family workshop and to train apprentices. In some places women came to dominate certain crafts (silk making in Paris), and a few women became successful entrepreneurs, handling the work of others.

If the modern notion of the artist has little relevance to the medieval practice of painting, sculpture, architecture, ceramics, embroidery, and the other visual arts, it is equally far from the dominant practice of poetry in the Middle Ages. The Middle Ages is an enormously long and complex period, and this is especially true with respect to language and literature, which saw a split between Latin as the only written language, known primarily to the clergy, and the many vernaculars that only gradually came to assume a written form. Poetry as learned in the schools was a necessary part of mastering Latin for those who wished to be a *clericus* or *litteras*. To be a poet in the Middle Ages was more often associated with sweat than inspiration. And the motive for mastering Latin versification, when it went beyond preparing for examinations was often to enable one to "turn out compliments, epitaphs, petitions, dedications and thus gain favor with the powerful or correspond with equals" (Curtius 1953, 468). Of course, the scholar-poets complained of the need to earn a living by seeking service to a patron or locating a benefice, and the ancient commonplace about poetic frenzy was dutifully handed on and would bear fruit in the Renaissance. Although the vernacular troubadour-sung poetry of southern France was much freer than the poetics taught in the schools, it would be anachronistic to speak of it in terms of romantic conceptions of originality, nor was the troubadour tradition normative for the general idea of poetry. By the end of the thirteenth century, the first great work of vernacular poetry appeared: Dante's *Divine Comedy*, which opened the way for the more self-consciously "literary" writings of Petrarch and Boccaccio. Yet the art of rhetoric still provided the framework within which these writers made such inventive use of forms and tropes. Like the sculptor or painter, the medieval poet was neither the modern literary artist preoccupied with originality and self-expression nor the mere craftsman applying scholastic rules (Auerbach 1993).

Our notion of the musician as artist-composer is also as distant from medieval conceptions and practices as modern ideas of the poet. As a liberal art, of course, music was a theoretical science concerning general ideas of cosmic harmony and mathematical relations. Although some of the preceptors in the cathedral schools became well known, and their hymns and settings for parts of the mass were circulated, there was little hesitation about altering and improving them in the process. In music, as in the realm of poetry and prose, women composers in religious houses were as productive and respected as those of men, as the recent revival of the remarkable musical compositions of Hildegard of Bingen reminds us. In secular music, the general distinction between the liberal and mechanical also held sway. The highborn enjoyed singing and might accompany themselves on an instrument for private pleasure, but they also had court entertainers, the jongleurs, that loose category of jugglers, acrobats, dancers, animal trainers, singers, and instrumentalists who provided diversion. Because these employed musicians composed and played for pay, they belonged to the mechanical arts and, vis-à-vis the nobility, had the same lowly status as hired poets, painters, or tailors. Such musical servants often went on the road seeking employment in other aristocratic or merchant households, and many settled down as town musicians, where duties might include watchman and sounding the hours as well as playing for weddings, funerals, and other ceremonial occasions. Thus, the higher status medieval musician was a pure theoretician, an aristocratic amateur, or a church or court official, including the leading composer/performers, whereas most "professional" musicians were regarded as part of the mass of artisan/artists working with their hands for pay. Instead of the self-conscious modern composer creating independent musical "works of art," the majority of musicians were composer-performers whose music was meant to accompany social and religious life (Raynor 1978).

When we put together all the evidence about stone carvers, glassblowers, embroiderers, architects, poets, religious, and secular musicians, it is clear that despite isolated cases, both the modern concept of "the artist" and its polar opposite, the "mere artisan," are concepts deeply inappropriate to this disparate group. In the long medieval period, which blends seamlessly into the early Renaissance, there were neither "artists" nor "artisans" but artisan/artists of varied ranks and statuses.

## The Idea of Beauty

Medieval thinking was also as far removed from modern conceptions of the aesthetic as it was from modern ideas of art and the artist. This does not mean that medieval people were blind to the beauty of line, shape, or color or that they found no pleasure in harmony, rhyme, or trope but only that appearance was not systematically separated from content and function. Poetry, for example, was still conceived to have the dual function of instruction and pleasure (Horace) and one of the main justifications for allowing images in Western churches was their didactic function. Music was still primarily devised to accompany texts, and even secular music was largely tied to social function.

As for the idea of beauty, many medieval philosophers and theologians reflected on it, but most discussions of beauty dwelt on the beauty of God and Nature, not the beauty of the products and performances of human art. As in antiquity, the term "beauty" had a much wider meaning than it does today, embracing moral value and utility along with pleasing appearance. Among those theologians who did discuss the beauty of mundane things, the harmony of parts or proportion within an object was not enough to make it beautiful; only right proportion in relation to purpose could do that. "Stained glass, music, and sculpture were not beautiful simply because they gave pleasure. They might give pleasure, or they might give instruction; but in either case, the medievals took the view that their true beauty lay in their conformity with their purpose" (Eco 1988, 183).

Nevertheless, well-meaning historians eager to rescue the Middle Ages from enlightened opprobrium have reinterpreted theological texts against their obvious meaning, looking everywhere for signs of a "secular" aesthetic attitude. But to read the modern idea of aesthetic disinterest into passing comments of Scotus Erigena or into the creation of gargoyles or Romanesque capitals is as false to the general outlook of the Middle Ages as is the stereotype of a relentless religious functionalism.[4] This constant search for signs of a purely aesthetic response reveals the stultifying restriction produced by the modern art-versus-craft polarity. As David Freedberg has shown, historians under its spell tend to dismiss those pieces designed to arouse an immediate emotional response as craft or religious kitsch (1989). It seems more plausible to suggest that in the Middle Ages there was neither fine art nor craft in the modern sense but only arts and that people responded to function, content, and form together rather than holding one or the other in suspension.

If an artificer, Aquinas said, should decide to make a saw more beautiful by constructing it out of glass, the result would not only be useless as a saw and thus a failed piece of art, it would not be beautiful either (*Summa Theologica* I–II, 57, 3c). Today, of course, making a saw out of glass would guarantee it to be a work of art, perhaps exhibited under the title *Aquinas's Saw.* And no doubt this glass saw would inspire an equally clever artist, in imitation of Duchamp, to purchase an ordinary saw at the nearest hardware and offer it as a counterexhibit, perhaps as *Occam's Saw.*

CHAPTER 3

# Michelangelo and Shakespeare

## *Art on the Rise*

ON APRIL 25, 1483, Leonardo da Vinci signed a contract with the Confraternity of the Conception of the Virgin in Milan to "deliver by December 8" an altar painting with "mountains and rocks" in the background and "Our Lady in the middle . . . her upper garments of ultramarine blue, brocaded with Gold" and to repair any degradation that might occur (Glasser 1977, 164–69). The requirements to which Leonardo submitted for *Virgin of the Rocks* hardly fit our idea of the artist's total autonomy (fig. 4). But what happened next fits our modern assumptions even less. Leonardo was only one of at least three people working on the altarpiece, as we learn from court records that show he and the other painter sued because the carver of the wooden framework for the altar, Giacomo del Maino, was being paid more than they were. They finally got 1,000 ducats to his 700 (Kemp 1997). Giacomo was not the only Renaissance carver to be paid more than painters for the kind of ornate frameworks, with arches, pinnacles, and sculpted figures, that surrounded pictures.[1] We are so used to thinking of paintings as autonomous art objects and painters as lone creators that it comes as a shock to learn that the typical Renaissance painter was simply one member of the teams that decorated altarpieces, council chambers, townhouses, and palaces.

### Opening up the Liberal Arts

Even so, the period between roughly 1350 and 1600 that we call the Renaissance also saw the beginnings of a long and gradual transition from the old art/craft system toward our modern fine art system. But the beginning of a transition is not an establishment; the assumptions of the old art system continued to regulate most practices despite the appearance of new ideas and attitudes among a small elite. Unfortunately, popularizers and historians preoccupied with the quest for "origins" have treated this elite as typical and presented what were important but fragmentary beginnings as if they were normative. As a result, we

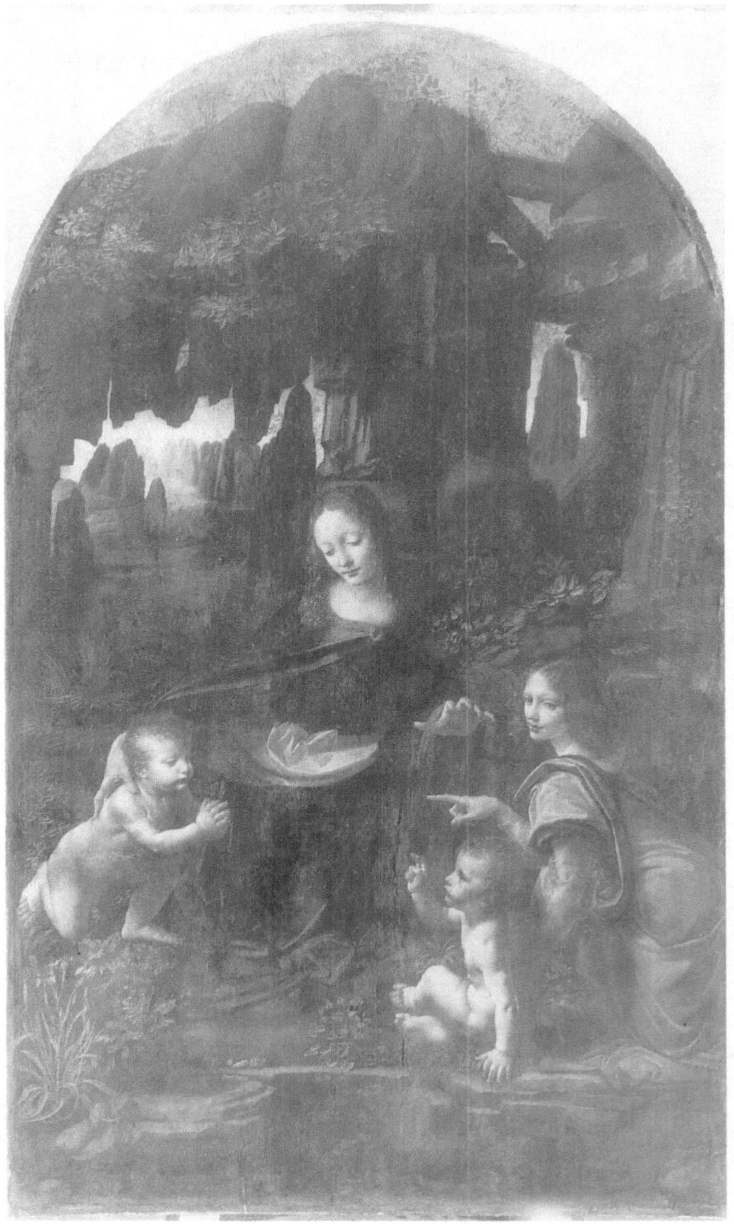

Figure 4. Leonardo da Vinci, *Virgin of the Rocks* (1483). Courtesy Réunion des Musées Nationaux, Paris. Believed to be the picture painted in response to the contract of 1483 even though it lacks the gold brocade that the contract called for on the blue robe. Now in the Louvre.

have become so accustomed to viewing Renaissance paintings as isolated works of art or reading Elizabethan plays as autonomous works of literature that we are surprised to discover that the Renaissance did not even possess the category of fine art.

Certainly, painting, sculpture, and architecture, along with their makers, achieved a higher prestige than in the Middle Ages, and some people explored the kinship between the visual and verbal arts. But the three visual arts were not joined with poetry and music to form a distinct new category under a general title. Down through most of the seventeenth century, leading scholars still adhered to the liberal versus mechanical arts scheme, associating poetry with grammar and rhetoric, music theory with geometry and astronomy, among the liberal arts, and placing painting and sculpture among the mechanical arts, along with cloth making, metalwork, and agriculture. The humanist teachers did create a new pedagogical grouping, called the *studia humanitatis,* by expanding the old medieval trivium of grammar, rhetoric, and logic. They kept grammar and rhetoric, replaced logic with poetry, and added history and moral philosophy. But in general the Renaissance had "no real equivalent of our 'Fine Art'" (Kemp 1997, 226; see also Kristeller 1990; Farago 1991) (table 2).

TABLE 2
The Liberal Arts and the *Studia Humanitatis* in the Renaissance

| | Disciplines |
|---|---|
| Liberal arts: | |
| Trivium | Grammar, rhetoric, logic |
| Quadrivium | Arithmetic, geometry, astronomy, music |
| *Studia humanitatis* | Grammar, rhetoric, poetry, history, moral philosophy |

Although the modern category of fine art had not yet arrived, there were some significant steps in the modern direction. Horace's phrase, "poetry is like painting" *(ut pictura poesis),* for example, was used by a number of painters and humanist scholars to justify making painting one of the liberal arts, and an aristocratic dialogue like *The Courtier* could praise painting as worthy of a gentleman's attention (Castiglione 1959; Lee 1967). On the institutional side, a group of Florentine painters and sculptors led by Giorgio Vasari set up an "Academy of Design" in 1563, giving the members exemption from guild regulations and emphasizing their claim to liberal arts status. But not only did the phrase "arts of design" not include music and poetry, it did "not entail any aesthetic

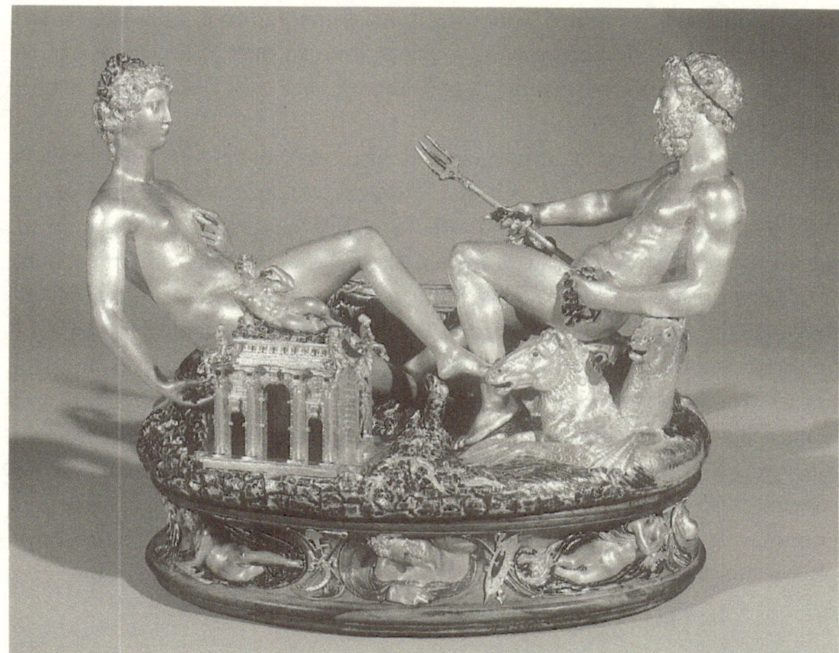

Figure 5. Benvenuto Cellini, saliera (saltcellar): Neptune (sea) and Tellus (earth); gold, niello work, and ebony base (1540–43). Kunsthistorisches Museum, Kunstkammer, Vienna. Courtesy Erich Lessing/Art Resource, New York. The saltcellar was set on wheels, and in his autobiography, Cellini describes how he and some friends enjoyed rolling it to each other around the table before he delivered it.

statement" (Barasch 1985, 114). Moreover, many of the wealthiest and best-informed Renaissance patrons throughout Italy and Northern Europe were avid sponsors of what we would call craft or decorative arts—miniatures, carved gems, medals, majolica ware, fancy inkwells, sumptuous inlaid coffers—which are often valued more highly in Renaissance inventories than paintings or sculptures (Robertson 1992). Of course, some of these utilitarian items were indeed bravura performances, such as Cellini's elaborately wrought silver saltcellar for Francis I (fig. 5). But neither wealthy patrons nor the average Florentine or Venetian saw an enormous gulf between the work of the best ceramists or cabinetmakers and that of the painters and sculptors (Goldthwaite 1980).

## The Changing Status of Artisan/Artists

Just as the Renaissance lacked our category of fine art, so it lacked our ideal of the autonomous artist pursuing self-expression and originality. For several decades now the old emphasis on Renaissance secularism, individualism, and subjectivity has been rejected by historians who see a greater continuity with the Middle Ages than with our modern age (Burke 1997).[2] What made it easy for some nineteenth-century historians to project the modern image of the autonomous artist back on the Renaissance is that there *were* important improvements in the status and image of musicians, painters, and writers. In the case of music, for example, Italian princes like the Estes, Sforzas, Gonzagas, and Medici put on lavish court spectacles that enlarged the scope and prestige of secular music and provided regular employment to scores of musicians. The slightly disreputable medieval jongleur wandering from court to court was turning into the uniformed minstrel, housed and fed in the palace with other domestic servants. Although the modern separation of composer and performer was not yet normative, the beginning of music printing in 1501 would eventually make it possible. The most celebrated musicians, such as Adrian Willaert and Josquin des Prez, were known for their compositions and had considerable freedom to move from court to court. This increased status was reinforced by the humanist scholars' discovery of ancient texts that suggested the Greeks had sung their tragedies, leading to a new emphasis on the need for music to express the sense of the text, a trend especially evident in the four-part madrigals that were sung as part of upper-class sociality. Some musicologists, impressed with these developments and with the fact that Listenius wrote of the "artificer" leaving behind an "absolute and perfect work," have been led to claim that music became a "fine art" in the Renaissance (Lippman 1992). But the occasional Renaissance use of the term "work," while it suggests a step in the modern direction, hardly amounts to the arrival of the modern concepts of the autonomous "work of art" and the sovereign artist. Most musicians remained composer/players who turned out functional pieces on schedule for their employers and freely recycled parts of their own pieces and borrowed from others (Goehr 1992).[3]

In the arts of painting, sculpture, and architecture there was an even greater advance in the status and image of the artisan/artist. Unfortunately, popular accounts have blown this out of proportion, casting figures like Michelangelo in the role of a tortured genius striving for self-expression, a kind of Van Gogh with ears intact. Not only is this postromantic image wide of the mark for Michelangelo, it applies even less to the majority of Renaissance painters and sculptors. Once we set aside these romantic simplifications, we can more objectively assess the modernity of the Renaissance idea of the artist.[4] Three kinds of evidence suggest the beginnings of the modern concept of the artist: the emergence of the genre of the "artist's biography," the development of the self-portrait, and the rise of the "court artist."

The new literary genre of the artist's biography treated the painter, sculptor, or architect as a hero figure after the pattern of the poet, celebrating individual accomplishments that exceeded traditional workshop skills (Soussloff 1997). Several Renaissance artisan/artists such as Ghiberti and Cellini even wrote autobiographies. The most famous and influential collection of artists' biographies were those produced by Vasari, also the central figure in founding the Florentine Academy, and it is no surprise that his book reflects an animus toward the guilds and production for everyday use. Yet there are aspects of even Vasari's book that undercut the popular image of the "Renaissance Artist." Vasari, for example, did not—and could not—write a book called *Lives of the Artists* as some translations have it, but *Lives of the Most Excellent Painters, Sculptors, and Architects.* It is a small but crucial difference. During the Renaissance there was no regulative concept of "the artist" that separated painters, sculptors, and architects collectively from glassblowers, ceramists, and embroiders. The term often used by Vasari and others was still *artifice,* "artificer." Some translations of Vasari render *artifice* as "artist," but others translate it as "craftsman" or "artisan" and at least one popular English abridgment arbitrarily switches between the two terms, sometimes in the same sentence. Here is such a translation of Vasari's description of his reaction at the first sight of Michelangelo's Sistine Chapel frescoes: "What a happy age we live in! And how fortunate are our craftsmen *[artifice]* who have been given light and vision by Michelangelo and whose difficulties have been smoothed away by this marvelous and incomparable artist *[artifice]*!" (Vasari 1965, 360). Although Vasari uses the same root, "artificer" *(artifice),* for Michelangelo and other painters, the translator couldn't bring himself to call Michelangelo a craftsman, but set up a verbal opposition that was not regulative in Vasari's time (Vasari 1991a). None of the major European languages at this time made a systematic conceptual distinction between "artist" and "craftsman" in the modern sense.[5]

Although early Renaissance painters had occasionally shown themselves among the crowd of worshipers in devotional paintings, by 1450 the new genre of the independent self-portrait had emerged in Italy. A recent study of these self-portraits has shown that most were by a small group of court artists who were clearly making high status claims by the way they presented themselves—dressed like gentlemen and looking directly at the viewer, often with no sign of the manual aspect of their work (Woods-Marsden 1998). But the most famous self-portraits of the Renaissance came not from Italy but Germany where Albrecht Dürer not only showed himself in the leisurely pose and dress of a fine gentleman in one of them but also assumed, in the famous *Self-Portrait* of 1500, a Christ-like pose (fig. 6). There are conflicting interpretations of this

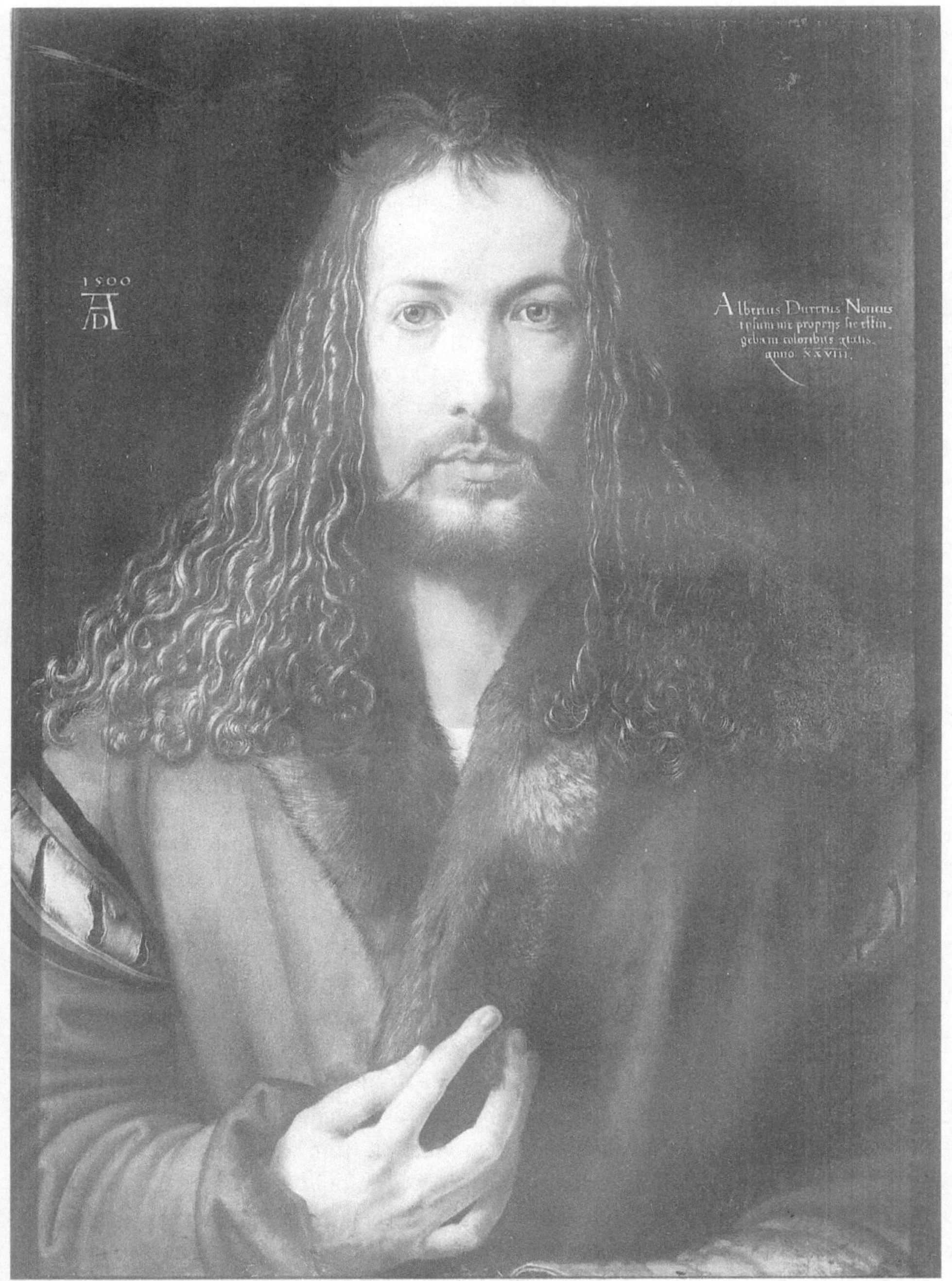


Figure 6. Albrecht Dürer, *Self Portrait at Twenty-Eight Years Old Wearing a Coat with Fur Collar* (1500). Alte Pinakothek, Munich. Courtesy Giraudon/Art Resource, New York.

*Self-Portrait,* with some seeing it in the religious tradition of the Imitation of Christ, others arguing that it makes an audacious claim for the painter as a divine creator (Koerner 1993). Important as the Italian and German self-portraits are in showing the beginnings of the claim to an exalted status for artisan/artist, we must remember that the majority of self-portraits of this type were done by a small elite know as "court artists."

What art historians call court artists were those painters, sculptors, and architects who managed to separate themselves from the majority of their fellow artisan/artists by appointments to reigning princes and to elaborate a justification for their high status (Warnke 1993). Renaissance princes needed enormous numbers of artificers to adorn their palaces with the result that some painters and sculptors were raised from among the palace barbers and tailors to the rank of *valet de chambre* and a few even ennobled. These artisan/artists not only dressed the part of courtiers but also engaged in various fictions, such as not placing a price on their works—although they would accept an "honorarium"—in order to be worthy of associating with nobles who did not work for pay. But the most sought-after painters or sculptors like Leonardo, Michelangelo, Titian, and Dürer, whether or not they were on a princely payroll and ennobled, could move from city to city without having to pay membership fees in the local guild or follow its limitations on materials and prices. It is this handful of "purveyors to the courts" who have often been treated as the typical "Renaissance Artist." In reality, even most court artists were given an annual salary, along with free board and room, and their employers expected them to paint portraits and decorate rooms or in some cases to paint furniture and guild caskets (Cosimo Tura), design tapestries and bowls (Mantegna), or do festivals and costumes (Leonardo). Unlike the modern artist, most of the court artists made their works on order for a specific function rather than creating them as a purely personal expression (Baxandall 1972; Burke 1986).

The genre of the "artist's biography," the development of the self-portrait, and the position of court artist were important steps toward the modern status and image of the artist. But to speak of Renaissance artisan/artists in general as "autonomous," "sovereign," or "absolute" is certainly an exaggeration. The Renaissance norm was cooperative production from workshops that fulfilled specific contracts for decorating churches, civic buildings, banners, wedding chests, and furniture. Even painters and sculptors who did not have permanent workshops often accepted joint commissions (Mantegna) or agreed to complete a half-finished sculpture (Michelangelo) with no sense that this was an offense to their "creative individuality." The workshop, with associates and apprentices doing backgrounds, feet, torsos, and often whole panels, continued to be typical from Raphael down through Rubens in the seventeenth century, and painters generally continued to work on decorative commissions along-side carvers, glassmakers, ceramists, and weavers (Cole 1983; Burke 1986; Welch 1997).

The situation of the architect was even more complex. Although early Renaissance buildings were still planned by master masons working from traditional pattern books, the building boom of the fifteenth century, combined with the enthusiasm for the remains of ancient Rome and the rediscovery of Vitruvius, led patrons to seek out painters and sculptors who were more likely to be familiar with the new style. Achievements such as Brunelleschi's daring design for the dome of the Duomo in Florence raised the prestige of the architect as engineer/designer, and Alberti's treatise and work claimed gentlemanly status for the architect as artist/intellectual. Yet, despite the claims of Alberti, Palladio, and Delorme for the ascendancy of architects over masons and carpenters, the latter were not treated as mere laborers carrying out orders but were often given considerable freedom to modify designs on the job.[6]

But the most striking evidence that the typical Renaissance painter, sculptor, or architect was not a modern individualist imposing claims to absolute autonomy are the many surviving contracts. Such contracts usually stipulated not only the size of the painting or statue, the price, and date of delivery but also the subject matter and materials. I have already mentioned the contract Leonardo signed in 1483. Many contracts gave even more detailed instructions, and a few Renaissance clients thought it appropriate to pay according to time and materials, and one even contracted for his frescos by the foot! This sort of attitude led to the famous incident in which Donatello, infuriated at a Genoan merchant who refused to pay the asked price for a bronze head because it hadn't taken that long to finish, threw it into the street where it shattered, declaring that the merchant was more used to bargaining for beans than for bronzes. It's a nice story that art writers have loved to repeat, but rather than illustrating an established "autonomy" of the artist in the modern sense it shows that the regulative assumptions during the Renaissance were quite different from ours. For every Leonardo whose hand was reputedly held at the moment of death by Francis I (Francis was out of town) or Titian whose dropped paint brush was supposedly picked up by Charles V (reprise of an ancient story), there were thousands of others whose workshops went on year after year faithfully executing the terms of their contracts (Kemp 1997; Welch 1997).

Another area where some steps toward the modern separation of artist and artisan were taken merits special attention because of its gender implications—the changing status of the "needle arts," especially embroidery. In the Middle

Ages, as we have seen, not only were the needle arts the province of both men and women, but in addition, women worked in all the arts. Women were still active in almost every art during the Renaissance, including the newly prestigious arts of painting and sculpture, although most were the daughters of painters (Lavinia Fontana and Marietta Robusti) or worked within the convent setting (Catherina dei Virgi). One female painter even came from a noble background (Sofonisba Anguissola). We know little of Marietta Robusti because her father Jacopo (called Tintoretto) refused to let her marry or accept commissions on her own, keeping her as a valued member of his large workshop. Sofonisba Anguissola's career, in contrast, is well documented since her father had her trained as a painter as part of a successful scheme to get her a court position—hence her many self-portraits that the father sent to various princes as gifts (fig. 7). Widely admired as a kind of "miracle"—a noblewoman who paints and paints well—she eventually became lady-in-waiting and painting instructor to the young Queen of Spain, and her stipend was regularly sent to her father (Chadwick 1996; Woods-Marsden 1998).

Despite the presence of these exceptional women, the fourteenth and fifteenth centuries saw the beginning of a general decline in the number of women in the higher status arts. Male-dominated guilds in most arts increasingly excluded women from full membership and obtained city ordinances forbidding independent work by women. As time went on, more and more arts of all kinds, including professional embroidery, were organized into guilds that excluded or restricted women. Apart from the unstated goal of eliminating economic competition, an indirect cause of the exclusion of women from higher forms of production was the beginning of the long transformation of the family from a work unit into the modern domestic household. Whereas medieval theories of sexual difference had seen women as the dangerous daughters of Eve, the Renaissance developed an ideology of sex role differences in which women's primary function was child care and household management.

This sex role differentiation began to show up in the attitudes toward embroidery. In the early Renaissance when the respected painter Antonio Pollaiuolo and the embroiderer Paolo da Verona jointly produced a piece such as *The Birth of John the Baptist,* with its fine perspectival and shading effects, the difficulty of the embroidering technique was as challenging as the drawing; it would take several generations for professional embroidery to be seen as merely close and patient handwork. At the same time, Italian conduct manuals were already stressing the importance of embroidery in keeping the noblewoman's idle hours occupied, thereby preserving chastity and enhancing femininity. Thus,

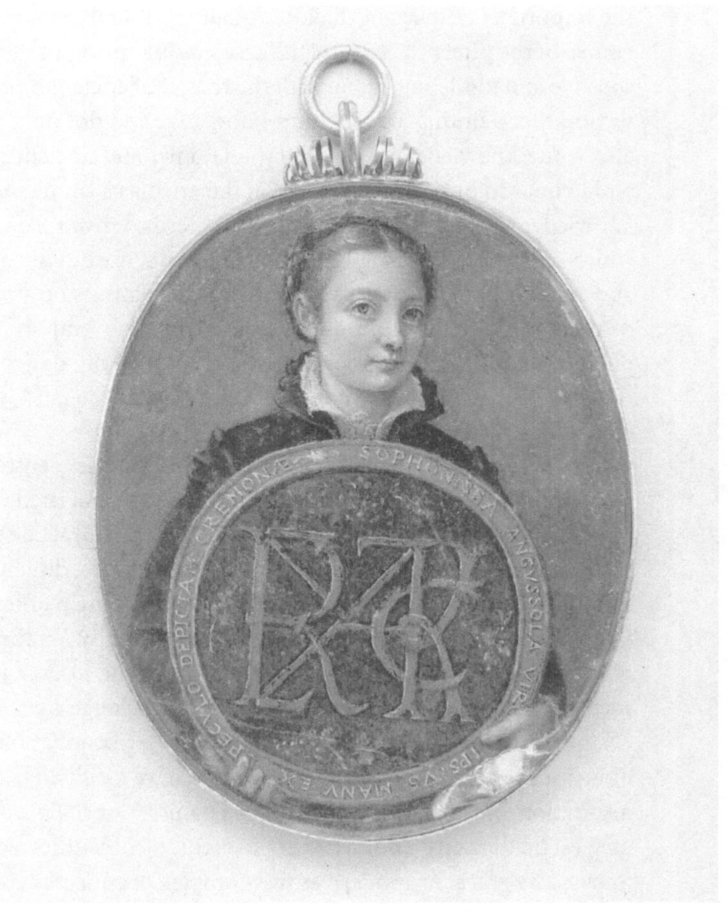


Figure 7. Sofonisba Anguissola, *Self Portrait* (ca. 1555); oil on parchment, 8.2 × 6.3 centimeters. Emma F. Munroe Fund, 60.155. Courtesy Museum of Fine Arts, Boston. Reproduced with permission. © 2000 Museum of Fine Arts, Boston. All Rights Reserved.

the Renaissance saw the beginning of a "process that not only divided embroidery from painting, but subdivided embroidery into a public . . . and a domestic art" (Parker 1984, 81).

## The Ideal Qualities of the Artisan/Artist

The workshop, contract, and gender practices we have considered show that, despite important steps in the modern direction, the normative practices and concepts of the artisan/artist in the Renaissance were still far from modern ideals of the autonomous creator. This becomes even clearer when we look at the important changes in the ideal qualities desirable in artisan/artists. In the course of the fifteenth century, the accelerating spread of the knowledge of perspective and modeling, along with the revival of ancient models, led to the conviction that painting and sculpture now required not only apprenticeship but also some knowledge of geometry, anatomy, and ancient mythology. Alberti and Leonardo projected an image of the artist as a "craftsman-scientist." Such knowledge was crucial to "invention," a term derived from classical rhetoric, which did not mean "creation" in the modern sense but the discovery, selection, and arrangement of content. Although some patrons proposed an "invention" of their own (or by a humanist scholar in their employ), a highly reputed painter, like Bellini, for example, might successfully dodge the attempt of an Isabella d'Este to have him use a drawing she sent as a guide to the composition of a painting she was ordering.

By the late sixteenth century this rather "scientific" sense of "invention" began to be supplemented by qualities more often associated with the idea of the poet such as "imagination," "inspiration," and "natural talent." Talent or natural brilliance *(ingegno)* was said to show itself as grace, difficulty, facility, and inspiration. Grace was believed to result only when the painter's or sculptor's activity was not labored but flowed from natural ability. Yet the highest praise was reserved for those who set themselves tasks of the utmost technical difficulty, such as the unusual foreshortening of Michelangelo's *Jonah* in the Sistine Chapel. When such feats of craftsmanship were brought off with ease and rapidity of execution, the painter was said to have facility. The remaining quality, inspiration *(furia),* was believed to fill a painter's or sculptor's imagination with images that facility could use to overcome difficulties and produce works touched by grace. As modern as this complex of concepts appears when looked back on through the veil of Romanticism, what makes these Renaissance ideas so unlike our "creative imagination" is that invention, inspiration, and grace were inseparable from skill and the imitation of nature for a particular purpose. And such imitations, for all the allowances to the painter's fantasy and individual initiative, were still to be under the restraint of "decorum," the rule of verisimilitude, and appropriateness. Similarly, Renaissance references to melancholy or personal idiosyncracies (much exaggerated in popular biographies) were not equivalent to modern ideas of bohemianism and rebellion.[7]

When Michelangelo mentioned in a letter of 1523 that Pope Julius II let him "do what I wished" in the Sistine Chapel, it did not mean "that he could paint whatever he wanted, rather . . . that he could treat his theme in whatever manner he chose," a theme in all likelihood agreed to in advance by his notoriously strong-willed patron (Summers 1981, 453). Renaissance painting and sculpture were not evaluated in their own time by modern standards of originality but by whether they gracefully overcame difficulties in invention and execution. Despite his pride in never keeping a workshop, Michelangelo's practice and outlook were closer to that of his fellow artisan/artists than to that of the modern artist who places self-expression and originality above skill and service. If we feel uncomfortable calling Michelangelo an artisan/artist, it is because the older idea of the artisan/artist was definitively separated in the eighteenth century, reserving imagination, grace, and freedom to the artist-creator and leaving only skill, labor, and useful service to those called artisans. If the popular image of the "Renaissance Artist" distorts the career of Michelangelo, how much less does it fit the majority of painters, sculptors, and architects of the Renaissance?

## Shakespeare, Jonson, and the "Work"

Just as traditional textbooks and popular histories have often given us a one-sided picture of the typical painter or sculptor of the Renaissance, so we have often been treated to a false idea of the Renaissance poet—and of Shakespeare, in particular. Literary historians identify two main types of writers of poetry in Elizabethan England: "amateurs" and "professionals" (Auberlen 1984; Wall 1993). The largest group, the amateurs, were the educated gentlemen and ladies who wrote for pleasure and circulated their poetry privately since print would bring an exposure unbecoming their station. John Donne, about to leave England on a diplomatic mission, asked a friend to keep a manuscript copy of his poems, declaring "I forbid it the Presse, and the Fire: publish it not, but yet burn it not; and between those, do what you will with it" (Marotti 1986). Donne's instructions nicely capture the nature of what is called "coterie poetry," writings that circulated in manuscript among friends and associates who might make revisions or additions before sending them on but were not meant for print where they might be fingered over by anyone at the bookstalls. As a result "authorship tended to disappear," and the poems often came to be "owned" as much by the social group as by the initial writer (Marotti 1991, 35). Among upper-class males, poetry was usually regarded as something to be indulged in during one's youth or used in a quest for position and then given up. Deflating as it may be to our sense of the artist, a good deal of John Donne's poetry, like that of many other Elizabethans, was not produced because he wanted to make art but because he was looking for a job.

The type of Elizabethan writers that literary historians loosely call professionals were people who either sought or were forced to make a living by writing, usually combining support from patrons with the sale of manuscripts to printers. To make a living through patronage occasionally meant actual employment as secretary or tutor in a household but more often involved the use of obsequious dedications in an endless hustling of small gratuities. To make a living by selling manuscripts directly to printers was almost impossible due to the small size of the market for books and the absence of copyright. The only kind of writing that actually paid well enough to sustain a living for a few was the steady writing of plays for companies of actors.

After an initial try at living from patronage (he wrote a fawning dedication of *Venus and Adonis* to the Earl of Southampton), Shakespeare turned to writing exclusively for the theater. *Sonnet* 111 seems to allude to it:

> O, for my sake do you with Fortune chide,
> The guilty goddess of my harmful deeds,
> That did not better for my life provide
> Than public means which public manners breeds.
> Thence comes it my name receives a brand.
>
> (Lines 1–5)

The "brand" Shakespeare's name received from the public theater came from the low status of actors and plays. Elizabethan plays still had acrobats, musicians, gaudy costumes, dancing, and sword fights, and the theaters themselves were noisy, open air affairs where food was hawked and clowns might interrupt the action by engaging in repartee with the audience. Written for such a lively theatrical setting, Shakespeare's plays were not fixed texts or "works of art" in our sense, but malleable scripts constantly revised for public performance (Loewenstein 1985; Patterson 1989).

Elizabethan plays were usually made on commission for theater companies who freely revised them for performance as long as they could get an audience, after which they might have them printed to make a few extra shillings. Most of Shakespeare's plays that ended up in print were not prepared for publication by him but were either printed by his company, the Lord Chamberlain's Men, or by pirates who wrote them down piecemeal from memory (Bentley 1971). Printed plays often mentioned the players on the cover and omitted the author's name, as on the 1597 cover of *Romeo and Juliet,* which says: "As it hath been often (with great applause) plaid publiquely, by the right Honorable the L. of *Hunsdon* his Servants" (fig. 8). The usual procedure for getting a new play was for the company to commission a plot outline and then farm out different acts to several writers for completion; it is estimated that at least 50 percent of the

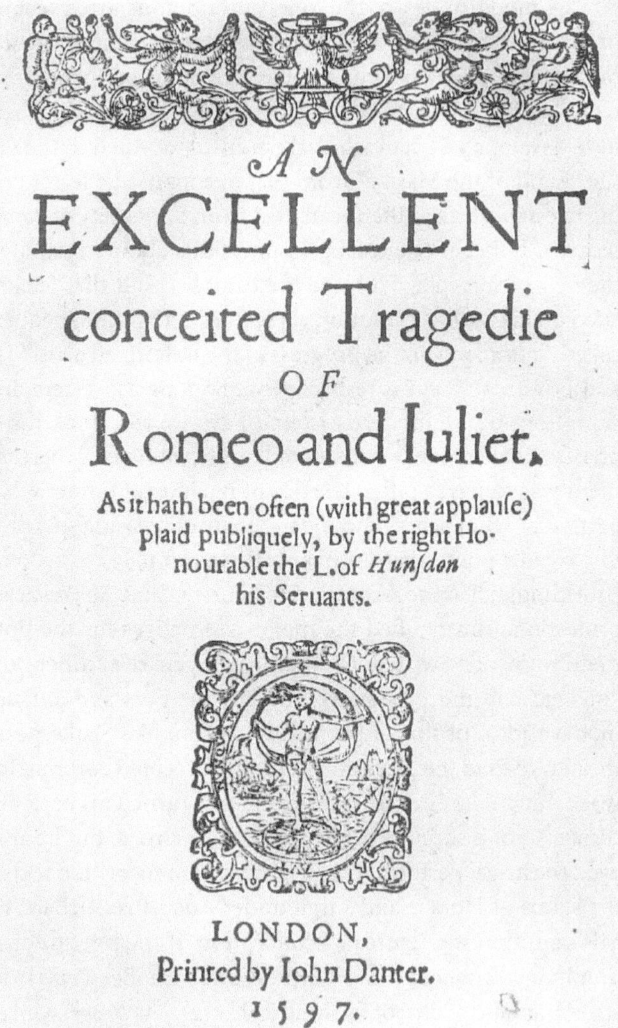

AN

EXCELLENT

conceited Tragedie

OF

Romeo and Iuliet.

As it hath been often (with great applauſe)
plaid publiquely, by the right Ho-
nourable the L. of *Hunſdon*
his Seruants.

LONDON,
Printed by Iohn Danter.
1597.

Figure 8. William Shakespeare, cover of *Romeo and Juliet* (London, 1597). Courtesy Rare Book and Special Collections, University of Illinois Library, Urbana-Champaign. Shakespeare's name is not mentioned, only the company and its patron.

extant Elizabethan plays were collaborative affairs, and Shakespeare himself engaged in several of them (Muir 1960). Moreover, Shakespeare, as an actor-shareholder in the Lord Chamberlain's Men, was not at complete liberty but clearly tailored his plays to the number of actors and variety of abilities in the company.[8] And when the Lord's Chamberlain's Men became the King's Men on the accession of James I, Shakespeare chose themes that would please the royal court (Kernan 1995).

The modern idea of the lone, autonomous artist seeking to create a fixed, original work of "art" is frustrated by this sixteenth-century practice of collaboration and of writing changeable scripts for performance rather than permanent "works." Accordingly, historians of literature, like historians of painting, have developed a small scholarly industry devoted to the task of separating out the "hand of the Master" from that of supposedly lesser collaborators and trying to establish an authentic ur-text from the variety of competing performance records. Other modernizing assumptions about creativity and independence then come into play with the predictable result that Shakespeare is congratulated on his "subtle evolution . . . toward artistic independence" or his plays are called "landmarks in the progress of the unfettered artist" (Rudnytsky 1991, 154; and Edwards 1968, 84, respectively). So long as we remain in thrall to the assumptions of the modern system of art, we will think it a compliment to emphasize Shakespeare's "unfettered" independence, whereas his actual achievement was to have crafted a series of magnificent dramas within the limits of a particular set of actors and the necessity of pleasing socially complex audiences in a volatile political atmosphere (Patterson 1989).

Although Donne's coterie amateurism and Shakespeare's entrepreneurial professionalism typified the major alternatives for the poet's self-conception, there were a few writers like Edmund Spenser and Ben Jonson who wanted a "higher" and more "serious" role for the poet and anticipated aspects of the modern ideal of the author/artist. Jonson, like Shakespeare, had acted in the theater, revised the plays of others, and accepted commissions for collaborative work. Yet unlike Shakespeare he not only turned his back on an active life in the theater to find support from aristocratic patrons, but he also constantly disparaged theatrical performance in comparison to written texts, wanting to recover the status of Horace and Virgil under Augustus. Richard Helgerson has called this ambition the "laureate" conception of the poet to distinguish it from the dominant "amateur" and "professional" modes (1983). Jonson promised to strip dramatic poetry of its theatrical "rags," its songs, dances, and comic antics: there will be "no eggs broken, nor quaking custards," he assures us in the prologue to *Volpone* and emphasizes that the entire play is "from his own hand" (Jonson [1605] 1978, 72, 75).

The primary instrument of Jonson's campaign for "laureate" status, however, was the very thing amateurs like Donne (out of principle) and professionals like Shakespeare (out of necessity) denied themselves: print. Jonson was one of the few playwrights who consistently saw his own plays into print, insisting that they feature his name on the cover and adding notes in Latin to accentuate their character as texts for elite reading rather than popular perform-

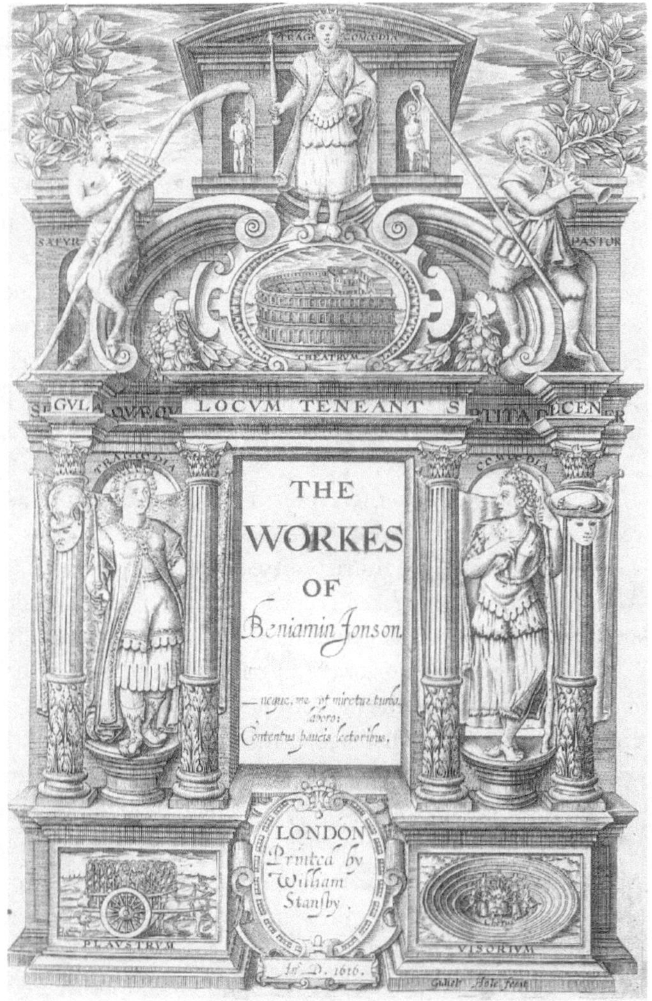


Figure 9. Benjamin Jonson, cover page of the *Workes of Benjamin Jonson* (London, 1616). Courtesy Rare Book and Special Collections, University of Illinois Library, Urbana-Champaign. The title page drawing of a grand piece of classical architecture and symbolic statuary, along with the Latin inscription, stresses Jonson's learning and superiority to those who write either for pay or for diversion.

ances. The apogee of Jonson's use of the printed text against the malleable script was his unprecedented publication of his collected plays, masques, and epigrams as *The Workes of Ben Jonson* (1616) (fig. 9) in an expensive folio edition of the kind normally reserved for writings like Latin classics (Jonson 1616; Murray 1987; Wall 1993). Calling a collection of mere plays "works," however, drew derisive comments from people like the gentleman amateur Sir John Suckling:

> And he told them plainly he deserv'd the Bayes
> For his were call'd Works, where others were but Plaies.
>
> (Spingarn 1968, 1:90)

A brief look at the role of women writers in Renaissance England can help put Jonson's laureate ideal in a wider perspective. The most influential sixteenth-century conduct manual for women, Juan de Vives's *Instruction of a Christian Woman,* underscored the belief that women had no place in public but should remain at home and keep silent. In this sort of atmosphere it is not surprising that few women were encouraged to write at all or few of those who did sought a "professional" career. Yet some aristocratic women like Mary Herbert, countess of Pembroke, or Lucy Russell, countess of Bedford, were not only patrons of writers but exchanged manuscript poetry with Donne, Spenser, and Jonson. But women who had their writings printed, and thus "exposed themselves" in public, were forced to engage in a variety of strategies of self-depreciation and self-justification, such as claiming a mother's obligation to provide a legacy of moral instruction for her children or to fulfill women's obligation to "redeem Eve" (Wall 1993).

Obviously, women writers' motives and self-conceptions were even further removed from the "laureate" conception of Jonson than Donne's or Shakespeare's. But even if we restrict ourselves to the handful of laureate writers like Jonson, we find they lacked crucial elements of the postromantic ideal of the artist, such as notions of genius and creative imagination. Jonson claimed that scholarship and hard work were a perfectly apt substitute for inspiration (Murray 1987). Contrary to the modern prejudice that radically separates the artist's creativity from the craftsperson's routine, the poetic craft in the Renaissance was learned "in the process of making, by innumerable examples, not by recipe and precept" (Bradbrook 1969, 67). Many of the Elizabethan playwrights were in fact the sons of craftsmen/tradesmen: Spenser's father was a clothmaker, Marlowe's a cobbler, Shakespeare's a glover, Jonson's stepfather a bricklayer (Miller 1959). Shakespeare, the son, was also a craftsman whose "models might be recognized and judged in the playing by his audience, as well as the actors' gild or fellowship" (Bradbrook 1968, 140). Shakespeare plied his craft for pay, making shrewd investments first in his own company, then as a property owner and a moneylender and was eventually able to buy a coat of arms, giving him gentlemanly status, and to leave his family a solid estate on his death. He rejected both the coterie amateurism of a Donne and the laureate pretensions of a Jonson. Rather than thinking of him as a forerunner of the modern author/artist, we might with equal justice think of him as a craftsman-entrepreneur who knew how to please an audience as he worked toward "a secure retirement at Stratford" (Schmidgall 1990, 97).

## A Proto-Aesthetic?

Just as the Renaissance did not have our category of fine art or our ideal of the autonomous artist, author, or composer, so it lacked the modern concept of the aesthetic as the contemplation of self-contained works. Architecture is, of course, by its very nature tied to utility, but in the Renaissance this was also true of music, poetry, and painting. Although there was a much more extensive development of secular music during the Renaissance, most music remained tied to texts and specific functions. As Vincenzo Galilei (Galileo's father) wrote, "If a musician has not the power to direct the minds of his listeners to their benefit, his science and knowledge are to be reputed null and vain, since the art of music was instituted and numbered among the liberal arts for no other purpose" (Strunk 1950, 319). Just as most music was written to accompany particular ceremonies or situations, most poetry, as we have seen, was also "occasional" and the Horatian motto of "please and instruct" prevailed. Sir Phillip Sidney's *Defense of Poetry* (1595) stressed the moral utility of poetry as able to teach by examples rather than mere precepts. Since most of us get our taste of Renaissance poetry out of anthologies or citations, we are seldom aware of the practical functions and political contexts of many individual poems. The typical modern anthology either omits the most obviously occasional poems or fails to note the original purpose of those it does include, producing an effect similar to seeing Renaissance panels from altars, wedding chests, or bedroom niches framed and hung as autonomous works in the museum.

Indeed, we are so used to viewing Renaissance paintings on the walls of museums or in book illustrations or slides that it takes some effort to remember that nearly everything now in our museums was originally made on commission and often designed to fit a specific location. It is particularly difficult in the museum setting to imagine the original context of the religious works that were "surrounded by screens, baldachins, flying angels and suspended ostrich eggs, candles and lamps" (Kempers 1992, 11). In some of the smaller churches of Venice, like San Sebastiano, where Veronese did the ceiling, frieze, choir, chancel, and the doors and insets of the organ, it seems every inch is decorated, and nearly every chapel abounds in statuary, paintings, carving, inlays, fine candleholders, monstrances, and reliquaries (fig. 10). Even the more secular works that are still on the walls or ceilings of Florentine or Venetian council chambers are seldom shown by our art books in their setting and framework; everything is cropped out but what *we* define as the "work." But anyone who has visited the Palazzo Vecchio in Florence or the Doge's Palace in Venice knows what a different sense and feeling these huge civic and religious paintings have in their

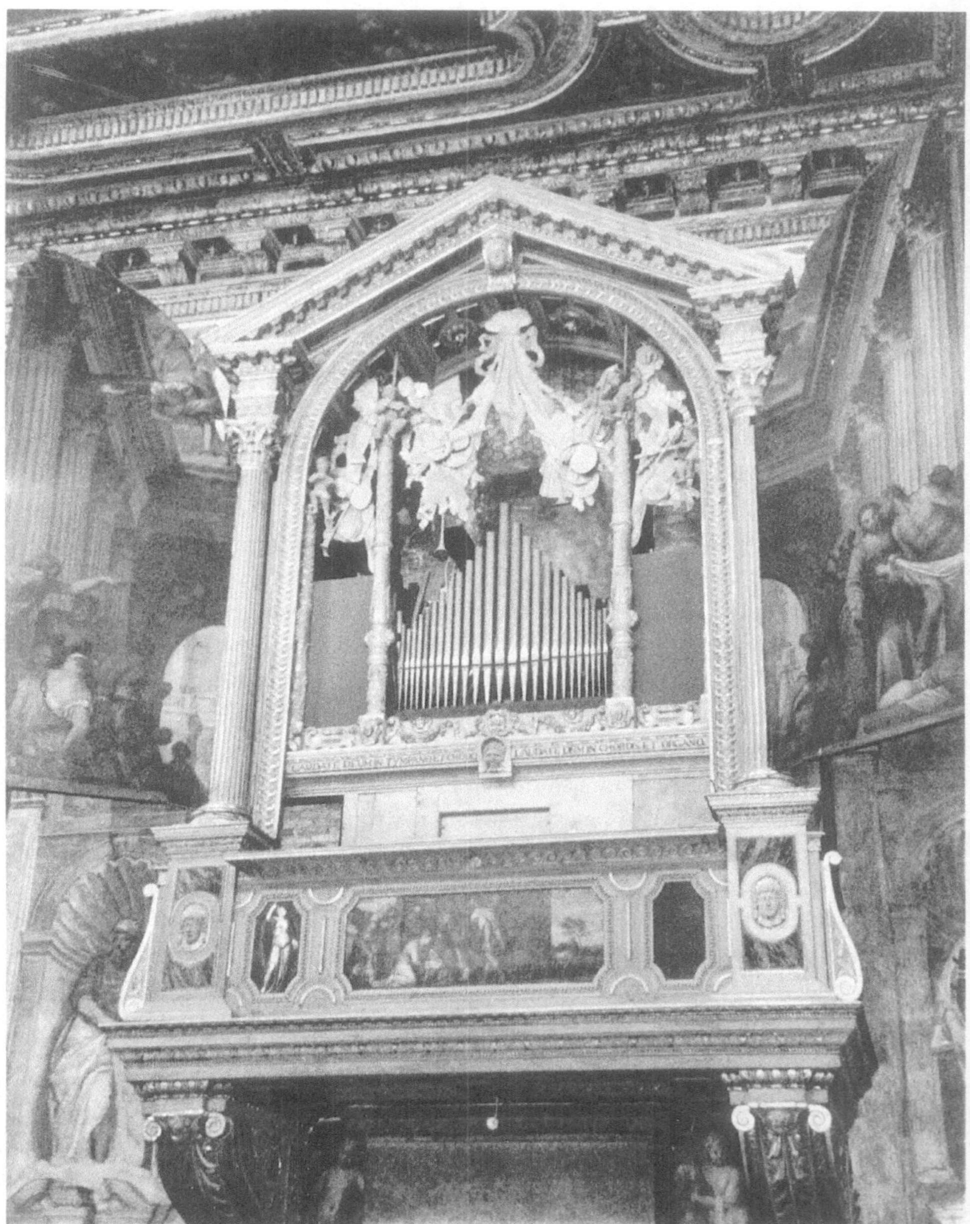

Figure 10. Paolo Veronese, organ doors *(Christ Healing at the Pool)* and panel *(Nativity)* (1560). Church of San Sebastiano, Venice. Photograph by author.

original setting. For those who lived in the Renaissance, the ornamented facades, frescos, panel paintings, carvings, statuary, tapestries, banners, fountains, fine furniture, and ceramics were not simply art to be looked at for itself but products of human skill and instruments of social, religious, and political life (Kemp 1997, 163; Paoletti and Radke 1997; Welch 1997).

Evidence that paintings and sculptures were sometimes acquired or contemplated simply "for themselves" is of two kinds: the revival of collecting and the development of a vocabulary for the appreciation of the purely visual qualities of such works (Alsop 1982; Gombrich 1987). By the sixteenth century, there was a small body of connoisseurs who wanted not just a devotional or bedroom panel but a painting by the hand of a celebrated master like Titian, Raphael, or del Sarto. Yet the wealthy and powerful of the Renaissance had collections of all kinds, and often mixed objects we would call art with oddities of technology or natural history. Collecting was as much motivated by impulses of piety, prestige, and show as by pleasure in purely pictorial qualities (Burke 1986; Baxandall 1988). Yet Renaissance naturalism did invite the development of a vocabulary for discussing the artist's success in capturing likeness as in Vasari's striking account of a progression from the "correct but dry" painting of the early Renaissance to the "fluent and graceful" painting of the sixteenth century. There was a parallel progression in the writings of a variety or artists and connoisseurs, from fifteenth-century theories of correct imitation and beauty as ideal proportion (Alberti) to the more poetic notions of expressiveness and grace (Varchi). By the 1550s Venetians like Lodovico Dolche could stress the viewer's pleasure and occasionally speak of "taste." Yet even Michelangelo, who placed the highest value on such qualities as imagination, difficulty, and judgment of the eye, saw them as leading us toward the divine beauty. Insistence on the moral and spiritual function of painting and sculpture was a constant in treatises on painting from Alberti in the fifthteenth century to Lomazzo at the end of the sixteenth. The Renaissance had a "proto-aesthetic" in the restricted, generic meaning of a "judgment of sense," but very few people took up the detached aesthetic attitude typical of the modern discourse of fine art (Summers 1987).

Despite the emergence of several characteristics that we associate with the modern fine art system, the dominant meaning of the terms "art" and "artist" in the Renaissance remained distinctly premodern, and taste, when discussed, was not generally separated from function. The greatness of Michelangelo and Shakespeare was not that they separated art from craft but that they created their incomparable pieces while holding together imagination and technique, form and function, freedom and service. If one is not satisfied with enumerating precedents for the supposedly inevitable triumph of the modern ideas of art, artist, and aesthetic, these changes during the early modern period, important as they were, will betoken major steps in the direction of the modern system of art, not its arrival. Perhaps the strongest evidence that art had not been definitively separated from craft in the Renaissance is the fact that the status of the arts and of artisan/artists were still being debated throughout the seventeenth century. But the continued rise in the status of artisan/artists along with the increasingly important role played by painting, poetry, and music in the emerging absolutist monarchies helped make the seventeenth century an important period of transition to the modern fine art system.

CHAPTER 4

# Artemisia's Allegory

## *Art in Transition*

LIKE MANY women painters of the seventeenth century, Artemisia Gentileschi was trained in her father's workshop, as we learn from the trial of Augustino Tassi, who had been hired to teach her perspective and was charged with raping her. Although it is tempting to see her *Judith Decapitating Holofernes* as an expression of her feelings about Tassi, Artemisia's biblical commissions were equally important as female achievements in the male-dominated genre of narrative painting. Her *Self-Portrait as the Allegory of Painting* (ca.1630–40) is also important as an assertion of women's intellectual and technical equality as painters (fig. 11). To appreciate her self-portrait's uniqueness, we need to understand Artemisia's use of Cesar Ripa's *Iconology,* a widely accepted handbook of symbols that specified that *Pittura,* or painting, should be personified as a woman wearing a gold chain with a pendant mask to stand for imitation, unruly locks of hair for inspiration, a colorful gown for skill, and a gagged mouth symbolizing the ancient saying that painting is "mute poetry." What makes Artemisia's self-portrait unique, as Mary Garrard points out, is that male painters could not use a self-portrait to personify painting since by established convention *Pittura* had to be a woman. Artemisia paints *herself* as *Pittura,* with the gold chain of imitation, the loose locks of inspiration, and the deftly colored shadows on her dress signifying technical skill. Of course, in a naturalistic self-portrait, the gag signifying "mute poetry" is absent, although it is hard not to imagine that this freeing of the female voice had an intentional significance. But most important of all Artemisia shows herself at an angle, leaning into her work, making it one of the most dynamic seventeenth-century self-portraits (Garrad 1989).

I have dwelt on Artemisia's self-portrait because we can learn a great deal about the changing state of the old system of art by comparing her self-portrait to a much more famous one painted twenty years later by Velázquez. Although the monumental *Las Meninas* (1656) (fig. 12) has been frequently analyzed as a profound meditation on the nature of representation, it is also a self-portrait that asserts the nobility of the painter in the context of the rigidly hierarchical

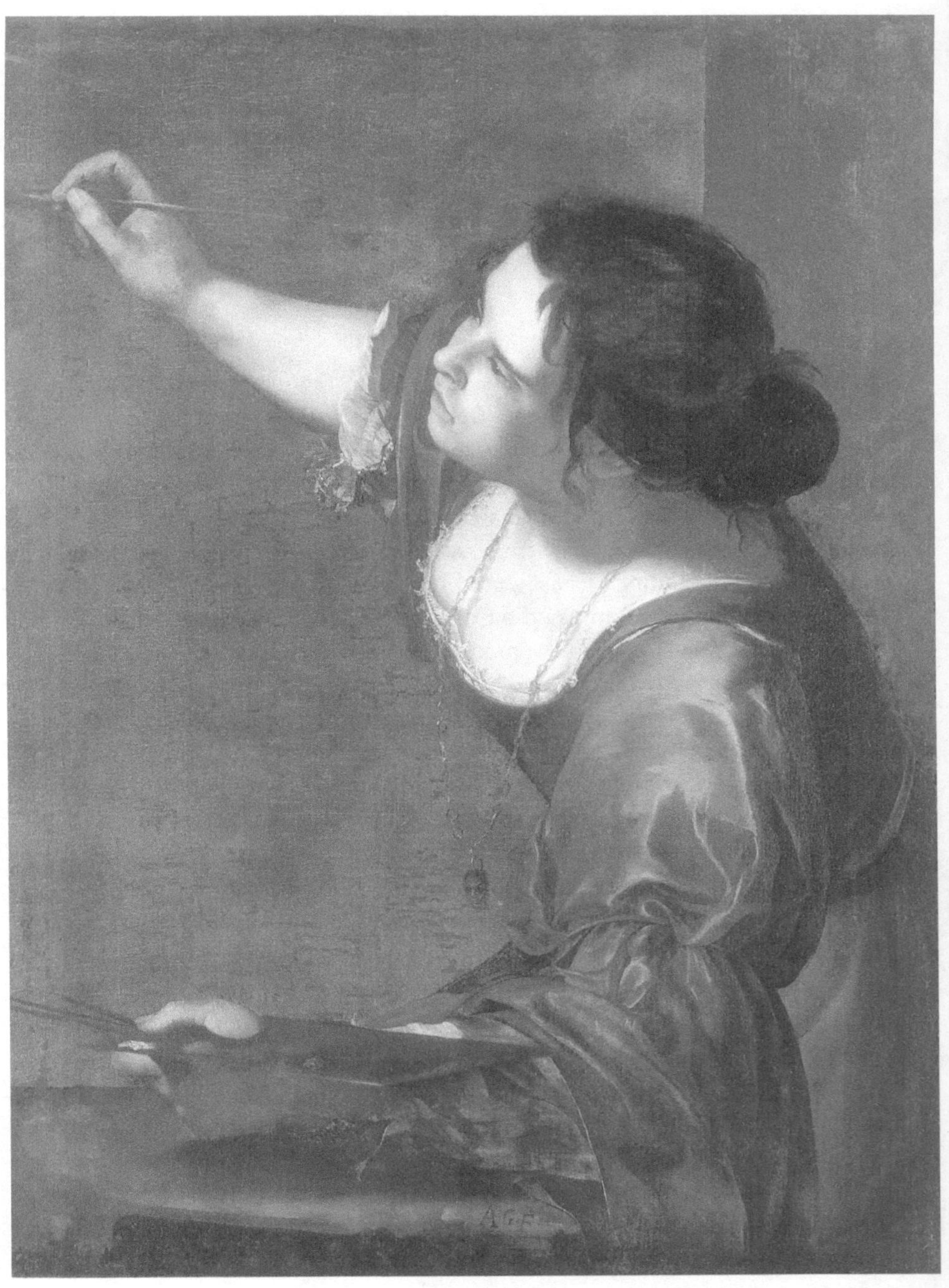

Figure 11. Artemisia Gentileschi, *Self Portrait as La Pittura* (ca. 1630). Courtesy The Royal Collection, © 2000 Her Majesty Queen Elizabeth II.

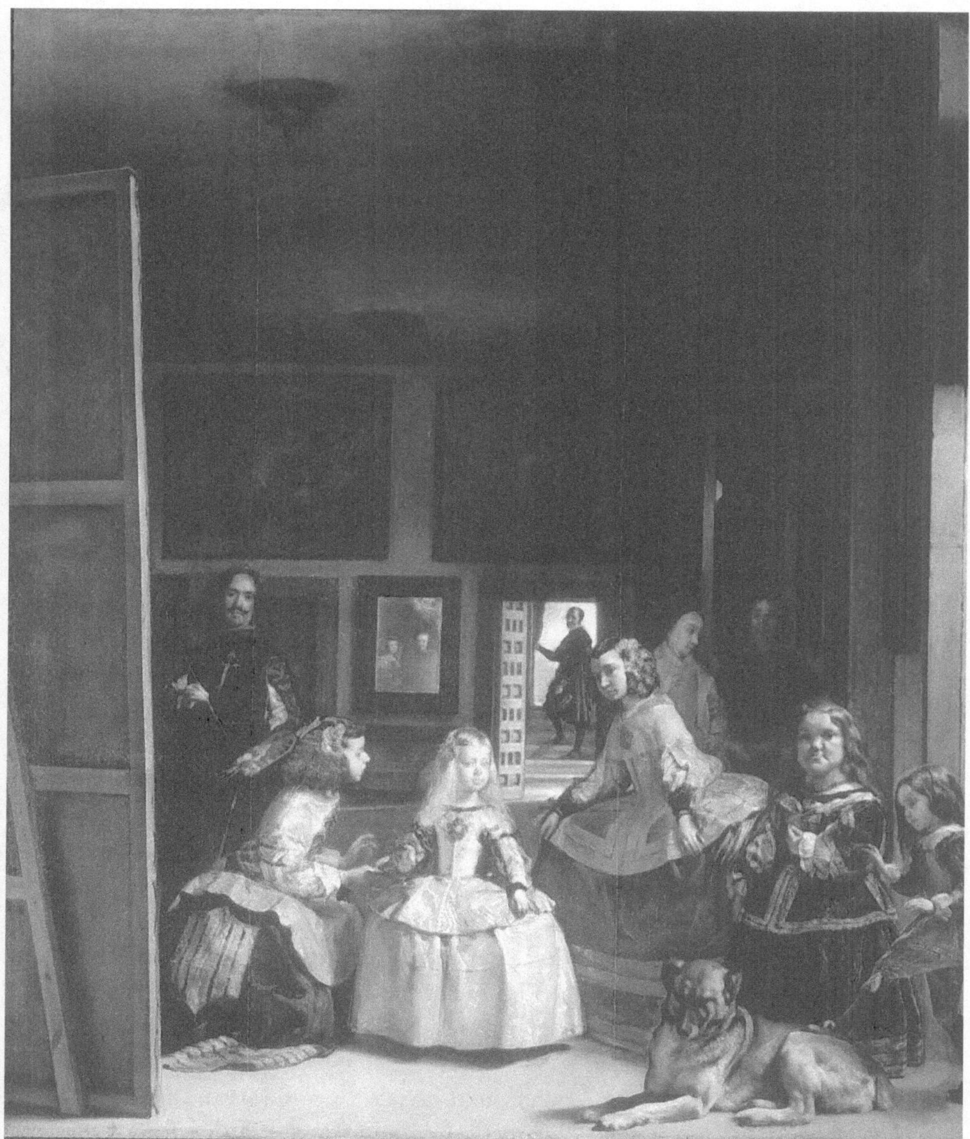

Figure 12. Diego Velázquez, *Las Meninas or the Family of Phillip IV* (1665). Museo del Prado, Madrid. Courtesy Erich Lessing/Art Resource, New York. The Infanta Margarita (accompanied by two maids of honor, a duenna, and two dwarfs) visits Velazquez in his studio. The two figures in the mirror on the back wall are believed to be the king and queen.

court of Philip IV "where painters were assigned a low rank" (Brown 1986, 264). Here the painter stands motionless in his fine clothes, the cross of the order of Santiago (sign of his ennoblement) on his chest, staring out at the king and queen who are honoring him with a visit; the Infanta and her entourage have been with him in the studio. Although he is holding his palette and brush, there is little in his demeanor or his surroundings to remind us that painting is an act of manual labor; on the contrary everything points to the elevated status of the court artist. Not so Artemisia; although finely dressed, she represents herself alone with her canvas, absorbed in her work, applying the brush in a vigorous movement. With her, mind and hand are one; artist and artisan are still united in a self-portrait that says "the worth of the art of painting derives neither from a precious temperament nor from theoretical pretensions, but from the simple business of the artist doing her work" (Garrard 1989, 361).

## The Artisan/Artist's Continuing Struggle for Status

The contrast of these two self-portraits nicely reflects the transitional state of the old system of art in the seventeenth century when both the image of the artisan/artist and the category of art were changing, yet the values and practices of the old system still dominated. Although a few painters achieved a high standing—Velázquez as court painter, Bernini and Rubens through prestigious commissions from Popes and princes across Europe—most painters still remained tied to workshops and regional commissions. The most dramatic institutional gains in status for painters and painting occurred in France where the monarchy created the Académie Royale de Peinture et de Sculpture in 1648. Although it is possible to treat the founding of the academy as simply another step in an inevitable liberation of art from craft, its creation at the time of the Fronde revolt of 1648–53 was also a political and economic riposte to the Paris Guild, which was trying to restrict the freedom of the king's painters at the very moment many French nobles were also in revolt. After the Fronde was defeated in 1653, the academy obtained an even more crushing set of privileges over the guild, yet the new regulations made no reference to economic and political advantages but portrayed the academy painters and sculptors as idealistically defending "two arts, which ignorance has almost confused with lesser professions" (Pevsner 1940, 87). Yet the high status of the French academy painters came at the price of independence since they were essentially state functionaries.

In Italy where court painters had already achieved a high standing by the sixteenth century, the Roman painter Salvator Rosa is reputed to have told a client who came to him with some specific ideas for a painting, "go to a brick maker . . . they work to order" (Haskell 1980, 22). Rosa was known for such outbursts, which show that 150 years after Donatello things had not changed much. Rosa sounds so familiar to us—yet he was completely untypical. Rosa's claims to independence expressed "an image of the artist that was to be fully appreciated only by the romantics of the nineteenth century. In his own day he stood alone" (Haskell 1980, 23). The typical Italian painter or sculptor was still part of a workshop taking commissions.

In England and in the tiny Dutch Republic, we find painters even more closely tied to the workshop tradition. Most English painters continued to be guild members, decorating furniture and carriages and painting elaborate shop signs along with portraits, flowers, and animals. Most Dutch painters maintained a close professional and social alliance with goldsmiths, glassblowers, and embroiderers (Montias 1982). So little was painting seen as a high-flown spiritual vocation that painters like Meindert Hobbema or Judith Leyster did little or no painting after they came into money or began managing the family business. No doubt Dutch painters and sculptors were as concerned for their social status as anyone else, but they were concerned to distinguish themselves *among* artisans, not *from* them (Alpers 1983).

One of the most often noted characteristics of the Dutch artist's situation in the seventeenth century was the emergence of an "art market." Although patronage still existed, a large proportion of Dutch still lifes, landscapes, seascapes, and genre paintings were done in advance for sale in shops or weekly markets like other craft products (Montias 1982). Yet the Dutch painter working for the market was no more the modern individualist than was the typical French or Italian painter fulfilling contracts. There were exceptions, of course, such as Rembrandt, but he was as unusual in the Netherlands as Rosa was in Italy (Alpers 1988). Even the most celebrated and financially independent painters and sculptors of the seventeenth century, like Rubens or Bernini, relied on workshop assistants. Rubens turned out paintings in a regular factory atmosphere at Antwerp, where a visitor in 1621 described "many young painters . . . working on different pieces that Rubens had sketched out in chalk and on which he had here and there added a spot of color" (Warnke 1980, 165). Rubens even paid local specialists to put in landscape, animal, or flower segments, after which he would touch up the final version.

The difference in the pace at which Italian and French painters achieved a higher status and self-image vis-à-vis the English and Dutch painters' stronger ties to the guild and workshop traditions was also true of architects. France's

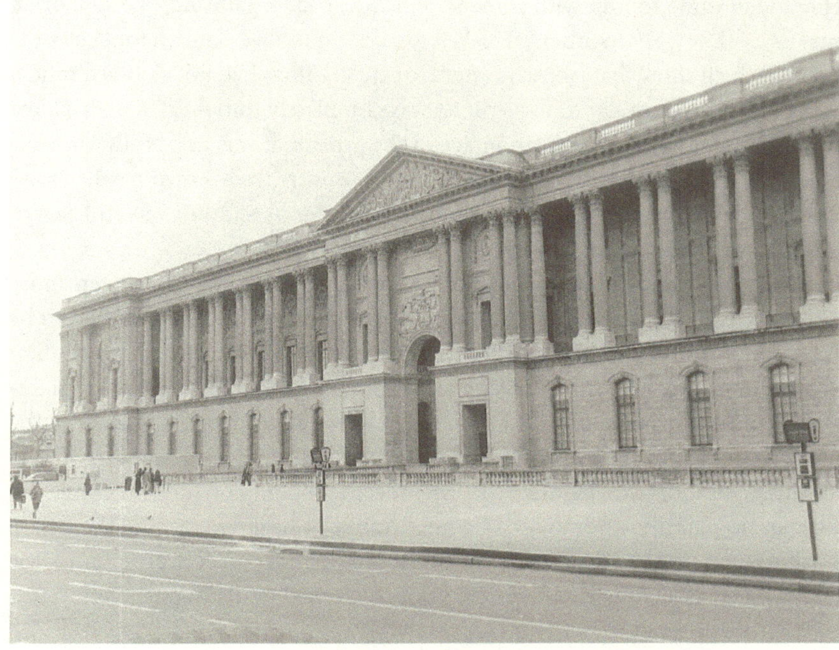

Figure 13. Claude Perrault, Louis Le Vau, and Charles Lebrun, east front of the Louvre (1667–74). Photograph by the author.

Académie Royale d'Architecture (1671) grew in part out of the famous struggle of French architects like Le Vau, Le Brun, and Claude Perrault to wrest responsibility for the east facade of the Louvre (1667) from the Italian Bernini (fig. 13). But the significance of the academy went far beyond asserting the independence of French architecture. The academy took an important step in developing the modern figure of the architect by reversing previous methods of training through the workshop and apprenticeship. Students were now taught abstract principles of design before acquiring practical experience in the stone yards and on building sites. Of course, the architects of the Royal Academy were hardly trained to be autonomous artists but were, in actuality, loyal state functionaries (Rosenfeld 1977). England, in contrast, had notable individual designers, such as Inigo Jones and Christopher Wren, but also kept alive the tradition of the mason-architect and the gentleman-architect directing his own bricklayers and carpenters. As in the Renaissance, many architects like Wren gave some leeway to masons and carpenters to modify designs on the job (Wilton-Ely 1977).

The status and image of the poet also rose with the new social and political role assigned to poetry by the French and English monarchies. But to write for money still sullied one's status, whereas to depend on patronage seriously limited the independence we think essential to the artist's existence. Cyrano de Bergerac (the real one) wrote a juicy satire in favor of the Fronde revolt, attacking Cardinal Mazarin as an atheist and sodomite, only to have his princely patron switch sides, upon which Cyrano dutifully produced a withering *Letter against the Frondeurs.* Even in England, where there was still no copyright, few writers made a decent living from printers, and in France dramatic writers were notoriously less well off than the actors themselves. As La Bruyère's line had it, "The actor, snuggled in his carriage, splashes mud in the face of Corneille who must walk" (Viala 1985, 95). Only Molière, like Shakespeare, an actor with his own company, sometimes prospered at it. Aristocratic disdain and the precariousness of making a living led writers like Racine to give up what we would consider his true "literary" vocation as a playwright to become an official historiographer to the king. Boileau accepted a similar position, referring to it as "the glorious activity that rescued me from the job of poetry" (Lough 1978, 130).

If the seventeenth-century situation of the poet lacked the autonomy characteristic of the modern idea of the author/artist, it did include many of the modern gender prejudices. Timothy Reiss has suggested that the modern idea of literature as it began to emerge in the late seventeenth century was male gendered from the beginning (1992). In the early seventeenth century, even aristocratic women ran afoul of gender stereotypes. Lord Denny attacked Lady Mary Wroth for her romance, *The Countess of Montgomeries' Urania* (1621), calling her a "hermaphrodite in show, in deed a monster" and abjured her to "leave idle books alone / For wiser and worthyer women have writte none" (Miller and Waller 1991, 6) (fig. 14). Later in the century some male writers argued that if women did write, they should not attempt epic or tragedy but should stick to "female" genres, such as letter writing or the romance. For Boileau and La Bruyère women were especially equipped to write popular novels because of a supposed female tendency to emotionalism and fixation on matters of intimacy. A few male writers, however, celebrated women's "soundness of discernment for fine and delicate things" (Perrault 1971, 31, 38). Reiss sums up the dominant seventeenth-century position: "Ideal consumers of high culture, admitted producers of subordinate cultural artifacts (short novels, fairy tales, letters), women now had their role essentially set for a long time to come" (1992, 217).

Women's position as consumers of high culture and producers of low can clearly be seen in the role the needle arts played in seventeenth-century debates over womens' place in society. The identification of amateur embroidery as a special province of women's expression that began in the Renaissance became

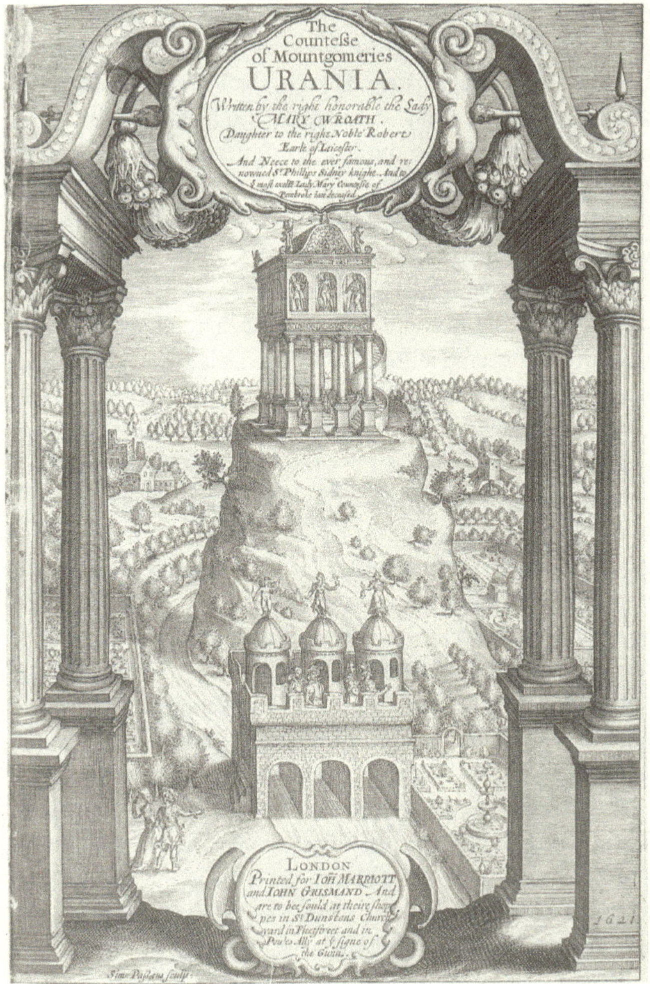


Figure 14. Title page, Lady Mary Wroth, *The Countesse of Montgomeries Urania* (1621). Courtesy Rare Book and Special Collections, University of Illinois Library, Urbana-Champaign. The balloon at the top stresses Lady Mary's pedigree as daughter of the Earl of Leicester and niece of Sir Phillip Sidney, the poet.

even more pronounced in the seventeenth century, and education for noble and middle-class women almost always included embroidery alongside singing, dancing, and the rudiments of reading. The contrast of the needle and the pen would endure through the eighteenth century, and some women saw the hours spent in amateur embroidery as a major impediment to intellectual development. The poet Anne Finch, Countess of Winchilsea, put it bluntly:

> I am obnoxious to each carping tongue
> Who says my hand a needle better fits.
>
> (Parker 1984, 105)

Despite these handicaps, increasing numbers of women published novels in both France and England and a few, like Aphra Behn, made a living writing for the theater during the Restoration. But many women who published still felt they must apologize for it.

As for musicians, composing and performing for pay remained lower-status jobs compared to the liberal arts of scholarly speculation on music theory or of aristocrats playing for diversion. Most musicians were even more dependent than the majority of painters and writers, employed by churches, towns, and aristocratic courts under contracts that specified their duties of composition, playing, education, and maintenance of instruments. Several monarchs and a few grand nobles had their own stable of court musicians, among whom a director, like Lully under Louis XIV, might achieve considerable prestige, yet in general court composer/players were simply part of the vast array of palace servants. Musical scores belonged to those who commissioned them or, if published, to the printer who purchased them since there was no copyright (Raynor 1988).

## The Image of the Artisan/Artist

When we turn from the social situation of artisan/artists to the image or ideal qualities desired, we find that the term "artist" could still be applied to anyone who practiced "an art," but more especially to alchemists. Examples of typical "artists" in Furetière's 1690 French dictionary (1968) were not Raphael or Corneille, but the alchemists Raymond Lull and Paracelsus![1] We also find little trace of the occasional Renaissance image of the unconventional melancholic whose bizarre actions, driven by the vapors, are to be tolerated as a sign of natural talent *(ingenium)*. This was particularly true of manual arts, such as painting and sculpture, whose most famous seventeenth-century practitioners—Rubens, Velázquez, or Bernini, for instance—all wished to be viewed as superior gentlemen (including Caravaggio, who killed two men in knife fights). Although poets did not have to overcome the stain of manual labor, most were as desirous as painters of achieving at least minor noble status. Once Racine was made historiographer to the king, for example, he quickly learned to play his proper role at court, earning the supreme compliment from the Duc de Saint-Simon: there was "nothing of the poet in his dealings, but everything of the gentleman" (Lough 1978, 126).

The key elements of the Renaissance image of the artisan/artist remained in force: facility, talent, enthusiasm, imagination, and invention. Yet here too the seventeenth century was a time of transition, especially in the concepts of talent *(ingegno)* and genius *(genius)*. The two Latin terms behind our word "genius" had quite different meanings: *genius* (a guardian spirit, "genie") and *ingenium* (natural talent). The dominant term, *ingenium*, or innate talent, was usually translated *esprit* in French and "wit" in English, words that had an important career in seventeenth- and eighteenth-century philosophy and literature. In the course of the seventeenth century, however, the term "genius" in English and French came to cover a blend of both its mythological meaning and the meaning of natural talent or wit. The cliché that the good poet needed both rules and talent or wit *(ingenium)* could now be expressed as a need for rules and genius. Like genius, the idea of "enthusiasm" or "inspiration" was also further secularized. The lingering supernatural associations deriving from biblical models or the Platonic tradition were largely eliminated. The skeptical Hobbes ridiculed the invocation of external spirits, saying he could not understand why a man "enabled to speak wisely from the principles of nature . . . loves rather to be thought to speak by inspiration, like a Bagpipe" (Spingarn 1968, 2:59). Yet even when genius and inspiration were declared indispensable by seventeenth-century writers, they were not placed above reason and judgment but in coordination with them (Becq 1994a).

In the seventeenth century, the notion of imagination in the arts had none of today's elevated connotations. Quite the contrary. As a general faculty of the mind, the imagination was still either treated as a receptive storehouse of sensory traces or given a workaday mediating role between body and mind. But when the imagination was not performing its normal image-retention functions and turned to invention or fantasy, thinkers as varied as Hobbes, Descartes, and Pascal declared it liable to fanaticism, madness, or illusion. According to England's poet laureate, John Dryden, "imagination in a poet is a faculty so wild and lawless, that like a high-ranging spaniel, it must have clogs tied to it, lest it outrun the judgment" (Dryden 1961, 8).[2]

The notion of invention, derived from rhetoric, also lacked the crucial modern elements of originality and subjectivity that later turned invention into "creation." Given the central place of imitation in seventeenth-century art theory, poets, painters, and composers were not viewed as "creating" beauty but as discovering what was already there. Only the ignorant, Boileau wrote, would think that having a new thought was a matter of having an idea that no one ever had before; on the contrary, "it is a thought that ought to come to everyone and which someone happened to be the first to express" (Ferry 1990, 54). André Félibien and Roger de Piles took a similar position on invention in painting, viewing the painter's work as an inventive imitation of nature not an imaginative creation in the modern sense (Becq 1994a). Thus, although the status and image of painters, poets, and musicians continued to improve, it still remained far from the modern postromantic ideal of the artist.

## Steps toward the Category of Fine Art

If the idea of the artisan/artist was still in transition toward its modern meaning, the same was true of the category of art itself. "Art" still had the older, more inclusive meaning of "an art," and the old scheme of liberal versus mechanical arts was still widely used even if it was increasingly inadequate to the changing conceptions and relations among the various disciplines, especially the sciences. The term "science" itself was still used for knowledge in general, although our more restricted meaning of science (physics, chemistry, biology, etc.) was beginning to emerge. Even then, the group of disciplines we call "natural science" was often referred to as "natural philosophy." Certainly, the division of knowledge into the sciences, fine arts, and humanities that seems so natural to us was not yet established, although it was approximated by a few individual thinkers. Francis Bacon's tree of knowledge, based on the three faculties of memory, reason, and imagination, placed history under memory, philosophy under reason, and poetry under imagination. Yet Bacon had no category of fine art that joined poetry, painting, and music under a single head. His former assistant, Thomas Hobbes, created a table of knowledge that put poetry, mineralogy, optics, music, ethics, and rhetoric together in the same subdivision under "civil philosophy," whereas it has architecture with navigation and astronomy under "natural philosophy" (Hobbes [1651] 1955, 54–55). Most other seventeenth-century classifications were equally far from our modern conception of the fine arts (Kristeller 1990). Yet even if there was no settled category of fine arts in the seventeenth century, there were some important transitional steps toward it within the individual arts of painting, music, and literature.

Painting and sculpture had already achieved something like liberal arts status in Florence with the creation of the Academy of Design in 1563, and the Pope had granted members of the Roman Academy of St. Luke liberal status in 1600. The creation of the French academy in 1648 clearly elevated painting's cultural prestige in France, although in Spain it took until 1677 for painters to attain a tax-free liberal ranking for their profession. Elsewhere (Portugal, England, the Dutch Republic), it was necessary to fight for the liberal arts status of painting down into the eighteenth century (Da Costa [1696] 1967; Pears 1988). French advocates of the intellectual worth of painting, such as Charles Du Fresnoy, continued to stress the similarity of painting to poetry, whereas the lay president of the Roman academy of painting, Giovanni Bellori, emphasized the high spiritual aspirations of painting through his vigorous reaffirmation of the notion that painting represents ideal beauty.

Music theory had been one of the liberal arts since antiquity, and musical practice (playing) and poetics (composing) had risen in status from the late Middle Ages onward as music became an increasingly important element of court ritual and entertainment. But an even more significant change in the conception of music occurred in the course of the seventeenth century. The older polyphonic ideal of music as a harmony based on mathematical ratios and the concord of the spheres began to be challenged by a new ideal of a monodic music (melody with accompaniment) that could more adequately represent human feelings, an idea already found in Vincenzo Galilei's *Dialogue on Ancient and Modern Music* of 1581. Galilei had argued in good Renaissance humanist fashion that composers should return to the practice of the ancients, who subordinated music to the ideas and feelings expressed in the text. The growing acceptance of the ideal of representing feelings led from madrigals written as voiced melody with instrumental accompaniment to the beginnings of opera around 1600. The first operas in Florence were a sober attempt to revive Greek tragedy, but as opera moved from the princely courts and aristocratic palaces to public theaters, first in Venice, later in northern capitals, it increasingly became an elaborate entertainment spectacle subordinating written scores to virtuoso arias and scenic effects. The older polyphonic style did not go away but tended to retreat into church music, although even there the Reformation and Counter Reformation churches encouraged a music that served texts.

This new emphasis on the representational and expressive aspects of music made an important contribution to reshaping the classification of the arts. In the running debate between adherents of the old polyphony and the proponents of the new melodic expressiveness, the polyphonists continued to stress music's relation to mathematics and astronomy within the liberal arts quadrivium, whereas the expressivists tended to draw analogies between music and rhetoric or poetry within the trivium. By moving music closer to rhetoric and poetry, the newer melodic and representational trend helped weaken the ties within the quadrivium and foreshadowed the later grouping of poetry, rhetoric, and music with painting sculpture and architecture that would be called the fine arts.

There were also some important seventeenth-century steps toward the modern category of literature (imaginative poetry, drama, fiction) that helped prepare the way for the emergence of the category of fine art. Cardinal Richelieu's creation of the Académie Française (1635) with the charge to purify the French language and Charles II's restoration of the theaters and naming of John

Dryden as England's poet laureate were recognitions of poetry's serious status as contributor to political stability and monarchic glory. No one better summed up the seventeenth-century union of the political, ethical, and artistic than the noted classicist Anne Dacier: "Belles-lettres are the source of good taste, good manners and all good government" (Reiss 1992, 37). Yet terms like "belles lettres," "poetry," and "literature" were still not fixed in their modern sense, and "literature" continued to be used primarily to mean book learning in general. Late in the century, however, an additional meaning began to attach to the term "literature," as reflected in Pierre Richelet's *Dictionnaire françois* of 1680, which defined it as "knowledge of belles-lettres," or the work of "Orators, Poets and Historians" (Reiss 1992, 231). Even so, Antoine Furetière, compiler of a competing dictionary a few years later, said of the term "belles lettres" (no doubt with Richelet in mind): "People call humane letters, or erroneously belles-lettres, the knowledge of poets and orators, whereas true Belles-Lettres are physics, geometry and the solid sciences" (Viala 1985, 282).

As Marc Fumaroli has shown, these conflicting attitudes toward the terms "belles lettres" and "literature" reflected their marginal status compared to the continuing prestige of eloquence and rhetorical theory. "Age of Eloquence, age of rhetoric, the seventeenth century saw the birth of Belles-Lettres: it is not yet the age of Literature. . . . The Literary only becomes perceptible after the fact, in the revealing and deforming light of a later stage of culture" (Fumaroli 1980, 31–32). Although Fumaroli emphasizes the difference between late seventeenth-century practices and modern ideas, and Timothy Reiss focuses on the similarities, the two positions are not incompatible. Erica Harth has argued that although a separate realm of literature was not fully established, changes in both the novel and travel writing show that the old category of literature was beginning to divide into more or less distinct realms of "truthful fictions" (poetry, novel, drama) and "truthful facts" (travel, mechanics, zoology), a division that Douglas Patey and Alvin Kernan see as complete only a full century later (Harth 1983; Patey 1988; Kernan 1990). Even more important than linguistic signs of the beginning of the modern idea of literature is evidence of a nascent literary public and vernacular criticism in the 1680s, especially in France. Prior to 1678 most literary debate in France took place among a small Parisian aristocracy and upper bourgeoisie, and what few journals existed were either political or highly academic. But in 1678, the monthly *Le mercure gallant* began to add excerpts and reviews of current novels, especially the controversial *La princesse de Clèves* by Madame de La Fayette. Her novel was controversial, at least, after the editor of *Le mercure gallant* invited his readers to form discussion groups and send in letters summarizing their reaction to it, thus treating his lay "public" as if their individual opinions mattered (DeJean 1997). The eventual expansion of this embryonic public for literature in the eighteenth century, combined with the emergence of similar publics for music and the visual arts, would play a key role in establishing the modern system of fine arts.

Although a category of literature was beginning to emerge in the late seventeenth century and many people were beginning to associate music with rhetoric and poetry, and although painting, sculpture, and architecture were widely accepted as liberal arts, the modern category of fine art still did not appear. Before it could emerge, the old liberal arts–versus–mechanical arts scheme itself had to be broken apart and reorganized. That began to happen through two other seventeenth-century developments: the increasing recognition of the sciences as a distinct realm of knowledge and practice and a transformation in the understanding of rhetoric that reduced it from a mode of practical knowledge and persuasive reasoning to a matter of style and ornament.

The founding of the Royal Society in London (1660) and the Académie Royale des Sciences in France (1663) were only the most visible signs of the institutionalization of science as a distinct realm of activity (Briggs 1991; Shapin 1996). Whereas many twentieth-century art historians have stressed the liberation of the individual artist from the workshops and guilds, some historians of science have stressed the cooperation of scientists with the workshops. The importance of the mechanical arts to the rise of science was not simply that they provided Galileo with a telescope; they also offered scientists a model of knowledge based on experience and collaborative effort (Rossi 1970). Of course, Galileo's insistence on mathematics as a key to a mechanical understanding of nature was as important as his emphasis on physical experiments. By joining the experimental and mathematical methods, seventeenth-century scientists not only laid the basis for the sciences to achieve an autonomous identity but also drove a wedge into the liberal arts, pushing geometry and astronomy toward disciplines like mechanics and physiology that seemed more appropriate company than music, which was itself moving toward rhetoric and poetry.

A parallel threat to the coherence of the liberal arts system in the seventeenth century came from changes in the conception of rhetoric, especially Descartes's rigorous separation of logic, as a "geometric" method of reasoning leading to certainty, from rhetoric, the "art" of reasoning toward the probable. Although "rhetoric" is a pejorative term today, from Aristotle and Cicero down through Montaigne and Erasmus, rhetoric, as the art of persuasion, had given fairly equal place to each of its three components: invention (developing arguments), disposition (ordering arguments), and eloquence (style and delivery). In the seventeenth century, Descartes's pursuit of certainty reinforced Petrus Ramus's earlier claim that invention and disposition should be transferred from rhetoric to logic and that rhetoric should henceforth concern itself only with style and delivery. One effect of Cartesianism was to hasten the breakup of the old liberal arts trivium that had grouped grammar and rhetoric with logic by pushing a rhetoric reduced to style even closer to poetry and by associating logic with geometry and the physical sciences.

Although all the elements for the emergence of the category of fine art were in place by the 1690s, such a reorganization of categories did not occur for another fifty years. Even at the end of the seventeenth century, for example, many people still associated music with mathematics and astronomy rather than with rhetoric and poetry; the English scholar William Wotton even called music a "physico-mathematical science" (Wotton [1694] 1968, 284). And although painting, sculpture, and architecture were often grouped together using names like "arts of design," "figurative arts," even "beaux-arts," no single name or concept became dominant even for the visual arts as a group (Brunot 1966). Horace's dictum linking poetry and painting was a commonplace, as were vague invocations of the "sister arts," but most of the new groupings of the arts were passing remarks, never worked out in any consistent fashion, let alone generally accepted.[3] A vivid example of the uncertainty about the new ways of classifying the arts is Charles Perrault's 1690 essay describing a nobleman's collection of eight allegorical paintings of the liberal arts. Perrault suggested that these eight arts should really be called "beaux arts" since they were "worthy of being admired and cultivated by a gentleman" and marked by "taste and genius," comments that make his idea of beaux arts sound remarkably like the modern category of fine art (Kristeller 1990, 195). But the arts depicted in the paintings included not only poetry, oratory, music, architecture, painting, and sculpture but also optics and mechanics. Perrault's mixture of what we would radically separate as art and science nicely exemplifies the transitional state of classifications at the end of the seventeenth century. It was to be another fifty years before the modern category of fine art was worked out in a way that gained general assent and became regulative for subsequent generations, a story we will pick up at the beginning of the next chapter.

## The Role of Taste

If seventeenth-century classifications of the arts were still in transition toward our modern categories, so were notions of how we should respond to the arts. Poetry, painting, music, and other arts were still seen as serving useful functions such as instruction, prestige, accompaniment, decoration, and diversion, whereas the number of people who began to appreciate painting or sculpture "for its own sake" were a tiny elite. Even in Italy, where "a body of connoisseurs was coming into being prepared to judge pictures on their aesthetic merits," such an attitude was one "that only generally becomes apparent in the eighteenth century" (Haskell 1980, 130).

A telling indicator of the continuing functionalism of the arts was the absence of institutions like the art museum, the secular concert, or copyright, which today help set works of art apart from other cultural artifacts. Yet one can identify some predecessors of these institutions. The beginnings of the secular concert have been traced to amateur musical groups such as the German *collegium musicum* and to the occasional concerts offered in London taverns from the 1660s on. Forerunners of the art museum, of course, were the large princely collections of paintings or sculpture, although most were closed to all but a few artists or connoisseurs on invitation. The other precursor of the art museum was the "cabinet of curiosities," *studiolo,* or *Kunstkammer,* a specially designed building or room in a princely palace for exhibiting clocks, scientific instruments, rare plants, and minerals alongside paintings, sculptures, and precious jewels. These assemblages were conceived on an encyclopedic principle reflecting the humanist ideal of knowledge, and the inclusion of painting and sculpture in them is one more sign that there was not yet a separate category of fine art (Hooper-Greenhill 1992; Bredekamp 1995). Of course, two other major art institutions already existed by the seventeenth century: the theater, which went back to the late Middle Ages, and the opera, which came into being at the beginning of the century. As the opera moved from its function as court diversion into public theaters, it became an entertainment medium for the well-off, in which the libretto was increasingly subordinated to virtuoso arias, orchestral interludes, ballets, and spectacular scenic effects.

Although the arts were still regarded primarily in terms of purpose in the seventeenth century, there is also evidence of an increased emphasis on the role of taste. The metaphorical use of "taste" goes as far back as the Hebrew Scriptures, and we have noted its application to Renaissance painting by a few Italian connoisseurs. In the seventeenth century, "taste" was even more extensively used for the ability to make discriminating choices in social life and the arts (Barnouw 1993).[4] Debates over taste in the arts centered around a generalized classicism, the belief in following ancient models and ideals shared by leading Italian (Giovanni Bellori), French (Nicolas Boileau), and English (John Dryden) writers whose views on poetry and painting remained a powerful force through much of the eighteenth century. The core beliefs of classicism were that painting, poetry, and music are arts of imitation, for which the object is the beautiful in nature, the means is reason, and the end is to instruct through pleasure.[5]

> Love reason then; that whate'er you write
> Borrow always from her its prize and light.
>
> (Boileau 1972, 47)

During the last half of the century, there was a growing resistance to these classicist positions in the name of feeling, individual judgment, and modern genres such as the novel. It was frequently said that members of the public, who knew little of the rules of art, might still make a correct response to theater or painting through feeling (Piles 1708, 94; Reiss 1992, 92). Yet these champions of feeling were not so much antireason as they were trying to enlarge the scope of reason itself (Becq 1994a). The idea of feeling was in its own way as broad and complex as the idea of reason, changing gradually in the course of the century from the notions of passion and emotion (Descartes's treatise on the emotions) to tenderness (Madelaine de Scudéry's famous "map" of the feelings), and culminating in the idea of sentiment, which became so important in the eighteenth century (DeJean 1997). "Sentiment" covered a territory ranging from the sentimental all the way up to a notion of tacit knowledge or spiritual intuition. Earlier in the century, Pascal had already claimed that the "heart has its reasons the reason knows not," for it reasons "tacitly, naturally and without art" (Pascal 1958, 73).

Among late seventeenth-century writers, Dominique Bouhours is best known for insisting on the role of feeling in our spontaneous response to social situations and poetic works, using the cliché, *je ne sais quoi* (I know not what) (Bouhours 1920). Most of Bouhours examples of the *je ne sais quoi* were not taken from the arts but from the social realm, such as the way we recognize a face, detect a fever, or find another person noble or lovable. Yet, so little was Bouhours an anti-intellectualist that he spoke of the *je ne sais quoi* experience as itself a kind of "rapid reason" (200). Bouhours and the others who emphasized grace, heart, delicacy, and feeling were suggesting that there might be a third way of responding to poetry, painting, or music between discursive reason and pure sensory enjoyment.

This attempt to combine reason with feeling also had important gender implications. Although Perrault and others admired women as both writers and judges of literature, for a philosopher like Malebranche it was the same emotional sensitivity that made women unfit to produce serious poetry that enabled them to appreciate its sentiments (Malebranche 1970, 266). Yet if some writers were willing to make women natural arbiters of taste, for still others, women's inconstant reason limited them to an appreciation of the merely ornamental and sentimental aspect of the arts. It is perhaps no accident that one male writer dismissed Bouhours as a ridiculous *précieuse* who had spent too much time with "women and minor teachers," whereas Madame de Sévigné found Bouhours a man of many-faceted intelligence (Ferry 1990, 54).

In attempting to enlarge the idea of reason, the partisans of feeling and visual immediacy took an important step toward the modern idea of the aesthetic, but few offered a theoretical elaboration of their position. The major thinker besides Pascal to formulate the philosophical implications of the cognitive role of feeling or rapid reason was Leibniz. Whereas Descartes had spoken of the discovery of "clear and distinct" ideas as the guarantee of certainty, Leibniz argued that there are ideas that are clear and yet not distinct; that is, we clearly perceive them but cannot distinctly separate them into parts for analysis. Such ideas are "fused" or compact, like the perception of red, the taste of a lemon, or the sound of a chord.

Rather than thinking of each musical note distinctly, we grasp harmony and melody all at once in a fused way (Leibniz 1969, 291; Barnouw 1993). Similarly, "we sometimes know *clearly*, without the slightest doubt, that a poem or a picture is well or badly done, because there is in it an *I know not what* which satisfies or shocks us" (Leibniz 1951, 325). Yet Leibniz did not limit tacit knowing or the *je ne sais quoi* to the arts any more than Bouhours had. Before ideas like those of Bouhour's and Leibniz's could lead to the modern idea of the aesthetic, the fine arts would have to be separated from both the crafts and the sciences and reconceived as an autonomous category requiring a distinct faculty of judgment. The late seventeenth century remained in these respects, as in so many others, a transitional period.

PART II

# Art Divided

## Overview

J. H. Plumb describes the cultural scene of mid-seventeenth-century England this way: "No public libraries, no concerts, . . . no museums" (Plumb 1972, 30). By the end of the eighteenth century, all these cultural institutions and more had appeared across Europe along with the rise of a distinct market and public for the fine arts and the new concepts of fine art, artist, and the aesthetic. The convergence of these social, institutional, and intellectual changes gave us the modern system of fine arts. There were actually three stages of convergence: an initial one from around 1680 to 1750 during which many elements of the modern system of art that had emerged piecemeal since the late Middle Ages began to be more closely integrated; a second and crucial one from around 1750 to 1800 that definitively separated fine art from craft, artist from artisan, and the aesthetic from other modes of experience; and a final stage of consolidation and elevation, from around 1800 to 1830, during which the term "art" began to signify an autonomous spiritual domain, the artistic vocation was sanctified, and the concept of the aesthetic began to replace taste. Although the word "art" also continued to be used in its older and broader sense, by the time the new system of fine art was firmly established in the nineteenth century, the adjective "fine" could be dropped, leaving the term "art" ambiguous when context did not make clear whether the older sense of "an art" was intended or the new fine art sense.

But *why* was the art system of the previous centuries replaced by a fine art system at just this time? At one level, the reasons were intellectual: ideas of fine art, artist, and aesthetic provided solutions to a series of conceptual problems inherited from previous centuries. But an exclusively conceptual study focused on "great thinkers" would be false to the extent that changes in concepts were also justifications for the new institutions that embodied them and the new cultural class that believed in them. Tracing how the use of terms changed and how various thinkers worked out the meaning of new ideas is necessary, but it does not by itself account for why one regulative system (art) was replaced by another system (fine art) at this time.

Another way of explaining why the modern system of fine arts only became fully established between 1680 and 1830 would take a long-term sociological view and consider it the final stage of a process of social differentiation beginning in the late Middle Ages. Viewed from such a distance, art's becoming an independent domain simply looks like part of a natural dissolution of the integrated activities of medieval society into distinct spheres of politics, economics, religion, science, and art. Unlike essentialist views, which treat the modern idea of art as a human universal or a historical destiny, the concept of differentiation does not see the modern fine art system as the unfolding of an essence but as a contingent response to the general forces of modernization and secularization. Unfortunately, the differentiation model operates at such a high level of generality that it gives us little sense of the specific mechanisms by which art became an autonomous realm.

A third approach is also needed, one that links conceptual changes to specific social and economic factors, such as the rise of a market economy, the growth and status aspirations of the middle class, the increase in literacy, and the preservation of gender roles. The point is not that these factors "caused" the invention of fine art, a claim that would simply be the converse of assuming that ideas like fine art and the aesthetic are the result of discussions among a few philosophers. Yet there is clear evidence that many of those who articulated the new ideas of fine art, artist, and aesthetic were not merely completing the conceptual developments of their predecessors but were also reacting to the expanded role of the market and the middle class and to new institutions and practices. The new art institutions played a key mediating role between changing concepts and socioeconomic contexts. Institutions such as the art museum, the secular concert, and literary criticism were the point at which the social and ideational met, mutually constituting and reinforcing each other.

Each of the following three chapters describes this interplay among intellectual, institutional, and social-economic factors in the emergence of the fine art system. Chapter 5 begins with the conceptual and semantic evidence for the division of the older idea of art into fine art versus craft, then looks at the institutions and behaviors that embodied that division and connects them to the growth of a market system for the arts and the expansion of a middle-class art public. Chapter 6 relates the new ideal of the artist to artists' need to assert independence of the new art market and art public in the wake of the breakdown of the old patronage system. With the emergence of institutions like separate exhibitions and dealers for painting, regular secular concerts, and the establishment of copyright, a new image of the artist as creative genius was consecrated along with a new concept of the "work" as a self-contained world. Chapter 6 also looks at the gendering of genius and the fate of the artisan and closes with an analytical comparison of the patronage and market systems. Chapter 7 shows how the idea of a distinct aesthetic experience for fine art emerged from the problem of taste and describes the institutional expression of this new sensibility through such things as the elimination of stage seating in the theater and the development of the picturesque tour. Although a book of this size cannot attempt to follow particular theories of art or the aesthetic—only the general assumptions that underlie such theories—I close chapter 7 with a brief discussion of the views of Immanuel Kant and Friedrich Schiller, whose writings on aesthetics offered influential justifications for the modern system of art as it had developed up to the end of the eighteenth century.

CHAPTER 5

# Polite Arts for the Polite Classes

ON JANUARY 22, 1687, Charles Perrault read a long didactic poem to the Académie Française declaring modern writers to be the equal of the ancients, citing as one of his proofs the superiority of modern science to Aristotle and throwing in a few criticisms of Homer along the way. Many of the "forty immortals," as the members of the academy were called, could hardly sit still. The leading poet and critic Nicolas Boileau muttered throughout the session and had something like a nervous breakdown afterward. The famous Quarrel of the Ancients and Moderns was on, a "Battle of the Books," as Swift satirized the English version, which flared up periodically from 1690 to 1730. Perrault was not the first to claim that just as Galileo's physics was superior to Aristotle's, so modern writers might equal or excel the ancients. But to suggest to a generation brought up on Homer and Virgil that a work such as Jean Chapelain's 1656 epic *The Maid of Orleans*, was the equal of the *Aeneid* could induce sputtering outrage.

Yet the issues at stake were much deeper than a mere squabble among academics. One issue was the question of whether the emerging art public rather than the scholarly elite are to be judges of literature and, more specifically, whether a new (female-identified) genre, such as the novel, was to be accepted as a successor of epic poetry (DeJean 1997). Above all, the quarrel brought into the open the shake up of the old liberal arts system by the rise in prestige of the sciences and the decline of rhetoric that had been taking place during the last half of the seventeenth century. By 1700, the old liberal arts scheme was undergoing a reorganization that would eventually lead to the separate categories of fine art, science, and humanities. The traditional core of the liberal arts, it will be remembered, included the trivium of grammar, rhetoric, and logic and the quadrivium of arithmetic, geometry, astronomy, and music theory. Of the modern fine arts, poetry had long been taught as a subdivision of rhetoric, and by the beginning of the eighteenth century, music was seen by many as closer to rhetoric than to mathematics, and painting, sculpture, and architecture were also widely accepted as liberal arts. Before the modern category of fine arts could be constructed, however, painting, sculpture, and architecture not only had to join poetry and music as liberal arts, but these five then had to be separated from the other liberal arts of grammar, rhetoric, logic, mathematics, and astronomy and regrouped under a new name. The success of the experimental sciences and the reduction of rhetoric to style in the course of the seventeenth century were crucial to this process of dissolving the old liberal arts scheme, and the Quarrel of the Ancients and Moderns pushed it along.

## Constructing the Category of Fine Art

Even before the dust had settled on the quarrel, there was a general recognition of the deep differences between the sciences and the arts. Leading "moderns" were ready to concede that progress may be easier to discern in those areas that depend on calculation than in arts, which depend on individual talent. William Wotton lists "Natural History, Physiology and Mathematics" as typical of disciplines in which the moderns have clearly excelled over the ancients but admits that in "Poesie, Oratory, Architecture, Painting, and Statuary" the moderns can at best equal their predecessors. (Notice that he omits music, which he still regarded as connected to mathematics [Wotton (1694) 1968, 18].) Although the quarrel merely dramatized changes that had longer-term causes, the period from 1730 to 1750 following the quarrel saw various proposals for new groupings until the new category of fine arts became firmly established in the 1750s.

The state of classification in the early decades of the eighteenth century is well illustrated by the abbé Dubos's widely read *Critical Reflections on Poetry and Painting* (1719), which talked of painting, poetry, and music within the same book yet did not make a fixed category of them, even occasionally joining them to the arts of military leadership or medicine ([1719] 1993). Similarly, the tree of knowledge at the head of Chamber's *Cyclopedia* of 1728 broke out a category of science from the old liberal arts scheme—but not one of fine art. Chambers grouped arithmetic and geometry with the new disciplines of physics, mineralogy, and zoology under "Natural or Scientifical" knowledge, but he nowhere hints at the modern category of the fine arts, scattering painting, sculpture, architecture, and music among fortification, hydraulics, and navigation, all under the general rubric of "mixed-mathematics," and still locating poetry next to grammar and rhetoric (Chambers 1728) (fig. 15). Before the modern category of fine art could be established, three things needed to come together and gain wide acceptance: a limited *set* of arts, a commonly accepted *term* to easily identify the set, and some generally agreed upon *principle(s)* or criteria for distinguishing that set from all others.

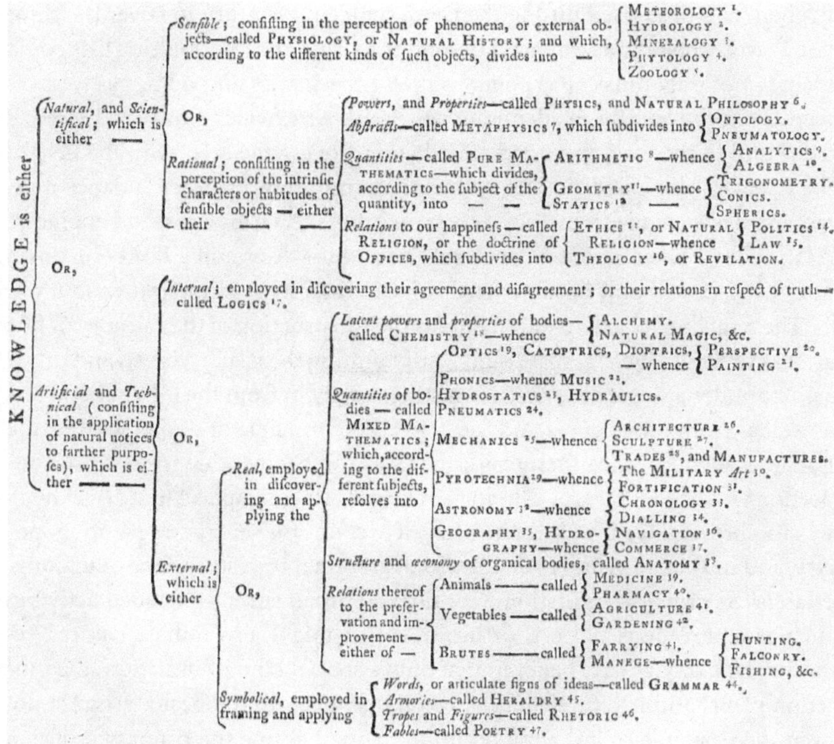


Figure 15. Ephraim Chambers, table of knowledge from *Cyclopedia* (1728). Courtesy Rare Book and Special Collections, University of Illinois Library, Urbana-Champaign.

The *set* that formed the modern category of fine art had at its core poetry, painting, sculpture, architecture, and music, to which one or more arts might be added such as dance, rhetoric, or landscape gardening. This core set, which was formalized in the 1740s, was not without partial and scattered precedents in the Renaissance and seventeenth century, such as invocations of Horace's *ut pictura poesis* or vague references to the "sister arts," but none of these lists were consistently put forward as an articulated category using an identifying term and a unifying principle, nor did any of them become regulative of discourse about the arts as was now about to happen (Kristeller 1990).

The *term* that eventually won out over such phrases as "elegant arts," "noble arts," or "higher arts," of course, was the French "beaux-arts" (beautiful arts), which was translated directly into German, Spanish, and Italian, as well as into English as "polite arts" or "fine arts." Although "beaux arts," often without the hyphen, had been used during the late seventeenth century to cover the three visual arts, when it was extended beyond the visual arts the resulting lists could include not only music and poetry but also mechanics and optics, as we have seen. Even the Société Académique des Beaux-Arts, which flourished in Paris from 1726 to the early 1730s and aimed at improving the arts "with the help of the sciences," included, among its members, not only a painter, a dance master, and a few engravers but also several watchmakers, surgeons, and engineers (Hahn 1981). The referent of the term "beaux-arts" was still a fluid one down into the 1730s and only become fixed in its modern sense in the 1740s and 1750s.

The final intellectual requirement for the construction of the category of fine art was some *principle(s)* that could justify uniting the visual, verbal, and musical arts under a single head yet also distinguish them from the other liberal arts as well as from the sciences and the crafts. The principle of design used by the Italian academies since the Renaissance was too narrow due to its close connection with the visual arts. The ancient liberal arts principle of mind over body was too broad since it would not by itself account for separating painting, poetry, and music as a group from the arts of grammar or history. One other long-established principle, imitation, was also too broad since it included activities such as embroidery, pottery, or birdcalls that might also imitate nature. Accordingly, many writers believed that only a special kind of imitation, the imitation of Beautiful Nature *(la belle Nature)*, applied to the beaux-arts. Yet not even the principle of imitating beautiful nature became the primary criterion justifying the new set and term.

Some combination of at least four other principles was regularly invoked. Two of these principles—"genius" and "imagination"—concerned the production of works of fine art; the other two—"pleasure versus utility" and "taste"—concerned the aims and mode of reception of the beaux-arts. The combination of pleasure versus utility with genius and imagination was frequently employed to distinguish the beaux-arts from the mechanical arts or crafts. The combination of pleasure versus utility with taste was employed to distinguish the beaux-arts from the sciences and from other liberal arts like grammar or logic. Among these principles, pleasure versus utility played a pivotal role. As we have seen, the old Horatian commonplace that the arts aim to "instruct and please" had been current since the Renaissance. Sometimes the two aims were seen as parallel and equally valid functions; more often, pleasure was seen as subordinate to the aim of instruction or utility. But in the eighteenth century, pleasure began to be systematically opposed to utility as a criterion for distinguishing one group of the liberal arts from the rest under the name "beaux-arts." But not just any kind of pleasure was involved. Over the course of the century, the notion of a special kind of refined pleasure or taste would be transformed into the modern idea of the aesthetic, a process we will discuss in chapter 7 on the construction of the aesthetic.

Obviously, a cultural transformation as broad as the construction of the modern category of fine art cannot be dated or tied to any individual. But intellectual historians often cite Charles Batteux's *Les beaux arts réduit à un même principe* (The fine arts reduced to a single principle) (1746) as the first widely read book to integrate the term "beaux-arts" with a restricted set of arts, in this case music, poetry, painting, sculpture, and dance, and to group them on the basis of an explicit principle, the imitation of beautiful nature (Batteux [1746] 1989). Although Batteux made imitation his central criteria, he also gave an important place to the opposition between pleasure and utility. On this basis, Batteux claimed there are actually three classes of arts: those that simply minister to our needs (the mechanical arts); those whose aim is pleasure (the beaux-arts par excellence); and those that combine utility and pleasure (eloquence and architecture). Batteux also used two other criteria for separating the beaux-arts from the rest: genius, which he calls "the father of the arts," because it imitates beautiful nature, and taste, which judges how well beautiful nature has been imitated (Batteux 1989, 82–83).

Batteux's treatise had an immediate effect not only in France but also in Germany, where two translations appeared in 1751. His book made it into English even sooner, with a pirated translation/adaptation published in 1749 as *The Polite Arts; or, A Dissertation on Poetry, Painting, Musick, Architecture, and Eloquence (*Kristeller 1990, 210). Batteux had clearly managed to hit on a formulation that captured the direction toward which ideas about the classification of the arts had been moving for some time. This is nowhere more evident than in France itself, where another work destined to have even greater influence on elite thinking offered a more fully articulated case for the new category: the *Encyclopédie* (Diderot and d'Alembert 1751–72). At the head of the *Encyclopédie,* Diderot placed a comprehensive table of all knowledge based on Bacon's division of human faculties into memory (history), reason (science), and imagination (poetry). A comparison of the *Encylopédie*'s 1751 tree of knowledge with Chamber's *Cyclopedia* (1728) shows that a decisive turn toward the modern category of art had occurred. Whereas Chambers had placed poetry next to grammar and rhetoric and put sculpture with trades and manufacture, the *Encyclopédie* now grouped all five fine arts (poetry, painting, sculpture, engraving, and music) under the faculty of imagination as one of three main divisions of knowledge, splendidly isolated from all other arts, disciplines, and sciences (fig. 16).

D'Alembert's "Preliminary Discourse" in the *Encyclopédie,* justifying the new tree of knowledge, announced, in an obvious reference to Batteux, that some of the liberal arts had been "reduced to principles" and "called Beaux-Arts primarily because they have pleasure for their aim" (d'Alembert 1986, 108–9). D'Alembert's list of the newly classified and baptized beaux-arts included poetry, painting, sculpture, music, and architecture (from Batteux's list, he dropped dance and rhetoric and added architecture, abandoning without comment the category mixed arts). But pleasure was not the only thing by which d'Alembert distinguished the beaux-arts from the "more necessary or useful liberal arts such as Grammar, Logic or Ethics." These other liberal arts, he claimed, have fixed and established rules, but the beaux-arts are the product of an inventive genius. Above all, the beaux-arts are distinguished from other arts and sciences by belonging under the faculty of imagination rather than memory and reason. In a general summary of the tree of knowledge, d'Alembert explained why he and Diderot substituted the term "poetry" for "beaux-arts" in their table of knowledge: "Painting, Sculpture, Architecture, Poetry, Music and their different divisions, make up the third general distribution that is born of imagination, and whose parts are included under the name Beaux-Arts. One could also include them under the general title of Painting, since all the Beaux-Arts can be reduced to painting, and only differ by the means they employ; finally, one could relate them all to Poetry, taking that word in its natural signification, which is nothing else than invention or creation" (1986, 119).

There is a certain irony in the *Encyclopédie*'s role in spreading the new category of fine art since one aim of the encyclopedists was to celebrate and codify the mechanical arts, to which it devoted many articles and most of its plates. Diderot's article "Art" in the first volume of 1751, for example, is devoted entirely to an appreciation of the mechanical arts and makes no reference to the new category. "Beaux-arts" only gets a separate section in the 1776 supplement to the *Encyclopédie,* and it wasn't until 1798 that the Académie Française finally gave it official recognition in its dictionary (Robinet 1776).

Yet the new category and term spread steadily across Europe between 1750 and 1770. By the end of the eighteenth century, almost all discussions of the arts in Germany, England, and Italy used the new grouping and a version of the name. In Italian, "beaux-arts" became *belli-arti,* in German *schöenen künste,* and in English the term "fine arts" eventually won out over "elegant arts" and "polite arts." Americans also picked it up. Writing home from Paris in 1780, John Adams remarked that it was not "the fine Arts" America needed just then,

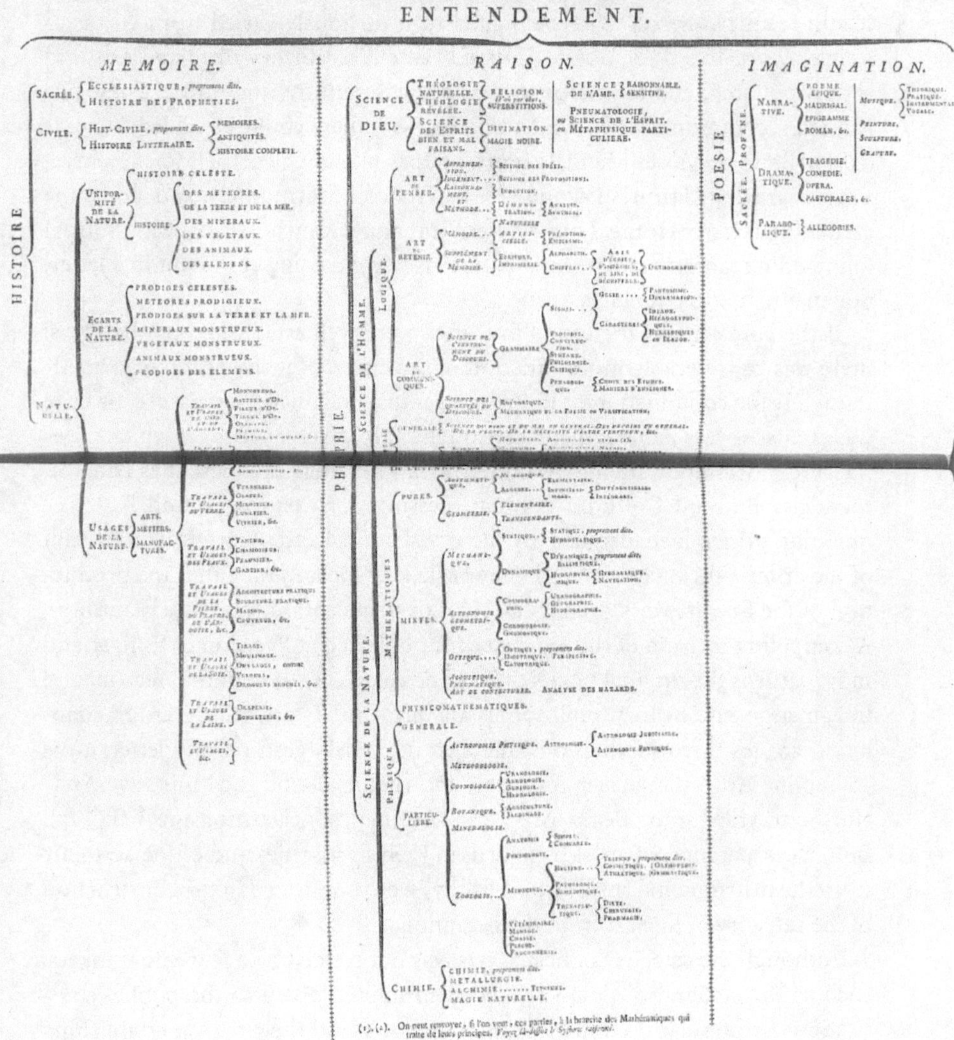


Figure 16. Denis Diderot and Jean le Rond d'Alembert, table of knowledge, *Encyclopédie* (1751). Courtesy Rare Book and Special Collections, University of Illinois Library, Urbana-Champaign. Although d'Alembert's preface uses the term "beaux-arts," the table puts the fine arts under the general rubric "Poésie" and substitutes engraving for architecture. The *Encyclopédie*'s concern to preserve and spread the knowledge of the crafts is reflected in the large list of entries under the subcategory of "Usages de la Nature" beneath "Mémoire"on the left, listing such things as working with gold, glass, leather, stone, silk, and so on.

but he must "study politics and war" in order that his grandchildren might study "painting, poetry, music, architecture, statuary, tapestry, and porcelaine" (Adams 1963, 3:342).

Although the term "fine arts" was firmly established by the end of the eighteenth century, the set of arts assigned to it obviously varied from writer to writer. Most, like d'Alembert, dropped Batteux's category of mixed arts and simply put architecture with poetry, painting, sculpture, and music. These five formed a common core to which one or two others could be added, such as dance (Batteux; Moses Mendelssohn), oratory (J. A. Schlegel; Thomas Robertson), engraving (Jacques Lacombe; Jean-François Marmontel), and landscape gardening (Henry Home, Lord Kames; Immanuel Kant).[1] Adams was unusual in including tapestry and porcelain, but his was a passing comment in a letter, not an attempt to enunciate a set.

If the core set and the term "fine arts" were well established by the 1770s, there was considerably more variation in the criteria for the new category. Although some combination of imitation, genius, imagination, pleasure, or taste was almost always named, there were often sharp divergences over which criteria were most important and what they meant. Writers as different as Diderot, Mendelssohn, and Gotthold Ephraim Lessing, for example, found Batteux's imitation principle inadequate. By the 1770s, critical and theoretical discussion of the criteria for inclusion in the new category focused on either the production of the fine art work (genius vs. rule) or its reception (pleasure vs. utility). A competing revision of the *Encyclopédie*, published at Yverdon in Switzerland in 1770, turns the original table's organizing categories of memory, reason, and imagination into history, philosophy, and art. Under "art," the Yverdon adaptation creates three subdivisions: the "Art of Signs" (gestures and letters), the "Symbolic Arts" (language, grammar, and rhetoric), and the "Imitative Arts" (further divided into "Beaux Arts" and "Aesthetics") (Darnton 1979) (fig. 17). Both the separation of artist from artisan (genius vs. rule) and of the aesthetic from the instrumental (pleasure vs. utility) were implicated in the construction of the category of fine art from the beginning.

Although the category of beaux-arts was not created by a few elite thinkers, such as Batteux and d'Alembert, and then filtered down to the public, codifications by popular dictionaries and handbooks did their part in establishing it. In 1752, for example, about the time the *Encyclopédie* began to appear in a costly edition, Jacques Lacombe published in Paris a far more accessible small book that deftly summed up the new assumptions: "*Arts* (Beaux); are distinguished from the Arts in general, insofar as the latter are destined for utility, the

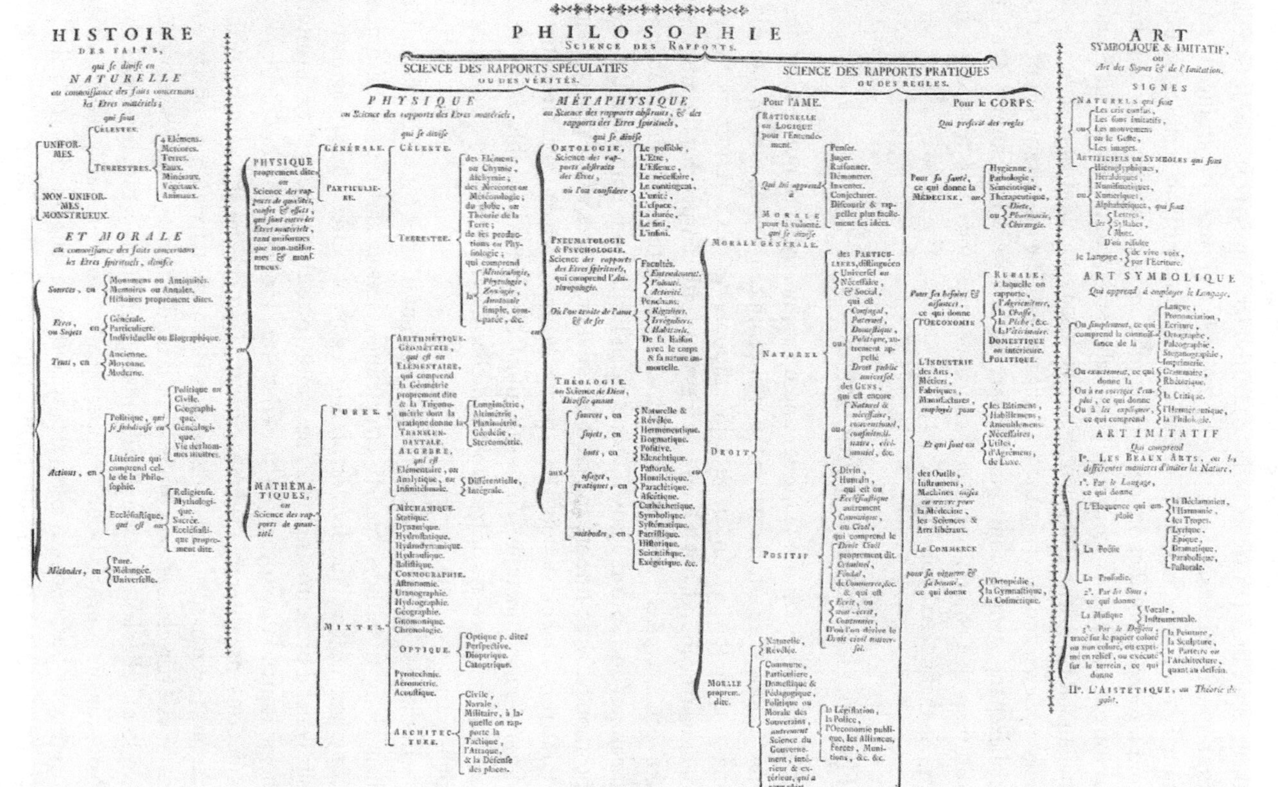


Figure 17. Table of knowledge, *Encyclopédie,* Yverdon, Switzerland (1770). Courtesy Rare Book and Special Collections, University of Illinois Library, Urbana-Champaign.

former for pleasure. The *Beaux-Arts* are the offspring of genius; they have nature for model, taste for master, pleasure for aim . . . the true rule for judging them is feeling" (Saisselin 1970, 18). Although hardly portable, J. G. Sulzer's four-volume *General Theory of the Fine Arts* (1771) was also arranged as a dictionary for the German public. But more important than treatises by Batteux and d'Alembert or dictionaries by Lacombe and Sulzer were informal conversations at exhibitions, concerts, bookstalls, and reading rooms, in French or Italian salons, British clubs, Dutch and German coffeehouses, and the many essays, reviews, and letters in the periodical press. The important role of such social exchanges will become more apparent when we look at some of the art institutions that embodied the new concepts and some characteristics of the art public that talked about them.

## The New Institutions of Fine Art

With the exception of the theater and opera, nearly all of our modern fine art institutions were established in the eighteenth century. Naturally, if one is trying to trace the "origin" of such institutions, various forerunners and precedents can be found, but it is only in the eighteenth century that the art museum, the secular concert, and literary criticism take on their modern functions and meanings and spread across Europe. Such institutions embodied the new opposition between fine art and craft by providing places where poetry, painting, or instrumental music could be experienced and discussed apart from their traditional social functions. This institutional separation probably did as much as any number of essays or treatises by intellectuals to establish a distinct category of fine art.

In the case of literature the rapid growth of the market for books and journals along with the spread of circulating libraries and the establishment of copyright hastened the division of the category of "letters" into imaginative versus general literature (fig. 18). These more directly market-related institutions helped spread three other practices that were more specifically "literary" in the modern sense: literary criticism, literary history, and the vernacular literary canons (Kernan 1989). Although general theoretical treatises on poetry go back as far as Aristotle, literary criticism in the modern sense of the review of current works of belles lettres was only fully institutionalized in the eighteenth century. Not only did journals begin to appear that focused primarily on the review of new books, but there was also a steady shift from religious titles to belles lettres (Berghahn 1988). In the early eighteenth century, the audience was still small enough to support heavily topical poetic satire of the kind written by Pope or

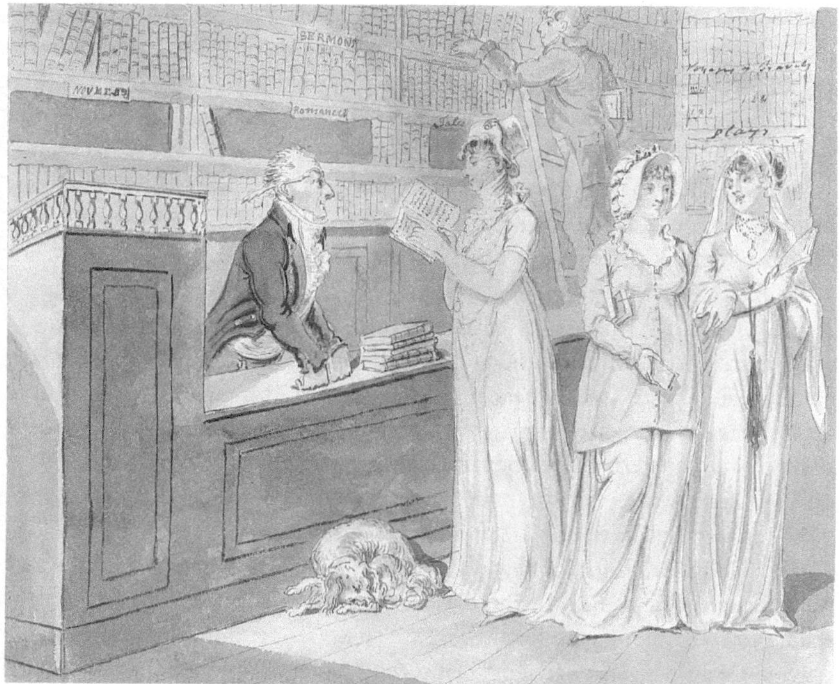

Figure 18. Isaac Cruikshank, *The Lending Library* (ca.1800–1811). Courtesy Yale Center for British Art, Paul Mellon Collection, New Haven, Conn.

Voltaire; poetry was a cudgel—and it got Voltaire literally cudgeled in return (Tompkins 1980). But by the second half of the century a few writers could even make part of their living from criticism as a growing audience of anonymous consumers sought advice on what to read amid the flood of new publications. It was only a step from this general critical practice to the emergence of journals like Schiller's *Horen* that set out to separate works of literary fine art from works of instruction or mere entertainment (Berghahn 1988).

Although there had been a recognition of authoritative texts in the ancient world and anthologies of model passages from Greece and Rome down through most of the seventeenth century, the modern vernacular canon began to take on additional functions in the eighteenth century. The passages chosen by the creators of ancient, medieval, or Renaissance anthologies were conceived of primarily as models of good style rather than as self-contained "works of art" in the modern sense. The vernacular anthologies of the seventeenth and early eighteenth century were also assembled from the most popular authors for teaching style, not as an authoritative selection of great masterpieces of literature (DeJean 1988). But the print explosion of the eighteenth century and the lack of sophistication of much of the new middle-class readership seemed to call for a triage of the fine from the ordinary, and it is in this situation that the religious notion of a "canon" of authoritative vernacular books began to take on its modern form.[2]

John Guillory has argued that vernacular canons have also operated as a form of "cultural capital" that helped separate the middle and upper classes from those that did not possess such cultural goods. In the British middle-class academies, for example, vernacular literature or "polite letters" was substituted for the aristocracy's badge of status, the Latin classics. Various anthologies of poetry and prose, with selections from Milton, Shakespeare, Addison, Gray, and Barbauld, were used for teaching composition. Although this new cultural capital was still being taught primarily as a way of learning eloquence in speech and writing, the vernacular linguistic canon later merged with the idea of the self-contained work of art to form the nineteenth-century curriculum of great works appreciated as exemplars of literature itself (Guillory 1993).

Paralleling the shift to a new classification system that placed painting in a separate category of fine art, there was an institutional shift from showing or selling canvases along with furniture, jewelry, and other domestic goods to displaying them in separate fine art institutions, such as art auctions, art exhibitions, and art museums. Here, too, the market played a key role. As the number of collectors increased, specialization became possible and the social standing of dealers improved with the result that "the organization of the [French] art market, as it exists in its current form came into being towards the middle of the eighteenth century" (Pomian 1987, 158).[3] In England commercial pressures also had the "effect of increasingly splitting art from other areas of trade" and fostering an "aura of exclusivity that began to distinguish [paintings] from other products" (Pears 1988, 64).

In the early eighteenth century, the few public exhibitions of paintings in Italy or France were usually of a few days duration on the occasion of religious festivals. But from 1737 on, the French academy began to hold annual salons, which became extremely popular with a mixed audience ranging from artisans and law clerks to rich bourgeois and members of the nobility, "the first regularly repeated, open, and free display of contemporary art in Europe to be offered in a completely secular setting" (Crow 1985, 3) (fig. 19). In England, in contrast, the early exhibitions of the 1760s charged an entrance fee in order to exclude "livery servants, foot-soldiers, porters, women with children, etc." (Pears 1988, 127).

It was but a natural step from the growth of a middle-class public for art ex-

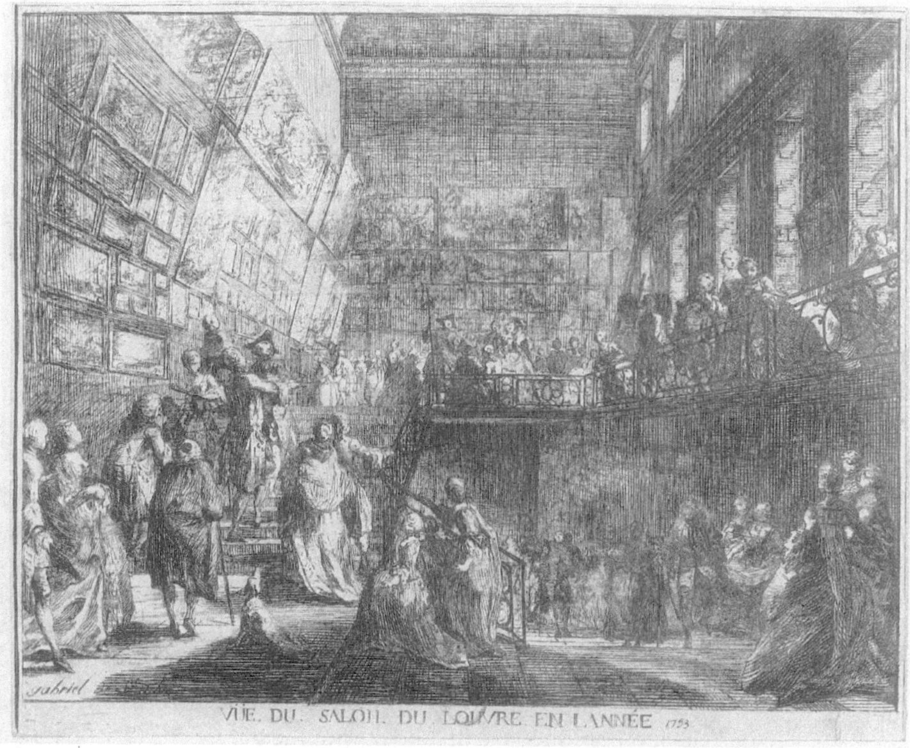

Figure 19. Gabriel de Saint Aubain, *Vue du Salon du Louvre en l'année 1753*. Courtesy Bibliothèque Nationale, Paris.

hibitions to the idea of a public art museum. Across Europe, parts of royal collections were opened to the public in the second half of the century (London, Paris, Munich, Vienna, and Rome). In Florence, the Uffizi gradually separated painting and sculpture from natural and scientific curiosities so that it had become essentially an art museum by the end of the century (Pomian 1987). Although many of these collections severely limited public access, their establishment is an important testimony to the idea of art as an autonomous realm since the works in them were torn away from their original functional contexts. The transformation of the Louvre into a fine art museum during the French Revolution engendered such an intense debate over the meaning and effects of this separation that it merits a special discussion in chapter 9.

Another indicator of the transformation of hitherto functional works into "art" is the upper-class educational experience that the English called the Continental Grand Tour and that the French and Germans referred to as the Italian

Journey. Hitherto limited to a few members of the aristocracy, the phenomenon grew in the eighteenth century and the arts claimed center stage. Painting and sculpture were viewed in detachment from their original purposes, especially for the nominally Protestant English or Germans or the Voltarian Frenchmen who visited St. Peters or the Duomo of Florence. The Grand Tour also encouraged the tendency to look at architecture, the most "utilitarian" of the fine arts, primarily in terms of beauty and style. Closely related to the Grand Tour of the nobility and the wealthy bourgeoisie was a desire for travel and "viewing" nature and other locales that developed among the middle class after mid-century. The new word "tourist" was coined, and the English, especially, traveled to see picturesque landscapes and to visit the great country houses and gardens of the aristocracy (Abrams 1989).

The new art tourist and museum visitor needed guidance as to what was famous and noteworthy. Most traditional treatises on painting, sculpture, or architecture had been written primarily for use by artisan/artists themselves or by small circles of connoisseur-collectors. But with the rise of the art exhibition, journalistic criticism developed to evaluate new works and exhibitions for the general public. Along with art criticism in the modern sense came the first modern art histories. Most previous histories had been organized biographically, but the construction of the category of fine art meant that it was now conceivable to write a history of the "art" of some limited period or place. In 1764 J. J. Winckelmann published the first book with the phrase "history of art" in its title (*History of Ancient Art* [1764] 1966).

At the beginning of the eighteenth century, music was still integrated into the fabric of social life, written and played for religious and civic occasions or for private and public entertainment. But over the course of the century the number and importance of public concerts grew steadily. The first advertised concerts for pay had been given in London in the 1670s; by the turn of the century, these small concerts were a regular feature of London life, and by the 1750s they had become socially fashionable. In France, where the state opera held a monopoly on public performance, the first regularly scheduled concerts were held from 1725 at the Tuileries Palace on the thirty-five holy days when opera performances were forbidden (Goubert and Roche 1991). In the small German principalities, there had already been subscription concerts in Frankfurt from 1712, Hamburg from 1721, and Leipzig from 1743 where the ground floor of the Leipzig *Gewandthaus* (cloth merchant's hall) was remodeled in 1781 to become the first European concert hall dedicated to an orchestra playing instrumental music (Raynor 1978). This new experience of listening to music for itself was also accompanied by the beginnings of modern music criticism, as well as the first general histories of music.

Although not a specifically musical institution, one of London's most celebrated eighteenth-century sites, Vauxhall Gardens, offers a good example of the institutionalization of the split between the so-called polite and vulgar arts. When Jonathan Tyers took over Vauxhall in 1728, it still had the reputation of being an outdoor brothel. Tyers cleaned it up physically and culturally by banning prostitutes, freelance vendors, and wandering musicians and by creating broad, well-lighted avenues lined with colonnades, arches, statues, and tastefully designed supper boxes. He also brought polite culture to Vauxhall by hiring an orchestra and well-known London singers to perform the music of J. C. Bach and George Frederick Handel. Of course, Vauxhall was primarily an outdoor pleasure garden, and for most people the music was background rather than something to listen to in silence (fig. 20). Yet already by 1735 there was also an orchestra housed above ground level in a cylindrical pavilion that "imposed

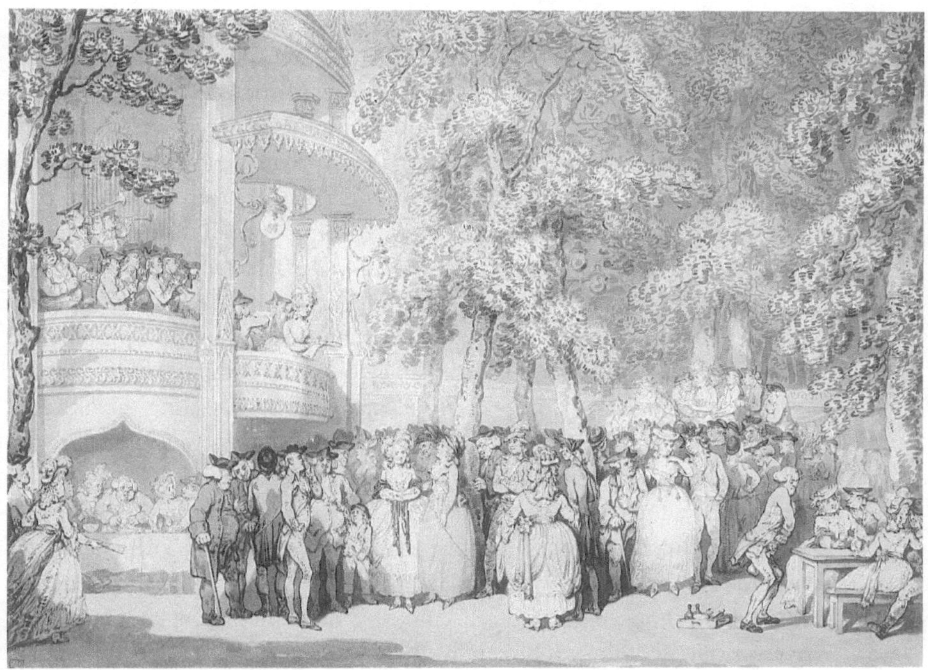

Figure 20. Thomas Rowlandson, *Vauxhall Gardens* (ca. 1784). Courtesy Yale Center for British Art, Paul Mellon Collection, New Haven, Conn.

a gulf between players and their listeners." The social and cultural message of Vauxhall was not lost on contemporaries who explicitly contrasted its refined pleasures with the vulgar amusements of the fairs and taverns (Solkin 1992, 115).

## The New Art Public

In the seventeenth century, the audience for most writers, composers, or painters had been a small one of patrons, connoisseurs, and amateurs whose demands were specific and tastes well known. In the eighteenth century, the new art institutions of secular concert, painting exhibition, and literary review helped bring a far larger and more varied public into being, one whose increasing diversity and anonymity forced a recasting of the terms in which the arts were conceived. The audiences that came to the exhibitions and concerts, read books and criticism, and met in coffeehouses and clubs to discuss them were now large enough to subsidize artistic production through their combined individual choices.[4] Eighteenth-century writers were deeply divided over who should be listened to among this new art public—were divided, in fact, over who was even to be counted as part of it. For the term "public" could sometimes mean all the people, but more often it distinguished the worthy part of society *from* "the people." The "people" in this restricted sense had various names, ranging from the merely pejorative ("multitude," *populace*) to the outright hostile ("mob," "rabble," *canaille, Pöbel*), who were said to be easily swayed by emotion, prejudice, and selfish interests. The true "public," in contrast, were those whose property and education empowered them to judge political and cultural matters impartially (Barrell 1986; Chartier 1991).

Obviously, the increasing involvement of people from the middle and lower ranges of the social order in the new art institutions posed an acute problem for those trying to define the appropriate public for the fine arts. If there was broad agreement that the lowest orders were incapable of appreciating the fine arts, there was no clear point at which middle became lower-middle and lower-middle became lowest. What we call the middle class in England and the bourgeoisie on the Continent was actually a hierarchy of great disproportion in wealth, education, status, and experience, ranging from rich merchants or financiers at the top down through layer after layer of decreasing wealth to the law clerk, shopkeeper, and self-employed artisan or independent farmer. Wherever one stood in this hierarchy, there was a tendency to ape those in the ranks above, whether by attending a concert or exhibition or, in the case of the more affluent, by acquiring a harpsichord or hiring a portrait painter. Some reacted to this emulation and its inevitable mixing of lower and higher art forms with patronizing amusement as in Horace Walpole's description of his experiences as a parliamentary candidate in 1761: "Think of me . . . dining with two hundred of them . . . amid . . . huzzas, songs, and tobacco, and finishing with country dancing at a ball and six penny whist! I have borne it all cheerfully . . . have sat hours to hear misses play on the harpsichord, and see an Alderman's copies of Rubens" (Porter 1990, 65). Hogarth, Swift, and Pope were not so gentle with the cultural pretensions of the upwardly mobile.

The result of the use of cultural choices to mark social ascension was not only middle-class aping of aristocratic tastes in the fine arts but also a gradual withdrawal from lower-class culture. One expression of this withdrawal was a tendency to stigmatize popular cultural forms as "mere recreation" when compared to the elite pleasures of the fine arts. In *Joseph Andrews,* Fielding humorously called attention to the eighteenth-century split between elite and popular culture: "Whilst the People of Fashion seized places to their own use, such as courts, assemblies, operas, balls, etc; the people of no fashion, beside one Royal Palace, called his Majesty's Bear Garden, have been in constant possession of all hops, fairs, revels, etc. . . . So far from looking on each other as brethren in the Christian Language, they seem scarce to regard each other as of the same species" ([1742] 1961, 136). As Peter Burke sums up his study of this separation, "In 1500, popular culture was everyone's culture; a second culture for the educated, and the only culture for everyone else. By 1800, however, in most parts of Europe, the clergy, the nobility, the merchants, the professional men—and their wives—had abandoned popular culture to the lower classes" (1978, 270). Of course, frequent borrowing and visitation between high and low culture continued in the eighteenth century and since, but the new ideas and institutions of fine art made the difference palpable (Burke 1993) (fig. 21).

Fraternization between the aristocracy and the upper reaches of the British middle class had already occurred to a limited degree in politics, where both groups had a stake in order; it happened even more frequently in charities, scientific clubs, book circles, and musical societies, as well as in coffeehouses or public gardens like Vauxhall. A key term for those able to participate in this social and cultural stratum in Britain was "the polite." Although the term "politeness" suggests a minor virtue to us, in the eighteenth century it was a crucial social and cultural term of broad application. It signified not only good manners but also the cultured outlook of a gentleman or lady. The polite were people who could converse knowingly but not pedantically about the "polite arts," "polite letters," and "polite learning" in the coffeehouses, clubs, and societies (Klein 1994).

It could be argued that one small factor contributing to England's social

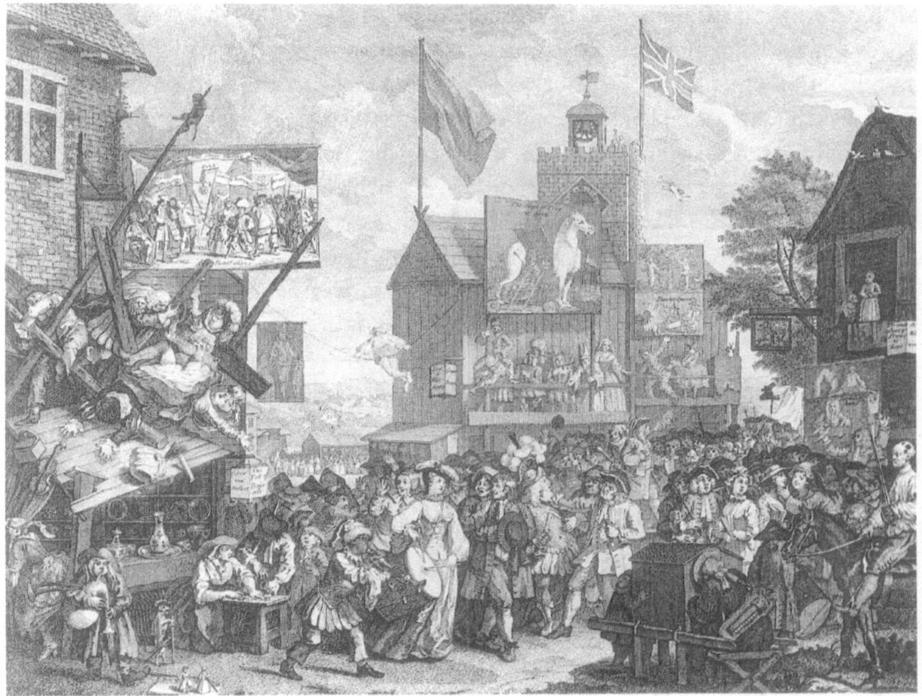

Figure 21. William Hogarth, *Southwark Fair* (1733). The print shows the mixed crowd drawn to the fair by the chance for gaming, flirting, getting their pockets picked, and watching ropedancers, tumblers, fire-eaters, magicians, and sundry theater companies; the tall young woman beating the drum is advertising a troop of players.

stability in the eighteenth century was the creation of a common arena of high culture and fine art in which the nobility, gentry, and educated middle class could share. The point was stated openly in Lord Kames's *Elements of Criticism:* "The Fine Arts have ever been encouraged by wise Princes not simply for private amusement, but for their beneficial influence in society. By uniting different ranks in the same elegant pleasures, they promote benevolence; by cherishing love of order, they enforce submission to government" (1762, iii). As Kames makes clear elsewhere, laborers and artisans were definitely not included. However wearying Walpole found the endless harpsichord recitals and the copies of Rubens, in their modest way, they were tokens of a common belief in the solidarity of the "polite" through a participation in "the same elegant pleasures."

Although social divisions in France and Germany were more pronounced than in England, those parts of the nobility and bourgeoisie most affected by Enlightenment ideas also began to find a common ground in high culture institutions, such as the salons and academies. Although touching only a handful of people, these institutions were seen by philosophes such as d'Alembert as a place apart where the members, whatever their social standing, temporarily became part of the "republic of letters" without compromising the society of orders and privileges (Goodman 1994). A large middle class was even slower to emerge in the various German states, but even there one can discern a limited meeting on the terrain of fine art between the aristocracy and the wealthier and more educated parts of the middle class. Kant, for example, begins his *Observations on the Feeling of the Beautiful and Sublime* with a contrast between those of grosser appetites who look at things in terms of money or sex and persons "of noble sensitivity" who are concerned with "finer feeling" (Kant 1960, 46).

If the middling orders could ascend into the polite public in part by shunning the crude amusements of the poor and frequenting fine art institutions, some of the nobility and bourgeoisie might exclude themselves from the cultured public by failing to exhibit an acquaintance with the fine arts and/or indulging in low entertainments like cockfights (fig. 22). Obviously, the untutored French noble buried in the provinces, the English "booby squire" who cared for nothing but meat, drink, and the hunt, or the Prussian Junker preoccupied with his horses and rank were little more sensitive or knowledgeable in the fine arts than some of the populace. The cultured middle class and nobility who made up the fine art public could be as scathing about their more boorish social equals as about the ignorant populace. In 1746 the Earl of Egmont and two well-off members of the middle class entertained themselves in a coffeehouse by ridiculing an ennobled merchant "worth a hundred thousand pound if not two" who "brags that in his whole life he never bought a book, picture or print" (Pears 1988, 14).

The category of fine art and its criterion of refined pleasure and informed judgment was neither a purely intellectual construct nor the simple expression of an existing social division but part of an effort to institute a new distinction at once social and cultural. On this high cultural ground, noble and bourgeois could meet as a fine art public, rejecting both the frivolous diversions of the rich and highborn as well as the vulgar amusements of the populace. There is a line in Diderot's *Salon of 1767* that nicely draws on both these rejections at once: "Money . . . degrades and destroys the fine arts . . . [which] are subordinated to the fantasy and caprice of a handful of rich men . . . or abandoned to the mercy of the indigent multitude, which strives, by poor work in every genre, to give itself the credit and lustre of wealth" (Diderot [1767] 1995, 77). It is no accident that when Batteux's book *Les beaux arts réduit à un même principe* appeared in its pirated English paraphrase, the term "beaux-arts" was translated as "polite

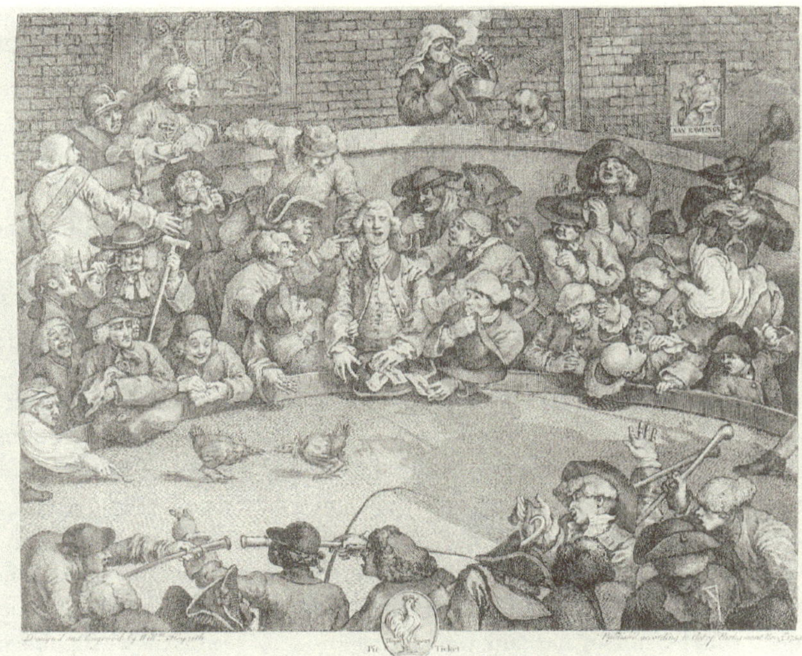

Figure 22. William Hogarth, *The Cockpit* (1759). Betting on cockfights was one of the most popular eighteenth-century pastimes in England. Here, the blind Lord Albemarle Bertie is shown at the center of a raucous crowd gathered in the "Royal Cockpit" of St. James' Park.

arts," with its strong social-class connotations (Kristeller 1990). Initially, both "polite arts" and "elegant arts" alternated with "fine arts" as the name of the new category, although "polite arts" was the more widely used and remained current throughout the century. The new category of polite or fine arts would henceforth serve European and American societies as a crucial marker for a new kind of social refinement and cultural distinction.

CHAPTER 6

# The Artist, the Work, and the Market

NOTHING BETTER illustrates the changing status of the artist in the eighteenth century than the career of Voltaire, who was beaten up in 1726 by the lackeys of a nobleman he had insulted, thrown in the Bastille when he complained, and exiled from Paris—all with little show of sympathy from the Parisian aristocracy, whose salons he had frequented. But when he returned to Paris fifty years later (1778), he was not only cheered in the streets and lionized by the Académie Française, the aristocracy now competed for his favor. When Voltaire died the next year, having wavered about receiving but finally refusing the last rites of the church, he had to be secretly buried to avoid his body being thrown into a common pit with prostitutes, thieves, and actors. Yet a decade later, after the Revolution had secularized church property and turned the huge, neoclassical church of St. Geneviève into a Panthéon to France's "great men," Voltaire's remains were among the first to enter (fig. 23).

## The Separation of the Artist from the Artisan

By the time Voltaire entered the Panthéon, the old idea of the artisan/artist had been definitively pulled apart. This can be vividly seen in a change in the meaning of the terms themselves. Dubos's widely read *Critical Reflections on Poetry and Painting* of 1719 refers to painters and poets throughout as "artisans," although Dubos apologized for the term, explaining that it would have been too clumsy to always combine "artisan" with adjectives like "illustrious or some other appropriate epithet" (Dubos 1993, 2). Obviously, he did not consider the word "artist" an alternative. As late as 1740 the official dictionary of the Académie Française still defined "artist" as "one who works in an art . . . in particular those who perform chemical operations." Nor did eighteenth-century English, Italian, or Spanish definitions of the terms "artist" and "artisan" sharply distinguish them.[1]

Yet by the 1750s there were unmistakable signs that the modern polarity of artist versus artisan was taking hold. Lacombe's popularizing *Portable Dictionary*

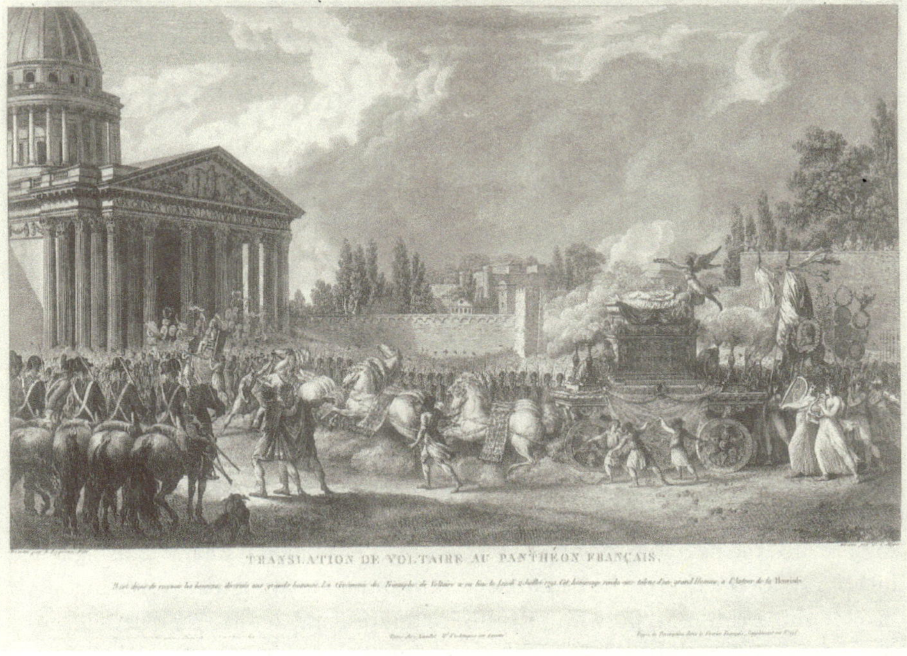


Figure 23. Jean-Jacques Lagrenée fils, *Transfer of Voltaire's Remains to the French Panthéon* (1791). Courtesy Bibliothèque Nationale, Paris.

*of the Fine Arts* (1752) showed no hesitation: "One gives this name [Artist] to those who exercise one of the liberal arts and especially to painters, sculptors and engravers" (1752). Soon other dictionaries and encyclopedias began to define "artist" and "artisan" as opposites (Heinich 1993). Rousseau recognized the new polarity in *Émile* (1762), mocking "these self-important fellows who are called artists instead of artisans and work solely for the idle rich" (Rousseau [1762] 1957, 186). Initially, examples of artists, in the new sense, were drawn from the visual arts, but the term came to have such prestige that it was soon extended to musical and literary creators as well (Watelet 1788, 286). In fact, so many professions laid claim to the title artist that a shrewd observer like Mercier began to make fun of it, suggesting that "the reign of the word Artist" may have come to an end thanks to "the trial brought by the Artists-poulterers of La Flèche against the Artists-poulterers of Le Mans" (Shroder 1961, 5).

Before looking at how the ideal qualities of the older image of the artisan/artist were divided between the two concepts, we need to consider the social and institutional conditions that were pushing artist and artisan farther apart.

Despite the rise in status of court painters from Leonardo to Velasquez and the prestige brought by the French Academy, the Marquis d'Argens could still complain in 1730 that most of the French "cannot tell a painter from a shoemaker" (Chatelus 1991, 277). One of the difficulties in generalizing about painters in the eighteenth century is that their condition varied enormously, ranging from a handful of wealthy and ennobled academicians at the top to the humblest decorators of furniture, coaches, and signs at the bottom. Several factors regularized the already more elevated status of easel painters and further demoted the more directly functional genres. One institutional factor was a sudden spurt in the founding of academies, which numbered ten in 1740 but over a hundred by 1790. The most notable of these, the British Royal Academy (1769), was intended to raise the status of artists by association with the French model. Its first president, Joshua Reynolds, exhorted his colleagues and students to pursue "ideal beauty" lest they fall to the level of the "mere mechanick" (Reynolds [1770] 1975, 43) (fig. 24). Most of the new academies had royal protectors, officers with high-sounding titles, freedom from guild restrictions, and regular

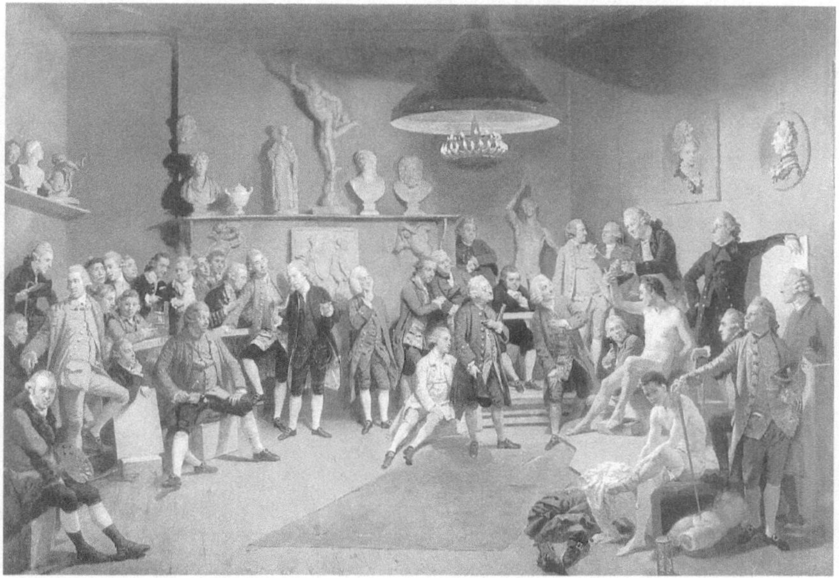

Figure 24. Johann Zoffany, *The Academicians of the Royal Academy* (1771–72). Courtesy The Royal Collection, © 2000 Her Majesty Queen Elizabeth II. Although two women painters, Angelica Kauffmann and Mary Moser, both daughters of foreigners, were admitted as founding members of the British Royal Academy, they are present at this discussion of the nude model only by portraits on the wall. No more women were admitted to the academy until 1922.

exhibitions of member's work. Thanks to their new academies, Dresden (1764), Copenhagen (1769), Stockholm (1784), and Berlin (1786) had their first official art exhibitions (Pevsner 1940).

If the creation of so many academies tended to elevate the status of some painters at the expense of others, an even more important factor was the expanding art market that led to increased specialization. In the first half of the eighteenth century, many painters still worked at a variety of tasks, often beginning as coach or sign painters and gradually working their way up to more complex and difficult genres, including the large-scale figurative scenes with which a François Boucher or Jean Honoré Fragonard decorated the walls of aristocratic houses (Chatelus 1991). In the second half of the century, the lesser-ranked specializations fell farther in status due to specific changes in the decoration of houses, carriages, and signs. The painting of elaborate pictorial signs, which had been done by people as distinguished as Jean Antoine Watteau in France or Godfrey Kneller in England, was almost eliminated in London by a 1768 law forbidding large overhanging signs that impeded traffic (fig. 25). Because of changes in domestic tastes, the figural parts of house decoration became smaller and painted in the studio, further diminishing contact between

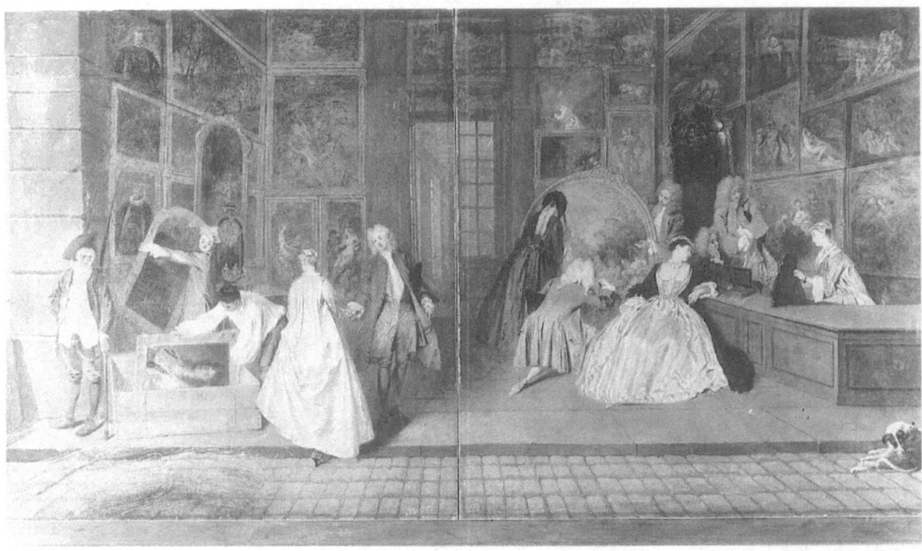

Figure 25. Jean Antoine Watteau, *The Shop Sign of Gersaint* (1720). Charlottenburg Castle, Berlin. Courtesy Foto Marburg/Art Resource, New York. Gersaint was a picture dealer, and Watteau's painting actually hung outside his shop as an advertisement.

easel and decorative painters. Finally, as commercial paint manufacture developed, decorative painters no longer needed to know how to grind pigments but were mostly selling their labor (Pears 1988). By the century's end "artist" and "artisan" had been separated not only semantically but also in daily practice and contact.

At the same time that social and technological changes were driving down the status of utilitarian painters, other market forces were further lifting the status of easel painters. Under the patronage/commission system the owner of a painting obviously knew who produced it and may have even suggested its subject matter. But the increasing resale of paintings through dealers and exhibitions led to an increase in the number of paintings done in advance for the market, which led in turn to a greater interest in the painter's individual style and signature. As Krystoff Pomian has discovered, catalogs of French painting sales in the first half of the eighteenth century typically described paintings by size, framing, and subject matter, mentioning the name of the painter only at the end of the description. This reflected the fact that subject matter and "beauty," as evaluated by the connoisseurs, were often considered more important in a contemporary painting than the identity of the painter or workshop (fig. 26). By the late 1750s, however, sale catalogs began placing the names of painters at the beginning of descriptions of paintings. Something similar happened with the catalogs for the French Academy's biennial exhibitions called "Salons" (after the Louvre's Salon d'Apollon, where they were held). Salon catalogs, which had once listed paintings by the order of their placement on the walls, also switched to the painter's name in the 1750s (Pomian 1987). It does not seem a mere accident that at the same time this practical and circumstantial need to know the provenance of a painting was developing, critics and theorists were increasingly stressing originality and creative expression.[2]

Institutional factors not unlike those influencing the image of painters also helped transform the image and status of the architect. In early eighteenth-century Britain, there were still master mason-architects as well as many aristocratic amateurs who designed their own buildings, but the modern professional architect was already emerging as a result of the growth of cities and the increasing wealth of the middle class. The surge in urban construction led to the creation of building committees that sought the services of professional architects, and market competition began to replace the older relation between the individual architect and their aristocratic patron. The new type of professionals not only developed well-organized offices and negotiated substantial fees but also insisted on controlling all details of the construction of their designs. Other

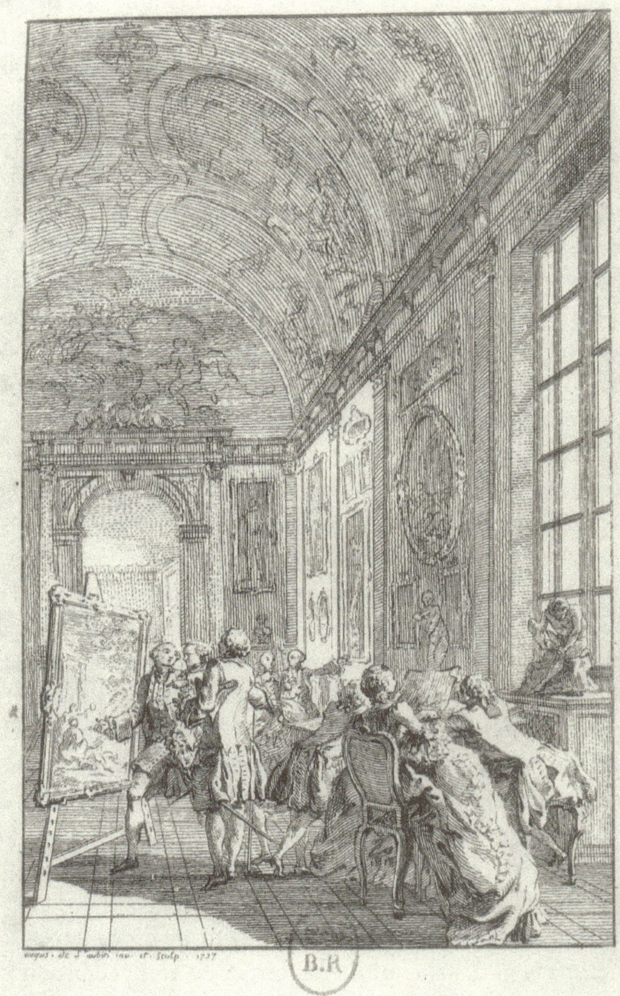

Figure 26. Augustin de Saint Aubain, frontispiece, sales catalog (1757). Courtesy Bibliothèque Nationale, Paris.

institutional signs of the growing separation of the architect from master masons, surveyors, and engineers were the British government's abolition of the positions of surveyor general and master mason (1782) and the emergence of such distinct organizations as the Society of Civil Engineers (1771), the Surveyor's Club (1792), and the Institute of British Architects (1834). Between 1800 and 1830 another great change resulting from rapid urban growth was the increasing importance of the "general contractor," who now stepped between the client and architect on the one side and the various master craftsmen on the other, leading to "a gradual decline in both skill and initiative among the building crafts" and an increased dependence on the architect's detailed drawings and specifications (Wilton-Ely 1977, 194). Just as "artist" and "craft" painters were further separated by social and economic changes as much as by the spread of new ideas, so architects were further elevated above master masons by changes in construction practices.

In France the elevation of the architect above the master masons had already received a great boost in the late seventeenth century with the creation of the Académie Royale d'Architecture in 1671, where students received a purely intellectual instruction before being introduced to the stone yards and building sites. By 1747, the year Batteux's treatise codified the new category of fine arts versus crafts (with architecture and rhetoric among the "mixed arts"), the creation of the Ècole des Ponts et Chaussées (School of Bridges and Roads) marked the beginning of a separation of engineers from architects, a separation further accentuated with the establishment of the Ècole Polytechnique in 1794. Yet both the Ècole Polytechnique and the Ècole des Beaux-Arts (successor to the academies of painting, sculpture, and architecture after the Revolution) offered courses in architecture, a fact reflecting architecture's "mixed" status.

One result of this dual teaching was a tendency for some French architects to see themselves primarily as engineer-builders and others to see themselves primarily as artists and architecture as the creation of works of art. For Ètienne-Louis Boullée, whose designs for colossal ideal structures have recently become celebrated, architecture was a species of poetry, something to be looked at rather than lived or worked in, and the architect was primarily an artist who creates images (fig. 27). Actual building was "secondary" to Boullée, and he envisaged an eventual "museum of architecture" that would contain everything of significance to the art. Obviously, this exalted image of the architect-as-artist had little room for either the craftsperson's practical knowledge or the engineer's calculations (Rosenau 1974). Speaking from a position similar to Boullée's, Claude-Nicolas Ledoux wrote of the architect in 1804: "The craftsman is the machine of the Creator; the man of genius is the Creator himself" (Kruft 1994, 162).

The rise in the status and self-conception of writers like Voltaire or Alexander Pope also went hand in hand with the gradual replacement of patronage relations by a market system. At the beginning of the eighteenth century, many British writers still found jobs as secretaries, librarians, and hired pens, turning out encomiums or vitriol as needed. By mid-century the British reading public was large enough to provide a precarious but independent living for a growing

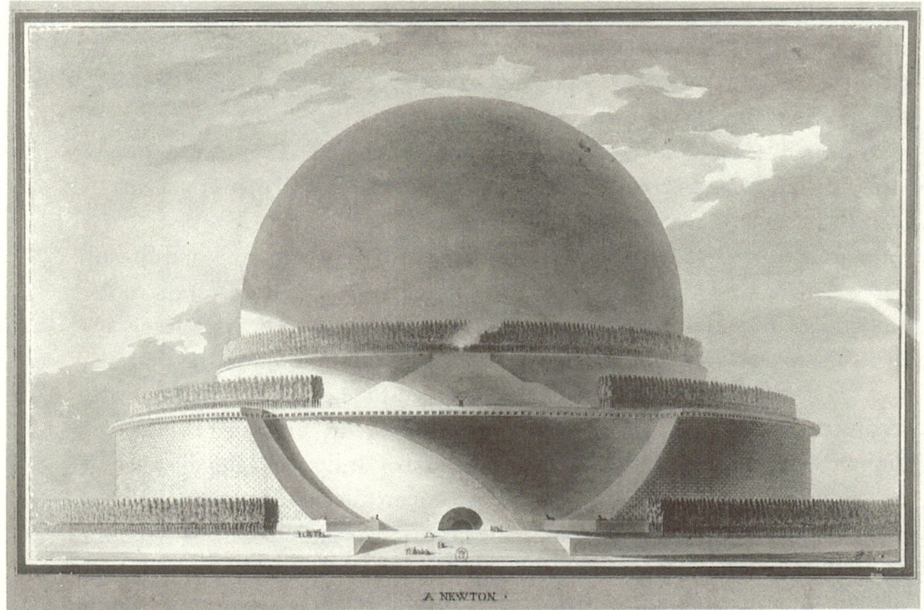


Figure 27. Étienne-Louis Boullée, *Cenotaph for Newton* (1784). Courtesy Bibliothèque Nationale, Paris. As one may judge from the relative size of the trees and the tiny figures on the front stairway, the Cenotaph was enormous and unbuildable.

number of writers. In France and Germany, most writers remained more dependent on patronage, yet as Voltaire's reception in Paris shows, by the 1760s the French "man of letters" began to take on a spiritual authority higher than the clergy (Bénichou 1973). A telling instance of the shift from patronage to market-based independence is Samuel Johnson's famous letter telling off Lord Chesterfield, who had pretended to have supported the preparation of Johnson's *Dictionary:* "A patron is someone who looks on with unconcern at a man struggling for life in the water, and when he reaches the bank, encumbers him with help." But more important than this famous quip was the fact that by publishing the *Dictionary* in his own name and basing it not on the language of the court or "polite society" but on examples drawn from other writers, Johnson had made the "The King's English" into "The Author's English" (Kernan 1989, 202).

Yet whatever the market gave in terms of momentary fame or temporary income, it often took away in dignity, as writers competed for such scraps as "Grub Street" might throw their way. It is not surprising that Alexander Pope,

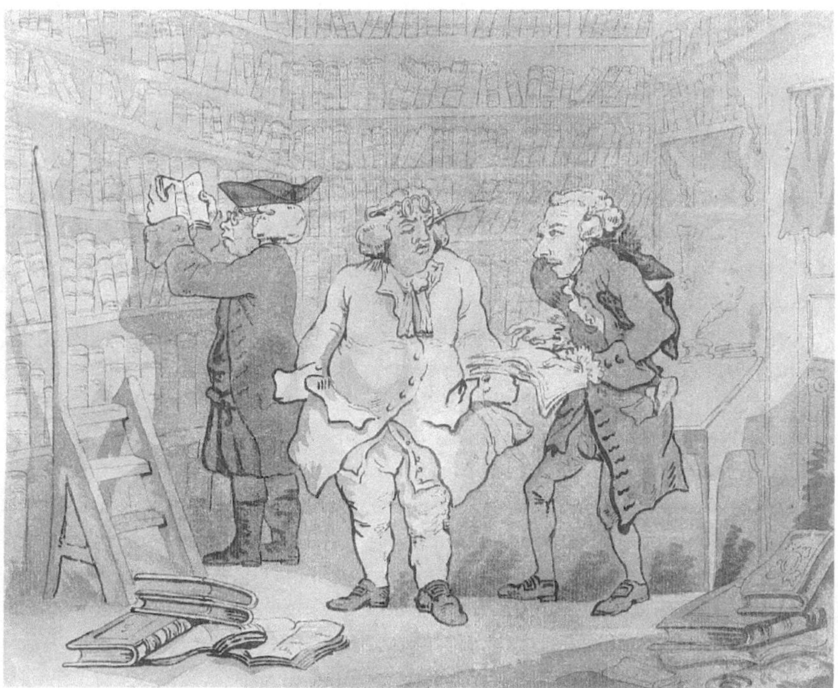

Figure 28. Thomas Rowlandson, *The Author and His Publisher (Bookseller)* (1784). Courtesy Yale Center for British Art, Paul Mellon Collection, New Haven, Conn.

one of the first writers to actually earn a living from print, presented himself as an old-style gentleman-amateur and mercilessly ridiculed the tribe of hacks and scribblers who worked for pay (fig. 28). In France, the combination of censorship and tight restrictions on the number of printers forced many writers to labor for clandestine publishers. High above these jobbers were a few successful entrepreneurs (Voltaire) and a handful of government-subsidized editors (Jean-Baptiste-Antoine Suard) who looked with contempt on "the literary rabble." The rabble returned their contempt and several—Jacques-Pierre Brissot, Jean Paul Marat, Jean-Marie Collot d'Herbois—later played out their resentment during the Revolution. In between the high flyers and the rabble were writers like Diderot and Rousseau, who relied on small inheritances, occasional patrons, and an always uncertain income from print (Darnton 1982).

A legal innovation at the beginning of the century had a profound effect on the writer's status and self-esteem: copyright. In England the Licensencing Act, which granted printers perpetual rights, was replaced in 1709 by the world's first copyright law that vested the ownership of a manuscript with the writer, who could sell it for two consecutive fourteen-year terms. Contrary to what one might think, the law was not advocated by writers themselves but by printers desirous of stifling pirates, and at the time, "no one . . . seems to have recognized the radical change of ownership from printer to writer that had occurred in the statute." Samuel Johnson was one of the first to articulate the implications of copyright laws, observing that writers have "a stronger right of property than that by occupancy; a metaphysical right, a right, as it were, of creation, which should from its nature be perpetual" (Kernan 1989, 99, 101).

Copyright laws did not come to France and Germany until the end of the century, but comments similar to those of Johnson were made by Diderot and Johann Gottlieb Fichte, the latter arguing that the content of ideas may not be protected, but the form is original and belongs to the author as its "creator" (Woodmansee 1994, 52). Whatever intellectual antecedents we can find for the ideas of genius, originality, and creation, the print market and the development of copyright obviously needed something like them. In the old patronage system the piece produced was often seen as the property of the patron. But as patronage gave way to the market, the writer, by selling his or her work, publicly affirmed both ownership and authorizing power (Becq 1994a, 766).

Musicians remained dependent on the system of patronage longer than either writers or painters. Playing for pay remained a lower-status employment, whereas playing by aristocratic or bourgeois amateurs was a sign of cultivation (fig. 29). With the exception of Handel in England and some vain efforts by Haydn and Mozart, it was not until Beethoven, at the end of the century, that composers began to gain what we consider the artist's natural right to independence. A glance at the contracts governing Bach, Haydn, and Mozart confirms the musician's dependency: most musicians needed permission to travel or compose for others, might be asked to compose in a certain style or to compose on a day's or even a few hour's notice, and, finally, might be reprimanded for taking liberties not approved in advance (Geiringer 1946; David and Mendel 1966; Elias 1993).

But with the rise of the secular concert and the increasing middle-class demand for lessons and sheet music, it became possible for a few musicians to envisage survival without a full-time patronage position. Handel was able to take on numerous private and university commissions, embark on ventures in the production of operas and subscription concerts, and, finally, die well off. In 1749, for example, twelve thousand people paid to hear the final open rehearsal of Handel's *Music for the Royal Fireworks* at Vauxhall Gardens. Handel was present at Vauxhall not only through his music but also by virtue of a fine marble

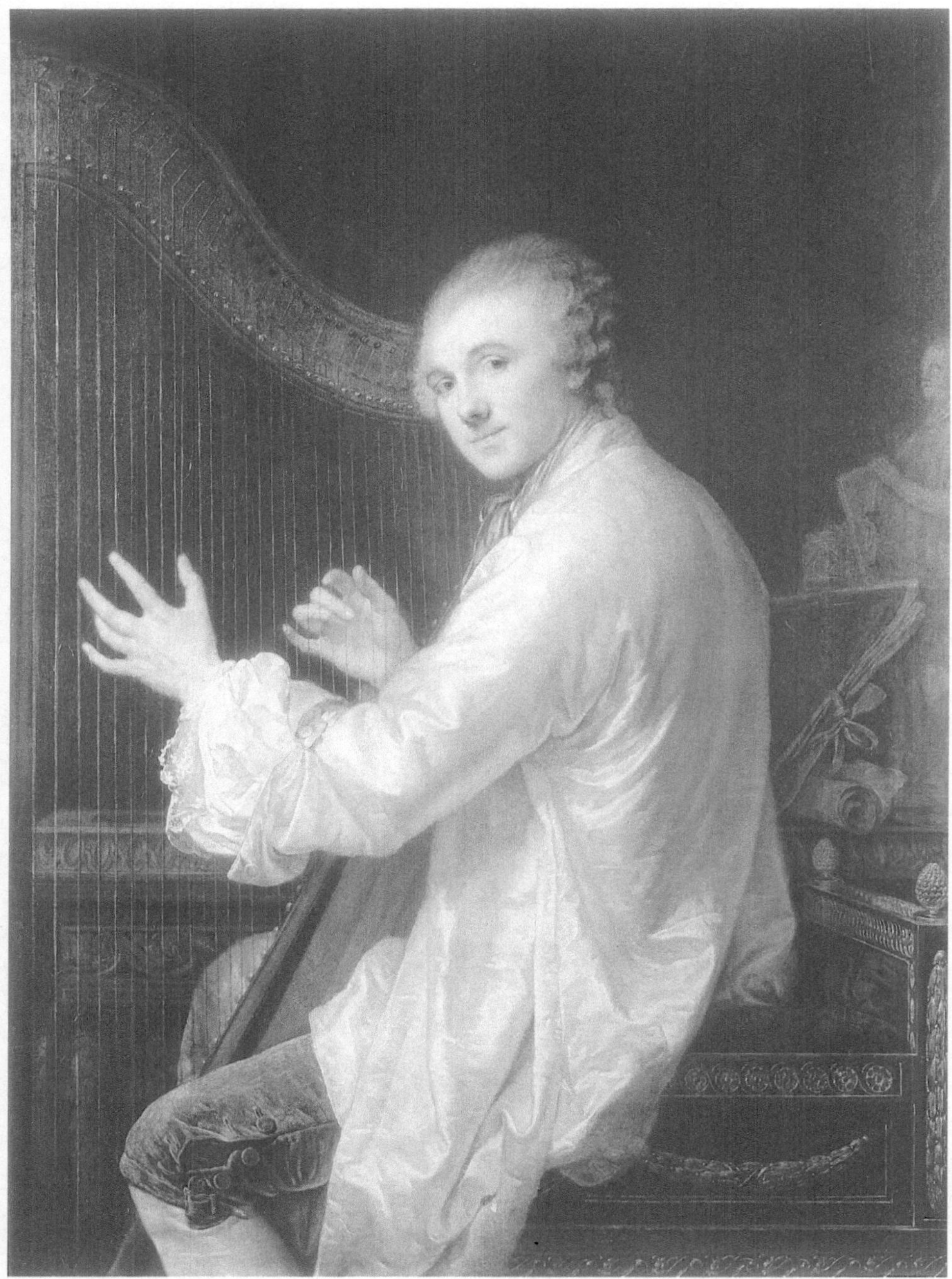

Figure 29. Jean-Baptiste Greuze, *Ange-Laurent de Lalive de Jully* (1759). Courtesy National Gallery of Art, Washington, D.C., Samuel H. Kress Collection. © 2000 Board of Trustees, National Gallery of Art, Washington, D.C. Lalive de Jully not only is shown as an amateur musician but also sits in a finely carved neoclassical-style chair with a statue and a sheaf of prints behind him.

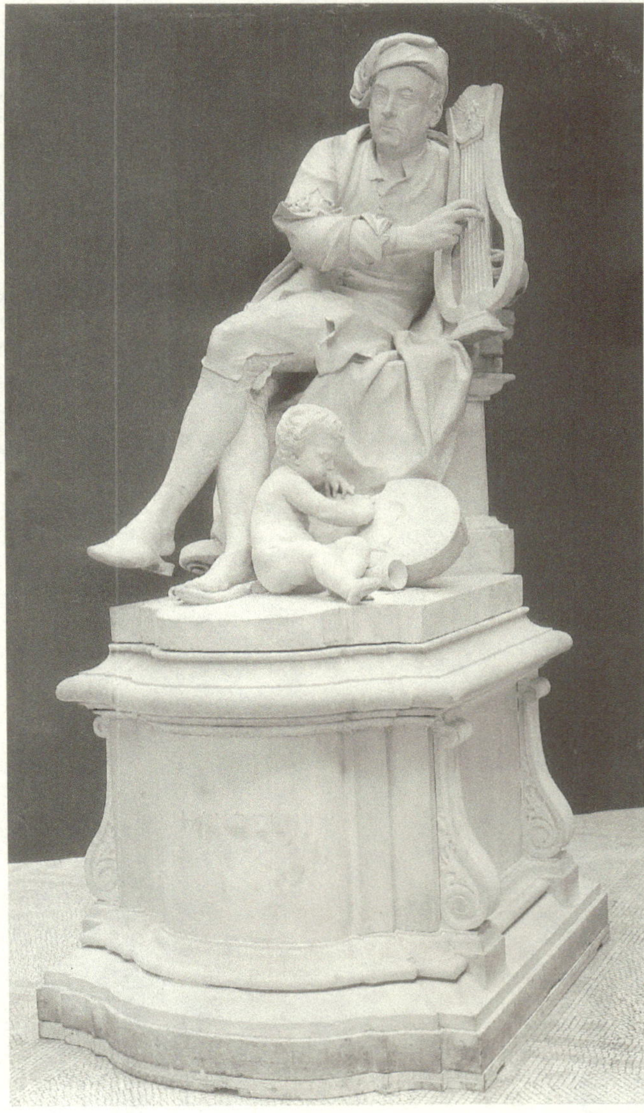

Figure 30. François Roubiliac, *George Frederick Handel* (1738), 4 × 5¼ feet. Courtesy Victoria and Albert Museum, London/Art Resource, New York.

statue carved by the celebrated sculptor, François Roubiliac (fig. 30). By the 1790s Franz Josef Haydn was given a leave by his princely patron to go to London, where he had no difficulty living from his concerts, commissions, and teaching and reveled in his new freedom: "How sweet is some degree of liberty!" (Geiringer 1946, 104). But when Prince Esterhazy summoned him back to Austria, Haydn went.

Among those who gave up a regular position out of exasperation, Mozart is the most famous, and for the first few years he made ends meet from lessons, subscription concerts, and commissioned operas, although he failed to please one of his patrons, the Emperor Joseph II, who made the famous complaint, "Too many notes, my dear Mozart, too many notes" (Elias 1993, 130). The aristocratic connoisseurs and the bourgeois patriciate who followed their lead in matters of taste were often themselves amateur composers and players who sometimes regarded their judgment in music as the equal of the musicians themselves. Mozart ran up against the problem awaiting all musicians who launched out on a freelance career in the early stages of the art market. If an archbishop or town board could curb one's freedom, so could the "public"—simply by staying away. Norbert Elias has suggested that Mozart attempted the freelance mode a decade too soon. To have comfortably succeeded would have required a further development of the public concert, a more extensive and secure market for printed scores, some system of royalty payment, and a larger and more varied audience. By the late 1790s, the situation had improved enough so that Beethoven, fifteen years Mozart's junior, was able to maintain his independence, although he too had aristocratic patronage along the way. It is also striking that Beethoven made explicit use of the idea of the artist as the "unfettered genius" to justify his demands for independence (Beethoven 1951, 72).

## The Ideal Image of the Artist

Whereas the ideal qualities desired in an artisan/artist in the old system combined genius and rule, inspiration and facility, innovation and imitation, freedom and service, these qualities were finally pulled apart in the course of the eighteenth century. As this happened, all the "poetic" attributes—such as inspiration, imagination, freedom, and genius—were ascribed to the artist and all the "mechanical" attributes—such as skill, rules, imitation, and service—went to the artisan. The 1762 dictionary of the Académie Française, for example, defined an "artist" as "he who works in an art where genius and hand must concur" whereas the artisan is simply called "a worker in a mechanical art, a man with a trade" (Brunot 1966, 682). Among the many attributes of the artist, genius and freedom seemed to sum up all the superlative qualities that now separated the free, creative artist from the supposedly dependent and routine craftsperson.

At the beginning of the eighteenth century it was widely believed that everyone had a genius or talent for something and that their particular genius could only be perfected by the guidance of reason and rule. By the end of the century, not only had the balance between genius and rule been reversed, but in addition, genius itself had become the opposite of talent and instead of everyone *having* a genius for something, a few people were said to *be* geniuses (Duff 1767; Gerard [1774] 1966). Among the key qualities of genius in the fine arts, freedom held a unique place. Although there had long been an elite among artists who claimed freedom from the dictates of patrons, artists' claims to independence were now extended and intensified. The idea of the artist's freedom versus the artisan's dependence underlay each of the other ideal qualities ascribed to the artist: freedom from the imitation of traditional models (originality), freedom from the dictates of reason and rule (inspiration), freedom from restrictions on fantasy (imagination), freedom from the exact imitation of nature (creation) (Sommer 1950; Jaffee 1992; Zilsel 1993).

*Originality.* Two very different kinds of imitation were debated in the eighteenth century: the imitation of nature and the imitation of great predecessors. Although the latter kind of imitation had always left room for innovation, the following of past masters now began to be roundly condemned. "Great genius is mere strength of natural parts . . . an imitation of the best authors is not to compare with a good original," wrote Addison in the *Spectator* (1711, no. 160).[3] The enormous change that took place over the next forty years is apparent in Edward Young's *Conjectures on Original Composition:* "Shakespeare mingled no water with his wine, lowered his genius by no vapid imitation" ([1759] 1965, 34). The turn toward originality was shared across the continent and went hand in hand with a new emphasis on feeling (Mortier 1982).

*Inspiration/Enthusiasm.* The enthusiasm of genius was variously described as irregular, wild, untamable, a devouring fire. "Don't ask, young artist, what genius is," Rousseau declared, "if you have it, you will know. If you do not have it, you will never know" ([1768] 1969, 227). But it was in Germany that the small world of arts and letters was swept by a "cult of genius." In *The Sorrows of Young Werther,* Goethe writes of the "torrent of genius" that "thunders and overwhelms . . . the soul" and strikes fear in the "respectable" ([1774] 1989, 33). It was only a short step from the view that the genius is above the "rules of art" to the belief that the genius is also above the "rules of society." As Diderot said of the playwright Racine, "If we have to choose either Racine the mean husband and father and false friend but sublime poet, or Racine the good father, husband and friend but mediocre poet," the choice is easy. "What is left of the mean Racine? Nothing. Of Racine the genius? The work is eternal" (Dieckmann 1940, 108).

Not everyone jumped on the genius/enthusiasm bandwagon. Samuel Johnson grumbled in *Rambler* (no. 154) that "the mental disease of the present generation" is "a disposition to rely wholly upon unassisted genius" (Johnson [1750–52] 1969, 3:55). Voltaire cautioned that while enthusiasm may be a "racehorse carried away in its course, the course is regularly drawn" (Becq 1994a, 698). By the 1790s Goethe had also turned away from the "torrent of genius" idea, as had Diderot, who now described genius as "the spirit of observation . . . exercised without effort, without argument . . . a sort of sense which others do not have" (Diderot 1968, 20).

In addition to developing a more nuanced understanding of the enthusiasm of genius, eighteenth-century writers modified another concept that was to play an important role in the nineteenth century: expression. In the seventeenth century, to praise an artist for "expression" in painting or music usually meant to praise their skill in depicting the feelings of others. But the new emphasis on sensibility gradually developed into the idea of the artist's empathy with their subjects. Writers on genius such as Giambattista Vico, Johann Gottfried Herder, and Karl Philipp Moritz often mentioned "sympathy" as an important sensitive power of the artist (Herder 1955). The shift toward sympathy marked an inward turn in the ideal of the artist that would eventually lead to the Romantic's emphasis on self-expression (Engell 1981; Marshall 1988).

*Imagination.* So completely has the idea of the "creative imagination" triumphed since the end of the eighteenth century that it requires a disciplined effort to remember that "imagination" previously referred either to a general image-storing faculty or to a dangerous power of fantasy. The first steps toward the idea of the *creative* imagination were taken not by philosophers but by poets and critics such as Addison in his 1712 essays titled "The Pleasures of the Imagination," where he can even say that the imagination "has something in it like creation" (*Spectator*, no. 417). The numerous poetic and critical invocations of the imagination in the following generation culminated in Joseph Warton's claim that "a creative and glowing imagination, and that *alone* . . . makes a poet" (Engell 1981). At the same time that critics and poets were celebrating the imagination, philosophers like Hume, Étienne Bonnot de Condillac, and Kant were increasing its scope in the theory of knowledge. It only remained for Alexander Gerard and Kant, in their very different ways, to push the idea of the imagination's integrative power over the line that separates the "combination" of images from "creation." Once the productive rather than merely reproductive power of the imagination had been established, the old idea of invention in the service of imitation could be replaced by the stronger idea of creation as an end in itself (Gerard [1774] 1966, 29, 43; Kant 1987, 182; Sweeney 1998).

*Creation.* Today, when corporations hire the services of "creativity consultants," the idea of creation has become so banalized that it is difficult to appreciate the reluctance of eighteenth-century critics and philosophers to call artistic activity "creation." In the early eighteenth century, the dominant term was still "invention," and the artisan/artist's activity was still seen as construction. That is the way Batteux and many others understood the difference between invention and creation: "The human spirit cannot properly create. . . . To invent in the arts isn't to give being to an object, but to recognize where and how it is . . . [that] the men of genius who dig deepest, discover only what existed before" (Batteux [1746] 1989, 85).

In order to become "creation," invention first had to be separated from the imitation of nature. Two factors contributed to diminishing the role of imitation. First, the claim that the fine arts imitate only "beautiful nature" had already downgraded the exact imitation of existing nature. Second, a number of writers argued that imitation in any form is irrelevant to architecture and music or even to lyric poetry (Abrams 1958; Becq 1994a). Yet many thinkers still hesitated to substitute "creation" for "invention" on religious grounds. In the Old Testament, God creates by bringing order out of chaos; in Christian dogma God creates ex nihilo, out of nothing. Many people, like Batteux, believed that creation ex nihilo by a human being is a logical impossibility. Without sharing Batteux's theological view, Diderot agreed: "The imagination creates nothing, it imitates, it composes, combines, exaggerates, expands, and contracts" (Diderot [1767] 1995, 113). Other writers used cautious phrases, such as Addison's "something . . . like creation," Johnson's "a right, as it were, of creation," Yves Marie André's "human creation, if I dare speak thus," and Kant's "creates, as it were."[4] When "creation" was taken in the limited sense of ordering a chaos of existing impressions, eighteenth-century writers seemed more comfortable with it. As a demiurge shaping new beings out of a material already given, the artist could be seen not as equal to God but at least bearing the honorific divinity of a lesser god. Shaftesbury likened the true poet to "a second *Maker;* a just Prometheus under Jove" ([1711] 1963, 136).

The spontaneous creativity of the artist did not entirely exclude the old value of facility since painting still required skill of hand, music a gift for harmony and melody, and poetry the ability to versify and follow meters. But the old union of facility with invention had now become the subordination of facility to spontaneous creation. In the old system of art, facility meant gracefully overcoming difficulties in the imitation of created nature; in the new system, the artist-genius was granted the creative power of nature itself, or in Kant's famous phrase, "through genius nature gives the rule to art" ([1790] 1987, 175–76).

What happened to the image of the "artisan" or craftsperson as the old union of facility and inspiration, genius and rule, innovation and imitation, freedom and service were pulled apart? Once divided from inspiration, facility was easily stigmatized as mere technique; once separated from genius, rule became the routine imitation of past models; once separated from freedom, service could be depreciated as mercenary trade. Whereas the artist was said to act with the spontaneity of nature, the artisan was said to act "mechanically," following rules, using imagination only to combine, serving only by filling orders. As a result, the former virtues of rule, skill, imitation, invention, and service were gradually turned into reproaches if not vices. Table 3 summarizes the separation of qualities that had gradually emerged since the Renaissance and was codified in treatises, encyclopedias, and various practices and institutions during the eighteenth century.

TABLE 3
From Artisan/Artist to Artist versus Artisan

| Before the Split (Artisan/Artist) | After the Split | |
|---|---|---|
| | Artist | Artisan |
| Talent or wit | Genius | Rule |
| Inspiration | Inspiration/sensibility | Calculation |
| Facility (mind and body) | Spontaneity (mind over body) | Skill (body) |
| Reproductive imagination | Creative imagination | Reproductive imagination |
| Emulation (of past masters) | Originality | Imitation (of models) |
| Imitation (nature) | Creation | Copying (nature) |
| Service | Freedom (play) | Trade (pay) |

## The Fate of the Artisan

Yet this lowly image of the artisan/craftsperson did not come to dominate all at once even in the eighteenth century. There were many who resisted one or another aspect of the idealization of the artist at the expense of the artisan, attempting to maintain something of the integration characteristic of the old system of art. Yet even some of those who resisted the increasing separation of artist and artisan were ambivalent since there seemed so much to be gained from the new direction. In music, Handel's borrowing and recycling tied him to the old ways, but his manipulation of patrons and the market and his successful achievement of public status signaled what was to come. Samuel Johnson retained much of the older craft approach to writing, yet his *Lives of the Poets* was one of the first literary histories in the modern sense, and he went on to articulate the implication of copyright for the ideal of the artist as creator (Johnson [1781] 1961). To give a fuller sense of ambivalent practices and attitudes toward the separation of artist and artisan in the eighteenth-century, I will look more closely at an artist—William Hogarth, the English engraver and painter of subjects depicting the mores of eighteenth-century London—and a craftsman-entrepreneur—Josiah Wedgwood, the Staffordshire potter turned industrialist and supplier of fine ceramics.

Hogarth began as a silver engraver, but his talent for satire soon led him to the original satirical prints of "modern moral subjects" for which he is famous. His two innovative series, *Harlot's Progress* (1732) and *A Rake's Progress* (1735), also reflected his status ambitions as an artist since they were originally done as paintings to be engraved by others, thereby setting Hogarth off as the artist-painter from the artisan-copyist (although fortunately for us he ended up engraving them himself) (Paulson 1991–93, vol. 1). Hogarth's aspiration to the status of artist was also expressed in his sponsorship of a copyright law protecting original engravings. Hogarth shrewdly decided to hold up the release of *A Rake's Progress* until the Engraver's Act went into effect, but when pirates brought out their own cheap series of the same title, Hogarth had even cheaper copies made and beat the print sellers at their own game. This last move hardly jibes with our modern myth of the artist driven solely by the inner fire of genius and disdaining all commercial calculations. Hogarth is an exemplary figure for the present study just because he straddles two worlds, the old world of the artisan/artist who worked alongside other craftspeople and the new world of the artist who wanted to widen the distance from craftspeople as far as possible. Although Hogarth insisted on the importance of invention and not imitating the work of others, he seems to have had no truck with the new "genius" talk. Like most craftspeople, he carefully considered the tastes of his potential buyers, calibrated his prices to different classes, and made shrewd use of newspaper advertising. For all his status aspirations, Hogarth remained an artisan/artist, keeping in uneasy alliance the two aspects of the artistic career that were being pulled apart in his time (Paulson 1991–93, vol. 2).

Hogarth's ambivalence can best be seen in his attitude toward the art exhibitions organized by the new Society of Artists. In the Spring of 1762 Hogarth, who admired the large figural tavern signs then in vogue, seems to have been involved in a mock "Sign-Painters Exhibition" that satirized the pretensions of the Society of Artists with advertisements and a catalog containing doctored pub sign titles like "The Hen and Chicken, a Landscape" and "Adam and Eve, an Historical Sign." What Hogarth found most objectionable about the direction some of his fellow painters were taking was their quest for a national academy on the hierarchical French model. Hogarth wanted free academies, democratically organized and supportive of an indigenous art that responded to the real society around it (Paulson 1991–93, vol. 3). This is suggested by his artist satires, such as *The Distressed Poet* or *The Enraged Musician,* which gently mock the poet's high art pretensions that leave his wife and child facing the milk bill, or the well-coifed violinist with his hands over his ears vainly trying to shut out the cacophony of daily life (fig. 31). By 1769 when the Royal Academy finally opened, Hogarth was dead and Reynold's version of fine art theory was in the ascendant. It is perhaps significant that the year 1768 saw both the final steps in the organization of the Royal Academy and the parliamentary act forbidding large overhanging signs that spelled the end of sign painting as a pictorial art.

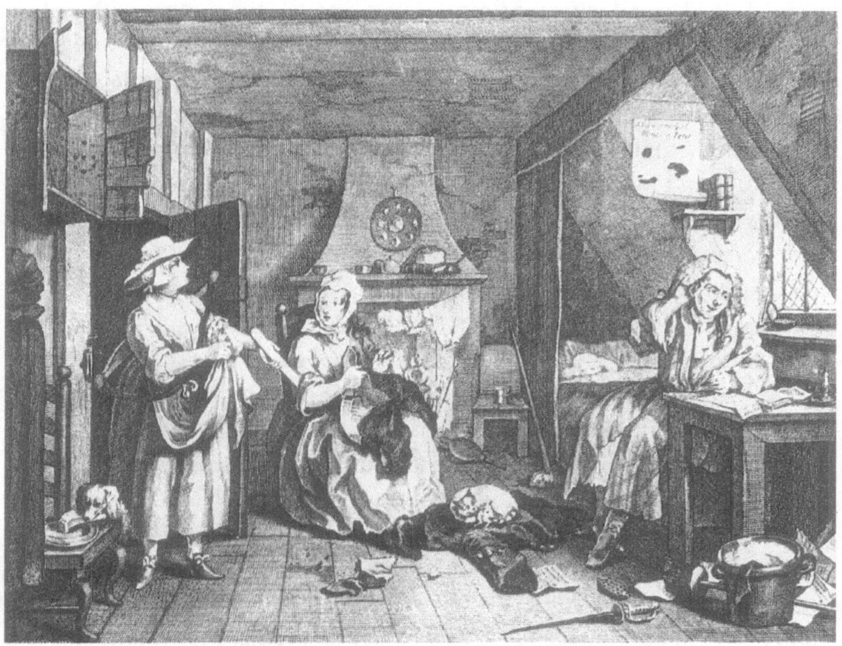

Figure 31. William Hogarth, *The Distressed Poet* (1740).

If Hogarth rose to prominence as an artist-painter from the craft of silver engraving, Josiah Wedgwood rose from the craft of potter to become a world-renowned manufacturer of decorative arts. Hogarth, secure in his reputation as a successful painter and engraver, could safely embrace many of the ideals and practices of the older system of art/craft. Wedgwood, as one engaged in the "craft" and "manufacture" of utilitarian and ornamental products, yearned for a status closer to fine art for his products. Wedgwood was apprenticed at fourteen in one of the many Staffordshire potteries, finally setting up on his own in 1759 and quickly learning to create new forms and glazes that won him a wide following. His very success, however, foretold the end of the old style craftsperson who knew all aspects of the ceramic process. When Wedgwood built his new pottery, Etruria, in 1769, it was a pioneering venture in a kind of assembly line. In order to break his craftspeople of their old habits of working at all aspects of production, he hired artists to design for him and segregated the modeling, molding, handle making, painting, and firing in separate buildings arranged in a semicircle. The clay arrived at one end and the finished products emerged at the other. His workers were to be specialists, not only for efficiency and quality but also for executing each step in precisely the way Wedgwood demanded. Wedgwood is famous for striding through the pottery with a stick, smashing work he considered inferior and scrawling "not good enough for Josiah Wedgwood" on the wall (McKendrick 1961; Burton 1976). Although many of his workers did in fact become more skilled at their specialty, the old freedom of the craftsperson to work at their own pace, to conceive of their work as a whole, and to shift from modeling, to glazing to firing was gone. Wedgwood's practices show one way in which the all-around artisan/artist of the old workshop system was being forced either to become an artisan executing orders and designs of others or to venture the precarious independence of the artist (McKendrick, Brewer, and Plumb 1982).

Wedgwood scored some of his greatest triumphs with the Etruscan and Portland vases, which caught the neoclassical tide in the fine arts (fig. 32). But his clearest play for fine art status were his jasper tablets, which were made of a material he developed himself, were almost as fine as china, and needed no glazing but were easily able to take luminescent color. The jasper bas-reliefs with their cool blue or green backgrounds and raised white neoclassical figures are now considered among his finest pieces, but he could not convince the most respected architects of the day, like Robert Adam, to incorporate them into their buildings. Ann Bermingham believes it is significant that shortly after this failure Wedgwood commissioned a painting of *The Corinthian Maid* from Joseph Wright of Derby (1778). The subject of the painting was chosen by Wedgwood

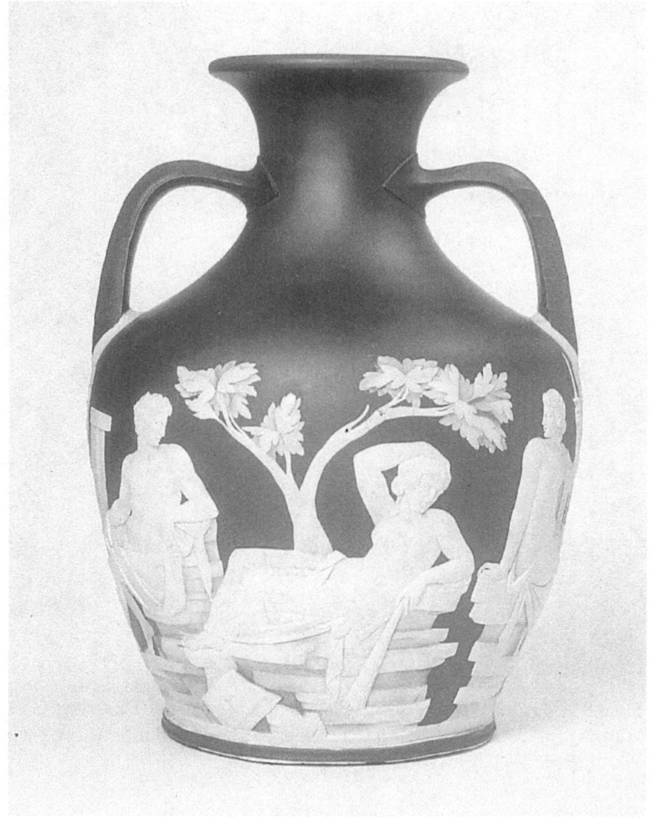

Figure 32. Josiah Wedgwood, *Portland Vase* (1790); blue-black jasper ware with jasper dip and white relief. Courtesy Victoria and Albert Museum, London/Art Resource, New York.

himself from Pliny's tale of the origin of ceramic bas-reliefs: a Corinthian maid, in love with a youth who was leaving the country, traced the outline of his shadow on the wall and her father later filled it in with clay and fired it with his other pottery (fig. 33). Wedgwood's commission seems intended to connect ceramic bas-reliefs to the origin of painting itself in order to give the craftsperson a central role in its invention. Bermingham wonders if the architects' resistance to Wedgwood's jasper tablets was the result of "their own growing pretensions of being 'artists' and a corresponding wariness on their part about supporting the manufacturer of 'Queen's ware' in what may have seemed to be a vulgarization and even feminization of the neo-classical taste" (1992, 148).

The "feminization" Bermingham mentions is suggested by the connection between the maid tracing a shadow and the still prominent idea of women's "accomplishments" in drawing, music, and dance. Wedgwood's factory made

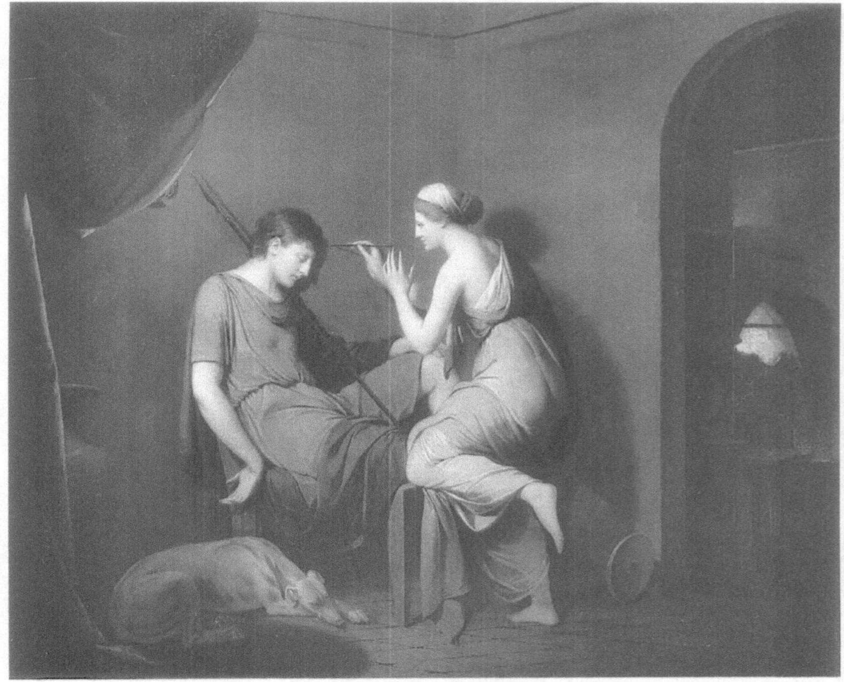

Figure 33. Joseph Wright, *The Corinthian Maid* (1782–84). Courtesy National Gallery of Art, Washington, D.C., Paul Mellon Collection. © 2000 Board of Trustees, National Gallery of Art, Washington, D.C.

unglazed vases, bowls, and other pieces for decoration at home, and his 1781 catalog lists lady's paint boxes in jasper, complete with color cups and a small palette. Eighteenth-century drawing manuals for ladies provided designs to copy, just as many of the artisans in Wedgwood's factory were copying the designs of the artists he hired. Bermingham concludes that "the denigration of craft in the late eighteenth and early nineteenth centuries by both industrial capitalism and the Academy facilitated its feminization, and this feminization of craft ensured its marginalization as 'women's art'" (1992, 162). Wedgwood and Wright of Derby, like Hogarth, were trying to hold together an older art system that was being pulled apart by the market and by the new ideals and institutions of fine art and the artist. Of course, Wedgwood's tablets and vases are now found in fine art museums, although often still separated from painting and sculpture by their relegation to departments of decorative arts.

## The Gender of Genius

The issue of the feminization of craft shows how deeply involved gender prejudices were in the split between artist and artisan. Christine Battersby (1989) has approached the gender issue from the side of the artist's attributes, showing how the modern concept of artistic genius was strongly gendered from the beginning. When genius and talent were still close in meaning, women and artisans could be said to have a genius for some particular activity. Of course, writing great poetry, composing operas, or painting historical canvases were not likely to be one of them. A writer in Addison's *Spectator* suggests that needlework is "the most proper way wherein a Lady can shew a fine Genius" and adds the wish "that several Writers of the Sex had chosen to apply themselves rather to Tapestry than Rime" (1712, no. 606). This dig is firmly in the tradition of developing men's intellectual powers but teaching women amateur "accomplishments" in needlework, dancing, singing, and drawing (fig. 34).[5] In suggesting needlework as women's proper sphere of production, the *Spectator* writer also reflected the further demotion and feminization of embroidery and other needle arts that began with the Renaissance. Women who did venture into professional work as painters or writers were still considered capable of only the lesser genres, for example, portraits and flowers or the novel and short lyrics. But as the ideas of originality, imagination, and creation came together to form the modern ideal of the artist-genius, new arguments were now available to deny genius to women.

Since French writers such as Diderot or Rousseau gave pride of place to enthusiasm in genius, it is not surprising to hear Rousseau argue that "women in general possess no . . . genius . . . [because] the celestial fire that emblazons and ignites the soul, the inspiration that comes and devours . . . are always lacking" (Rousseau 1954, 206). English writers of the time, such as William Duff, who made imagination the central attribute of genius, found women incapable of genius because they lacked the "creative power and energy of imagination" (Battersby 1989, 78). Kant shared Duff's perspective and said that if a woman did possess a vigorous mind, it would be against nature were she to express it publicly; a woman scholar "might as well even have a beard." Kant makes women's strength (and deficiency) just the opposite of Rousseau's: women can respond to what is emotional in art but lack a strong understanding, without which an artist produces only nonsense (Kant 1960, 78–80).

Nothing better illustrates the gendering of genius in the late eighteenth century than Mary Wollstonecraft's hesitancy concerning female genius in her

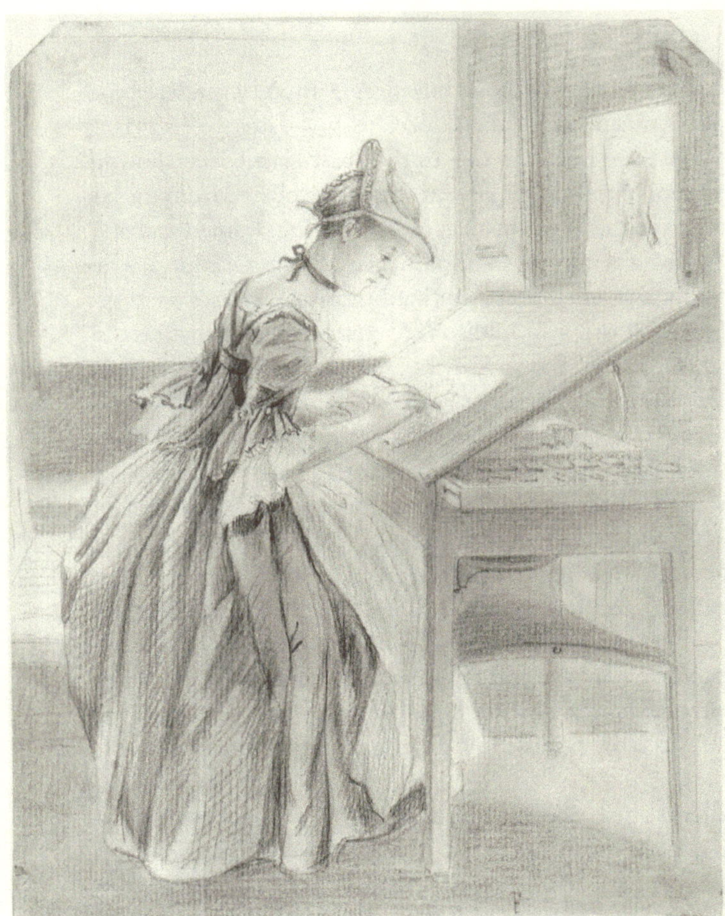

Figure 34. Paul Sandby, *A Lady Copying at a Drawing Table* (ca. 1760–70). Courtesy Yale Center for British Art, Paul Mellon Collection, New Haven, Conn.

*Vindication of the Rights of Woman* (1792). Accepting the idea that genius requires physical vigor, she wonders whether "the few extraordinary women" who have appeared in history "were *male* spirits, confined by mistake in female frames" (Wollstonecraft [1792] 1989, 5 : 66). The redoubtable Germaine de Staël had no such hesitation, and in her novel *Corrine, or Italy* (1807) makes her heroine a poet "joyously devoting herself to genius" who is crowned with the laurel by the Senators and people of Rome (1987, 32). But by the end of the novel, Corrine has succumbed to the lot of woman and dies for love. Another example of the tension between genius and womanhood can be found in the career of Sophie La Roche, a widely read and admired German novelist of the second half of the century. Her better-known friend, the poet Christoph Wieland, wrote a preface to her first novel in which he patronizingly tells critics to address their complaints to him since La Roche "never intended to write for the world or to create a work of art" (Woodmansee 1994, 107).

The new idea of genius in the eighteenth century seemed to set before women the choice of being a genius or being a woman. That is the implicit message in Diderot's hailing of Racine as the artist who must follow his genius, whatever the cost to those around him. Accordingly, following this line of thinking, while nature has destined males for the public sphere, there is no exception to traditional female roles even for the woman of great natural gifts. Women in "male" vocations such as one of the fine arts either were suspect as a threat to social order or were accepted only because they were "really" male spirits in a female body.

## The Ideal of the "Work of Art"

It is striking that when Wieland wanted to "protect" Sophie La Roche from critics, he assured them she did not intend to create a "work of art." The counterpart of the male artist's creative power was the work of art as genial creation. In the old system of art, the phrase "work of art" meant the product of "an art," something constructed rather than created, although the best of such constructions, like Sophocles' *Oedipus,* had always been praised for achieving unity (Aristotle, *Poetics*). But such works were not necessarily conceived of as fixed, self-contained creations. As we saw in the case of the seventeenth-century theater, Ben Jonson was one of the first to insist on publishing his plays under the title of "works." Paintings and statues were more obviously fixed works even in the old system of art/craft, yet most were not thought of as self-contained but as connected to a purpose and place. By the beginning of the eighteenth century, however, Roger de Piles was emphasizing the internal unity and total impression made by a painting rather than the painting's subject matter, message, or fitness to purpose (Piles [1708] 1969). But it is musical practice that most dramatically reveals the depth of the break between the older idea of a work of art (construction) and the modern idea of a work of Art (creation).

Paradoxical as it may sound, the old system of art produced an enormous number of beautiful pieces of music, but people seldom thought of these pieces as "works" in the modern sense of fixed, self-contained "worlds." Lydia Goehr lists a network of practices still regulative in the early eighteenth century that make the application of our modern notion of the work to the musical practice of this period anachronistic. First, most early eighteenth-century music was composed as a vehicle for specific occasions by people who usually performed the pieces they wrote, sometimes composing *as* they performed. Second, the enormous demands placed on musicians by their employers often led them to recycle chunks of their own pieces and borrow freely from each other with few compunctions about originality. Third, notation was not always complete and performers sometimes "finished" the work to their own understanding as they played it. Finally, most composers did not think of their music as lasting beyond their lifetime in the form of discrete works—they simply composed a quantity of music to be used on various occasions. Bach turned out an enormous amount of music year after year at the Thomas-Kirche in Leipzig and assumed that those who followed him would not use the pieces he wrote any more than he used theirs and "indeed his works were as promptly laid aside when he died as theirs had been" (David and Mendel 1966, 43). Goehr concludes, "In a practice that demanded . . . functional music, and which allowed an open interchange of musical material . . . musicians did not see works as much as they saw individual performances" (1992, 186).[6]

But as the new ideas of fine art and the artist spread from the mid-eighteenth century on, the open borrowing and free recycling of musical elements gradually ended. Some writers on music now began to criticize earlier composers for what had once been normal practice, complaining that Handel "has pilfered from all Manner of Authors . . . putting even his own subjects in so many different Works over and over again" (Goehr 1992, 185). The changed situation is reflected in Beethoven's claim in 1797 that he never attended Mozart's operas nor did he like "to hear the music of others lest I forfeit some of my originality" (Sonneck 1954, 22). An equally sure sign that the work concept had begun to be accepted was the increasing concern to provide exact notation of dynamics and the insistence that performers follow them. Beethoven began replacing tempo notations such as "andante" with precise metronome marks, asserting in a letter that "the performers must now obey the ideas of the unfettered genius" (Beethoven 1951, 254). Finally, just as Shakespeare's malleable play scripts quickly came to be treated as fixed works after his death, so at the end of the eighteenth century, the pieces that Bach or Haydn wrote for specific occasions began to be treated as self-contained works and given opus numbers in place of the old title page references to their original purpose (Goehr 1992).

The concept of the literary work inaugurated by Ben Jonson in the seventeenth century was reinforced in the eighteenth from two directions, one theory using the idea of supernatural or romantic worlds, the other the idea of fictional versions of the empirical world. According to Richard Hurd in *Letters on Chivalry and Romance* (1762) the poet does not "follow . . . the known and experienced course of affairs" but "has a world of his own" (Abrams 1958, 272).

By severing supernatural poetry from the natural world, the work of art could become a "second nature" or creation, and the Swiss critics Johann Jakob Bodmer and Johann Jakob Breitinger explained it with the help of Leibniz's concept of "possible worlds." As Leibniz's famous phrase has it, given all the things he wished to include in it, God made this "the best of all possible worlds." Similarly, the artist as creator conceives of each artwork as a kind of "possible world" and, like God, must make this work/world an internally consistent whole (Abrams 1958).

But other writers on the arts argued that the artist creates a fictionalized version of our actual world: "He forms a whole, coherent and proportioned in itself, with due subjection and subordinancy of the constituent parts [and] . . . can thus imitate the Creator" (Shaftesbury [1711] 1963, 136). In Shaftesbury's view the artist's creation is defined primarily by its internal fictional content and formal organization rather than by an external purpose. Later in the century, the German playwright Lessing claimed that works done for some external purpose do not deserve the name "art" at all since they are more about "meaning than Beauty"—such a work is "not made for itself, but as a mere auxiliary to religion" (1987, 80–81).

The strongest expression of the modern idea of the work of art as a self-contained world was offered by the German novelist and philosopher Karl Philipp Moritz in his 1785 essay "Toward a Unification of All the Fine Arts and Letters under the Concept of Self-Sufficiency." Moritz contrasted craft works that "have their purposes outside themselves" with works of art that "are complete in themselves" and exist only for the sake of their "own internal perfection" (Woodmansee 1994, 18). In the traditional idea of unity, a work's internal coherence was still affected by what was external to it—the imitation of nature and the work's function. In the new idea of the work of art as a self-sufficient creation, the unity is completely internal and the work forms "a little world in itself," as Goethe put it (Abrams 1958, 278).

Closely connected to the emergence of the idea of the work as creation was a final transformation in the idea of the "masterpiece." Originally a masterpiece was the piece by which an artisan/artist demonstrated to the guild that he or she was now a master of the art. These demonstration pieces—which continued to be required down to the eighteenth century—were often set problems, such as a 1496 Lyon statuary requirement for a "Jesus Christ in stone, entirely naked, showing his wounds, wearing a little loin cloth . . . a crown of thorns on his head" (Cahn 1979, 11). By the late Renaissance, the term "masterpiece," although still referring to demonstration pieces, was already used for any superlative achievement in the arts. But a further transformation occurred in the eighteenth century when the notion of masterpiece merged with the new idea of the work of art as creation. The notion of masterpiece became attached to it as signaling a particularly exceptional work in the new sense of a fixed and self-contained world. With the decline and eventual disappearance of the guilds in the nineteenth century, the older sense of masterpiece disappeared with them. The modern idea of a masterpiece was then completely absorbed into the concept of the artist as creator, with the result that art, music, and literary history often came to be written as the story of a series of artist-geniuses and their "masterpieces."

## From Patronage to the Market

Although writers, painters, and musicians experienced the transition from the patronage to the market system at different rates from country to country, there are enough features in common that we can draw up a general comparison of the situation before and after the separation of artist from artisan and the work as creation from the work as construction. There were obviously many varieties of patronage/commission relations in the old system of art, some of which approached features of a market economy, just as the market system today still leaves room for commissions and patron sponsorship, as well as government sinecures and grants. The following comparison of the two systems of art practice sets in relief the structural differences by sketching the most typical characteristics of each.

In the old system of art, patrons or clients normally commissioned poems, paintings, or compositions for particular places or contexts, often prescribing subject matter, size, form, materials, or instrumentation. Even in cases where producers were left considerable freedom, they still made their pieces in response to specific requests of clients or regular needs of employers. The criteria of success for poems, paintings, or music produced within this system obviously included how well the piece satisfied its purpose(s), along with such traditional tests of beauty as harmony and proportion. The "price" of the resulting piece was usually determined by materials, difficulty, and time, along with the reputation of the workshop or master and the function the piece was to serve.

In the purest form of a market system, in contrast, writers, painters, and composers produce in advance and then attempt to sell their work to an audience of more or less anonymous buyers, often using a dealer or agent. The absence of a specific order or a prescribed context of use gives the impression that the artists are completely free to follow their own inclinations. Works produced under the market system are viewed as the expression of a personality, and the receiver is buying not only a self-contained work but also the producer's imagination and creativity expressed as reputation. The criteria of success are largely internal to the work, such as originality, expressiveness, and formal perfection, although the creator's reputation and current fashions play a role. Hence, the "price" of the work of fine art seldom has any basis in the work itself—not in its materials, not in the amount of labor, not even in the difficulty of execution since it is no longer a construction but a spontaneous "creation." In itself, the work of fine art is literally "priceless," its actual price set by the artist's reputation and the buyer's desire and willingness to pay.

Historians have often described the transition from the old system of art to the new system of fine art as a "liberation." In the old system, patrons were generally in a superior position and the artisan/artists often had to submit to their wishes; in the new market system, artists and buyers come closer to being on equal footing. The new art institutions, such as criticism, histories, academies, and conservatories, along with the artists themselves, attempt to guide the public's taste, and the public is more susceptible because it is no longer gathering as a corporate group in church or palace or private salon where the art works serve well-understood purposes that anyone can judge. Now people come as individuals to exhibitions, concert halls, and theaters, where they encounter works that are often complex and strange to those not familiar with the latest trends in the various arts (Elias 1993). Obviously, the modern image of "the artist," with its notions of genial freedom and creative imagination, helps convince this fragmented public that artists, critics, and other specialists know best what should be appreciated and paid for. Yet we should not exaggerate the freedom of the artist in the new market system. If artists want to earn a living from their work, they will have to offer works within a range that some audiences and critics will accept or else join forces with other artists and critics to impose a new direction. The insistence on artistic independence and freedom, which has been a leitmotif since the late eighteenth century, is in part a reaction to a new kind of dependence.

The French literary historian Annie Becq has described the transition from patronage to the market as a move from "concrete labor" to "abstract labor," necessitated by the shift from use value to exchange value. In the older system of art, the producer's labor was concrete in the sense that facility, intelligence, and inventiveness were employed in executing a commission that often had a specific use and an agreed on subject matter. In the emerging market system, labor becomes abstract in the sense that it has no tie to a specific place or purpose, no predetermined subject matter and, therefore, no specific tasks of execution but only a generalized creativity. Table 4 shows the differences Becq discerns.

TABLE 4
From the "Piece" to the "Work": Two Systems of Art Production and Reception

| Aspect | Old "Art" System (Patronage/Commission) | New "Fine Art" System (Free Market) |
|---|---|---|
| Production | Concrete labor | Abstract labor |
| Product | Piece | Work |
| Representation | Imitation | Creation |
| Reception | Use; enjoyment | Exchange; contemplation |

Of course, this table describes ideal types; the actual situation of producers seldom approached either model in its purity. This was especially true of the long eighteenth century (1680–1830), which saw a gradual transition from the dominance of a patronage model in the late seventeenth century to the dominance of a market model in the early nineteenth. The shift was more rapid in some parts of Europe than others, with England moving earliest to the market system and France lagging behind until the Revolution swept away many of the old elements of patronage. Figures such as Hogarth and Wedgwood in the visual arts, Diderot and Johnson in literature, Haydn and Mozart in music show the difficulties and ambivalence of those who lived through this transformation.

Initially, many eighteenth-century artists and critics regarded the shift from patronage to the market as a liberation. Such a response was especially characteristic of England where people like Johnson, Hogarth, and the visiting Haydn all exclaimed of their freedom. Nor did Johnson feel any conflict between art and money: "No man but a blockhead ever wrote except for money." Of course, by the time of the early Romantics, even the new public audience for fine art would be scorned as a shackle. "Where any view of money exists, art cannot be carried on," William Blake would declare (Porter 1990, 242–49). The dialectic of art and money had already taken on the form it has retained to this day: the artist's need to show independence of the very people whose approval is necessary to success (Mattick 1993).

For our purposes what is important about the displacement of patronage by the market is that it occurred at the same time that the new ideas of fine art, the artist, and the aesthetic were being constructed and new institutions such as the museum, concert, and copyright were being established. Set apart from contexts or use or entertainment and insulated from the realities of the market by the ideals of the artist's creativity and the work as a world, the work of fine art invited a unique mode of attention that came to be called "aesthetic." Only when we have put the ideas and institutions of fine art, artist, and work of art together with the concepts and practices of the aesthetic will we have a complete picture of the modern system of art.

CHAPTER 7

# From Taste to the Aesthetic

On May 1, 1778, Mozart wrote his father about a salon concert he gave at the duchesse de Chabot's in Paris: "Madame and her gentlemen never interrupted their drawing for a moment . . . so that I had to play to chairs, tables and walls" (Johnson 1995, 76). Even when the music was not intended as background for other activities, salon audiences were seldom very attentive (fig. 35). If people didn't listen in the salons, the situation was no better in the opera houses, where the aristocrats who sat on the stage and the mixed company that stood in the pit talked, blew whistles, threw apples, or started fights. At the Paris Opera, the rowdiness was such that forty soldiers carrying muskets were assigned to patrol the halls. Orchestra conductors tried to keep time above the noise by beating a wooden stick against the podium, scene changes took place in full view, and the hall was brightly lit by thousands of candles that maximized the spectator's view of each other, although the smoke sometimes obscured the stage. Even the physical layout favored socializing over listening because the boxes along the sides of the second and third levels were deep and had floor to ceiling walls set at right angles rather than slanting toward the stage, making it easier to carry out liaisons or to see people across the way than to attend to the actors on the stage (Johnson 1995, 10) (fig. 36). The situation was no better in London. Hogarth's painting of a climactic scene in the *Beggar's Opera* of 1728 humorously exploits the fact that some of the aristocracy sat on stage by having Lavinia Fenton, playing Polly, look past the other actors toward her lover, the duke of Bolton at a table along the side (Paulson 1991–93, vol. 1) (fig. 37).

In 1759 the French eliminated stage seating, and the English followed in 1762; later in the century the walls of boxes in new theaters were slanted toward the stage and fixed seats were installed in the pit, although this did not quiet audiences as much as hoped (Rougement 1988). The removal of aristocrats from the stage not only signaled an attempt to eliminate distraction but also swept away one of the last vestiges of the social/ritual aspect of the theater. Serious operas and plays were now supposed to be the experience of an art illusion, and theater audiences began to be encouraged to sit in respectful and attentive silence

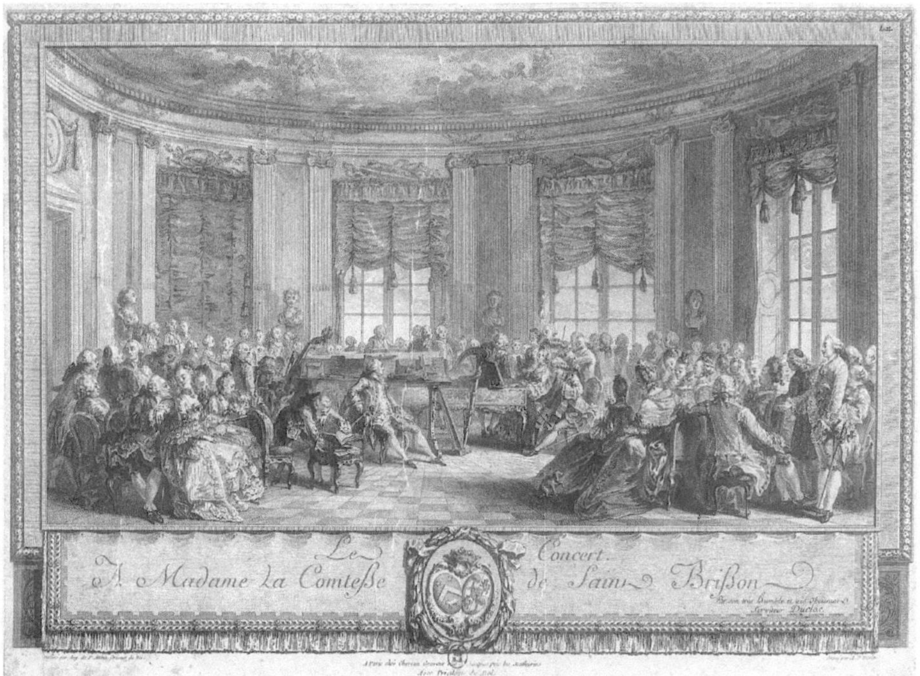


Figure 35. Augustin de Saint Aubain, *Le Concert à Madame la Comtesse de Saint Brisson* (n.d.). Courtesy Bibliothèque Nationale, Paris.

(Caplan 1989). It would take until the mid-nineteenth century for the new behavior to become typical; meanwhile, the physical changes and the exhortations to silent attention helped prepare the way for theories of the aesthetic.[1]

This is not the place to trace the history of particular theories of the aesthetic since Alexander Baumgarten first coined the term in 1735; instead I will describe some signs of a split in the traditional responses to the arts that divided the satisfactions of utility and diversion from the special kind of pleasure that came to be called aesthetic. The crucial difference between taste and the aesthetic is that taste has always been an irremediably social concept, concerned as much with food, dress, and manners as with the beauty or meaning of nature or art. From the ancient Greeks through the nineteenth century, literal taste, as facilitated by the tongue, as well as the senses of touch and smell, were downgraded as too sensual and bodily compared to vision and hearing (Korsmeyer 1999). In the eighteenth century, for example, Lord Kames begins his influential discussion of taste by distinguishing the dignified and "elevated" senses of sight and

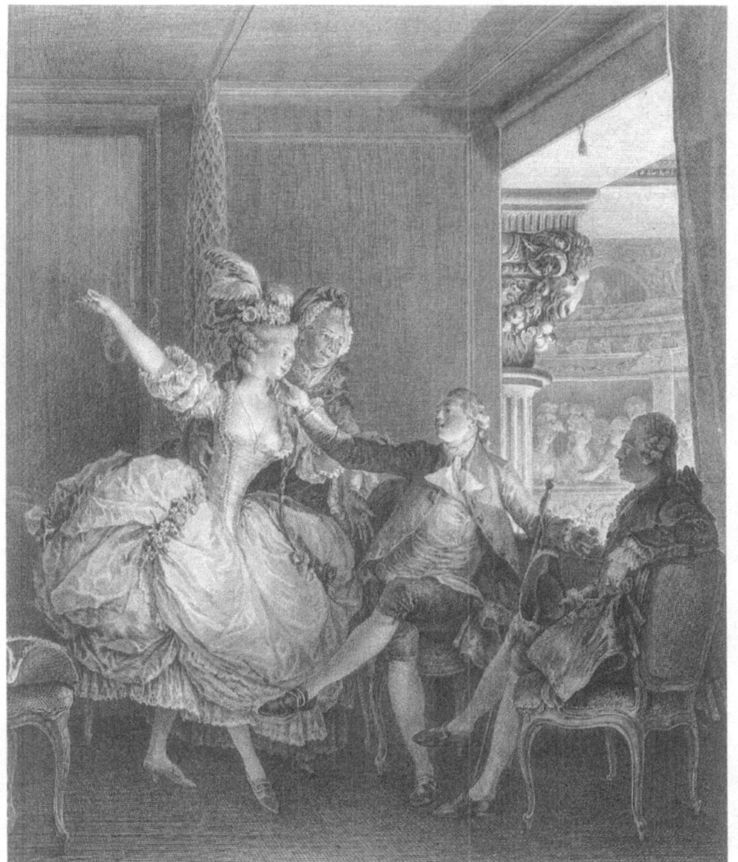

Figure 36. Jean Michel Moreau le Jeune, *La Petit Loge* (1777). Two gentlemen receive a dancer in their box at the Paris Opera. Courtesy Bibliothèque Nationale, Paris.

hearing from the "inferior" bodily senses of tasting, touching, and smelling (Kames 1762, 1–6). Most of those who contributed to the theory of taste in the eighteenth century similarly tried to separate taste in the fine arts from the word's natural association with ordinary sensual pleasures or the satisfactions of utility. The advantage of the new term "aesthetic" was that it did not carry such metaphorical baggage. But before examining the intellectual process by which taste was transformed into the aesthetic, we need to consider the emergence of certain "aesthetic" behaviors—like the calmer attention aimed at by eliminating aristocrats from the stage or by installing seats in the pit.

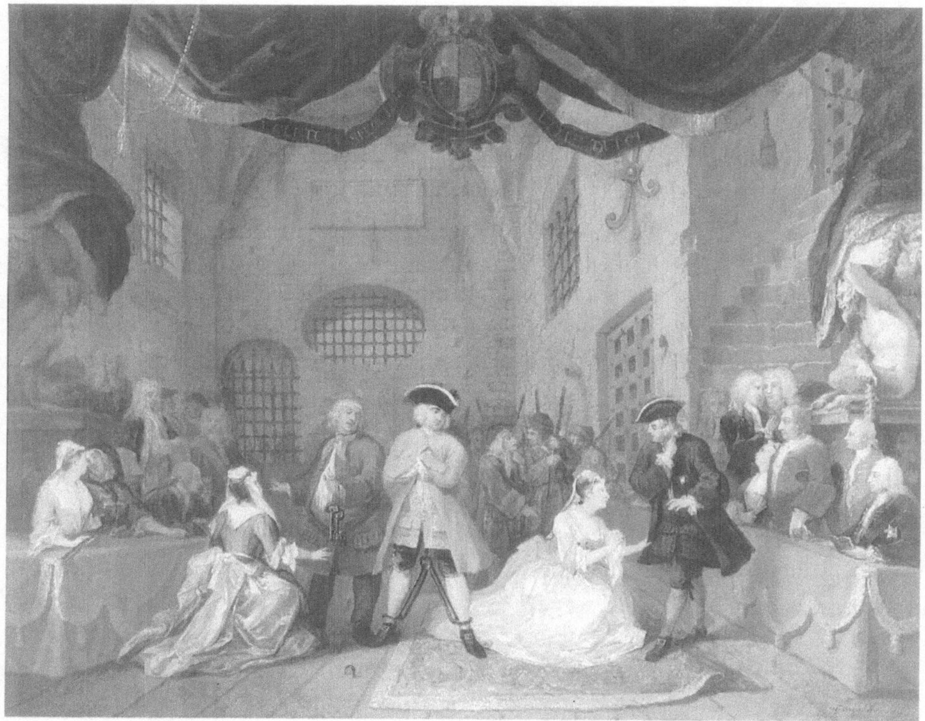

Figure 37. William Hogarth, *The Beggar's Opera, III* (1729). Courtesy Yale Center for British Art, Paul Mellon Collection, New Haven, Conn.

## Learning Aesthetic Behavior

A particularly telling example of this new kind of behavior was the "picturesque tour" so popular in Britain during the last third of the century. To experience a landscape as "picturesque" was to look at it in the way one looked at a painting. This purely visual attitude seems so natural to us that it is easy to overlook the change from a moral and utilitarian to an aesthetic behavior. Early eighteenth-century estate grounds were often laid out with quiet vales for meditation and adorned with exemplary statuary and structures such as Stowe garden's neoclassical "Temple of Virtue," conceived after the old Horatian ideal for poetry: "The End and Design of a good Garden is to be both profitable and delightful" (Andrews 1989, 52). By mid-century, however, many newer designs eliminated exemplary statuary and laid out estates to provide a gallery of landscape views solely to please the eye.

According to William Gilpin's influential guidebooks on the picturesque, regular fields and well-built houses might give us moral satisfaction, but they excite no "pleasure in the Imagination" (Andrews 1989, 48). Appreciating picturesque beauty meant attending to the purely visual factors of lighting, distances, rough contours, and ruins (Gilpin 1782). Moreover, only certain kinds of people could appear in a genuinely picturesque scene without spoiling the effect: "Milk-maids . . . ploughmen, reapers, and all peasants *engaged in their several professions,* we disallow . . . they are valued, for what in real life they are despised—loitering idly about" (Bohls 1995, 96). Coached by writers like Gilpin to eliminate moral and utilitarian interests in favor of purely pictorial ones, the new domestic tourists set off for the river Wye and other sites armed with guidebooks, sketchpads, journals, and a most telling piece of aesthetic equipment: the "Claude glass," a dark tinted, convex mirror that conveniently reduced a scene to the scale and tonality of a miniature Claude Lorrain painting (fig. 38). Today, we are likely to sympathize with Jane Austen's parody of the picturesque tourist in *Northanger Abbey* where Catherine Morland looks down from the top of Beechen Cliff and rejects "the whole city of Bath, as unworthy to make part of a landscape" (Austen 1995, 99). However banal it now seems, picturesque tourism, with its Claude glasses, guidebooks, and journals, was an important step toward the behavior we call aesthetic.

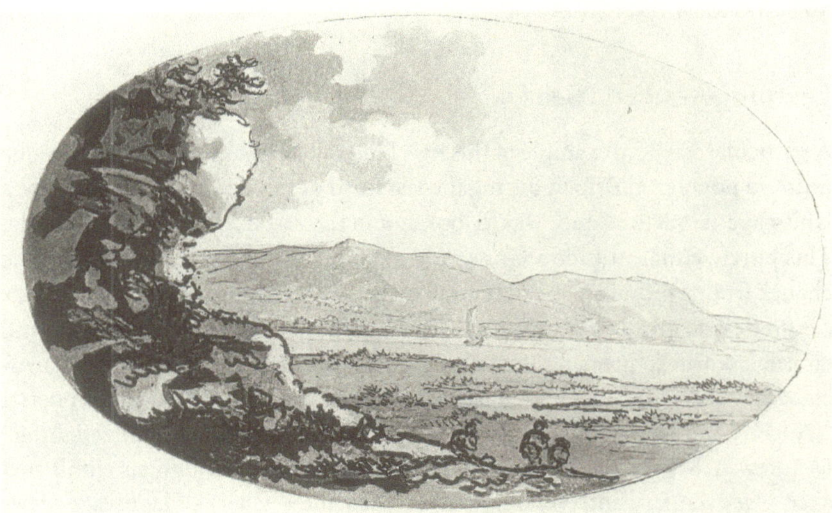

Figure 38. William Gilpin, sketch from *Observations on the River Wye* (1782). Courtesy Rare Book and Special Collections, University of Illinois Library, Urbana-Champaign.

The rapid growth in the number of readers for poetry and the novel also led to attempts at shaping appropriate attitudes, beginning with Addison's series titled "Pleasures of the Imagination" in the *Spectator.* In chapter 4, we noted the beginning of a literary exchange in the French journal, *Le mercure gallant,* from the 1680s on (fig. 39). In Germany, the burgeoning market for secular literature in the late eighteenth century led to a vigorous public discussion in which pastors and officials were alarmed about morals and political stability, while Fichte, Goethe, and Schiller complained of the taste for sentimentalism and cheap thrillers. The new literary criticism not only attempted to guide readers toward which books to read but, in some cases, how to read them. Periodicals like Schiller's *Horen* or books like Johann Bergk's *The Art of Reading* attempted to inculcate a contemplative reading focused on the literary form of the sort of books Christoph Wieland called works of art (Woodmansee 1994).

The public also had to be coached on proper behavior in the new art museums. When part of the Louvre Palace was turned into a public art museum during the Revolution, signs had to be posted asking people not to sing, joke, or play games in the galleries but to respect them as "the sanctuary of silence and meditation" (Mantion 1988, 113). The more sophisticated members of the emerging art public needed no such prodding to treat painting and sculpture as the object of a refined, even spiritual, pleasure. Parts of the British nobility had understood painting in the traditional way as having a public, even political, purpose, but this view was gradually modified over the century as writers like Adam Smith and David Hume argued that the primary aim of the arts is pleasure not instruction (Barrell 1986). If painting was to have a positive effect on morals, henceforth it would only be indirectly. Although a Gilpin could argue against bringing moral considerations into the experience of landscapes, he did believe there was an indirect moral benefit to fine art experiences: "When I sit ravished at an Oratorio, or stand astonished before the [Raphael] Cartoons, or enjoy myself in these happy Walks, I can feel my Mind expand . . . and my Heart better disposed . . . a Taste for these exalted Pleasures contributes towards making me a better Man" (Andrews 1989, 53). The literary critic, William Hazlitt was even more effusive in describing the spiritual thrill of visiting the collection of the duke of Orléans in 1799: "A mist passed away from my sight; the scales fell off . . . a new heaven and a new earth stood before me. We had all heard the names of Titian, Raphael, Guido, Domenichino, the Caracci—but to see them face to face, to be in the same room with their deathless productions, . . . from that time on I lived in a world of pictures" (Haskell 1976, 43). Similar reactions to painting were taking place in France, where one critic referred to the exhibition room of the Louvre, as "this temple of the arts," and another critic wrote

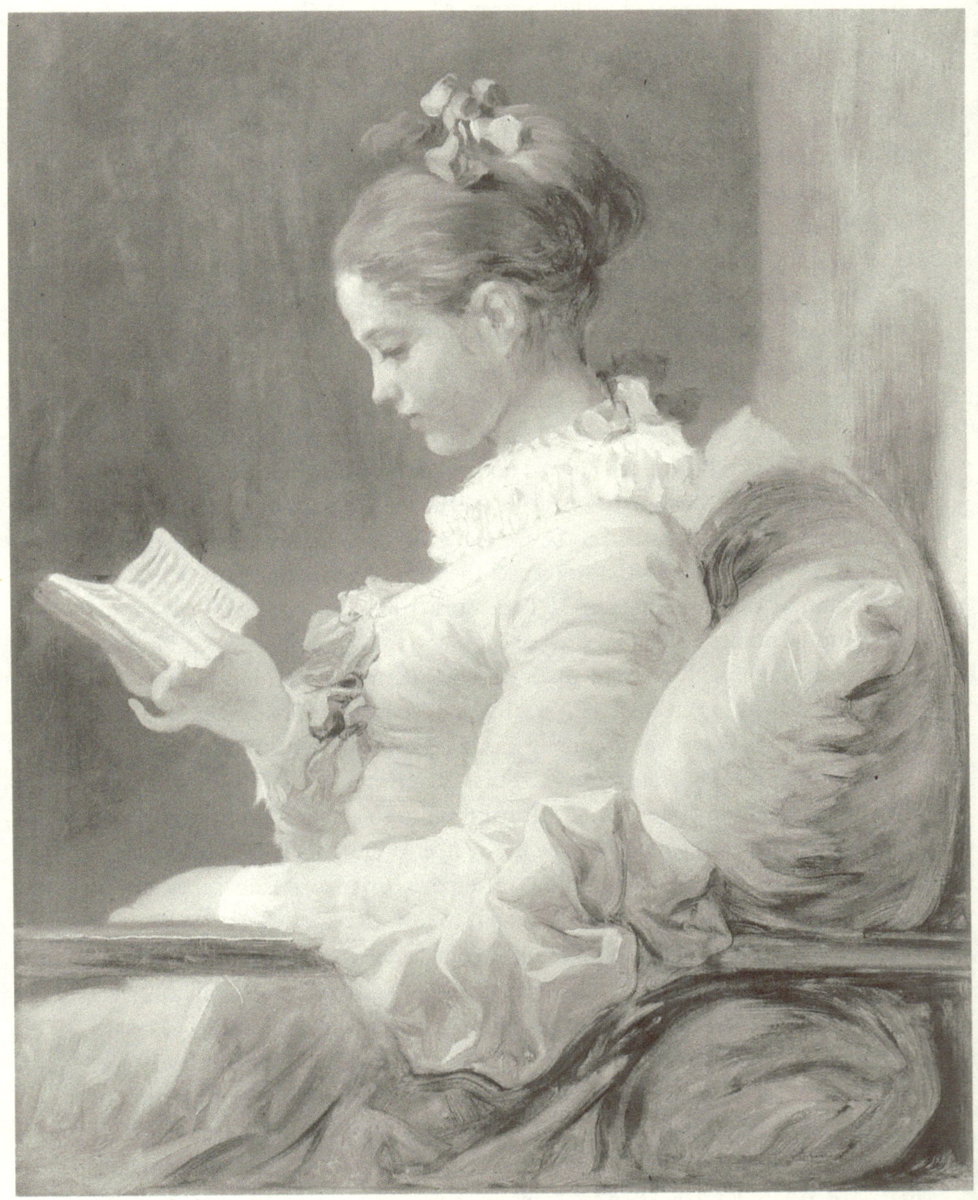

Figure 39. Jean-Honoré Fragonard, *A Young Girl Reading* (1776). Courtesy National Gallery of Art, Washington, D.C. Gift of Mrs. Mellon Bruce in memory of her father, Andrew W. Mellon. © 2000 Board of Trustees, National Gallery of Art, Washington, D.C.

of the academy's Salon exhibition of 1779, "I perceive a sentiment worthy of unifying the human species . . . the passionate love for the Fine Arts" (Crow 1985, 4, 19). Already the cult of art was beginning and the inflated, quasi-religious rhetoric that goes with it.

In Hazlitt's response we recognize the late eighteen-century Romantic sensibility of a cultivated gentleman. But what of the motley assortment of Louvre Salon visitors earlier in the century that included a great noble, a lady, a Savoyard odd-job man, a fishwife, and a "rough artisan," the latter, "guided only by natural feeling" yet coming out with "a just observation"? (Crow 1985, 4). Was that "natural feeling" something universal, something common to both Mairobet and the rough artisan? And if it was common, why did people disagree so widely in their tastes? These questions formed part of what historians of aesthetics call the "problem of taste," the issue of whether there is an objective or inborn standard of taste. If the fishwife or artisan already possesses this subtle judgment, it would seem so. However, if people had to learn how to behave toward the fine arts, taste would seem to be a social matter requiring education and leisure.

## The Art Public and the Problem of Taste

In chapter 5 on the category of fine art, we saw that a major criterion for separating fine art from craft was fine art's appeal to the finer pleasures of taste rather than to utility or sensual enjoyment. Moreover, frequent experiences of this refined sort distinguished the polite public from the ignorant poor or the boorish rich and their "grosser" pleasures. Yet it was not only the laboring poor or the booby squires who were believed to lack the fine sensibility requisite to good taste but also the colored races, most women, and, on the wealthier side, the idle rich who mixed art and luxury.

Although many eighteenth-century writers on taste suggested that laborers lacked the capacity or means to acquire a refined taste, others, like Kant, believed that literacy would eventually make almost everyone part of the public. A good example of the differences over who was capable of refined taste was the debate over who was qualified to judge the French Academy's annual Salon exhibition. At one extreme, Louis de Carmontelle could idealistically declare that "all classes of citizens come to pack the Salon . . . [and] the public, natural judge of the fine arts, . . . renders its verdict" (Crow 1985, 18). But the academy director, Charles Coypel, declared that "the public changes twenty times a day. . . . What the public admires at ten o'clock . . . is publicly condemned at noon. . . .

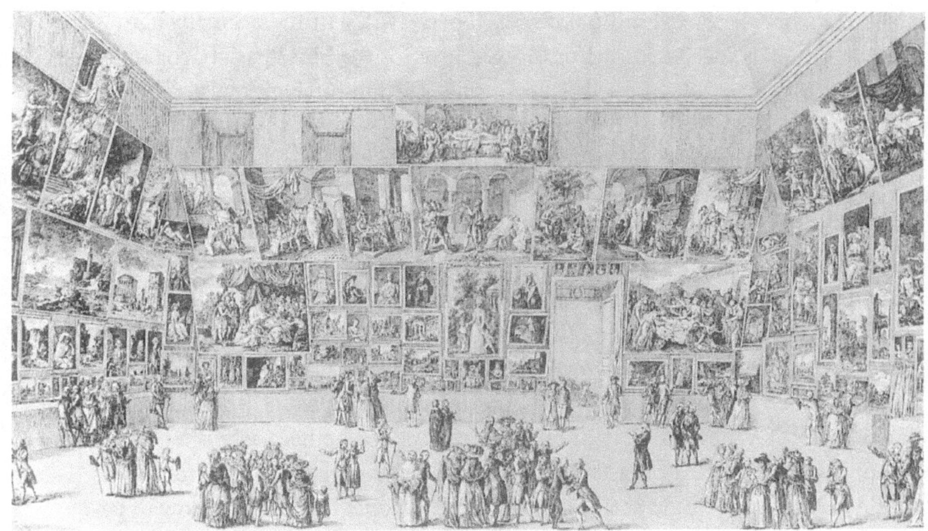

Figure 40. Pietro Antonio Martini, *Le Salon du Louvre 1785*. Courtesy Bibliothèque Nationale, Paris. By 1785 the annual salons of the academy drew large crowds and vigorous critical commentary; Jacques-Louis David, whose *Oath of the Horatii* of that year has often been described as a harbinger of several Revolutionary ideals, knew how to play off parts of this public against the more conservative leaders of the academy.

After having heard them all, you will have heard not a true public, but only the mob" (Crow 1985, 10) (fig. 40). A similar distinction was made with regard to the audience at the theater and concerts. In the first half of the century, the noisy parterre continued to be the place of cheap standing-room-only tickets, filled by merchants, students, law clerks, and a smattering of shop assistants, self-employed artisans, and servants (Rougemont 1988). Dubos asserted that the public of "the *parterre,* without knowing the rules, judges a play as well as the playwrights," but immediately added that he did not "include in the public the lower classes . . . but only people who have acquired . . . taste through comparison" (Dubos 1993, 279). Many observers in the second half of the century claimed that the judgment of the parterre was declining because too many of the working classes were showing up: "Workmen and mercenaries decide the fate of music. They fill the theaters; they attend the musical competitions and they set themselves up as arbiters of taste" (le Huray and Day 1988, 125). Although these alarms were probably exaggerated, they are evidence of a combined cultural and class anxiety.

A small but significant segment of the European working population in the eighteenth century were African slaves and servants who can be seen in paintings of the time as a sign of their owner's wealth and status. Two of the leading eighteenth-century writers on aesthetics offered the opinion that people of color were by nature incapable of a refined taste for the arts. David Hume's comments are the most notorious and sweeping: "I am apt to suspect the negroes to be naturally inferior to the whites. There scarcely ever was a civilized nation of that complexion . . . no ingenious manufactures amongst them, no arts, no sciences. . . . Not to mention our colonies, there are NEGROE slaves dispersed all over EUROPE, of whom none ever discovered any symptoms of ingenuity" (1993, 360). Although James Beattie and others refuted Hume's inaccuracies and prejudices, Kant thought enough of Hume's essay to cite it in support of his own contention that "the Negroes of Africa have by nature no feeling that rises above the trifling" (Kant 1960, 110; Eze 1997, 63).

The exclusion of women from those capable of the "fine taste" was not as sweeping as the exclusion of the dark-skinned races or the laboring class. Although a few male writers believed women were actually more discriminating than men, others, such as Shaftesbury and Kant, for example, believed women lacked the requisite intellectual powers to go with their sensibility. Instead of becoming connoisseurs of the fine arts, women were generally expected to become practitioners of the lesser arts or crafts. In Jane Austen's unfinished novel, *Sanditon,* the "two Miss Beauforts" have been brought by their parents to a seaside resort to display their female attainments in the search for husbands: "They were very accomplished and very Ignorant," Austen writes, "with the hire of a Harp for one, and the purchase of some Drawing paper for the other" (Bermingham 1992, 14).

Of course, it was not only the vulgar poor, the colored races, and the majority of women who were identified as lacking the intellectual capacity for a sound comparative taste but also the vulgar rich who had no interest in the fine arts. Yet there was still another group of the rich and high born who, although they did collect paintings or host salons for noted writers and musicians, nevertheless still failed to exhibit a properly aesthetic attitude. Although highly sophisticated, they were excluded from that class of people with good taste by writers on the subject because they misused their fine taste for display, decoration, and diversion—what the eighteenth century called "luxury." The critique of upper-class luxury was probably as important to the construction of the modern idea of the aesthetic as the rejection of the lower-class and female-identified pleasures of sense and utility. Of course, luxury in the simpler meaning of conspicuous expenditure had its eighteenth-century defenders—for example, Hume, Bernard Mandeville, Adam Smith, and Charles-Louis Secondat de Montesquieu. But from mid-century on, many critics began to focus on luxury's deleterious effects on the arts, attacking conspicuous consumption and rococo prettiness in the name of nature, morality, and the ancients. When Lord Kames described the sort of people who are in touch with the universal standard of taste, he eliminated not only those "who depend for food on bodily labour" but also the sensualists, especially the opulent who use riches "to make a figure in the public eye" (1762, 369).

An important subtext in the attack on luxury was the blame many authors laid on women. Shaftesbury faulted women for the success of a rococo style that appealed primarily to the senses rather than to "rational" pleasures (Barrell 1986, 38). Gabriel Sénac de Milhan warned that women, particularly mistresses, were threatening the survival of the French nobility by encouraging the acquisition of lavish houses, gardens, furniture, paintings, and statuary (Saisselin 1992, 41). Louis-Sébastien Mercier attacked the prevalence of portraits over history painting in the annual salons, declaring that "as long as the brush sells itself to idle opulence, to mincing *coquetterie*, . . . the portrait should remain in the boudoir" (Crow 1985, 21).

But once the dark-skinned savages, the ignorant poor, the boorish middle class, the luxurious rich, and the frivolous or merely accomplished women were eliminated, there still remained the problem of identifying the characteristics of a "fine taste" on the part of the small group of upper-class men and women who were left. Writers like Hume or Kames were content to identify further characteristics of the kind of *person* who would exercise such a taste, whereas a Dubos or Mendelssohn attempted to define the nature and operations of the fine taste itself. Thus the "problem" of taste involved not only the question of universality and innateness but also the question of what special social or mental characteristics were requisite to a fine taste. This was not an entirely new problem, of course, since taste had long been defined as a special kind of tacit knowledge, an "I know not what." Now, however, a distinct category of fine arts had been constructed and had been conceptually and institutionally separated from contexts of use and everyday pleasure, inviting a similar separation of the experience of fine art from other kinds of experience. Over the course of the eighteenth century, innumerable artists, critics, and philosophers tried their hand at answering these questions in a flood of books, essays, and letters and, in the process, constructed the modern idea of the aesthetic.

## The Elements of the Aesthetic

Three major elements of the older idea of taste were transformed into the modern idea of the aesthetic: (1) ordinary pleasure in beauty developed into a special kind of refined and intellectualized pleasure, (2) the idea of unprejudiced judgment became an ideal of disinterested contemplation, and (3) the preoccupation with beauty was displaced by the sublime and eventually by the idea of the self-contained work of art as creation.[2] The most important of these elements was the idea of a special refined pleasure that set polite or fine taste apart from the older notion of taste as preference. In the old system of art, pleasure, as well as use, was conceived of instrumentally; the pleasures of the arts provided diversions and amusements that contributed to health and civic peace. And something useful that fulfilled its purpose gracefully was also a source of satisfaction. But once the new system of fine art versus craft had been codified, the crafts were said to aim at a merely sensual pleasure or at bare utility, whereas the fine arts were said to be the object of a higher, contemplative pleasure. This was already suggested by the tendency of the polite classes to withdraw from popular culture and stigmatize it as "mere" recreation compared to the more refined pleasures of the imagination. The refined pleasures of polite taste now became the object of close psychological and philosophical analysis.

Early in the century, many writers argued that the pleasure of taste was something like a distinct faculty, an "inward eye" (Shaftesbury), an "internal sense" (Francis Hutcheson), a "sixth sense" (Dubos). Yet the idea of taste as a spontaneous faculty jostled uneasily with the need to develop taste by social experience. Addison assured his *Spectator* readers that if they wanted to know whether their spontaneous response showed *good* taste, they need only compare their reactions to "The Politer Part of Our Contemporaries" (1712, no. 409). A remark by Anne-Thérèse de Lambert nicely captures the tension between taste as a social attainment and taste as a quality of mind: "Up to now people have defined good taste as *a usage established by the polite and spiritual people of high society.* I believe that it depends on two things: a very delicate sentiment in the heart, and a great precision in the mind" (Lambert [1747] 1990, 241). Lambert's call for combining "sentiment in the heart" with "precision in the mind" shows that the shift from "taste" to the "aesthetic" came about partly as a result of giving a more intellectual character to the pleasures of the "higher" senses of the eye and ear in order to further distance them from ordinary sensual enjoyments.

Here again Addison was prescient in describing the "pleasures of the imagination" in the *Spectator* as located somewhere between the grosser satisfactions of sense and the more abstract enjoyments of the intellect (1712, no. 411). A number of writers, including Hume, Diderot, Rousseau, and Sulzer, not only distinguished sentiment from sensuality and feeling from emotion but also joined sentiment and reason in a kind of spontaneous or tacit knowledge, suggesting a third kind of experience combining elements of both. D'Alembert, for example, speaks of taste as having its own kind of "logic," which discovers the "truths of feeling" (Becq 1994a, 687). Hume claimed that taste for the "polite arts . . . improves our sensibility for all the tender and agreeable passions; at the same time that it renders the mind incapable of the rougher and more boisterous emotions" (Hume 1993, 12). Diderot contrasted those who cry over any sad story with the true judges of art who possess "that gentle emotion in which feeling does not injure comparison" (Becq 1994a, 680).

If we want to get a sense of what the broader public was experiencing, two visual representations of refined taste can be of help. Anne-Marie Link (1992) has explored the representation of taste in the *Goettingen Pocket Calendar* of 1780, a middle-class almanac filled with maxims for everyday living. This almanac featured a set of twelve essays accompanied by engravings that contrasted the "Natural" with the "Affected Practices in Life," a sort of compendium of good and bad taste. The March/April section had two sets of drawings and essays comparing natural versus affected "Sentiment" *(Empfindsamkeit)* in relation to nature and to art, respectively. The engraving depicting a "natural" sentiment or feeling in the presence of nature shows a middle-class man and woman with heads bowed before a sunset, and the accompanying essay by Georg Christoph Lichtenberg speaks of their "quiet," "innocent," "un-self-conscious" behavior. The contrasting engraving, depicting an "affected" sentiment toward nature, in contrast, shows a similarly dressed couple wildly gesticulating at the sunset (fig. 41). When we turn to the drawing depicting a "natural" sentiment toward art, we see two middle-class men standing side by side, their arms folded, as they gaze up respectfully at the statue of a woman. But in the contrasting "affected" sentiment engraving, one of the men points to the bunch of grapes held by the statue while exclaiming to the other man who is throwing up his hands in enthusiasm (fig. 42). The almanac illustrations and text reject irrational outbursts of feeling in favor of a calmer, more reflective sentiment of just the sort Diderot described—"that gentle emotion in which feeling does not injure comparison."

A less direct but equally telling example of the new experience of refined sentiment can be found in the changed behaviors and attitudes toward music in France from the mid-1770s onward. In the first half of the century, when purely instrumental music was still regarded as inferior, the passages in operas and symphonies considered most thrilling were the imitations of sighs, shouts, cries, battle sounds, birdsongs, rushing streams, storms, and avalanches. Significantly, most of these passages could easily be heard above the din of con-

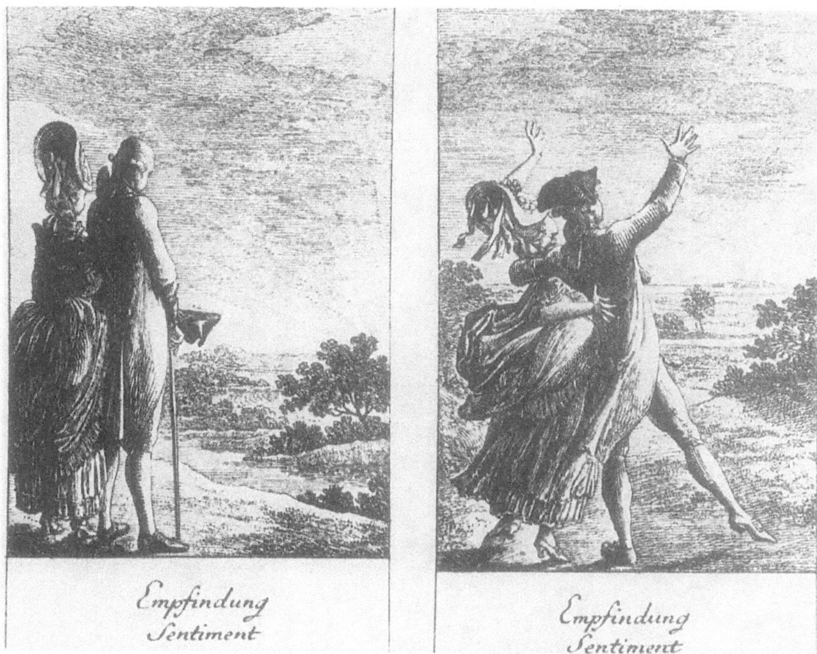


Figure 41. Daniel Chodowiecki, *Natural and Affected Sentiment* (1779). First published in the *Goettingen Pocket Calendar* of 1780.

versation and the beating of the conductor's stick. By the 1780s, as audiences began to quiet down, both the kind of music written and audiences' experience of it had begun to shift toward the musical expression of human feelings rather than the clamor of storms and battles. A turning point was the arrival in Paris of the composer Christoph Willibald Gluck, whose subtler scores and staging brought a shift from spectacular effects to expressive harmonics and orchestration. In describing an opera premier of 1779, one writer spoke of "an extreme and uninterrupted attentiveness" despite "the strongest emotions visible on every face" (Johnson 1995, 59). As in the case of the Goettingen drawings, these fine art spectators are at once moved yet calm, combining intellectual concentration with intense feeling, the sort of attitude later theorists would call "aesthetic."

Yet before the modern idea of a distinctive aesthetic experience could be fully formulated, two further refinements in the idea of taste had to occur. First, the attempt to specify more closely the nature of the pleasure involved in "fine

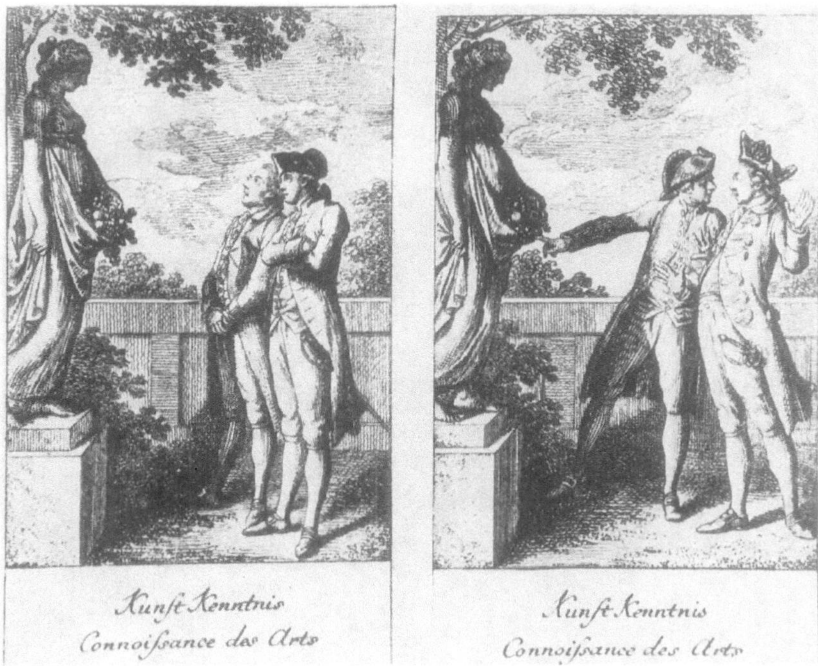


Figure 42. Daniel Chodowiecki, *Natural and Affected Knowledge of the Arts* (1780). First published in the *Goettingen Pocket Calendar* of 1780.

taste" led to the idea of disinterested contemplation. Second, the investigation of the objective qualities of the beautiful led to the separation of the beautiful from the sublime and the picturesque, opening the way toward a more general concept.

In the old system of art, taste was usually tied to an "interest" or stake in the purpose of works of art, whether moral, practical, or recreational; in the new system of fine arts, the response believed most appropriate became one of disinterested contemplation. Paradoxically, the idea of "disinterestedness" involved an intense "interest," in the sense of focused attention, but a complete absence of *an* interest, in the sense of a desire for possession or personal satisfaction, even of a moral or religious kind. There seem to be two sources for the general idea of disinterestedness, one aristocratic/political, the other philosophic/religious, each leading to a slightly different emphasis, although the two could be blended. According to the political perspective known as civic humanism, only those who have the wealth and leisure for reflection are able to rise above self-interest and take a view of society as a whole. Most British and

French writers adopted some form of this patrician ideal of disinterestedness.[3] It is assumed in Addison's often-cited line from the *Spectator,* "A Man of a Polite Imagination . . . often feels a greater Satisfaction in the Prospect of Fields and Meadows, than another does in the Possession. . . . He looks upon the World, as it were, in another Light" (1712, no. 411). Shaftesbury combined the aristocratic conception of disinterest with a Neoplatonic philosophy that encouraged the rational contemplation of the true, the good, and the beautiful. In an often-cited dialogue examining the proper response to the beauty of the ocean, a landscape, and a human body, he contrasted "eager desire" with a "rational and refined contemplation" (Shaftesbury [1711] 1963, 128). Sometimes, as in Dubos, Hutcheson, Hume, or Archibald Alison, disinterestedness seems to have meant little more than an ability to rise above prejudice or narrow self-regard (Townsend 1988, 137).

The religious and theological concept of disinterestedness goes back through medieval mysticism to Augustine, who emphasized that all genuine love of God must be for the sake of God alone. Karl Philipp Moritz, whose idea of the work of art as a "self-sufficient world" we have already considered, described the appropriate response to such works in the vocabulary of the contemplative love of God: "As the beautiful object draws our attention completely to itself, it makes us forget ourselves for a while so that we seem to loose ourselves in it; and precisely this loss, this forgetting of ourselves, is the highest degree of pure and disinterested pleasure that beauty grants us . . . a pleasure which must be ever closer to disinterested *love,* if it is to be genuine" (Moritz 1962, 5; Woodmansee 1994).

A third element that helped turn the notion of taste into the aesthetic was the addition of the ideas of the sublime and picturesque to the traditional focus on beauty. Rooted in theories of rhetorical or poetic style where it meant grandeur of effect, the "sublime" began to be widely used in the eighteenth century for anything in nature or art that produced an impression of overpowering greatness. At first the sublime was treated as an aspect of beauty but soon came to be contrasted with it. The sublime was variously described as an experience of something that is vast, awesome, or terrifying and yet gives pleasure because we contemplate it from safety—for example, an enormous mountain rising from a plain or a storm at sea or Milton's portrayal of Hell. When contrasted with the sublime, the beautiful was often described as charming, sympathetic, harmonious, something we experience as immediately pleasurable (De Bolla 1989). Like other components of the modern system of art, many versions of the sublime were male gendered from the beginning. Even some of Burke's male contemporaries noticed that his description of beauty, in contrast, was almost a caricature of stereotypes of femininity—delicate, timid, small, soft, light (Burke 1968, lxxv). Kant devoted an entire chapter of his early book on the beautiful and sublime to the idea that men are sublime (noble, heroic, powerful, deep), while women are beautiful (charming, sensitive, weak, superficial) (Kant 1960). Theories of the sublime achieved considerable complexity by the end of the century, and the sublime has been seen by many artists and philosophers from the Romantics to the present as far more powerful and aesthetically important than the merely beautiful (Ashfield and De Bolla 1996). The rise in importance of the sublime, the picturesque, and other qualities alongside the beautiful opened the way for a new concept and term that might embrace what was most important in the responses to each (Cassirer 1951).

Alexander Baumgarten originally coined the term "aesthetic" for the kind of response he believed appropriate to the "sensate discourse" of poetry; he wanted a name for sensation's own logic—and he called it "aesthetic" from the Greek *aiesthesis,* having to do with the senses (1954). By providing a separate term for the joint working of sense and imagination in the arts, Baumgarten did three things: he gave feeling or sentiment a more important role in the panoply of the mental powers; he provided a technical term whose range of meaning could be more easily stipulated than the word "taste," with its inevitable physiological and social associations; and he opened the way for the term "aesthetic" to become the name for a special mode of knowing. Since it was a new coinage, it could easily be given several significations, and there has been an equivocation from the beginning between the broad use of "aesthetic" for any sort of value system having to do with art or beauty and "the aesthetic" as a special form of disinterested knowledge, uniting feeling and reason.

## Kant and Schiller Sum up the Aesthetic

Although I have avoided following particular theorists of art or the aesthetic, I want to close this chapter by looking briefly at Kant's and Schiller's way of integrating the concept of the aesthetic with the new concepts of fine art and the artist. By doing so, they provided the first systematic justifications for the modern system of art as a whole.[4] According to Kant, theories that make taste the application of concepts or rules, of sensual pleasure or utility, all admit of an "interest" or desire, whereas true "aesthetic taste" is a pure, disinterested pleasure in which we only contemplate an object. Put positively, aesthetic experience, for Kant, is a "harmonious free play" of our imagination (percepts) and our understanding (concepts). In a true aesthetic experience, imagination and understanding do not gear into each other in their normal workaday fashion of classifying or concluding but spin freely in a pleasurable harmony. So long as understanding and imagination remain in this aesthetic mode they simply explore and enjoy the world contemplatively (Kant 1987, 45, 51–52, 61–62).

Although Kant's description of the aesthetic was almost completely taken up with what happens inside our heads, he did identify a quality in objects most conducive to stimulating this harmonious play of our faculties: "the form of purposiveness," or "purposiveness without a purpose." Some objects seem to be "purposefully" made, to have a form, yet we do not directly see *a* purpose or use for them. The forms of objects like "flowers, free designs, lines aimlessly intertwined" simply offer our mind an occasion to enjoy its own powers at play with no ulterior desire or interest (Kant 1987, 64–66, 49).

By making disinterestedness the key to the universality of aesthetic judgment, Kant distinguished the autonomy of aesthetic experience not only from the ordinary pleasures of sense or utility but also from science and morality. This seems to run counter to the many eighteenth-century writers on fine art who stressed art's moral functions and, also, to Kant's own conviction that moral freedom defines our dignity as human beings. Yet Kant did claim a highly indirect connection between the aesthetic and morality: beauty is a symbol of morality since both aesthetic and moral judgments are similarly free of external rules, and the sublime—our aesthetic pleasure in the midst of nature's overpowering force—reveals our dignity as rational-moral beings. An aesthetic experience of beauty or the sublime does not teach us particular "moral lessons" but makes us aware of our freedom as moral agents (Kant 1987, 225–30, 119–32). For Kant, there is no way to escape the fundamental paradoxes of aesthetic judgment: it is pleasurable yet disinterested, individual yet universal, spontaneous yet necessary, without concepts yet intellectual, without moral instruction yet a revelation of our moral nature.

Once Kant had established the specificity of the aesthetic, he used it to explain the new polarities of fine art versus craft and artist versus artisan. Kant's discussion of the fine art–versus-craft dichotomy remarkably recapitulates the history of the split in the older idea of art, although Kant presented the division as a logical rather than historical process. He begins by recognizing the older idea of art as any kind of human production in contrast to nature, then distinguishes within the general idea of art between the liberal and the mechanical arts. Next, Kant distinguishes two classes within the liberal arts: the "agreeable arts," which aim at ordinary sensory satisfaction, and the "fine arts," which aim at the properly aesthetic "pleasures of reflection." Kant's examples of merely agreeable arts are storytelling at a party, a nicely furnished table, or music at a banquet (Kant 1987, 170–73). Kant's list of fine arts includes the usual core of poetry, music, painting, sculpture, and architecture, to which he adds oratory and landscape gardening. Yet Kant also recognized that some things usually categorized as crafts because they aim at use *could* be treated as fine arts if they were intended "to be merely looked at, using ideas to entertain the imagination in free play, and occupying the aesthetic power of judgment without a determinate purpose" (Kant 1987, 193).

Kant also interpreted the ideal of the artist as creator in terms of the aesthetic by making works of fine art the product of spontaneous genius and works of craft the product of diligence and rules. Craft work *(Handwerk)*, Kant claims, is merely labor, something people do only if paid, whereas making fine art is an activity pleasurable in itself, a kind of "play." Unlike the artisan or craftsperson, who follows a specific concept, the artist uses his genius "aesthetically," exercising the imagination and understanding in free play (Kant 1987, 171–75).

By systematically integrating the polarities of aesthetic versus purpose, artist versus artisan, and fine art versus craft, Kant offered a powerful philosophical justification for the modern system of art. Even though Kant himself was as interested in the aesthetic response to nature as to fine art, those who built on his work connected the aesthetic almost exclusively to fine art. Moreover, despite Kant's attempt to show that the beautiful and sublime reveal our moral nature, the long-term effect of his work has been to reinforce the separation of art, science, and morality.

Kant's younger contemporary, the poet and playwright, Friedrich Schiller, was deeply impressed by Kant's formulation of the aesthetic but felt Kant had perpetuated a dualism between the spiritual and sensual that would be ruinous to society. When Kant's *Critique of Judgment* appeared in 1790, the French Revolution was in its first hopeful phase, and Schiller's warm support of liberty led the French Assembly to make him an honorary citizen. But when the Revolution took a bloody turn in 1792–93, Schiller rejected revolutionary politics in disgust, convinced that without authority the deep divisions in the human soul lead to chaos rather than freedom. Schiller's *Letters on the Aesthetic Education of Man,* written between 1793 and 1795, claim that it is not political revolution that will bring freedom without chaos but the aesthetic experience of fine art. Knowing that his claim for the redemptive power of aesthetic fine art would seem grandiose, he set out to prove it in a spiraling argument based in part on Kant, in part on a vision of human nature divided between spirit and sense and desperately needing integration (Schiller 1967).

In the genuine work of fine art there is already a harmony of freedom and necessity, duty and inclination, the "spiritual drive" and the "sensuous drive," a union that Schiller called "play." The artist-genius embodies the transcendent truth about life in the work of art as play, yet this truth is not a specific content but resides only in the *form* of the work. "In a truly successful work of Art the contents should effect nothing, the form everything, for only through form is the whole man affected . . . only from form is there true aesthetic freedom" (Schiller 1967, 155). True fine art never aims at some particular result like stimulating emotions, teaching beliefs, or improving morals. Only when people renounce all such instrumental aims and exercise "a disinterested and unconditional appreciation of pure semblance" will they have "started to become truly human" (Schiller 1967, 205).

But how can such idealized works of fine art bring the political freedom and equality that have escaped the grasp of political revolutionaries? Schiller believed that art would change society by healing the inner divisions within each individual so that moral and political actions would no longer be a self-imposed duty but a spontaneous expression of the whole person. The exemplary images of fine art would draw each person toward a harmonious life in which the good can flow from natural inclination. For Schiller, fine art was not merely a symbol of morality as in Kant but the incarnation of a higher truth that will transform us by restoring our lost unity. "Humanity has lost its dignity; but Art has rescued it. . . . Truth lives on in the illusion of Art, and it is from this copy, or after-image, that the original image will be restored" (Schiller 1967, 57).

Given Schiller's lofty understanding of aesthetic experience, it is not surprising that he considered only a few people capable of it. What Schiller called "the aesthetic state," in contrast to the purely political state, exists only among a saving remnant; it is like the "pure church or pure Republic," found only "in some few chosen circles . . . governed . . . by the aesthetic" (Schiller 1967, 219). The "aesthetic education" of Schiller's title, therefore, is not mere art appreciation but a dynamic process of salvation by art; art, just by being art, can redeem us by reuniting our sensual and spiritual natures. Schiller's *Letters on the Aesthetic Education of Man* exalted the new ideals of fine art, the artist, and the aesthetic to their highest pitch at the end of the eighteenth century. Whereas Moritz applied the language of the love of God to the love of art, Schiller gave fine art the redemptive power of God incarnate.

Although it would be nice to end our discussion of Kant and Schiller on this high note, we need to reconnect their elevated and exciting visions of aesthetic experience to more earthly realities. Both Kant and Schiller were admirable figures in many ways and more liberal than most of their contemporaries, but they were not immune to the prejudices of their time. We have already mentioned some of Kant's racial and gender attitudes, although the *Critique of Judgment,* like his other two critiques, moves on the high plane of analyzing the universal faculties of the human mind. Yet it seems fairly obvious that only those who have attained a certain level of middle-class comfort could easily adopt a purely disinterested attitude: "Only when their need is satisfied can we tell who . . . has taste and who does not" (Kant 1987, 52). One of Kant's examples of the type of person who lacks aesthetic disinterestedness, is "that Iroquois sachem who said that he liked nothing better in Paris than the eating-houses" (Kant 1987, 45; Shusterman 1993, 111–17).

Schiller's passionate and self-sacrificing devotion to fine art is legendary, and, partly because of his high ideals, he had trouble supporting himself through the market, finally accepting the patronage of the duke of Augustenburg to whom he dedicated the *Aesthetic Letters.* The *Letters'* main themes were not only a response to the Revolution, however, but had been worked out two years before in a fierce attack on the poetry of Gottfried Bürger, who was not only commercially successful but had even argued that poetry should be accessible to the broad public, invoking the old Horatian ideal of please and instruct (Woodmansee 1994). Schiller shot back that the true artist will appeal to "the *elect* of a nation" against "its *mass*" and claimed that the only permissible criterion for the success of a work of art is its internal perfection (Berghahn 1988, 79). Schiller was convinced that only a class freed from labor would have sound "aesthetic powers of judgment" and "maintain the beautiful entirety of human nature, which is . . . thoroughly destroyed by a life of work" (Hohendahl 1982, 56).

Obviously, the personal motives or class prejudices connected to Kant's and Schiller's ideas do not invalidate them as ideas, but it would be equally mistaken to ignore the specific historical context of their justification for the modern system of fine arts.[5] The larger issue is not whether Hume or Kames, Kant or Schiller shared the race, class, and gender prejudices of their time, but whether this kind of prejudice was an essential part of the new system of fine art and the aesthetic. Obviously, many of the same Enlightenment thinkers who held these social biases also believed in a universal human nature. In the French debate over who made up the true public for the Salon or the concert hall, there were not only those who systematically excluded the lower classes and most women as inferior by nature, but also others who believed that almost anyone could learn the proper behavior and attitudes. One writer claimed that any worker who saved up in order to frequent concerts of serious music had by that fact become part of the legitimate art public (Lough 1957, 218). On a more philosophical level, many British and German writers on taste often exhibited a universalizing commitment that implied everyone is in principle capable of refined judgment, even if in practice only the "politer parts" of society actually rise to it. Kant's use of the notion of a *sensus communis* (not "common sense" but the common sensory and intellectual powers of humanity) implied that at least some Africans and Native Americans, if well fed, would be capable of disinterested contemplation. Although it is perhaps an exaggeration to call this universalizing strain in writers from Shaftesbury to Schiller "aesthetic democracy," it is true that social, racial, and gender prejudices often stood in tension with a professed belief in a common humanity and aesthetic experience (Dowling 1996).

PART III

# Countercurrents

## Overview

During the century between Perrault's speech setting off the Quarrel of the Ancients and Moderns and Schiller's celebration of aesthetic fine art as humanity's salvation from inner division, an enormous change in the ideals and institutions of art had taken place across Europe. From a seventeenth-century world in which the arts were purposefully integrated into society and there were few separate art institutions, the expansion of the middle class and a market system for the arts led to the emergence of nearly all the modern institutions and practices of fine art: in painting, there were now art exhibitions, art auctions, art dealers, art criticism, art history, and a new emphasis on the signature; in music, there were now secular concerts, the elimination of stage seating in the opera, the development of music criticism and music history, the emergence of the "work" concept and its practices of exact notation, complete scores, and opus numbers, along with an end to borrowing and recycling; in literature there were circulating libraries, literary criticism, and history, the development of vernacular canons, the establishment of copyright, and a new status for the author as free creator. Accompanying these institutional and behavioral changes was a parallel revolution in the concepts and terms for the arts. The older and broader notion of art ("an art") was divided into the category of fine art versus craft, the older idea of the artisan/artist was divided into the ideal of the artist as creator versus the artisan as routine maker, and the older idea of taste was divided into the refined and intellectualized experience called "aesthetic" in contrast to the ordinary pleasures of sense and function. And within each of the three new categories of art, artist, and aesthetic, there were new component ideas or new meanings for older ones. In the case of the artist, for example, there were heightened ideals of freedom and genius, as well as profound shifts from imitation to originality, invention to creation, the reproductive to the creative imagination. Taken together all these changes in institutions, practices, ideals, and terms constituted the modern system of fine arts that is still largely in place today.

Of course, such an enormous cultural change did not sweep away older ideals and practices overnight, nor were the new categories fixed and monolithic. The shift from the older idea of taste to the aesthetic, for example, took several decades to penetrate all of Europe and its colonies, and even then there was a spectrum of opinion. The notion of "disinterested contemplation" so important in Kant and Schiller was not universally stressed. Writers from Hume to Kames to Alison were satisfied with something closer to "unprejudiced judgment" and remained more concerned with finding a universal standard of taste than in establishing the singularity of aesthetic experience. At a less sophisticated level Bernard Mandeville shocked public opinion by celebrating self-interest and luxury and even wrote a parody of Shaftesbury's dialogue on disinterestedness. In Mandeville's counterdialogue, the characters—who unlike Shaftesbury's include a woman—argue over the respective merits of Italian history painting, preferred by aristocrats, and Dutch still life, a genre that had a more popular appeal. The dialogue's Shaftesburian speaker tells the young woman, "Pray, Cousin, say no more in Defence of your low Taste . . . Great Masters don't paint for the common People, but for Persons of refined Understanding" (Mandeville 1729, 2:35).

There were, of course, intermediate positions on the aesthetic, especially among German writers. Herder championed folksong and poetry, explicitly criticized the Kantian notion of disinterestedness, and rejected—at least with regard to sculpture—the demotion of sensory touch in favor of distanced contemplation. By insisting that each of the arts be interpreted not only in relation to a different sensory register but also in terms of their cultural and historical context, Herder undercut the tendency of the contemplative aesthetic toward a detached formalism. For all his historicism, however, Herder embraced other aspects of the new fine art system such as the category of fine art, the exaltation of artistic genius, and the idea of a "science" of aesthetics that would discover universal principles of beauty (Herder 1955; Norton 1991).

In chapter 8, I will look briefly at three other writers who formulated alternatives to the emerging idea of an autonomous aesthetic: William Hogarth, Jean-Jacques Rousseau, and Mary Wollstonecraft. Each of them was drawn to the developing ideal of a refined and contemplative taste yet ultimately resisted it in favor of sensual pleasure and social utility. Hogarth's "hedonist aesthetics" approached the issue from the visual arts, Rousseau's "festival aesthetics" primarily from music and theater, and Wollstonecraft's "aesthetics of social justice" from a critique of the picturesque. Their ambivalence toward the emerging ideals of fine art and the aesthetic constitutes part of an alternative tradition that can help us assess what was lost as well as gained through the construction of the modern system of the fine arts.

But just as the fine art system was the result of institutional as well as intellectual changes, so it gave rise to institutional forms of resistance. Chapter 9 will explore the most dramatic instance of resistance to the growing autonomy and privatization of the fine arts: the attempt of the French Revolution to breathe new life into the old system of art for a purpose through the revolutionary festivals, the National Institute of Music, and a national museum of art. The revolutionaries aimed at something higher than merely using art for propaganda, although their failure to reintegrate art and life has helped to discredit subsequent efforts to create a politically engaged art. Of special importance in this respect was their creation of a national museum of art in the Louvre. Although the revolutionaries could hardly have taken the time to read Kant or Schiller, their actions in wresting art works from their functional contexts for gazing at in the museum uncannily enacted the new ideal of the aesthetic contemplation of "art for itself."

CHAPTER 8

# Hogarth, Rousseau, Wollstonecraft

## Hogarth's "Hedonist Aesthetics"

ALTHOUGH HOGARTH rejected Mandeville's celebration of luxury and self-interest, he wholeheartedly joined in the attack on the connoisseurs and self-styled "men of Taste." Hogarth's *The Analysis of Beauty* ([1753] 1997), aimed at settling "the fluctuating ideas of taste" by showing up the connoisseur's preference for the continental grand style yet also doing justice to the new emphasis on enjoying fine art for itself. As in his attitude toward the emerging ideal of the artist, Hogarth's approach to aesthetics was torn between two worlds, the old world of art/craft, which integrated instruction with common pleasures, and the new world of refined taste and art for itself. In fact, the first principle of beauty Hogarth discusses is fitness, not only the fitness of parts to whole but also fitness to purpose, for example, of bottles and knives, of windows and doors, of the design of a ship, and, above all, the fitness of the human body for its movements in work and play. Closely allied to fitness, according to Hogarth, are those central principles of the traditional art treatise, such as symmetry, proportion, and unity (Hogarth [1753] 1997, 25–26). But his greatest interest and enthusiasm are for two principles that hardly played a part in older treatises: variety and intricacy—principles that reflect not only the rococo style but especially the new emphasis on the viewer's pleasure. Variety concerns surface form or ornament rather than use, its aim primarily one of "entertaining the eye." Intricacy "leads the eye on a wanton chase" and "gives a pleasure" that "entitles it to the name of beauty" (27, 32–33). Here we seem to have a very different kind of beauty than the beauty of fitness to purpose, one to be enjoyed for itself. And when Hogarth speaks of the pleasure of the eye following intricate curving forms as the pleasure of "pursuit as pursuit" we might think him on the track of what Kant would later describe as the play of imagination and understanding, or of "purposefulness without a purpose."

But there is another side to Hogarth that runs counter to the main direction of modern aesthetics. One would never expect a Kames or a Kant to speak of intricacy leading the eye on a "wanton" chase. A key remark in the *Analysis of Beauty* is Hogarth's jibe at the connoisseurs' and academics' ideal of imitating classical forms: "Who but a bigot . . . will say that he has not seen faces and necks, hands and arms in living women, that even the Grecian Venus doth but coarsely imitate?" (Hogarth [1753] 1997, 59). For Hogarth beauty is sensuous, bodily, one could even say erotic—not as sexual possession but as ordinary, sensuous pleasure. Hogarth's "hedonistic aesthetics," as Paulson calls it, comes through especially in his examples, which are mostly drawn from the body, for example, "the beauty of a composed intricacy of form" is illustrated with the flowing curls of the hair whose "intermingling locks ravish the eye with the pleasure of the pursuit" (Paulson 1991–93, 3:94; Hogarth [1753] 1997, 34). Hogarth also calls this kind of intricate form "the true spirit of dancing." Although the true spirit of dancing can be seen in the theater, it is especially present in "country dancing," something that is neither part of the pompous fine arts nor an artless jumping around but simply an art in the older sense (109–11). Like the ordinary movements of the body, country dancing is made up of many serpentine lines, a "composed variety." But Hogarth finds his serpentine "line of beauty" not only in the curves of waving hair and men and women dancing but also in ordinary objects like candleholders or corsets or even in the worm gear of a fireplace control, an object to which he devotes two pages of the *Analysis* (33–34) (fig. 43).

And just as the objective forms of beauty reside in ordinary bodies and everyday objects, so the perception of their beauty is available to the ordinary eye. One needs neither the superior social and economic standing required for

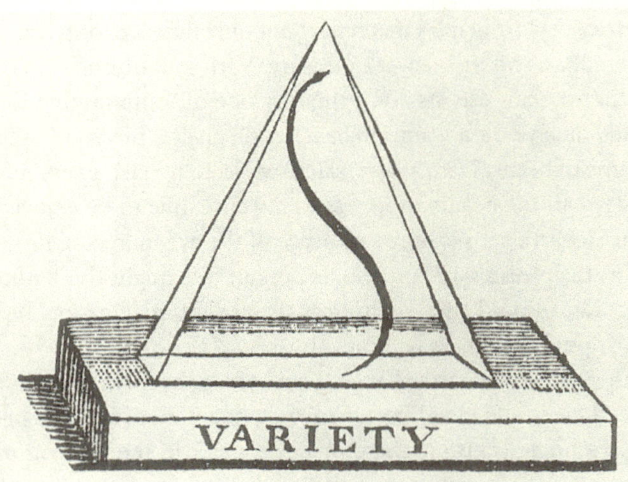


Figure 43. William Hogarth, symbol from the cover of *The Analysis of Beauty* (1753). Hogarth daringly uses the transparent pyramid, symbolizing the Trinity, but replaces the traditional Hebrew letters for the name of God with his "line of beauty." The curving line is given a serpent's head in allusion to a verse from Milton, also printed on the cover, describing Satan's temptation of Eve.

Dubos's or Kames's "taste of comparison" nor the ascetic and intellectual discipline required for Moritz's and Kant's "disinterested judgment" but only an unspoiled eye and ear and a mind unprejudiced by the attitudes of the "men of Taste." In the case of the human arts, Hogarth admits, the formal and utilitarian aspects may not always coincide, and something rather displeasing to the eye may be useful, but in "nature's machines, how wonderfully do we see beauty and use go hand in hand!" (62). Nature, especially the human body, combines the utmost in intricacy of line, proportion, and fitness as seen in graceful working, walking, or dancing. Such happy combinations of variety and proportion, intricacy and purpose are there for all to see. If Hogarth sometimes spoke of "men of greater penetration," he did not mean the disinterested spectator of later mainstream aesthetics but the person of critical intelligence able to read Hogarth's own intricate satires. His advertisement for the *Analysis of Beauty* declares it to be for "persons of both sexes" and written in a plain and entertaining manner (xvii). Paulson argues that Hogarth implicitly understood that taste is "a question of politics and power, of who has or should have the authority to judge" and aimed not so much to refine taste "as to democratize it" (Paulson 1991–93, 3:121). For the mainstream development of the modern system of fine art, the term "hedonist aesthetics" is an oxymoron. The whole point of what became the dominant strain in aesthetics was to distinguish "refined," "rational," or "aesthetic" taste from ordinary pleasures, whether of immediate sense or of satisfaction in purpose, and many leading writers on taste from Shaftesbury to Kant specifically excluded desire from the aesthetic. Hogarth felt the pull of the refined direction, but he also recognized its inherent elitism. He remained on the side of the "soldiers and porters and women with children" who were to be excluded from the new fine art exhibitions as persons "wholly inappropriate" (Pears 1988, 127).

## Rousseau's Festival Aesthetics

Hogarth was not alone in championing ordinary sensuality and equality. His outlook was shared by a figure so unlike him in temperament and interests as to make the linking of their names seem odd indeed, yet Jean-Jacques Rousseau was also torn between the old system of art and the new system of fine art. Even contemporaries charged Rousseau with paradox, if not contradiction, for denouncing the fine arts as a manifestation of moral corruption yet continuing to write operas, plays, and novels. Some scholars have tried to reconcile the two sides of Rousseau and make him more palatable to modern aesthetics, but I believe we have more to learn from his ambivalence.[1] I will focus on three issues in Roussseau: the social role of the fine arts, the nature of taste, and the ideal of the festival.

Like many other young men on the make in the eighteenth century, Rousseau hoped to use music and literature as his entrée to polite society. As a poor runaway from Geneva, he was forced to work as a music teacher and hired pen, tutoring recalcitrant children and writing digests and drafts until he made it to Paris, where Diderot and d'Alembert invited him to write articles on music for the *Encyclopédie* (Cranston 1991a). One day, while walking out to Vincennes prison to visit Diderot, who had been jailed by the censors, Rousseau read the Dijon Academy's essay competition question on whether the arts and sciences tended to "purify morals." Suddenly, he had an illumination and sank down under a tree as a swarm of visions passed before him on the theme that would become his life's work: humanity is naturally good but has been corrupted by its institutions.

Rousseau's prize-winning *First Discourse* (1751) was a thunderous "No!" to the question of moral benefits from the arts and sciences. One of the things that makes Rousseau's essay so interesting for our story is that he specifically attacked the new category of beaux arts, as well as the criterion of pleasure versus utility, in the very year d'Alembert was publicizing both in the preface to the *Encyclopédie.* Rousseau's critique drew on the familiar contrast between the decadent Athenians and the civic-minded Spartans: "While the vices led by the Fine Arts were introduced into Athens" the Spartans "chased the Arts and Artists" from their gates (1954, 9; 1992, 9).[2] Although friends like Diderot greeted the *First Discourse* as a clever paradox, Rousseau enthusiastically took up his new role of cultural scourge.

Rousseau's *First Discourse* drew many attacks, which forced him to reflect more deeply on the role of the fine arts in corrupting society. In the *Second Discourse* (1754), on the origins of inequality, he developed a hypothetical genealogy of the human arts, tracing a descent from the division of labor to private property and on to luxury and the fine arts. In this version of mankind's fall, Rousseau calls the period between the pure state of nature and the corrupt social state, "nascent society," a kind of golden age before private property when humanity enjoyed the simple pleasures of the arts as part of everyday life. "People grew accustomed to gathering in front of huts or around a large tree; song and dance, true children of love and leisure, became the amusement or rather the occupation of idle and assembled men and women" (1954, 71; 1992, 47). So long as people made and artfully adorned their own clothes, tools, and musical instruments, they were "free, healthy, good and happy," but once envy and the division of labor set in, the result was private property, inequality, labor, and misery. Now the long process began that would eventually lead to the modern world of luxury and display in which the fine arts are used to mark social differences (1954, 49).[3]

Rousseau's genealogy of the fine arts elicited little enthusiasm from Diderot and downright hostility from Voltaire, partly because it rejected the distinction between fine art and luxury that was crucial to the emerging idea of the aesthetic. In 1758 Rousseau also managed to alienate d'Alembert, who had written that the Genevans should establish a theater to improve taste. That was too much for Rousseau, whose *Letter to d'Alembert* attacks the supposed civic benefits of the theater, arguing that the theater must inevitably flatter the upper classes whose pity for suffering on the stage seldom translates into pity for real misery in the world outside. Since Rousseau had continued to write operas and plays ever since the *First Discourse,* he now looked the complete hypocrite. In reply he pleaded that he was prepared to tolerate fine art institutions as a moral palliative for already corrupt cities like Paris or London but not among the simple and wholesome Genevans.

Despite Rousseau's powerful critique of the fine arts in the *First* and *Second Discourses* and the *Letter to d'Alembert,* there is evidence in other writings—the *Dictionary of Music* ([1768] 1969), for instance—that he saw the fine arts as something greater than simply palliatives. Yet given his general outlook, for a work of fine art to be more than a palliative, it would have to be purified of the taint of vanity and serve a high moral purpose. The second preface to *Julie, or the New Heloise,* for example, presents his novel as a means of being "useful" by reaching a wider audience with its message of the simple life, and Rousseau even suggests that husbands and wives ought to read it together to gladden their marriage ([1761] 1997, 16). A few years later, Rousseau's article on opera in his *Dictionary of Music* declared opera the most elevating of fine arts, although the operas Rousseau seems to have had in mind were those like Gluck's or his own *The Village Soothsayer,* which he believed would amend people's moral feelings by portraying simple actions through a music that served the poetry ([1768] 1969). Yet this praise of opera's potential moral effects is far from the idea of a disinterested appreciation of self-contained works.

Rousseau's idea of taste showed the same sort of ambivalence as his comments on the category of fine art. Occasionally, he sounds like those who were moving toward the kind of refined taste that became the aesthetic, as in his emphasis on the union of feeling and reason in taste. Moreover, he shared the gender prejudices of many of those who were developing the mainstream's ideas of refined taste, sometimes contrasting the moral understanding of males with the "physical" taste "natural" to females (who should not pretend to judge something so serious as literature). In his tract/novel on education, *Émile,* he even sends his fictional pupil, who has been brought up in the country in a completely "natural" way, to live in Paris for a time since there would be more opportunities there to learn fine discrimination in the arts (1957, 426; 1979, 341). Yet Rousseau's more settled opinion is that good taste is a matter of knowing how to enjoy the "tissue of little things" that make up "the agreeableness of life." It is through these little things that we learn to "fill life with the goods that are within our reach in all the truth they can have for us" (1957, 430; 1979, 344). It was, of course, precisely the agreeable or pleasant that Kant used as a foil for the "aesthetic," and it is no accident that one of Kant's examples of the failure to adopt a properly disinterested attitude is Rousseau protesting against "the vanity of the great who spend the sweat of the people on superfluous things" (Kant 1987, 46).

In contrast to the refined or disinterested pleasure later embraced by mainstream aesthetic theory, Rousseau made taste a form of ordinary pleasure that he called "temperate sensuality," or "voluptuousness." In his later writings he set up a running contrast between the sensuous and the refined, the simple and the sophisticated, the natural and the artificial, the ordinary pleasures anyone can experience and the elegant pleasures of the fine arts available to the cultured few. In *Julie* his heroine's way of dressing and eating are said to reflect a "sensuality without refinement," and she has arranged the country estate of Clarens so that simple and honest "occupations" replace the artificial and fashionable "amusements" of polite society ([1761] 1997, 412–18). Rousseau's ideal of the sensual enjoyment of everyday life is nicely conveyed by the opening lines of his account of the wine harvest at Clarens: "The sound of the barrels being banded on every side; the singing of the women picking grapes . . . of rustic instruments spurring them on; the endearing and touching tableau of a general exhilaration that seems at this moment to extend over the surface of the earth . . . everything conspires to give it a festive air, and this festivity becomes only the more beautiful upon reflection, when it occurs to us that it is the only one in which people have succeeded in combining the agreeable and the useful" (494).

But the full extent of Rousseau's resistance to the emerging ideals of fine art and the aesthetic will only become apparent when we join this idea of taste as temperate sensuality to his convictions about the crafts and the festival. Rousseau believed that traces of the original unity of the arts and everyday life could still be found among the craft practices of Native Americans and even in some Swiss villages. In the *Letter to d'Alembert,* he describes a mountain community near Lake Neufchatel where farm families spent the winter months making their own clothes, furniture, and entertainment, where almost everyone knew how to draw and paint and most could play the flute and sing. Rousseau also devoted an entire section of *Émile* to an attack on the invidious distinction between the artist and artisan and the "prejudice that despises a trade." Émile, who is being educated according to nature, is not given the gentleman's lessons in connoisseurship but learns the honorable craft of carpentry instead (1957, 213–34; 1979, 185–203).

At the end of the *Letter to d'Alembert,* after page upon page assailing the supposed benefits of theater, Rousseau finally asks, "Should there be no spectacles at all?" Yes, he replies, there should be many, but not "those exclusive spectacles that shut a few people up in a dark cavern . . . in silence and inaction. . . . No, happy peoples, those are not your festivals. It's in the open air, under the sky that you ought to gather and surrender to the sweet sentiment of your happiness." And what would be "shown" in these public spectacles? The people would show themselves to each other. "Plant a stake in the middle of a square and crown it with flowers, gather the people, and you will have a festival. Better yet; make the spectators themselves the spectacle; make them the actors; arrange it so that each sees and loves themselves in the other, so that all will be better united" (1954, 224–25; 1960, 125–26).

The most knowledgeable interpreter of Rousseau's views on the arts has called Rousseau's festival a "normative myth" (Robinson 1984, 252). But it was not a complete fantasy. The *Letter to d'Alembert* recalls a spontaneous celebration Rousseau saw in Geneva as a boy. One night after the militia exercises in the Saint-Gervais district, the men gathered around the fountain in the square and began to dance to the sound of drum and fife under torchlight. As some five or six hundred danced hand in hand, winding about the fountain, wives and children woke to watch through open windows, then descended into the streets with wine, and the evening ended in toasts, embraces, and laughter. Rousseau remembers his father saying, "Jean-Jacques love your country. Do you see these Genevans? They are all friends, all brothers, joy and peace reign among them" (1954, 232–33; 1960, 135–36). For Rousseau, avid theatergoer and lover of opera, the memory of this simple and spontaneous festival had a greater authenticity and charm than the most perfect work of fine art contemplated in silence. It was, of course, an idealized memory by 1758 when he wrote the *Letter.* How far this idealized version was from the real Geneva, with its class divisions and authoritarian oligarchy, he learned when his native city burned *Émile* and condemned its author just four years later (Cranston 1991b).

The simple arts of a festival shared in by everyone are the counterpart of

Rousseau's notion of taste as temperate sensuality. Rousseau's festival is a time of equality, spontaneous expression, a union of gentle pleasure and moral purpose. Inevitably, it invites comparison with Schiller's ideal of "play." There is much in common, especially in Schiller's notion of play as uniting pleasure and duty, the sensuous and the spiritual. But Schiller made fine art the highest form of play and turned away from ordinary sensuality and utility to the disinterested contemplation of form. Since mainstream aesthetics and fine art institutions have followed Schiller, it is no surprise that the twentieth-century art world keeps vainly trying to get Art and Life back together.

## Wollstonecraft and the Beauty of Justice

Mary Wollstonecraft's life and writings would have scandalized Rousseau and irritated Hogarth, whereas she was incensed by Rousseau's patriarchal views on women and thought Hogarth's serpentine line of beauty a "narrow rule" (Wollstonecraft 1989, 6:289) (fig. 44). Although we now think of her as primarily a writer on feminism and politics, Elizabeth Bohls has shown that Wollstonecraft, along with Helen Maria Williams, Dorothy Wordsworth, Ann Radcliffe, and Mary Shelley, worked out a penetrating critique of the eighteenth-century move toward a contemplative aesthetic (Bohls 1995). The writers Bohls examines rejected or seriously qualified different components of the aesthetic, but all shared a will to validate the taste of women (and in some cases of the lower classes or colonized peoples of color) and to resist the separation of taste from the particular interests of life. Mary Wollstonecraft's work not only contains a forceful critique of the idea of disinterested taste but also suggests an alternative vision of taste as sensual pleasure joined with a concern for social justice.[4]

The aesthetic implications of Wollstonecraft's political position are most memorably stated in *A Vindication of the Rights of Men,* her spirited riposte to Edmund Burke's enormously influential *Reflections on the French Revolution* ([1790] 1955). Wollstonecraft recognized immediately that Burke's conservative defense of ancien régime inequality was largely based on aesthetic positions he developed thirty years earlier in *Enquiry into the Origin of Our Ideas on the Sublime and Beautiful* ([1757] 1968). Burke set before his readers the alternative of the revolutionaries' barren abstractions or the beauties of an established order whose "pleasing illusions . . . made power gentle and obedience liberal." By comparison, Burke sneered, the revolutionaries' philosophy "is as void of solid wisdom as it is destitute of all taste and elegance" (Burke 1955, 87). Wollstonecraft saw that Burke was appealing in politics to the same kind of refined taste by which he claimed we intuitively perceive the beautiful in art or nature.

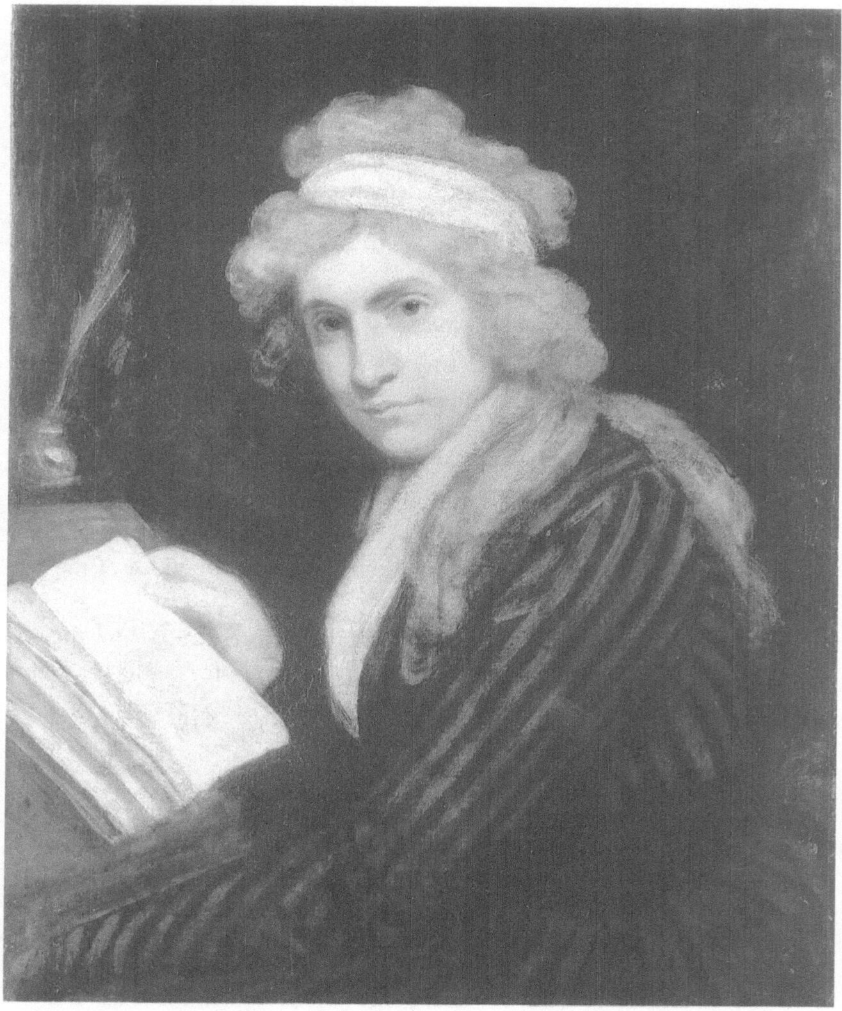

Figure 44. John Opie, *Mary Wollstonecraft* (ca. 1790–91). Courtesy Tate Gallery, London/Art Resource, New York.

The same spontaneous judgment that tells the ruling class which symphony is worthy of praise tells them which political system is worthy of emotional allegiance. Wollstonecraft's critique cuts through Burke's aestheticized political argument to show that his idea of a beautiful, organic society is only a rhetorical screen covering an existing power arrangement based on inherited property and status. She throws back at Burke his own aesthetic categories. Where, she asks, is the "infallible sensibility" of the upper-class colonial ladies who order their African slaves flogged and then "exercise their tender feelings by the perusal of the last imported novel"? No doubt, she continues, they have read Burke's *Enquiry into the Sublime and Beautiful* and have "labored to be pretty, by counterfeiting weakness." The effect of Burke's notion of women as beautiful ("little, smooth, delicate, fair") is to deny women the exercise of reason and correspondingly of morality and its sublime heroism (Wollstonecraft [1790] 1989, 5:45).

Rather than accept Burke's view of taste and claim for women an equal share in the sublime, Wollstonecraft argues that true beauty and sublimity lie in moral virtue and that pleasure in beauty requires a union of feeling and reason in which "reason must hold the rudder" (Wollstonecraft 1995, 48–50). Poetry and music indeed have the power to arouse our spontaneously felt response through the imagination, but they simultaneously affect our moral reason. But what most deeply separates Wollstonecraft's view of taste from the contemplation ideal is the direct link she establishes between the pleasure of taste and political morality. This becomes clearest in her handling of the idea of the picturesque in refuting Burke.

Wollstonecraft borrows the conventions of the picturesque to show that the beauty claimed for the well-laid-out English or French estate is at the cost of the ordinary people who work on them. This is something that the man of taste like Burke or Gilpin does not want to see.

> I know, indeed that there is often something disgusting in the distresses of poverty, at which the imagination revolts. . . . The rich man builds a house, art and taste give it the highest finish. His gardens are planted, and the trees grow to recreate the fancy of the planter. . . . Every thing on the estate is cherished but man;—yet, to contribute to the happiness of man, is the most sublime of all enjoyments. But if, instead of sweeping pleasure grounds, obelisks, temples, and elegant cottages, as *objects* for the eye, the heart was allowed to beat true to nature, decent farms would be scattered over the estate, and plenty smile around. (Wollstonecraft [1790] 1989, 5:56)

"True pleasure" is not to be found in the disinterested viewing of purely pictorial values but in the simple beauty of a countryside that reflects social justice. She continues her argument with a contrasting description of the gross inequality she saw on a trip to Portugal a few years before, precisely the kind of trip on which Gilpin and other theorists of the picturesque encouraged people to view—from a suitable distance—a landscape embellished with ruined castles, crumbling huts, and ragged peasants picturesquely loitering: "Returning once from a despotic country to a part of England well cultivated, but not very picturesque—with what delight did I not observe the poor man's garden!—The homely palings and twining woodbine, with all the rustic contrivances of simple, unlettered taste, was a sight that relieved the eye that had wandered indignant from the stately palace to the pestiferous hovel, and turned from the awful contrast into itself to mourn the fate of man, and curse the arts of civilization!" ([1790] 1989, 5:56–57). In place of the refined and contemplative taste of polite society's picturesque, Wollstonecraft puts a "simple, unlettered taste" that combines grace with utility. For Wollstonecraft, true pleasure is to be found by turning "the eyes from ideal regions of taste and elegance" to "give the earth . . . all the beauty it is capable of receiving" (61).

Bohls shows that Wollstonecraft's last published work—a travel memoir written to raise money—carried her belief in taste as the union of sensual pleasure and social justice directly onto the terrain of picturesque travel writing. The *Letters Written during a Short Residence in Sweden, Norway and Denmark* (1796) are unlike most travel descriptions of the picturesque, which typically omitted the human presence except as ornament and avoided mention of the economic uses of the land or the labors of the people who inhabited it. Even while exploiting the picturesque genre to sell her book, Wollstonecraft mixed in the economic and political aspects of the scenes she describes. She typically begins with a fairly conventional picturesque description, but soon veers off toward the practical and political. In Norway, for example,

> the rocks which tossed their fantastic heads so high were often covered with pines and firs, varied in the most picturesque manner. Little woods filled up the recesses . . . and vallies and glens, cleared of the trees, displayed a dazzling verdure which contrasted with the gloom of the shading pines. . . . The little cultivation which appeared did not break the enchantment, nor did castles rear their turrets aloft to crush the cottages, and prove that man is more savage than the natives of the woods. I heard of the bears, but never saw them stalk forth, which I was sorry for; I wished to have seen one in its wild state. In the winter, I am told, they sometimes catch a stray cow, which is a heavy loss to the owner. (Wollstonecraft [1796] 1989, 6:263)

Although the presence of cultivated fields did not break her "enchantment" with the rocky, pine covered landscape, the memory of feudal castles crushing cottages did. As Bohls points out, Wollstonecraft's concern over the farmer's loss of cattle completes the deflation of the picturesque conventions of aesthetic distance (Bohls 1995, 156).

Wollstonecraft's *Letters* reveal her to be a "woman of taste" but in a very different sense than the eighteenth-century "man of taste." Although she shared a number of new ideals of fine art and the artist-genius, and occasionally reveals some middle-class cultural prejudices, hers was not the distanced aesthetic of polite society but an everyday pleasure united with a concern for political justice.[5] As Bohls says of letter 8, which moves from a description of Wollstonecraft's pleasure in the landscape to a recollection of past love affairs and ends with her delight in rowing a boat out to a hidden grotto where she bathed: "All three kinds of pleasure, aesthetic enjoyment, sex, and exercise, are implicitly grouped together, contradicting theories that separate aesthetic experience from other pleasures as something qualitatively different, higher, and distinctively non-corporeal" (Bohls 1995, 165).

In 1798, when Wollstonecraft prematurely died, the triumph of the modern system of fine arts was not yet complete; that triumph would come in the early decades of the nineteenth century as the new ideas of fine art, the artist, and the aesthetic took deeper root through idealism and romanticism and through the expansion of the new art institutions and art public. By the early twentieth century, historians and philosophers of the aesthetic would treat the autonomy of art and the aesthetic as a destined outcome, and the tradition of resistance would drop out of most of our histories and anthologies. But the resistance to the modern system of art, like the system itself, was not only a matter of ideas; it was also embodied in institutions and practices. It is striking that Wollstonecraft's most vigorous assertion of the union of beauty and social justice came in her defense of the French Revolution against Burke. A consideration of the fate of the new ideals and institutions of fine art in the crucible of the Revolution will cast a revealing, if sometimes garish, light on the final struggles between the old and new systems of art.

CHAPTER 9

# Revolution

## *Music, Festival, Museum*

IN THE SUMMER of 1793 when revolutionary France was invaded by foreign armies and torn by internal revolts, its legislative arm, the Convention, called for the destruction of all signs of royalty. Mobs had toppled statues and burned royal portraits before, but now the most celebrated acts of official vandalism began. The beautiful tombs of the French kings at St. Denis were ordered broken open, the desiccated and stinking remains thrown into a common pit, and the bronze and lead melted down for ammunition. A few weeks later, the Paris Commune officially ordered twenty-two statues of crowned kings (actually kings of Judah but believed to be French) chiseled off the west portals of Notre Dame Cathedral. Meanwhile, coats of arms and fleurs-de-lis were being knocked off statues and offending covers ripped off books or the books simply burned. Although these scenes of destruction are often the first things that come to mind when we think of the arts in the Revolution, the reality was far more complex.[1]

## The Collapse of Patronage

The French not only debated and fought their Revolution, they sang and danced it (fig. 45). Paris and other large cities in Europe had always been noisy places, but the Revolution added the sounds of incendiary oratory, chanting demonstrators, marching bands, and festival choruses. Thanks to the end of restrictive privileges and monopolies for the royal theaters, music indoors also multiplied; by 1793 two dozen new venues for music and drama had been opened. The Revolution also provided new state-funded opportunities for musicians through the National Guard Band and the National Institute of Music. Prior to 1789, most musicians were employed by churches or by royal and aristocratic patrons and a handful of theaters; now there was a large, if uncertain, new market for their services (Franz 1988; Brevan 1989; Charlton 1992).

The Revolution had a more mixed effect on painters since many of the painters' natural patrons had emigrated and those who remained were financially

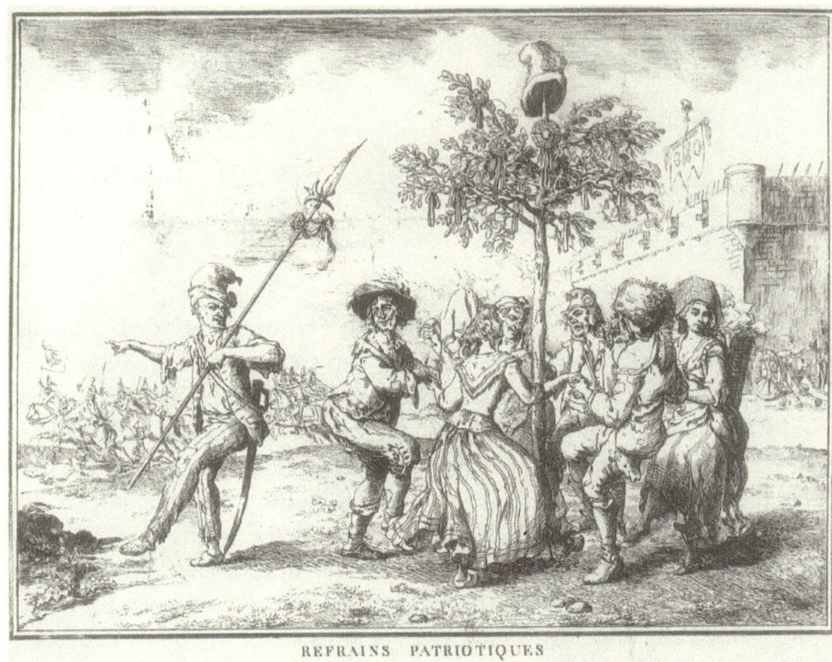


Figure 45. *Patriotic Refrains* (ca. 1792–93). Courtesy Bibliothèque Nationale, Paris. The songs "Dansons la carmognole" and "Ça ira," printed below the picture, were among the most popular of the Revolution. The liberty tree is decorated with the ribbons worn by supporters of the Revolution and topped with the radical revolutionaries' red cap.

pressed. In addition, as French, German, and Italian nobles began selling off paintings to raise money for exile or fines, the number of paintings on the market rapidly expanded until "it seemed as if the whole of Europe from dukes and generals to monks and common thieves was involved in a single vast campaign of speculative art dealing" (Haskell 1976, 44). The flood of paintings for sale along with the widespread social and economic disruption reduced many artists to near penury. A report to the Convention from the Committee on Public Instruction in 1795 concluded: "The Arts have lost a great deal from the Revolution. They have lost the decoration of churches, of religious houses; the decoration of the palaces of Kings and their pleasure, of royal monuments built from flattery or tombs from mourning, of statues and paintings for reception to the Academy; finally the Arts have lost all they might expect from the luxury purchases of individuals" (Pommier 1991, 250). There could be no better description of the rapid collapse of the old patronage/commission system.

As commissions declined and writers, musicians, and painters had to sell their services in an unstable market, they insisted all the more on the ideal of the free art of genius. The composer André Grétry saw the new situation as a culmination of trends already underway in the 1780s: "I saw the birth of a revolution by artist musicians, which came a little before the great political revolution . . . musicians, maltreated by public opinion, suddenly rose up and repulsed the humiliation weighted down upon them" (Attali 1985, 49). When Joseph Lakanal proposed the copyright law of 1793, he emphasized the special status of "the productions of genius" and the freedom that must be assured artists in their "quest for immortality" (Gribenski 1991, 26). The Commune of the Arts, an organization created by Jacques-Louis David and others to stalk the Academy of Painting and Sculpture, declared that artists "are free by nature: the essence of genius is independence; and certainly, one has seen them, in this memorable Revolution, among the most zealous partisans" (Pommier 1991, 168).

Yet at the same time as artists were covering their increasing market dependence with claims to absolute freedom, the Revolution inspired a counterthrust in favor of utility and service. Much of David's painting was directly in service of the Revolution, and he became the leading designer of its revolutionary festivals. He declared to the Convention in 1793, "Each of us is accountable to our country for the talents he has received from nature . . . the true patriot must ardently seize every means of enlightening his fellow citizens and constantly put before their eyes the sublime traits of heroism and virtue" (Soboul 1977, 3). Although many painters, writers, actors, and musicians threw themselves into the political turmoil with a fervor equal to David's, others served the Revolution out of conformity, opportunism, or prudence. Composers such as François Gossec or Étienne Méhul found it natural to shift from commissions for church or royal companies to writing hymns and marches for revolutionary governments.

## The Revolutionary Festivals

The key institutional forms of the Revolution's resistance to an increasingly privatized ideal of aesthetic experience were the revolutionary festivals and the National Institute of Music. As multiarts events, the festivals could be seen as part of an attempt to renew the old system of the arts for use at a moment when the new system of art for itself was already replacing it. Revolutionary leaders were

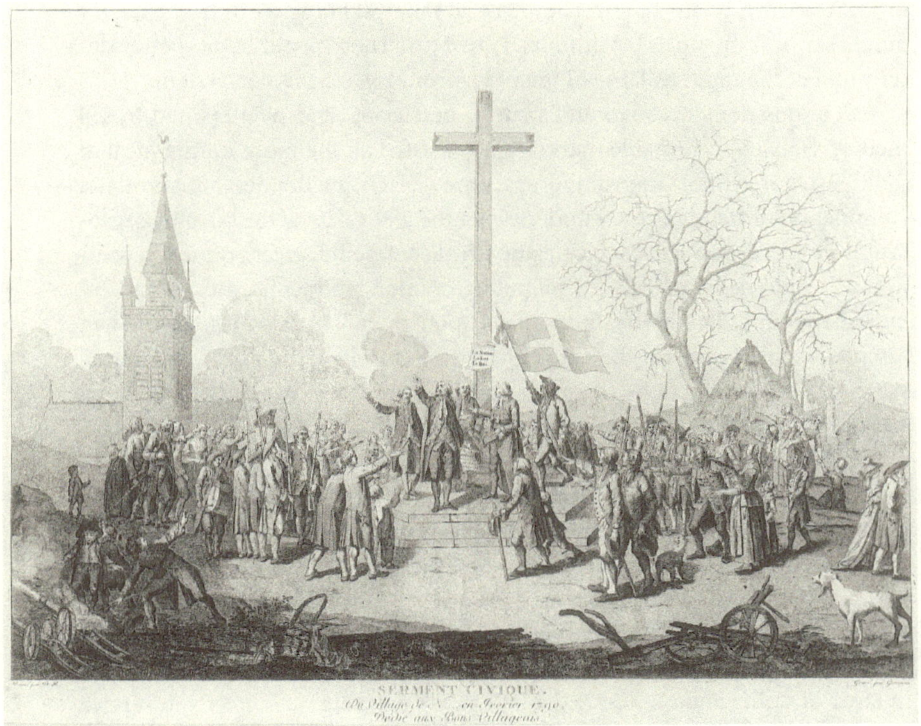

Figure 46. *Civic Oath: Of the Village of N . . . in February 1790; Dedicated to the Good Villagers.* Courtesy Bibliothèque Nationale, Paris. The sign pinned to the cross says, "The Nation, The Law, The King," reflecting the early days of the Revolution, when a peaceful transition from the absolute monarchy of a "kingdom" to the constitutional monarchy of a "nation" still seemed possible.

not simply trying to enact Rousseau's festival ideal, they were also looking for an alternative to the violent processions with bloody heads stuck on pikes or the rural riots that erected maypoles with signs that read: "All rents paid." The official festivals substituted busts of Voltaire or Franklin for the severed heads and planted liberty trees instead of maypoles. But the most immediate predecessors of the festivals were the provincial "federations" in the winter of 1790 in which neighboring village militias pledged cooperation by marching to an open-air mass, where there was a blessing of flags, an oath taking, and the signing of a federative pact, followed by dancing and bonfires (Ozouf 1988) (fig. 46).

Royal administrators tried to co-opt these local festivities by a "Great Federation" to be held in Paris before the king. The Paris ceremony of July 14, 1790, was rather austerely military, as fifty thousand troops and National Guard delegates from all over France stood in ranks on the great Champs de Mars parade ground (now site of the Eiffel Tower) to hear a mass by Talleyrand and take an oath led by Lafayette as the king and a huge crowd looked on. On the same day, far livelier festivals took place in the provinces, amalgamating all sorts of traditions: at Béziers a wine harvest dance was performed along with military exercises; at Chateau-Parcien the "queen" of the local girls gave the speech; at Denèze-sous-le Lude, the culminating bonfire surrounded a maypole. Processions often included children and young women, and the symbolism mixed Christian, classical, and revolutionary images as the Blessed Sacrament was carried among regimental banners or an angel waved a tricolor flag, and the day ended with drinking, singing, and dancing.

The difference between the carefree amalgam of the provincial festivals and the formality of Paris shows the difficult choices facing officials. Substituting reformed and purified processions for spontaneous popular ones or deeply rooted religious ones would have been difficult enough, but the task was made almost impossible by the Revolution's violent and chaotic course. The festival, meant to be a time of coming together to celebrate liberty, equality, and fraternity, often became a reminder of social fragmentation, as competing festival parades challenged each other. In 1792 rival processions were held a few weeks apart, one designed by the painter David, the other by the art theorist Quatremère de Quincy. The first was a "festival of liberty" organized by radical clubs to celebrate the liberation of some mutinous soldiers and included a Declaration of the Rights of Man, busts of Voltaire, Rousseau, and Franklin, a hymn to liberty, women in white carrying the soldiers' chains, and a large chariot with a seated statue of Liberty (fig. 47). The second procession, organized by the government to honor a mayor killed by food rioters, included a model of the Bastille, the sword of the Law, the dead mayor's bust, a hymn to Law, women in white, and a large chariot with a statue of the Law. Although the first procession was meant to inspire antigovernment sentiments and the second to honor legal authority, they used similar emblems, similar chariots and statues, similar women in white, similar music by Gossec—and both ended at the Champ-de-Mars, where the Great Federation had been held, to lay symbols of the Revolution on the altar of the nation (Ozouf 1988).

Revolutionary leaders such as Mirabeau, Robespierre, or David saw the festivals as a way to arouse patriotic feelings and seal emotional ties to the Revolution. David's festival programs (handed out in the streets) have an incantatory tone, not only describing how a statue of Wisdom will emerge from the ashes

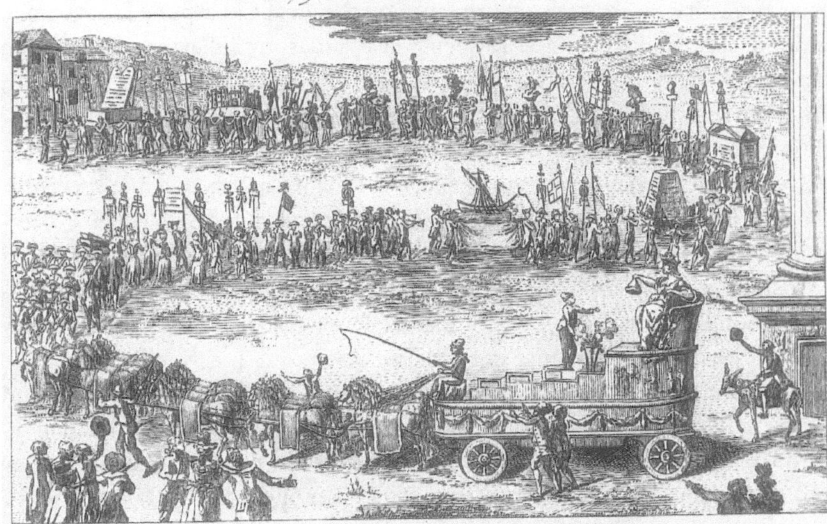


Figure 47. *Festival of Liberty, April 15, 1792.* Courtesy Bibliothèque Nationale, Paris. The lower inscription reads, "First festival of Liberty on the occasion of the release of forty soldiers of Château-Vieux from the galleys of Brest."

of a cardboard Atheism at a certain point but also declaring that "tears of joy and gratitude will flow from all eyes." The most difficult problem facing festival planners was how to find images and music that would kindle intense feelings without leading to violent excess. Their solution was classical allegory. But the neoclassical statues, friezes, columns, tripods, wreaths, and costumes puzzled and rebuffed the less educated and had to be supplemented with banners, labels, and a surfeit of oratory. Thus, David's proposal for a colossal statue of Hercules (representing the French people) called for the words "light" on its forehead, "nature" and "truth" on its chest, "force" on its arms, and "work" on its hands (Schlanger 1977; Hunt 1984).

Were the revolutionary festivals a fair test of the Rousseauist ideal? Probably no historical experiment is a fair test of a myth. Unfortunately, at the same time the revolutionaries were trying to reintegrate the arts in a natural festivity, they were also encouraging a market economy that was hastening the destruction of the old system in which making art for a purpose was a matter of course. Moreover, the deep ideological divisions and violence on all sides never let something more spontaneous develop and take root. Viewed from a later perspective that takes the autonomy of art for granted, the revolutionaries' attempt to reintegrate the fine arts into everyday life inevitably appears an act of manipulation. But such a criticism assumes the very separation of art and society the Revolution was contesting. Yet even if we look more sympathetically on their aims, their effort still seems doomed from the start. Two hundred years later it is easier to see the French Revolution itself as a dramatic moment in the coming of pluralistic societies for which a natural integration of the arts in shared rituals is only fully possible within smaller communities of belief. Many other experiences with government intervention in the arts and spiritual life since 1789 have also taught us that the role of the state must be very indirect. But the festivals were only one part of the Revolution's attempt to revivify the old system of art on a new basis.

## Revolutionary Music

"No Republic without national festivals; no festivals without music," declared Bernard Sarrette, founder of the National Guard Band (Jam 1991, 39). The National Institute of Music, the most important new musical institution to come out of the Revolution, was primarily intended to provide music and musicians for the band, the festivals, and the army. The institute's playing and teaching corps, which included many of the best-known composers of the day, instructed six hundred young musicians and wrote patriotic hymns, marches, and overtures, for example, Méhul's "Chant du Départ," Gossec's "Marche Lugubre," and Cherubini's "Hymne à la Fraternité." Prior to the Festival of the Supreme Being in the summer of 1794, musicians from the institute went into each of the forty-eight wards of Paris to teach everyone Gossec's "Hymn to the Supreme Being" (figs. 48 and 49). The compositions created for the institute were considered national property and printed for free distribution to every department of France and every battalion of the army. For a brief period, the traditional dominance of music production by the church, monarchy, and aristocracy was replaced by production for the "nation" (Jam 1989; Gessele 1992).

Of course, music's political role in the Revolution was not limited to these official experiments. Revolutionary and counterrevolutionary songs of every political stripe poured forth—often drawing on existing tunes from recent operas or dances, although there were striking new ones, such as Rouget de Lisle's "Marseillaise." Elite music also flourished with new operas and a variety of instrumental concerts in the theaters. But as the Revolution took an increasingly radical turn, the political conflict invaded the theaters, sometimes stopping

4

strophe, et l'instant où il devra chanter le refrein de chaque strophe les vieillards, les adolescens et mères de familles, ainsi que les jeunes filles, placés sur la montagne; seront guidées pour le chant de chaque strophe, par le chœur de musique, après la dernière strophe, une décharge générale d'artillerie interprète de la vengeance nationale, se fera entendre et tous les français confondront leurs sentimens et termineront la fête, en faisant retentir le airs des cris de vive la République Française une et indivisible.

Certifié conforme à l'original,
HUBERT, Architecte.

H Y M N E

Qui sera chanté par le Peuple au Champ de la Réunion Décadi prochain, en l'honneur de la Fête qui sera célébrée.

AIR simple et fait pour le peuple, par le Citoyen BRUNY.

O Dieu puissant, invisible à nos yeux,
Mais qu'en tes œuvres l'on contemple:
O toi, dont l'espace est le temple,
Qui dans tes mains tient la terre et les cieux.
Vers toi, dont il a reçu l'être,
Le Français élève sa voix.
S'il a rougi d'obéir à des Rois.,
Il est fier de t'avoir pour maitre.

REÇOIS de nous pour culte et pour autels
Nos cœurs tous remplis de toi-même.
Au sein de la grandeur suprême
D'un œil égal tu vois tous les mortels:
Mais nous suivrons ta loi premiere
Et nous serons tes vrais enfans
Si nous t'offrons des vertus pour encens,
Et des actions pour priere.

OU sont-ils ceux qui t'osoient menacer?
Qui sous le manteau du civisme,
Vils professeurs de l'athéisme,
Du cœur de l'homme espéroit t'effacer.
C'est à l'instant de leurs naufrages.
Qu'ils ont vu dans tous les esprits,
Leurs noms voués à d'éternels mépris;
Le tien à d'éternels hommages.

PENSOIENT-ILS donc lorsqu'il n'est plus d'erreur,
Qu'on croira à leurs impostures?
Qu'en revenant à la nature
De la nature on oublieroit l'auteur?
Tandis que chacun s'aime en frere
C'est Dieu seul qu'on rejetteroit!
Tous en famille on se réuniroit
Pour en méconnoitre le pere!

QUAND donc jamais des prodiges plus grands
Ont signalé ta puissance?
N'as-tu pas délivré la France
D'un joug antique et de ses vils brigans?
De leur famille avec audace.
S'élevoit l'arbre détesté,
Tu l'as proscrit.... et de la Liberté
C'est l'arbre qui croit à sa place.

LORSQUE vingt rois pour nous perdre aujourd'hui.
Unissent le fer et l'intrigue,
Contre leur détestable ligue,
Que de bienfaits nous prouvent ton appui?
Tu couvres nos armes de gloire
Et nos champs de riches moissons...
Tu fais pour nous combattre les saisons.
Et la nature et la victoire.

NOUS ne voulons que défendre nos droits,
Soutient une cause si juste!
Protege le Senat auguste,
L'appui de l'homme et la terreur des Rois!
Que tous les peuples de la terre
Reconnoissant leur longue erreur,
Au lieu d'avoir le François pour vainqueur,
S'empressent de l'avoir pour frere.

Vive la République.

Par J. M. DESCHAMPS
de la Section du Contrat Social, rue
J.J. Rousseau, N°. 40.

De l'Imprimerie de MILLIN, rue de Chartre, n°. 68

V É R I T A B L E

# DÉTAIL DE LA CERÉMONIE

QUI doit être célébrée DECADI 20 Prairial, l'indication des Places que doivent occuper la Convention Nationale, les Sections de Paris, la Cavalerie, la Musique, les Vieillards, les Meres de familles, les Filles et les Adolescens;

AVEC L'ORDRE, LA MARCHE ET LES NOMS DES RUES PAR LESQUELLES PASSERA CE CORTEGE.

S U I V I E

## DE L'HYMNE

QUI doit être chanté par le Peuple, au Champ de la Réunion, en l'honneur de L'ETRE SUPREME.

A cinq heures il se fera un rappel général dans les Sections.

Tous les Citoyens et Citoyennes seront invités par ce rappel, à décorer à l'instant leurs maisons de couleur chérie de la liberté, soit en renouvellant les petits drapaux, soit en les embélissant de guirlandes de fleurs et de verdures.

Ils se rendront ensuite aux chefs lieux de leurs Sections respectives, pour y attendre le signal du départ.

Tous les hommes seront sans armes, exceptés les adolescens de quatorze à dix-huit ans, qui seront armés de sabre et de fusils ou de piques.

Les adolescens formeront dans chaque Section, un Bataillon quarré, marchant sur douze de front, et au milieu duquel seront placés les flames et le drapaux de la force armée de la Section, portés par ceux qui en sont ordinairement chargés.

Tous les Citoyens et les jeunes garçons au-dessous de quatorze ans, tiendront à la main une branche de chêne.

Toutes les Citoyennes mères et filles seront parés des couleurs de la liberté les mères

Figure 48. *Details of the Ceremony of June 8 . . . Followed by the Hymn to the Supreme Being* (June 1794). Courtesy Bibliothèque Nationale, Paris. This festival program tells where various groups are to assemble, what route will be followed, and the division of the verses among the "elderly, the adolescents and mothers, as well as the young women who will stand on the mountain."

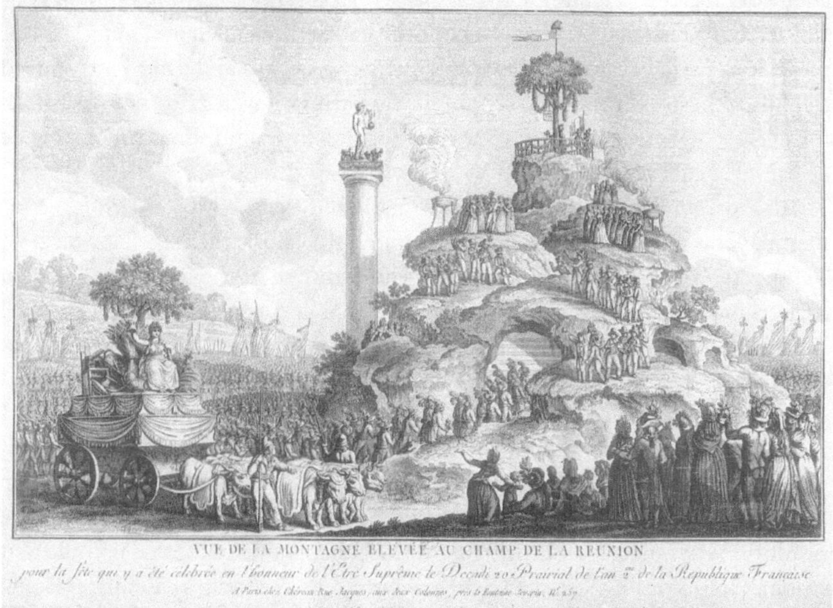


Figure 49. *View of the Mountain Raised on the Field of Reunion for the Festival in Honor of the Supreme Being, June 8, 1794.* Courtesy Bibliothèque Nationale, Paris. The chorus of young women can be seen halfway up the left side of the artificial mountain next to the burning brazier.

performances. In one celebrated instance at the Opéra-Comique, when a soloist turned to Marie Antoinette's box as she sang the lines "I love my mistress tenderly. Oh, how I love my mistress!" revolutionaries leaped onto the stage to throttle the singer and fellow actors rushed to her defense, ending in a free-for-all (Jam 1989).

The opera, identified with the monarchy and aristocracy, was especially hard-pressed to show its patriotic credentials. To help out, Gossec and the choreographer Gardel developed a brief tableau called, "Offrande à la Liberté (scène religieuse)" that could be presented in place of the usual divertissements at the end of most operas. It was an ingenious little piece consisting of a soloist announcing to villagers that the enemy is coming and calling on them to pay homage to Liberty; the villagers then rise up and sing the "Marseillaise." What made the piece so successful was Gossec's orchestration and Gardel's choreography. Gossec varied the accompaniment of each verse, emphasizing the sixth, "Amour sacré de la patrie" (sacred love of country), which was preceded by a solemn dance. In the dance, children in white brought incense to burn before a statue of Liberty as a trilling solo clarinet with a soft horn accompaniment continued the "Marseillaise" theme. The entire chorus then knelt as it sang "Amour sacré de la patrie" in reverential tones, rising up as bells and canon introduced the full orchestra for the final refrain of "Aux arms citoyens! Formez vos bataillons!" The "Offering to Liberty" was performed over a hundred times to wide acclaim (Bartlet 1991).

By 1793, when the revolutionaries instituted censorship and the Terror, many operas appeared based on contemporary patriotic themes: "The Siege of Thionville," "The Taking of Toulon," "The Triumph of the Republic." Actors, dressed in street clothes, played ordinary citizens and sang patriotic songs while citizens became actors when they joined in the choruses, using song sheets provided them. But this blurring of the line separating fiction and reality had dangerous consequences. Some theaters were shut down, and many actors were arrested as suspected traitors for their fictional portrayals of royalty, and at least one was sent to the guillotine for having uttered the line "Long live our noble King!" By demanding a "common exaltation beyond passive amusement," the revolutionaries placed a burden on musical and dramatic theater it could not sustain (Johnson 1995). Rather than exemplifying Rousseau's call for replacing fine art theater with public festivals in which "the spectators are themselves the spectacle," the attempt to transform the theater itself into a political ritual generated an ambiguous and deadly hybrid.

The most violent and eventful years of the Revolution throw into relief a set of intersecting issues on the role of music and the festivals: the problem of pleasure versus utility in the arts, the place of emotion in music, and the value of purely instrumental music. Despite the attempts of Diderot and others to define a third way between sensory pleasure and moral or social utility, most people in the France of 1790 still saw music and the festivals in terms of an either/or: either the agreeable (pleasure, amusement) or the useful (education, inspiration). Opera and ballet were especially suspect to many patriots since they were so closely associated with the "frivolous" pleasures *(agréments)* of the ancien régime. Had the revolutionaries been able to read and grasp Kant's *Critique of Judgment*, with its subtle proposal for a special kind of refined and intellectual pleasure that is neither sensory (agreeable) nor moral (useful), most of them would have found it too elitist and apolitical.[2] The Revolution tried to resist the drift toward a subjective aesthetic experience by emphasizing the moral utility of music. But the Revolution's political and moral use of music got tangled up in the other two issues: the status of instrumental music and the question of the way music affects the emotions.

As Johnson points out, what especially complicated the revolutionaries' task was the emergence, after the 1780s, of a belief that purely instrumental music was capable not only of imitating sounds (thunder, birdsongs) but also of conveying human emotions. As a result, one could no longer dismiss instrumental music as mere technical exercises, and many composers of the revolutionary period were praised for expressing patriotic enthusiasm or funereal solemnity through purely harmonic writing, although the titles or context of these instrumental pieces usually left little doubt as to what was to be felt (Johnson 1995, 138). Yet even this was not enough for some good republicans. In January of 1795 the Convention commemorated the second anniversary of the king's execution by a concert from the National Institute. The orchestra had played only a short way into a gentle and melodious introduction when a deputy jumped up demanding to know, "Are you for him or against him?" Poor Gossec had to explain his orchestral piece and then play the "Ça ira" and other patriotic tunes to save the day. Music without words was still suspect (Jam 1989, 23).

The fall of Robespierre and the end of the Terror brought not only a political but a social and artistic reaction as well. As Louis-Sébastien Mercier described it, after Thermidor, "luxury emerged from the smoking ruins more stunning than ever. The culture of the fine arts has recaptured all its luster" (Johnson 1995, 155). The theaters were full again and dropped their patriotic fare for traditional operas, instrumental concerts, and light entertainments. Commercial festivities based on the ability to pay took the place of public festivals. People filled the ballrooms, the cabarets, and the flourishing public gardens, where they could dine, dance, listen to a variety of music (including Haydn), and perhaps end the evening watching fireworks (Mongrédien 1986). Meanwhile, despite the government's establishment of an entire system of festivals for youth, old age, harvest, and so forth, interest and attendance steadily dwindled and Napoleon finally finished them off. Early on, the Revolution had swept away the dependence of music and musicians on church, royalty, and aristocracy; the collapse of both the festivals and the program for a national music left the field open to market forces and an aesthetic of musical autonomy. Many citizens were now ready to accept a separation of pleasure from politics and morals and to restrict music to the sphere of private enjoyment.

Although the return of pleasure was not always articulated as the higher, refined pleasure of the specifically Kantian and Schillerian aesthetic, it opened the way for a cultivated elite to develop just such an attitude. Signs of this were already surfacing in comments on the new subscription concerts that began as early as 1798. Writing of the Concert des Amateurs, one critic sighed, "There, all rivalries, party spirit, and animosities cease . . . one thinks only of art." By 1801 the National Conservatory's students and professors, once dedicated to providing revolutionary music for the people, had also established an instrumental concert series, and the players were praised in the press for their "radiant . . . fervor; their love for their art is a cult" (Johnson 1995, 198, 201). The era of Napoleon and the Restoration would bring some revival of traditional patronage, but the old patronage *system* in which music primarily served religious and social ends was fatally undermined, as was the Revolution's attempt to revive it on a secular and egalitarian basis.

## The Revolution and the Museum

The conflict between the old system of art and the new system of fine art was played out with equal drama in the debates surrounding the creation of a national art museum in the Louvre Palace. Unlike the attempt to create a national music through the festivals and the institute, the National Museum was one of the Revolution's most enduring creations—although paradoxically it was an institution that ended up promoting the idea of fine art for itself rather than art in service of the nation. The museum that opened in one wing of the Louvre in August of 1793 involved far more than the long-anticipated exhibition of a private royal collection (McClellan 1994). By 1793, the Revolution had careened through a series of radical transformations that gave the museum a powerful ideological charge. Two things served early on to implicate the museum in the struggles of the Revolution. The first was the nationalization of church and émigré properties, many of which contained rich furnishings, large libraries, and collections of scientific apparatus, musical instruments, paintings, and statues. The second was the omnipresence in Paris, Versailles, Fontainebleau, and elsewhere of artistic monuments and symbols of the royalty itself. In October of 1790, as the assembly debated the organization of the sale of church property to save the state from bankruptcy, an obscure scholar called for an inventory of all works of science and art and the creation of a museum to house what he called the "national heritage." By November, the Committee on the Disposal of National Property had created a special Commission on Monuments to oversee the inventory and determine what should be sold and what kept for an eventual museum of the sciences and the arts (the two not yet separated in many people's minds). One might think the matter settled, but the overthrow of the monarchy in August 1792 led to a fierce conflict over what to do with the innumerable signs of royal power found in every city and town—statues of Louis XIV and XV, paintings of princes or royal mistresses, and fleurs-de-lis everywhere.

Two incidents occurring within a month of each other in 1793 illustrate the opposed attitudes. A delegation from Fontainebleau proudly reported to the Convention that they had made a bonfire of all the royal portraits at the Chateau. They had briefly considered saving a finely done arm from a portrait of Louis XIII in honor of the artist, Philippe de Champaigne but finally decided to throw it on the fire with the rest. By contrast, a medallion of Louis XIV by the sculptor Girardon was saved when a government envoy at Troyes was able to snatch it from the "view of our fellow republicans, who by their hatred of despotism could not have long stood the sight of it." Such ornaments, he added, "ought to be conserved out of respect for art" (Pommier 1988, 138, 472).

The two attitudes just illustrated, one bent on destroying every sign of "despotism," whatever the artistry, the other determined to save the "art" however repugnant the symbol, struggled with each other—sometimes within the same person—throughout the decisive years of the Revolution. Some, like Charles-Maurice de Talleyrand or Jean-Marie Roland argued that despite their content, the best works of the past should be saved, but they were opposed by artists like David, who argued that the most offensive works should be ground into raw material for new works of liberty and virtue. It is striking that at each crucial stage of the Revolution the discourse of destruction was almost immediately followed by an equally passionate discourse of conservation and that the idea of an art museum became the key to its resolution.

The confrontation between the rhetoric of destruction and that of conservation crystallized around two moments, the first during the weeks immediately following the violent overthrow of the monarchy on August 10, 1792, and the second in the midst of war and the Terror in the summer of 1793. In the days following August 10, 1792, mobs toppled royal statues, and the assembly voted a decree calling for the destruction of all monuments and signs of royalty.[3] Over the next three weeks a vigorous debate took place amid reports that a number of masterpieces were being damaged or destroyed around the country. One deputy called for works of art to be saved as memorials of the Enlightenment; others railed against "barbarians" and "vandals."

The argument that was decisive in turning the assembly toward conservation was made by Pierre Cambon, who called for using the "monuments to royalty" to "form a museum." By putting them in a museum, Cambon emphasized, "we will destroy the idea of royalty" and at the same time "preserve the masterpieces." The new decree, passed on September 16, 1792, just a month after the first one, called for "the conservation of paintings, statues and other monuments related to the Fine Arts . . . which objects are to be gathered prior to dividing them between the museum of Paris and those which may be established in other departments." A museum commission was appointed to turn a wing of the Louvre Palace into a national museum (Pommier 1991, 104, 106). By placing the suspect works in a museum, the assembly recognized that the museum would neutralize them. Once in the museum, monuments to royalty would lose their sacred power. They would cease to be symbols pointing beyond themselves and become merely art. Out of the crucible of the Revolution had come an institution that "makes" art, that transforms works of art dedicated to a purpose and place into works of Art that are essentially purposeless and placeless. Or to use Kant's terms they are "purposeful without a purpose," having the purposefulness of being made by an artist but serving no particular purpose—except to be Art.

Although the museum's neutralizing power was officially recognized in the debates of 1792, the increasing radicalization of the Revolution in the spring and summer of 1793 once more revived a policy of destruction, leading to the desecration of the royal tombs at St. Denis and to chiseling the "kings" off Notre Dame. Once more the museum provided the solution. By mid-October of 1793, when the military threat to the Revolution was over, the Convention condemned recent excesses and decreed that if signs of royalty could not be removed from an art work without damage, the work "shall be transferred to the nearest museum" (Pommier 1991, 136). Meanwhile, the planning committee for the National Museum had continued its work, and the Louvre officially opened its doors as part of the August 10 anniversary of the overthrow of the monarchy, the same day a great Festival of Unity, designed by David, was winding through the city. A deputy presented the Convention with an "agate cup with a piece of jasper carved in the shape of two hands" to be used in the festival's ceremony of regeneration, and the Convention later voted that the cup should be deposited in the new museum "with an inscription recalling the sublime and moving use it served" (Pommier 1991, 66) (fig. 50).

Of course, the museum was viewed as far more than an expedient for solving the conflict between destruction and conservation; from the beginning it was seen as an instrument of civic education, and the commissions on conservation and on preparing the museum were placed under the Convention's Committee on Public Instruction. Félix Vicq d'Azyr, head of the special commission charged with inventorying the many kinds of confiscated objects, sent an "instruction" to all French departments in 1794 that included a revealing discussion of the classification of the arts under the pressure of the Revolution. During the Old Regime of "despotism," he wrote, painting, sculpture, and architecture were called either "agreeable arts" or else "fine arts." But neither name is correct, since the term "agreeable arts" trivializes the arts, whereas the

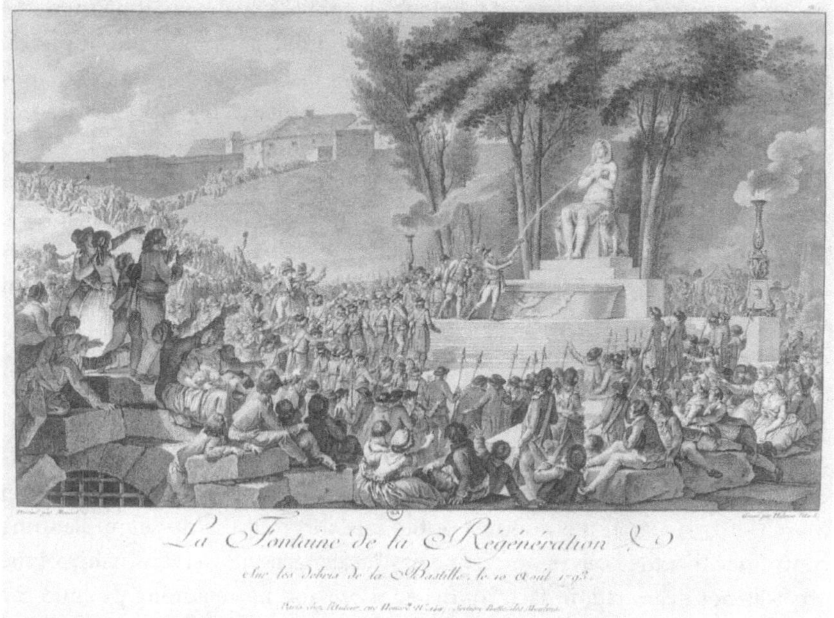


Figure 50. *The Fountain of Regeneration, Erected on the Debris of the Bastille, August 10, 1793.* Courtesy Bibliothèque Nationale, Paris. A representative of the Convention catches the water of regeneration pouring from the breast of a female statue. The Chalice of Regeneration in which he received the water was later placed in the Louvre by order of the Convention.

name "fine arts" "insults the *mechanical arts,* whose progress demands just as much invention and breadth of spirit as the others. More recently, painting, sculpture and architecture have been called *arts of imitation,* which is more exact, or *arts of history,* which is better yet, since it reflects their true aim. For the arts are asked to line the route of time with monuments aimed at keeping alive the meaning of useful actions and the benefactors of humanity" (Aboudrar 2000, 95). Although not specifically a program for the museum, Vicq d'Azyr's instruction on conservation is a striking rejection of the fine art–versus–mechanical arts polarity, which he sees as tied to aristocratic social divisions and political absolutism. Under the Revolution, he suggests, the fine arts and crafts will be reunited as "arts of history," the inspirers and educators of an egalitarian society. As for the arts of the past, Vicq d'Azyr suggests that a free people will be able to distinguish between their value as art and the reactionary purposes they once served. But Vicq d'Azyr doesn't see the danger inherent in using the museum to help people make that distinction. Given the museum's power to neutralize royalist and religious meanings, why would it not have the same effect on the monuments of the Revolution? The Convention implicitly recognized this in 1793 when it ordered that an inscription recalling the "sublime and moving use" of the Festival of Unity's chalice of regeneration accompany it into the Louvre. In subsequent years some revolutionaries began to doubt whether the art museum could be an effective instructor in republican virtue at all, and claimed that the Revolution would be better served by public murals or by statues of exemplary thinkers and heroes along the Champs Élysée. "By ceasing to imprison our monuments in Museums," one of them wrote, "we will lead the arts back to their true destination . . . speaking to the hearts of citizens" (Mantion 1988, 126).

But the museum was now firmly established and the revolutionary and Napoleonic military conquests provided another opportunity for its aestheticizing power to be reaffirmed, although a vigorous debate ensued that casts additional light on the museum's role in turning "arts" into "Art." Already in March of 1793 Garat, the minister of the interior, told the museum planning committee that the Louvre would one day "attest that the sacred worship of the arts was not neglected, in fact flourished more and more among us amid the terrible storms of revolution" (Pommier 1991, 118). Given this elevated view of the place of the museum in French glory, it is not surprising that there was widespread support for the policy of confiscating artistic masterpieces in conquered lands and sending them back to France. Bonaparte's exactions in Italy are the most famous, but the policy began with the conquest of Belgium in 1794, leading one deputy to declare: "The Flemish school rises en mass to come and adorn our museums" (Pommier 1991, 25). In 1798 a "Festival of Liberty and Triumphal Entry of Objects of the Sciences and the Arts Collected in Italy" was held in Paris with a great procession of chariots displaying paintings, statues, and manuscripts. Over the chariot carrying the famous bronze horses of St. Mark's of Venice a banner proclaimed: "They are now on free soil" (E. Kennedy 1989).

Yet there were many artists and writers who rejected the idea of confiscation. The most outspoken was Antoine-Chrysostome Quatremère de Quincy in his *Letters to [General] Miranda on the Removal of the Art Monuments of Italy* ([1796] 1989b). Quatremère's central argument was that the removal of ancient and Renaissance works from their living historical context destroys their meaning. Torn from their original setting and put in the museum, they become overvalued as sacred relics of Art—or undervalued as if they were merchandise laid out in a fancy store. Quatremère was not alone in these sentiments. Fifty artists, including David, signed a petition to the Directory executive supporting his theses. But there were also attacks on Quatremère's book, and two months later a petition defending confiscation, signed by thirty other artists, including François Gérard and Carle Vernet, was sent to the Directory. These artists used the revolutionary rhetoric of liberty and regeneration, claiming that France was the only appropriate place for works of free genius and adding that the Italians didn't really care for the historical associations of these works because they were selling them to France's enemies, the English and Austrians.

In subsequent years, Quatremère spelled out more fully the denaturing effect of the art museum ([1815] 1989a). Works of art, he asserted, only speak to our deepest feelings when they are made for a specific purpose and place. The relatively new idea of producing works without a commission but destined for the market or the museum results in our either treating art works as luxury

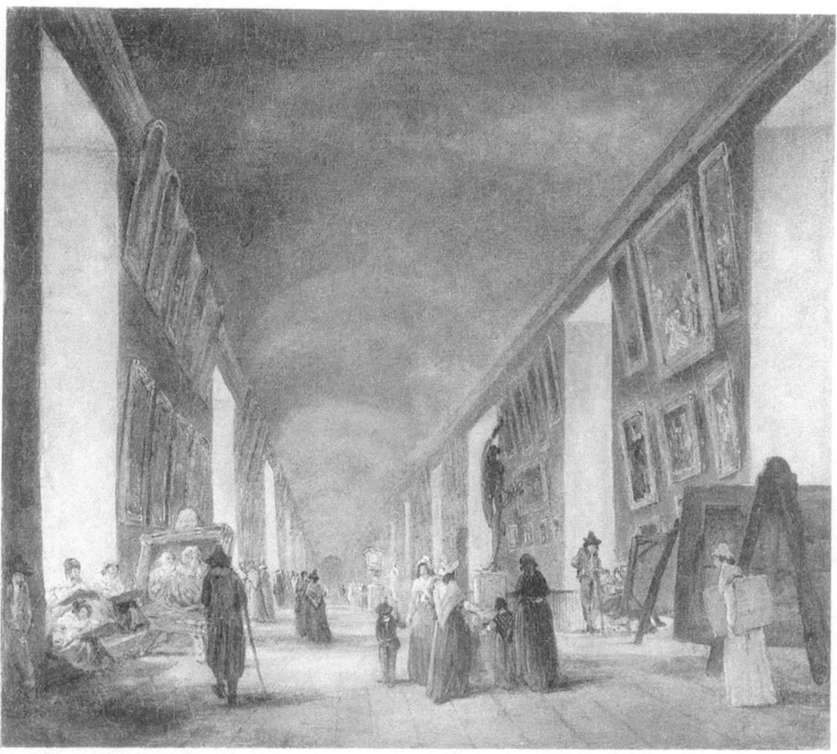

Figure 51. Hubert Robert, *The Grand Gallery of the Louvre* (1794–96). Courtesy Réunion des Musées Nationaux, Paris. This is the way the new national museum appeared in its first years; the presence of copyists fulfilled one of the aims of the museum, which was to offer artists access to great paintings as models.

goods or considering only their formal and technical merit. The museum sets up a vicious circle in which the only aim of a work of art is to engender other works of art. In the museum, art works become "bodies without soul, empty simulacra, deprived of action, feeling and life" (Quatremère 1989a, 26). Although several other writers seconded these arguments, they had little effect. Many of Napoleon's confiscated works had to be sent back after 1815, but the Louvre remained the sacred temple of fine art and the model for the modern art museum (fig. 51). Even more important, it was not long before some nineteenth-century painters and sculptors began to think of the true, the ultimate destination, of their works as the museum itself, a far more powerful impetus toward "Art for Art's sake" than any later aestheticist pronouncement. Meanwhile Quatremère's insights into the effects of separating works of art from their contexts of use were largely forgotten.[4]

PART IV

# The Apotheosis of Art

## Overview

If the French Revolution's failed attempt to reintegrate the fine arts with social and political life spurred on the idea of "art for itself," it was only possible because the tendency toward viewing fine art as a distinct realm had already been gaining momentum since the 1750s. Whereas the eighteenth century split the older idea of art into fine art versus craft; the nineteenth century transformed fine art itself into a reified "Art," an independent and privileged realm of spirit, truth, and creativity (chap. 10). Similarly, the concept of the artist, which had been definitively separated from that of the artisan in the eighteenth century, was now sanctified as one of humanity's highest spiritual callings. The status and image of the artisan, by contrast, continued to decline, as many small workshops were forced out of business by industrialization and many skilled craftspeople entered the factories as operatives performing prescribed routines (chap. 11). Finally, the "aesthetic," which had been constructed by transforming refined taste into a special form of detached contemplation, became for parts of the cultured elite a kind of experience superior to both science and morality (chap. 12). These elevations did not take place simply on the level of beliefs but were accompanied by corresponding changes in institutions and behaviors. As institutions like the museum, the secular concert, and vernacular literary curricula gradually spread across Europe and the Americas, increasing numbers of the middle class were learning proper aesthetic behavior. At the same time, the broader audience for the arts became more clearly divided and began to frequent different institutions. Although the elevation and consecration of the ideals of art, artist, and the aesthetic were largely complete by the 1830s, it took most of the rest of the century to build the art institutions, inculcate the new ideals, and modify behaviors. Similarly, the descent of the skilled and inventive craftspeople who had run their own shops and participated in all aspects of production stretched out over most of the century, varying from country to country with the pace of industrialization and affecting the different crafts unequally.

CHAPTER 10

# Art as Redemptive Revelation

IN 1830 ANOTHER revolution took place in Paris, touching off revolts and disturbances from Rome to Warsaw most of which were easily crushed. The German poet, Heinrich Heine, already in exile, quipped that the revolution may have failed in Germany, but "art has been saved": "Everything possible is now being done in Germany for art, especially in Prussia. The museums are ablaze with artful delight in color, the orchestras roar, the danseuses leap their loveliest *entrechats,* the public is enchanted with the Arabian Nights of novellas, and theater criticisms flourishes once more" ([1830] 1985, 34). The followers of Goethe, Heine noted in the same essay, already "regard art as an independent second world which they rank so highly that all activities of human beings—their religion, their morality—course along below it" (34). Heine was one of the first in the nineteenth century to note not only that "art" had become an autonomous realm but that it could also be used to distract people from political oppression.

## Art Becomes an Independent Realm

Although it would be impossible to say exactly when and where "an abstract, capitalized Art, with its own internal, but general principles" first emerged, such a concept was firmly in place by the 1830s (Williams 1976, 33). In 1835 one French critic remarked that "instead of the fine arts we have Art, the new king of the century" (Bénichou 1973, 423). That same year Théophile Gautier wrote of "Art for Art's" sake in the preface to *Mademoiselle de Maupin* and Emerson's 1836 lectures spoke of Art as a "department of life" alongside religion, science, and politics (Emerson 1966–72, 2:42). Yet Art was a separate realm not only in concept and language but in its separate institutions as well. In the visual arts, separate auctions, dealers, and museums had become an established feature of European life by the 1830s (fig. 52). Music and literature also underwent further changes in both conception and institutional forms, during the first half of

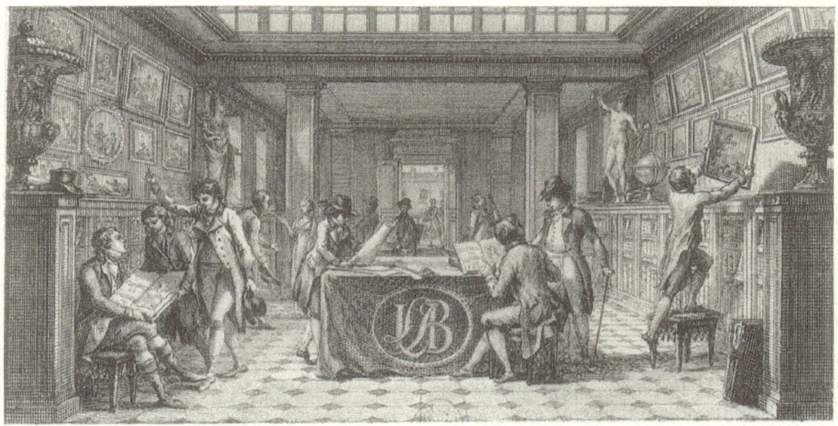

Figure 52. Pierre-Philippe Choffard, *The Print Gallery of Basan* (1805). Courtesy Bibliothèque Nationale, Paris.

the century, that accentuated their separation from their former functional contexts.

We have already explored the creation of a national art museum in the Louvre during the Revolution. In 1835, Franz Liszt called for a "museum" of musical works in the Louvre, proposing that every five years the best musical works should be performed every day in the Louvre for a month and the scores purchased and published at state expense. Although Liszt's musical museum did not materialize in the Louvre, a more generalized musical museum did, what Lydia Goehr calls the "imaginary museum of musical works." It consisted in the retrospective application of the "work" concept so as to create a historical series of great musical artists and their works of art as a reservoir for performance (Goehr 1992). Part of Liszt's dream was achieved by the gradual establishment of autonomous symphony orchestras and the building of separate concert halls where the great works of past and present could be performed (fig. 53).

The separation of music from religious and social contexts, which began in the eighteenth century, now took on a new form in the dramatic reversal in the status of instrumental music. Until the last third of the eighteenth century instrumental music had often been disparaged as a mere showcase for dexterity, but now some romantics turned the tables and argued that instrumental or "pure" music was the only kind deserving the name. "When we speak of music as an independent art," E. T. A. Hoffmann wrote in 1813, "should we not always restrict our meaning to instrumental music, which . . . gives pure expression to

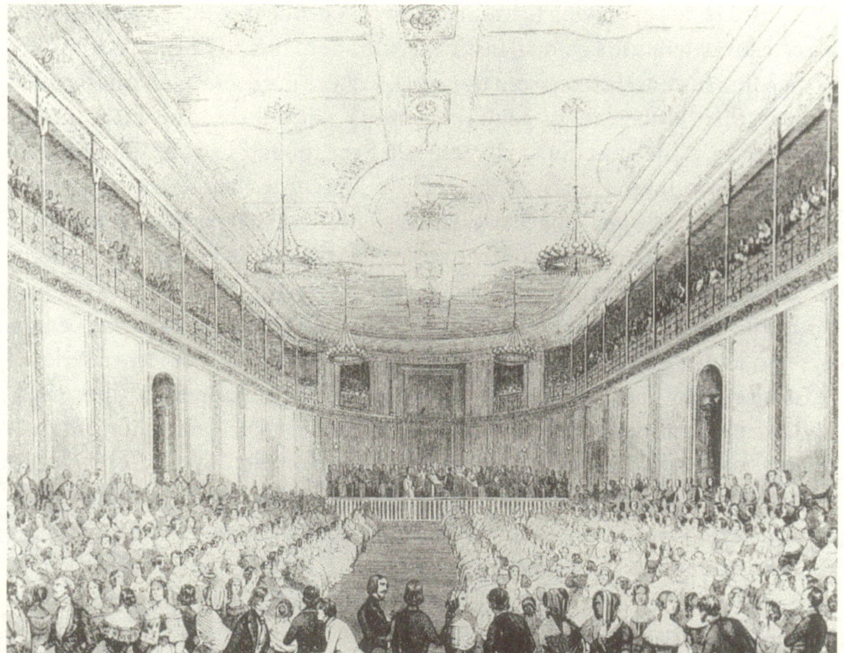

Figure 53. A concert in the old Gewandhaus (former Cloth Merchant's Hall), Leipzig (1845). Courtesy Bildarchiv Preussischer Kulturbesitz, Berlin. The women are seated in rows facing each other, the men stand behind them.

music's specific nature?" (Strunk 1950, 775). The apotheosis of instrumental music involved two claims: first, that music, as one of the fine arts, is not meant to serve specific social or religious uses but a generalized spirituality, and second, that instrumental music is able to do this better than any other art because its meaning is entirely within itself (Dahlhaus 1989).

The idea of literature underwent a similar transformation as one after another of the older components of literature in general began to drop out, first scientific writing, then history, and finally the sermon and the letter.[1] Several factors contributed to the final separation of the literature of imagination from literature in general. On the classificatory level, the term "literature" had already begun to replace poetry for speaking of imaginative writing once the novel was accepted as fine art.[2] But "literature" became more than a convenient category when German romantic theorists and English romantic poets began to celebrate imaginative literature as expressing deeper truths than reason or science can grasp (Schaeffer 1992).

A third factor in making literature as art independent of literature in general was creative literature's gradual institutionalization. Identifying the institutions of high literature as distinct from those of literature in general is obviously more difficult than in the case of painting or music since there is no exact literary counterpart of the museum or concert hall. Even though separate libraries were not created to house works of imaginative literature, there did emerge what Alvin Kernan calls an "Imaginary Library" of great literary works similar to Goehr's "imaginary museum" of musical works (1982). The canons of vernacular literature that began to develop in the eighteenth century became fully institutionalized in nineteenth-century education. These vernacular canons were no longer primarily grammatical and stylistic models but were a series of masterpieces forming an Imaginary Library whose "monuments," to use T. S. Eliot's famous phrase, "form an ideal order" (1989, 467). Removed from their original social and historical context they were mentally (or physically, in the case of anthologies or survey courses) assembled as exemplars of poetry or literature as fine art. The literature anthologies familiar to generations of college students taking the "sophomore survey" form a kind of literary equivalent to the art museum or the concert repertoire. Viewed in this light, the perennial debates over which works belong in the canon is less important than the recontextualizing function of modern canons when linked to an essentialist idea of literature.

Based on these imaginary libraries, the most important literary institutions of our time have been the literature departments of our schools, colleges, and universities. Although we take the discipline of literature for granted, literature as a separate academic subject is only a little over a hundred years old. At the beginning of the nineteenth century, the tiny European and American elite who attended colleges or universities studied Greek and Latin in order to read selections from classical authors as models of grammar, rhetoric, and civic behavior. In early nineteenth-century Britain, English literature appeared first in the adult education programs of mechanic's institutes, then in the "brick" universities attended by the middle classes, and only became a degree subject at Oxford in 1894 and at Cambridge after the turn of the century (Baldick 1983; Court 1992). French literature, in contrast, was viewed from the seventeenth century on as an instrument of national prestige and as a way of unifying a country where regional and local dialects remained strong. Nineteenth-century French literary culture included not only a centralized national curriculum but also salons and cenacles, literary prizes and government subsidies, the Académie Française and the Panthéon (Clark 1987).

In America, the gradual shift from Latin and Greek to English language and then literature is reflected in the changing title of the professorships at Yale: the 1817 title "rhetoric and oratory" became "rhetoric and the English language" in 1839 and finally turned into "rhetoric and English literature" in 1863 (Scholes 1998). These titles and the curriculum behind them were typical of an American higher education system in which rhetoric was more important than literature down through the Civil War. Moreover, literary study in the antebellum period often meant no more than examining short passages from Shakespeare and Milton along with speeches of the great orators. Not until the 1870s did literature cease to be subordinate to rhetoric, but even then many English departments were split between the more academically respectable historical linguists and the barely tolerated belletristic generalists, the latter teaching great works of literature as spiritual inspiration. By the 1890s, however, the missionary belleletrists were gaining the upper hand in many departments. Typical was a University of Chicago report claiming that English was not linguistics or the history of language but the study of "masterpieces of literature . . . as works of literary art" (Graff 1987, 101). By the end of the nineteenth century, a reified "literature" was institutionally established throughout the Americas, and by 1915 the Russian formalist critics were attempting to define the essence of "literarity" and thus scientifically separate literature as fine art from literature in general once and for all (Erlich 1981).

Of course, just as the term "art" could designate either all arts in general or "fine art" alone, so the small case "literature" or "music" could refer to either the general field of writing or music or to their specifically fine art forms. When a distinction between the fine art and popular art domains was needed, recourse was had to capitalization, or to adjectives such as "imaginative" or "creative" literature, or to "serious," "classical," or "art" music. One effect of art, music, and creative writing becoming distinct domains, each with its own real or imaginary museum of self-contained works, was that the term "art" frequently came to designate only the visual arts of painting, sculpture, and architecture, something already happening in Emerson's time (he spoke of "Literature and Art" as "co-ordinate terms") (1966–72, 2:55). But even more important for the future was the use of a capitalized "Art" to designate all the fine arts as forming an independent realm within the larger society. In the early nineteenth century, this usage was given a metaphysical and religious turn by a wide spectrum of writers, ranging from romantic poets and idealist philosophers to social prophets and Darwinian theorists. "Art" was no longer simply a generic term for any human making and performance, as under the old system of art, nor even shorthand for the category of Fine Art constructed in the late eighteenth century but had become the name of an autonomous realm and a transcendent force.

## The Spiritual Elevation of Art

Although one can find a number of nineteenth-century declarations such as Alfred de Vigny's "Art is the modern . . . spiritual belief," such utterances were hardly a sign that the average European bourgeois was about to give up Christianity for Art (Shroder 1961, 50). Yet an increasingly skeptical intellectual elite was finding in art and various social utopias a substitute for the old religious ideals and certainties (Charlton 1963; Honour 1979). This tendency to treat the realm of art as a religious substitute only gradually spread beyond those directly involved in the arts, without necessarily replacing religious belief in each case. Most writers who believed in the exalted role of art simply placed it on the same level as religion (Chateaubriand, Hugo, Goethe). From the secular side, Flaubert's letters contain some of the most ecstatic pronouncements on the spiritual role of art, such as his appeal to Louise Colet in 1853: "Let us love one another 'in Art' as the mystics love one another 'in God'" (1980, 196). In England, Matthew Arnold claimed that "most of what now passes with us for religion and philosophy will be replaced by poetry" (1966, 2). And in America, many writers and teachers "channeled into literature emotions that a half century earlier" would have gone into Christianity or transcendentalism (Graff 1987, 85). Of course, even in the mid-nineteenth century, ringing public declarations that Art or Literature should replace Christianity would have been incautious anywhere (both Flaubert's *Madame Bovary* and Baudelaire's *Les fleurs du mal* were publicly prosecuted for immorality and offense to religion in 1857).

Generally, the spiritual elevation of art took the Schillerian form of viewing art as the revelation of a superior truth with the power to redeem. The insights of the imagination and feeling, on this view, while they may lack the clarity and certainty of scientific or practical reasoning, give us immediate access to a spirituality that transcends the religious divisions of humankind. Shelley claimed that poetry alone brings "light and fire from those eternal regions where the owl-winged faculty of calculation dare not ever soar" (1930, 135). And Hoffmann said of instrumental music that it "discloses to man an unknown realm, a world that has nothing in common with the external sensual world that surrounds him" (Strunk 1950, 775). Although few of the poets or critics who made these claims for the transcendent truth of art gave any arguments for their position, several German romantic theorists and idealist philosophers turned these vague ideas into what Jean-Marie Schaeffer has called "the speculative theory of Art" (1992).[3]

The core of the speculative theory of Art is the claim that art reveals the ground of the universe (God, being, absolute) through the sensuous means of image, symbol, and sound. The philosopher F. W. J. Schelling called Art the self-externalization of the absolute which "opens up . . . the holy of holies where burns in eternal and original unity, as if in a single flame, that which nature and history has rent asunder" ([1800] 1978, 231). Hegel made art one of the three forms of "absolute spirit" in his system, although he believed that religion and philosophy are "more" spiritual than art because of art's sensuous aspect. But for that very reason Art's special task is to express "the most comprehensive truths of the Spirit . . . by displaying [them] sensuously" ([1823–29] 1975, 7). In America, Emerson developed a homegrown version of the speculative theory of Art, blending idealist influences with a down-to-earth mode of expression that reached a wide audience, although he also criticized the separation of art from life (see chap. 13).

Meanwhile, Arthur Schopenhauer was making equally grandiose claims for art using a metaphysics of the will. According to Schopenhauer, our ordinary existence, driven by will, is subject to an endless dialectic of desire and boredom, and the only way to escape it is either ascetic renunciation or art. Fine art can give us temporary relief from ceaseless striving by making us forget our desiring individuality in the aesthetic act of rapt contemplation (Schopenhauer 1969, 52). If Schopenhauer found in art the comfort and compensation of a momentary cessation of worldly desire, Friedrich Nietzsche used a metaphysics of will to define an aesthetics of joy and affirmation. For Nietzsche, in a world without God, it was "Art and nothing but art! It is the great means of making life possible, the great seduction to life . . . the *redemption of the man of knowledge . . . of the man of action . . . of the sufferer* . . . where suffering is a form of great delight" (1967, 452).

Although the Saint-Simonists, socialists, and Darwinists of the nineteenth century did not share the metaphysics of the speculative theorists of art, they often gave art a similarly exalted spiritual role. Both Claude-Henri Saint-Simon and Auguste Comte made art and artists central to their social vision of the future. Comte's "Positive Philosophy" put Art on the same level as science and his religion of humanity. At one point Comte even claimed that Art is higher than science because it is closer to feeling and unites the theoretical and practical (Comte 1968, 221). Even a Darwinian like Grant Allen concluded that once our basic needs are satisfied, aesthetic experiences make our lives not only happier but "brighter, higher and more ethereal" as well (Allen 1877, 55). Although the specifically idealist, vitalist, or social Darwinist forms of the speculative theory of art did not become part of the regulative assumptions of the modern system of art, what did become a commonplace was the belief that art is an autonomous realm and spiritual force. Even a formalist critic, like Clive Bell, who denied artworks any reference beyond themselves, could write in 1914 that the experience of art is "so valuable . . . that I have been tempted to believe that art might prove the world's salvation" (1958, 32).

One outgrowth of this reification of art was the attempt to identify which of the fine arts was closest to the essence of Art, whether conceived as spirit, will, life, feeling, or form. Many poets, but also several philosophers, such as Hegel and Comte, were deeply convinced that poetry most fully exemplified the essence of art. Hegel argued that poetry was closer to spirit than the sensuous media of sound, color, or stone. Schopenhauer, by contrast, is famous for making instrumental music the paradigmatic art because its pure sounds are a direct expression of the will. Schopenhauer's view was part of a general nineteenth-century tendency to elevate instrumental music to the supreme status once held by poetry or painting. The primary reason many writers gave for viewing instrumental music as the highest art was that it seemed the least worldly of all the arts, having no purpose beyond its intrinsic pleasures. This is perhaps the meaning of Walter Pater's oft quoted line, "All art constantly aspires towards the condition of music" ([1873] 1912).

A term closely related to "art" that also changed its meaning in the nineteenth century was "culture." In the eighteenth century, culture signified a social distinction between the cultivated and the ignorant or unmannered; culture was something one had more or less of as a cultivated person. Although some nineteenth-century writers, such as Matthew Arnold, made culture a near synonym for fine art, its more general meaning usually included all the higher intellectual activities, such as history, philosophy, or even the sciences. Late nineteenth-century historians and anthropologists made its scope even broader by reviving Herder's use of "culture" as a general term for the totality of behaviors, beliefs, and institutions of a society. In the twentieth century, of course, some of the most prominent debates about culture have turned around the distinction between high and low culture, a parallel to the art-versus-craft distinction, since "low" culture usually includes popular art, decorative art, and commercial art, which are also encompassed by "craft" in its broadest usage (Williams 1976; Clifford 1988).

CHAPTER 11

# The Artist

## *A Sacred Calling*

### The Exalted Image of the Artist

High is our calling, Friend—Creative Art!" Wordsworth wrote to the neoclassical painter Benjamin Robert Haydon in 1815 (1977, 317). As the industrial revolution drove more and more painters, musicians, and writers into the ranks of hired workers or paid entertainers, the ideal figure of the artist took on a more intense aura of spirituality. Of course many artists connected their sense of high spiritual vocation to traditional religious convictions. One such group was the "Nazarenes," young German painters living a semimonastic life in Rome devoted to Art and Catholicism. On the Protestant side, there was the English poet-painter William Blake, who wrote in 1820: "A Poet, a Painter, a Musician, an Architect: the Man or Woman who is not one of these is not a Christian. You must leave Father and Mother and House and Lands if they stand in the way of Art" (Eitner 1970, 19). Hector Berlioz renounced his medical studies in similar biblical terms after hearing one of Gluck's operas, vowing that, "in spite of father, mother, uncles, aunts, grand-parents, friends, I would be a musician." He immediately wrote to his father of "the imperious and irresistible nature of my vocation" (Honour 1979, 246). Composing, writing, and painting were not mere professions, but "higher" callings, demanding the kind of personal sacrifice once reserved for religion. As one critic remarked in 1834, "The despot of the day is the word *Artist*. . . . In the old days one said of good artists that they had beliefs. . . . But Art itself is a belief. The true artist is the priest of this eternal religion" (Bénichou 1973, 422). And lest we think this was only the view of an elite of successful painters and composers, we can turn to the literary remains of obscure nineteenth-century clerks and *functionaires* who speak of opening themselves to "the great wind of Art" in order to sail on a sea of beauty or of dying to the world for the sake of Art: "Divine Art, I carry you in my soul. Let me be worthy of you" (Grana 1964, 79).

Given the place of instrumental music in the early nineteenth century, it is no surprise that for many people the exemplary case of the artist as spiritual paragon was Beethoven. From 1835 on, monuments glorifying Beethoven began to appear in various German principalities, and later in the century Georges

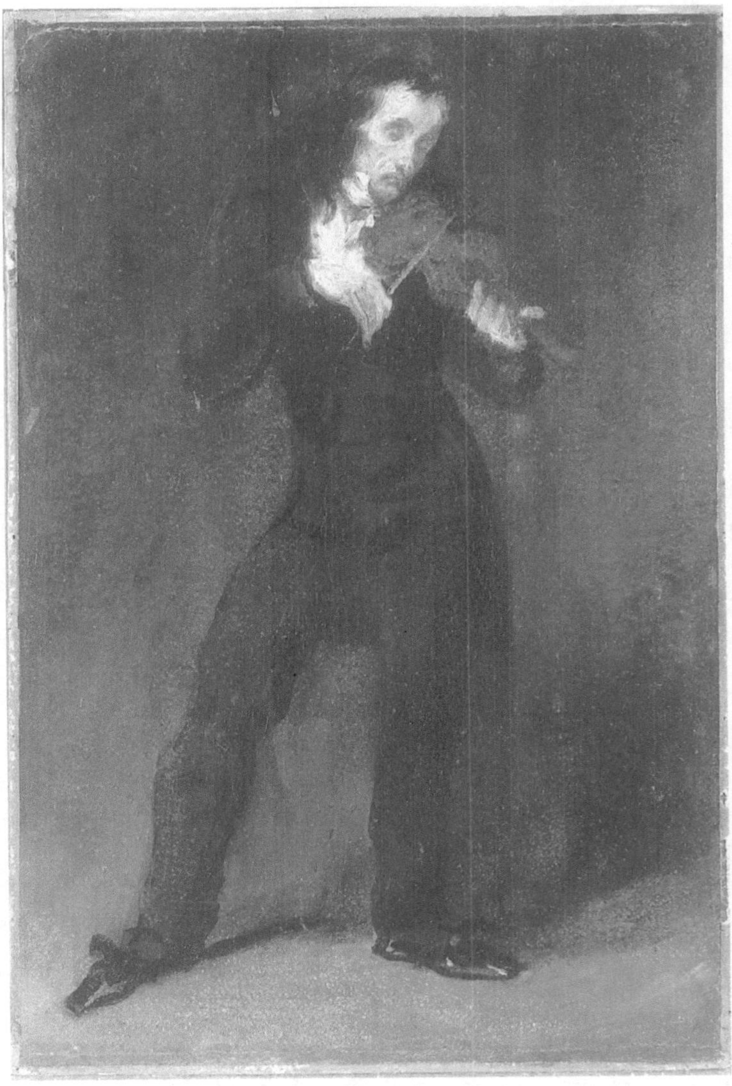

Figure 54. Eugène Delacroix, *Paganini* (1831). Oil on cardboard on wood panel. 17? × 11? inches. Courtesy Phillips Collection, Washington, D.C.

Bizet said simply: "Beethoven is not a human, he is a god" (Salmen 1983, 269). Paganini's virtuosity with the violin was seen by many as diabolical, although his flamboyant gestures, fantastical glissandos, and lighting execution were carefully calculated for effect (fig. 54). In literature, the most famous declaration of the artist's prophetic powers, remains the closing line of Shelley's *Defense of Poetry:* "Poets are the unacknowledged legislators of the world" (1930, 7:140).

As the "unacknowledged" in Shelley's peroration hints, however, the exalted ideal of the artist as seer was not universally accepted. A few writers even made fun of the more exaggerated prophetic claims. Thackeray mocked the Parisian "scribblers" of the 1830s who always have to tell you in their prefaces "of the *sacerdoce littéraire*" (Grana 1964, 57). Certainly, large swaths of the growing middle class remained immune to high-flown talk of the artist's calling, tending to see painters as manual workers and poets, novelists, and musicians as makers of amusing but dispensable frills. In a century of rapid commercial and industrial expansion, the elevation of the artistic vocation was in part a reaction to the utilitarianism and greed for which so many artists expressed disgust. One thinks of Dickens's portrayal of Gradgrind in *Hard Times,* driving fantasy and feeling out of his pupils' heads for the sake of fact, fact, fact. Later in the century, many artists tended to see themselves as belonging to a special subculture, with its own institutions, coteries, and conventions, a singular world of beauty and spiritual value within an uncomprehending, commercial society. Despite the numerous philistines (a term coined in Germany at this time), the *ideal* of the artist as a spiritual visionary endured and became the norm against which many artists, critics, and a part of the art public measured behavior and achievement.

The foundation for this exalted image of the artist had been laid in the eighteenth century with the ideal of the artist as genius of the creative imagination, an idea-complex now raised to new heights. Wordsworth's *Prelude* is nothing less than an autobiography of the poet's "Imagination . . . which in truth / Is but another name for absolute power" ([1850] 1959, 491). In France, Baudelaire declared the imagination "queen of the faculties," and "quasi-divine" (1986, 293; [1859] 1968, 184). Among poets and critics, Samuel Taylor Coleridge developed the most sophisticated theory of the imagination in his threefold distinction among a general imagination that all people share, the associative "fancy" of persons of mere talent or craft, and the truly creative imagination of the artist (1983).

Although the belief in the supreme power of the imagination received its most colorful expressions from romantic poets and critics, it was not merely a doctrine of romanticism. An 1825 Saint-Simonist dialogue comparing artists, scientists and industrialists announces: "*Artist* in this dialogue means the *man of imagination,* and it embraces at once the works of the painter, the musician, the poet, the man of letters" (Shroder 1961, 6). One can even find versions of the distinction between the reproductive and creative imagination in works as unromantic as Herbert Spencer's *Principles of Psychology* (1872), although Spencer, like John Stuart Mill, Auguste Comte, and others believed genius and imagination are characteristics of the best scientists as well as artists (Spencer [1872]

1881; Mill 1965; Comte [1851] 1968). Whatever the particular terms in which faith in creative imagination was expressed, it had become the central element in the modern ideal of the artist as genius.

Unfortunately, the nineteenth-century views on genius and imagination continued most of the gender prejudices of the eighteenth. "Women," Schopenhauer wrote, "can have remarkable talent, but not genius, for they always remain subjective" (1958, 2:392). John Ruskin contrasted man as "the creator, the discoverer" with woman whose "intellect is not for invention or creation but sweet ordering" (Parker and Pollock 1981, 9). Women who were obviously creative and artistically productive, such as George Eliot, George Sand, or Rosa Bonheur, were often regarded as not only socially deviant but also as physiological freaks. Even those males who had a somewhat more positive view of women often argued that female talent was suited only to crafts like embroidery or to minor arts like domestic poetry or flower painting (Comte 1968, 250). As Christine Battersby has pointed out, one of the striking things about the continuing insistence on the maleness of genius was that many of those who held to it also stressed the "feminine" aspects of creativity, such as heightened sensibility and the capacity to enter sympathetically into the feelings of others. But in order to create works of high art, it was claimed, this feminine sensibility had to be combined with the virile assertiveness of the male. These ideas received intermittent reinforcement from medical speculation and achieved a sort of apotheosis in Otto Weininger's notorious *Sex and Character* of 1903: "The man of genius possesses . . . the complete female in himself; but woman herself is only a part. . . . Femaleness can never include genius" (Battersby 1989, 112).

Apart from creative imagination, no article of faith has been more central to the modern ideal of the artist than freedom. The Russian composer Modeste Mussorgsky put it simply: "The Artist is a law unto himself" (Salmen 1983, 270). As the art market and the art public began to play an ever-increasing role in artistic recognition and financial success, the claims to autonomy became correspondingly more sweeping. The most dramatic effects of the market were in literature. As paper and printing technologies made books cheaper, newspapers from the 1840s onward dramatically lowered prices and increased readership by relying on advertising and serialized novels. By the late nineteenth century, the kind of multilevel culture with which we are now familiar began to emerge. One could identify a person's social class in part by what papers or books they read, what music they listened to, what plays they saw, what sort of pictures they preferred. In the case of the visual arts not only did the invention of lithography make relatively cheap reproductions available for the upper reaches of the working class, but there was also a growing middle class with the means of acquiring paintings and statues, if only copies. The emergence of not one but several art publics meant that a variety of styles and levels of art could coexist, but at any given level the tension between the ideal of independent genius and the demands of the market always had to be negotiated.

As important as the growth and differentiation of the art market was in fostering the rhetoric of autonomy, so was the parallel growth in the sheer number of aspiring writers, painters, and composers. The idea of Art as a high vocation and the relative prestige brought by academy exhibitions, the success of touring soloists like Paganini or Liszt, and the fame of a Balzac or Dickens contributed to a glut of would-be artists by the mid-nineteenth century (White and White 1965). The ritual complaint down to our day that artists are undeservedly neglected and unsupported may stem as much from a chronic oversupply as it does from the supposed philistinism of the middle class.

Attracted to the world of art by its spiritual aura, hero worship, and rhetoric of freedom, the aspiring artist in the nineteenth century found a ready-made discourse of "spirit versus money" to explain lack of success. Given such a climate, it is no wonder that George Sand would remember her decision to become a writer in just those terms: "To be an artist! Yes, I wanted to be one, not only to escape from the material jail, where property large or small, imprisons us in a circle of odious little preoccupations, but to isolate myself from the control of opinion . . . to live away from the prejudices of the world" (Pelles 1963, 18) (fig. 55). It is instructive to compare Sand's comment with the judgment of a decidedly unromantic source, the 1845 Select Committee of the British Parliament investigating institutions known as "art unions." Art unions were lotteries organized by artists in which the prizes were paintings. As one might expect, the paintings tended to be simple genre scenes that would sell the most tickets. The committee's report criticized the lotteries as degrading to the image of the artist: "Where the Artist himself consents to treat his profession as a trade, it is some time before the people will be induced to treat it as Art" (Gillett 1990, 49). It is no accident that art is here referred to as a "profession." Although it would be 1863 before Britain officially declared it so for census purposes, the ideal of a profession is that one's monetary reward is to be regarded as recompense for a general contribution to society not as payment for work done.

This deep-running belief in the artist's freedom manifested itself in a number of forms. The image of the bohemian who flaunts middle-class norms of ambition, decorum, and morality has retained a place in the popular imagination to this day, providing the standard caricature formula in the mass media. Its polar opposite in the nineteenth century was the figure of the dandy who

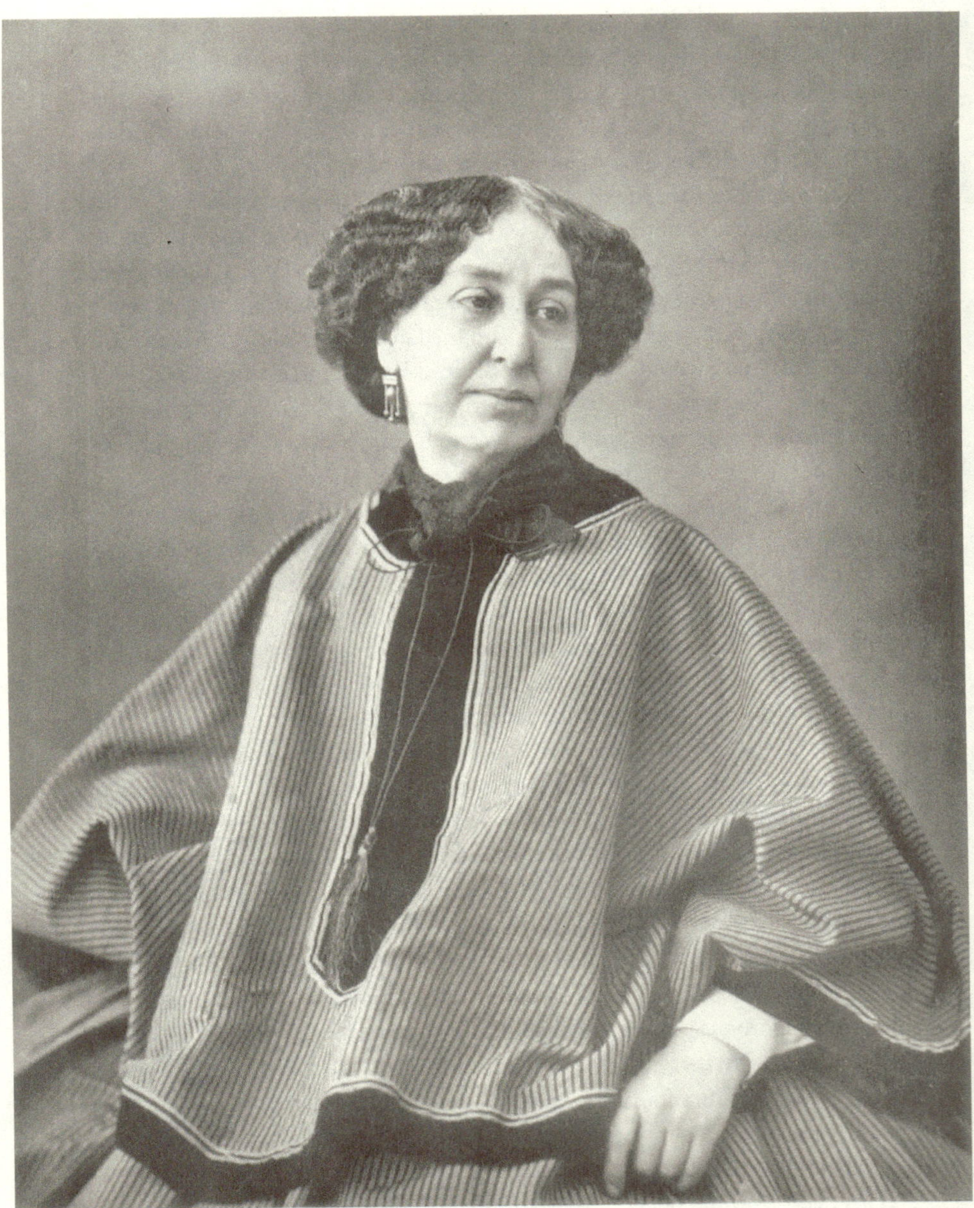

Figure 55. Nadar, *George Sand* (1866). Courtesy Gernsheim Collection, Harry Ransom Humanities Research Center, University of Texas at Austin. By this stage in her career Sand was very much the grand dame of French literature.

flaunts aristocratic superiority by outlandish dress and extravagant public gestures (Gautier's bright red waistcoat, Sand's riding habit and cigars, Wilde's green carnation, Gérard de Nerval's lobster on a leash). Although we owe the dandy to England and the bohemian to France, most British artists of the early nineteenth century could not afford to be dandies and were too desirous of social respectability to affect bohemianism. And although both the bohemian and dandy images eventually migrated to the rest of Europe and to the Americas, where they have remained part of the optional repertoire of artistic poses, they should not be mistaken for the normative belief in artistic autonomy shared by the sober middle-class writer and the bohemian poseur alike. The bohemian and the dandy are picturesque idioms of the modern system of art not structural components.

A more deeply rooted pair of stereotypes growing out of the ideal of artistic independence is that of sufferer and rebel. These are really the passive and aggressive sides of the same phenomenon, often dramatized as the "alienation of the Artist" (Shroder 1961, 38). The romantics tended to associate artistic rejection and suffering with the "curse of genius." Balzac intoned Cervantes and Dante in exile, Milton in poverty, Nicolas Poussin ignored, all "like Christ on the Cross . . . putting off mortal remains" (Honour 1979, 268). And Baudelaire claimed that we ought to say of Poe "what the catechism says of our God: 'He suffered greatly for us'" (1968, 147). Like the Christian saints, artists were to embrace their suffering as a sign of election. While some seemed to wallow in it, others saw rejection as a stimulus to defiance and heroic assertion. No one put the Promethean response better than the painter Théodore Géricault: "Everything that opposes the irresistible advance of genius irritates it, and gives it that fevered exaltation which conquers and dominates all, and which produces masterworks. Such are the men who are their nation's glory. External circumstance, poverty, or persecution will not slow their flight. Theirs is like the fire of a volcano which must absolutely burst into the open" (Eitner 1970, 101). Toward the end of the century, Paul Gauguin captured many of the contradictory facets of the artist's exalted image in a series of self-portraits, the most striking one showing him as both saint and Satan, although it also seems to have a touch of irony (fig. 56).

The reality of most artists' lives was rather more prosaic than Gauguin's. The Select Committee's complaint about artists' unions reflects the fact that many British painters of the early Victorian period sought commercial success by producing for the market in much the way seventeenth-century Dutch genre painters had. Most artists, writers, and composers tended to lead conventional

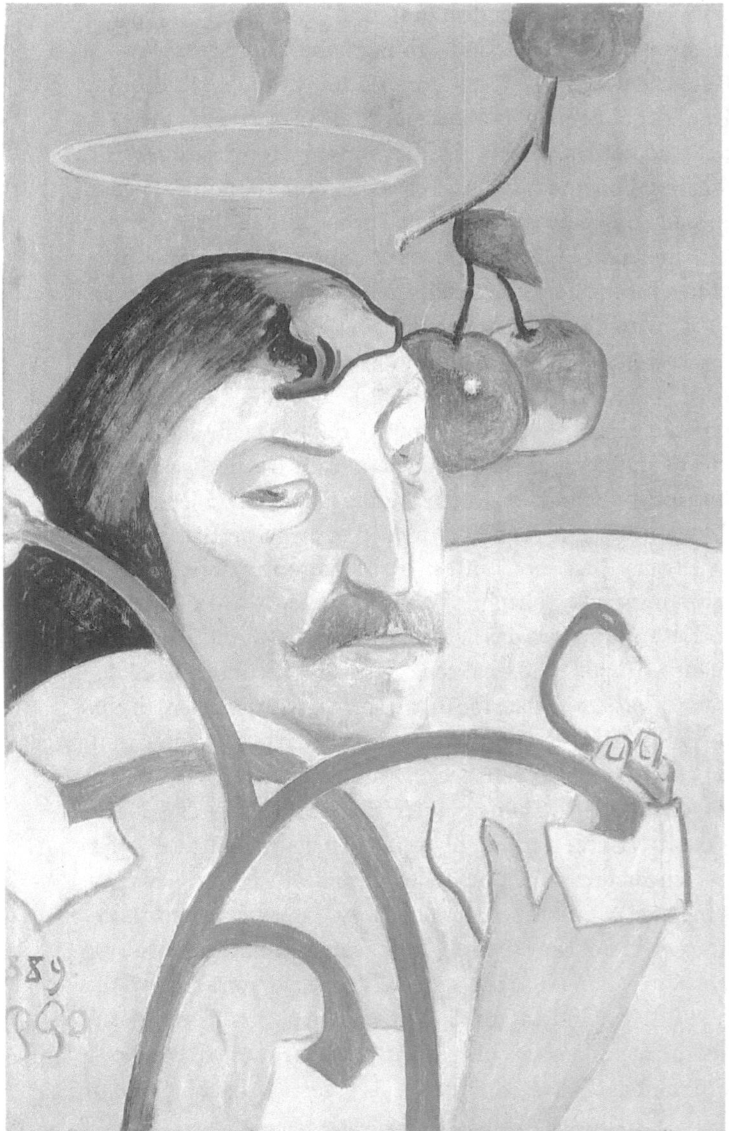

Figure 56. Paul Gauguin, *Self-Portrait* (1889). Courtesy National Gallery, Washington, D.C., Chester Dale Collection. Photograph © 2000 Board of Trustees, National Gallery of Art, Washington, D.C.

lives and seek social acceptance. By the 1860s, the income and status of both British and French painters had risen sufficiently for the profession to become a vehicle for modest social ascent. The economic and social rise of writers was even more dramatic thanks to the rapidly expanding literary market that could bring wealth and fame to a Sir Walter Scott or a Victor Hugo. But the image of the genius misunderstood and rejected was always there if needed, and it could be deliberately cultivated by a Whistler or a Wilde and has been regularly trotted out ever since.

Alongside these colorful images and poses, there was another tradition drawing, in part, on the old artisan/artist ideal: the artist as dedicated craftsman, sacrificing all for the perfection of the work, seeking to create a masterpiece. Flaubert's endless revisions and hesitations over every comma have become proverbial. But the willingness to work hard was a common theme among many nineteenth-century realists, such as Edmond and Jules de Goncourt or Émile Zola, and was embraced by many symbolists and aestheticists, as well as early modernists such as James Joyce or Thomas Mann. Although craftsmanship was always held subordinate to the supreme values of imagination and creativity, the sheer application of effort was one sign of artistic vocation—as compared to the nonchalance of the bohemian or dandy images—although dedicated craftsmanship could combine nicely with the secular saint-and-martyr syndrome. The Goncourts put it simply in a *Journal* entry of 1867: "The artist is a man who lives only for his art" (Goulemot and Oster 1992, 149).

By the time the symbolists in France and the aestheticists in Britain revived a version of "art for art's sake" at the end of the century, the notion of the artist's high spiritual calling and autonomy was a commonplace. By then independence of the materialistic bourgeoisie had come to embody superiority to the mob of the uncultured. Ironically, this was possible because the growth and differentiation of the market had by now created a network of publishers, impresarios, dealers, critics, and connoisseurs that could support this little world of ultrarefined high art (White and White 1965). The posture of "defiance" was, of course, reserved for the mass of the untutored middle and lower classes and increasingly took the form of producing works that were deliberately difficult if not obscure (Grivel 1989).

It was also in this period that the French military term "avant-garde" (literally, "advanced guard"), which had already become a metaphor for political radicalism, began to be used for the most advanced art. The term had been used by Saint-Simonian socialist visionaries in the 1820s and later by anarchists, such as Mikhail Bakunin, for instance, who called his paper, *L'avant-garde.* When applied to artists it suggested defiance of middle-class conventions and established art styles and institutions. By the early twentieth century, the idea of the artistic avant-garde had simply become conflated with modernism in its various forms and with the belief that the most important art, music, and poetry should be shockingly new. More recently, some social critics have argued that the only true avant-gardes of the past were the anti-art movements of the early twentieth century—dada or Russian constructivism, for instance (Bürger 1986).

## The Descent of the Artisan

If the image and status of the artist achieved new heights in the nineteenth century, that of the artisan or craftsperson sank even lower as many were forced to give up their independent workshops. Although the Industrial Revolution used to be talked of as if steam-powered machines swept away the old workshops system overnight, historians now describe a far more gradual process, varying from region to region, industry to industry. Nevertheless, the disappearance of tens of thousands of small workshops was inexorable even if it took most of the nineteenth century to complete. Traditional workshops had four characteristics that were steadily eroded and finally destroyed. First, they were intimate hierarchies based on the inventiveness, knowledge, and skill that together formed the "art" or "mystery" of the craft. Some crafts, such as shoemaking or glassblowing, required an apprenticeship of seven to ten years. Masters often worked alongside their journeymen and were expected to offer both guidance and protection to the apprentices, who usually lived on the premises. Second, although there was a certain division of labor in the larger shops, apprentices learned all aspects of production, and the individual journeyman often saw the entire product through from design to final finishing. In the early nineteenth century, the New Jersey hatter Henry Clark Wright, for instance, looked back on his career with "real satisfaction in being able to make a hat because I loved to contemplate the work, and because I felt pleasure in carrying through the various stages" (Laurie 1989, 36). Third, although the pace of work varied according to demand, it was generally leisurely, with time for frequent breaks and conversation—New England's shoemaking shops, for example, were known as centers of intellectual and political discussion. Finally, much of the work was still done with hand tools and by techniques that had been handed down from generation to generation.

Machines, steam power, and multistory, regimented factories came at later stages of industrialization; initially, there were simply larger shops and an increasing division of labor, followed by the introduction of a few machines at a time, then water and steam power and further mechanization until a point came where most of the old skills were no longer needed and the old way of organizing work impossible. In early nineteenth-century America, for example, most pottery for household use was dark-glazed, red earthenware made by small shops of one or two potters and a few assistants, all of whom might also engage in farming. Gradually, somewhat larger firms developed in the cities, and a few merchant importers of English stoneware decided to make their own fine ware and hired master potters to set up shops. Now the master potter was an employee, and the increasing size of the workforce allowed greater division of labor until the merchant owners began to control the organization of production and training. Such consolidations had already taken place in weaving, where the first factories appeared in England in the eighteenth century. In America, as late as the 1850s, small family weaving operations continued to thrive in some specialties, such as the making of coverlets (fig. 57).

In fields such as furniture making or shoemaking, the introduction of machinery not only sped up the pace and regimentation of work but eventually

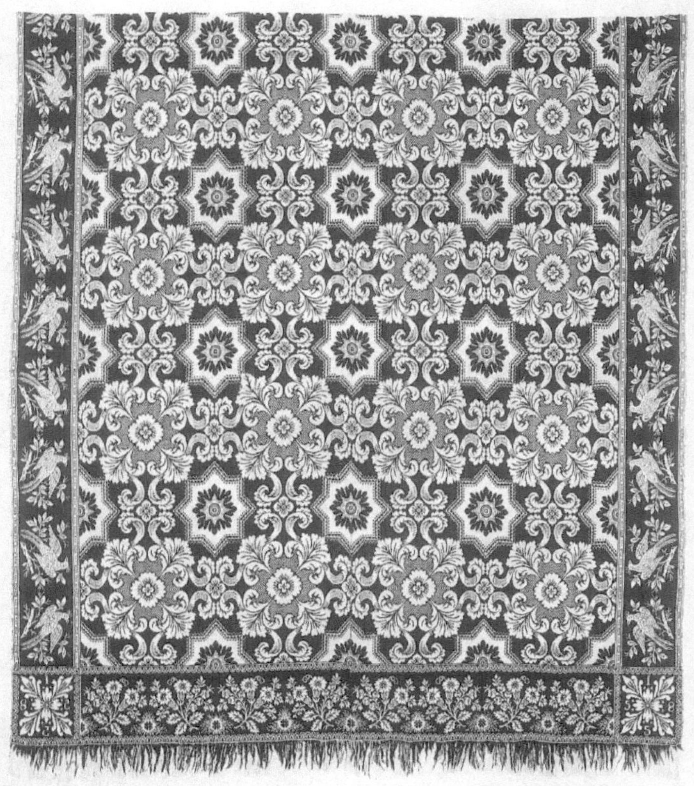

Figure 57. Coverlet (ca. 1855). This coverlet has a carpet medallion centerfield design, with birds along the side borders and a floral end border. Done by the Muir family of Greencastle, Indiana, using a Jacquard loom. Courtesy Illinois State Museum, Springfield. Marlin Roos photographer.

made judgment and skill with hand tools unnecessary. As late as the 1850s, cabinetmaking still had many "all around journeymen who turned rough-cut timber into elegant furniture," but they were a disappearing breed since more and more firms used one group of workers to cut uniform parts on steam-powered saws, had the pieces assembled by a second team, and finished by a third (Laurie 1989, 42). In Lynn, Massachusetts, down into the 1850s there were still many small shoemaking shops where five to six shoemakers, often entire families, worked together, each sitting at a bench. Between 1851 and 1883 one machine after another was invented for cutting, shaping, and stitching leather until there were forty distinct steps to making a shoe, none of which required an apprenticeship; the McKay Company claimed it could train an entire factory workforce on its machines in two days.

In a celebrated study of an 1895 strike by the glassmakers of Carmaux, a small town in southern France, Joan Wallach Scott explored a dramatic case of resistance to this destruction of the old craft ways. Because of the high cost of building a coal-fired glass-melting furnace, glassmaking was already organized into larger shops, often owned by a nobleman or wealthy bourgeois, such as the one at Carmaux, which made wine bottles. Yet within the Carmaux shop, the master craftsmen and journeymen controlled each step of production, including the pace of work and the quality of the product, and chose their own apprentices and assistants (usually family members). But by the 1880s the Carmaux glassworks not only had acquired new gas-powered furnaces that allowed around-the-clock production but had begun to use the new closed molds, which required far less judgment and dexterity for shaping bottles than the old open molds. The workers began to feel a loss of pride and power, and one report expressed fears that, although mechanization reduced fatigue, by "depriving glassworkers of difficult tasks we will destroy their skill as well as the artistic talents of which glassworkers have the right to be proud" (Scott 1974, 83). The strike of 1895 was ultimately over the survival of glassblowing as a skilled craft. The strike was crushed, most union members fired, and less-skilled workers trained to replace them. Yet even had the union won, a new invention in 1900 spelled the doom of glass bottle making as a craft: the Boucher blowing machine, which required only a few days training and produced more uniform bottles.

As traditional methods were displaced in glassblowing, weaving, shoemaking, and woodworking, many artisans were reduced to machine operators. Even so, some masters and journeymen were able to hang on with diminished income until they retired or moved to less industrialized regions. In North America, the visiting Alexis de Tocqueville was impressed by the thousands of small shops he saw in the 1830s, and there were still many in existence a hundred years later. As a boy in the late 1940s, I remember watching with fascination the blacksmiths in my grandparent's small Kansas farm town, sharpening plowshares, repairing machinery, and making ornamental ironwork. In the same era, cities such as Chicago or New York still had neighborhood bakers, tailors, and jewelry makers. Even as late as the 1990s, the independent artisan bakers of Paris, with their small family *boulangeries,* were successfully fighting off the arrival of chain operators. Despite such scattered survivals into the age of malls and franchises, the majority of the tens of thousands of small workshops and their handcraft ethos of the nineteenth century had disappeared by 1914.

If older craftspeople in the nineteenth century retired or moved to avoid becoming factory operatives, their children seemed to face the choice of submission to factory regimen or giving up the family craft tradition. Yet recent research has revealed a third outlet for craftspeople in the nineteenth century: the continued need for artistic skills in many of the newly mechanized factories themselves. Factories producing for the booming household demand in textiles, wallpaper, floor coverings, ceramics, and ironwork needed not only designers but also people who could handle the intermediate steps of applying the designs in machine production. British roller printing of calicoes in the 1830s, for example, required not only a constant flow of new patterns but at least four types of skilled workers to transfer them to the machine as well. Similarly, the development of electroplating for cast-iron household wares such as stoves, lighting fixtures, or tableware required modelers, dye sinkers, and engravers able to translate flat designs into three dimensions. Soon the demand for skilled workers who understood design and how to transfer it to mechanical processes could not be met simply by hiring existing journeymen from the workshops. As a result, there was a widespread discussion in Britain and elsewhere about how to provide arts education for workers, reflected first in British workers' own demand for classes in drawing and design at the new mechanics institutes, then in the creation of government schools of design from 1837 on (Schmiechen 1995; Goldstein 1996).

These new "art-laborers," as Schmiechen calls them, were neither the old-style craftsperson of the workshops nor autonomous artists but a new kind of artisan. Yet even as a relatively skilled elite among the majority of factory workers, they were still employees, their work pace and assignments subject to the employer's demands. The pure designers, especially those working under outside contracts, generally stood apart from the art workers who did the intermediate stages of application within the factory; yet not even the designers were viewed as independent artist-creators but, rather, occupied a status at the upper end of what were now called the "applied arts." In Europe, this extension of the artist-versus-artisan pattern was especially apparent in the creation of separate schools and museums for applied or decorative arts to parallel the academies and museums of fine art. The South Kensington Museum (now the Victoria and Albert) opened in 1862, and other museums of "applied arts" soon appeared in Vienna (1864), Paris (1864), and Berlin (1867) as part of a competitive "art and industry" movement (Richards 1927; Brunhammer 1992). In the United States, the split between fine art and craft was reflected in the internal organization of museums; painting and sculpture had their own separate departments, organized by period or culture, but work in clay, glass, wood, metal, and fiber was often lumped together in a department of decorative or applied arts. Established artists might occasionally design for private or industrial clients without sacrificing their elevated spiritual image as free and genial creators (Whistler's *Peacock Room*), but the image of the artisan or craftsperson remained associated with imitation, dependency, trade, and now the factory.

As the gap between artist and craftsperson increased, so did the tension within the one fine art profession still identified with making for a purpose: architecture. Although practicing architects could not turn their backs completely on serving human needs, many experienced a deep conflict between the ideal of the architect as autonomous artist, creating works for visual contemplation, and the architect as the designer of useful structures. Many early nineteenth-century architects, such as Karl Friedrich Schinkel, for example, began to publish collections of both their built and unbuilt designs, arranged without commentary as if they were fine engravings (fig. 58). Schinkel's writings on architecture show him torn between the fine art side and the craft side of the profession, claiming that although many aspects of architecture remained "a technical craft," architecture is a fine art and the architect's real task is to discover the "true aesthetic element" (Kruft 1994, 300). By contrast, Gottfried Semper, without denying the importance of beautiful forms, stressed the connections between architecture and the crafts, placing a high value on truth to materials and function (Semper 1989). In France, the architectural theorist Eugène-Emmanuel Viollet-le-Duc took a position similar to Semper's, emphasizing the relation of architectural form to purpose, materials, and construction techniques, something the architect Henri Labrouste beautifully demonstrated in his iron and glass reading room and top-lit stack cage of the Bibliothèque Nationale in 1868.

If machine technologies tended to reduce the skilled crafts of weaving, shoemaking, or glassblowing to routine labor, the new construction materials and techniques of iron, glass, and reinforced concrete required of the architect an

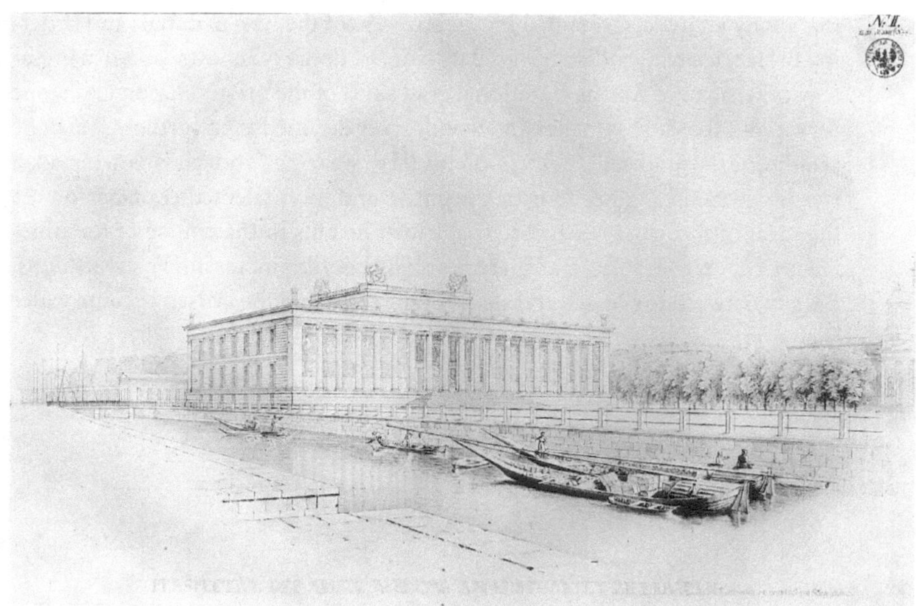

Figure 58. Karl Friedrich Schinkel, *Perspective View of the New Museum to Be Built in the Pleasure Garden* (1823–25). The building that was erected in Berlin from Schinkel's plans, now known as the Altes Museum, is considered a key monument of German neoclassicism. Courtesy Bildarchiv Preussischer Kulturbesitz, Berlin.

engineer's grasp of structural principles and created an even greater tension between the art and craft aspects of architecture. Nothing better illustrates this increased tension than the late nineteenth-century English debate over the call for professional engineering standards for architects. Many architects and art critics vehemently resisted these efforts in the name of fine art and the artist's autonomy, with even John Ruskin and William Morris joining the "antiengineering" side. After the Royal Institute of British Architects began requiring examinations for membership in 1887 and several Registration Bills came before Parliament, a letter to *The Times,* signed by seventy leading architects and artists, declared that "artistic qualifications . . . really make the architect" and these cannot be tested by examination. The next year, these views were vigorously defended in a collection of essays, aptly entitled *Architecture: A Profession or an Art?* (Wilton-Ely, 1977, 204).

By the end of the nineteenth century, those who thought of the architect primarily as an artist would come to view iron, glass, and reinforced concrete simply as new opportunities for individual artistic expression. But at the same time that many architects were making creative use of the new materials and ordering prefabricated wood or iron pillars, panels, doors, windows, and ornamental work, the need for the traditional craft skills of the master mason and stone carver and the cabinetmaker and woodcarver declined even further. Thus, the building arts followed the arts of pottery, weaving, and glassblowing in a steadily diminishing need for the inventive and multitalented craftsperson. As the ideal of the artist reached new spiritual heights in the course of the nineteenth century and the craftsperson's skills became increasingly superfluous, the gap between the image and status of the artist and the artisan became wider than ever.

CHAPTER 12

# Silences

## *Triumph of the Aesthetic*

IN ÉMILE ZOLA'S novel *L'assommoir* (1877), a working-class wedding party decides to celebrate by a visit to the Louvre, thinking the edifying majesty of the art museum accords well with the occasion. Only one of them has been in an art museum before and they are overwhelmed by the finely dressed guards, the sumptuous surroundings, the mirror finish of the parquet floors, the heavy gold frames. When they come on Ruben's painting of a country festival *(The Kermis),* showing drunken, vomiting, urinating peasants, many lewdly grabbing each other, the women "utter little cries; then turn away blushing deeply." The men stare and snicker, "looking closer for obscene details" ([1877] 1965, 92; [1877] 1995, 78). Finally, the wedding party gets lost in the labyrinth of galleries, and they scurry from room to room, numbed by the endless rows of paintings, etchings, drawings, statues, and cases full of figurines. Zola's working-class wedding party whirling through the Louvre strikes us as comic because they lack the rudiments of what we believe necessary to appreciating museum art—some knowledge of art history, some sense of aesthetic distance. They give way to their instinctive sensual or moral reactions and are captivated by eroticism or the riches of gold frames and mirror-finished floors. Yet despite their chatter and scurrying, they at least behave with a certain respect, no singing, shouting, or game playing of the kind that had to be forbidden seventy-five years before.

### Learning Aesthetic Behavior

In America, where the great public museums only began to appear in the 1870s, there is evidence that it took more time to teach visitors both proper respect and the beginnings of an aesthetic response. By 1897, however, the director of New York's Metropolitan Museum could proudly describe the success of vigilance, admonitions, and a few ejections: "You do not see any more persons in the picture galleries blowing their nose with their fingers; no more dogs brought in . . . no more spitting tobacco juice on the gallery floors . . . no more nurses taking children to some corner to defile the floors . . . no more whistling, singing, or calling aloud" (Tomkins 1989, 84–85). But the issue soon became not just middle-class decorum but the proper aesthetic attitude in the "temple of Art," as well. Even art education, always an aim of museums since the eighteenth century, was not enough. In the 1890s, many American art museums, such as those in Boston and Chicago, still exhibited plaster casts of ancient sculptures but finally put them in storage after younger curators and critics argued that only the finest "original" works belonged in the museum. The first aim of an art museum, the assistant director at Boston declared in 1903, is to "maintain a high standard of aesthetic taste" by choosing objects for their "aesthetic quality" and, thereby, afford its visitors "the pleasure derived from a contemplation of the perfect" (Whitehall 1970, 1:183, 201).

Similar behavioral norms were taught theater and concert audiences, although the lessons were aided by a gradual separation of the "legitimate" theaters and concert halls from venues for farce, melodrama, and popular music. In Europe Honoré Daumier caught the passionate reactions of lower-middle-class theater audiences in his "A Literary Discussion in the Second Balcony" (fig. 59). Lawrence Levine has recently traced the gradual separation of fine art theater from popular theater in America by examining the fortunes of Shakespeare in the nineteenth century. For the first two-thirds of the century, Shakespeare's plays were not only the most frequently performed but also drew large and socially varied crowds, many of whom stamped their feet, whistled, shouted, and demanded instant encores. One reason Shakespeare appealed to such a broad audience was the wholesale alteration of his plays that had begun in the eighteenth century, leaving some versions of *Richard III* with one-third fewer lines and *King Lear* with a happy ending in which both Cordelia and Lear live on! Nineteenth-century promoters also interspersed the acts with other entertainments and usually followed the play with a farce to assure an enthusiastic and demonstrative response. Naturally, the upper classes who sat in the orchestra and boxes were not always happy with the their clamorous inferiors in the balconies, especially when pelted with apple cores (Levine 1988).

Class tensions mixed with cultural differences throughout the century, sometimes to tragic effect, as in the Astor Place Riot of 1849. Twenty-two people were killed when the militia fired into a crowd attempting to storm the Astor Theater and break up a performance of *Macbeth* by the snobbish English actor William Charles Macready. Macready's highly publicized insults to America's noisy, plebeian audiences had ignited popular anger, whereas the same kind of gallery crowds gave standing ovations to Macready's American rival, Edwin Forrest, whose stentorian delivery was enormously popular. Yet only a dozen years later, the editor of *Harper's* derided Forrest's "rant, roar, and rigmarole"

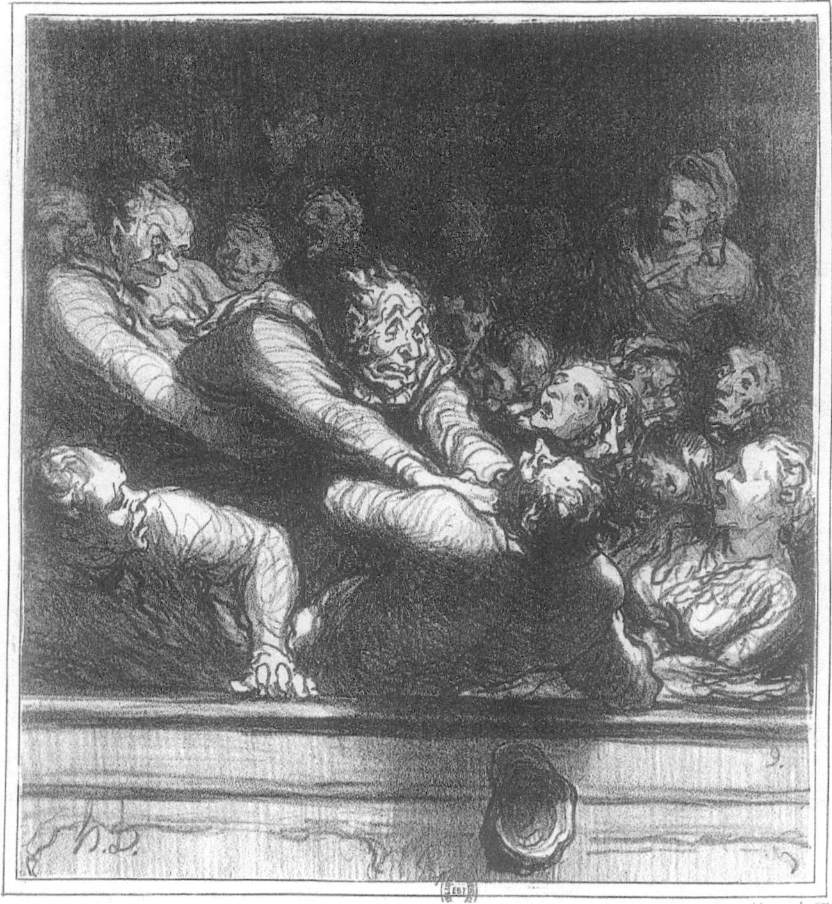

Figure 59. Honoré Daumier, *A Literary Discussion in the Second Balcony* (1864). Courtesy Bibliothèque Nationale, Paris. In Europe as in America the nineteenth-century lower classes took their theater seriously.

as good only for wringing tears out of working-class girls but praised the elegant performances of Edwin Booth for eliciting "refined attention rather than eager interest" (Levine 1988, 59). By the second half of the century, separate theaters for "art" performances began to appear in most of the larger American cities. By the 1890s, the theater audience had divided, and Shakespeare was performed uncut in "legitimate" theaters before silent and respectful audiences. Even if the term "aesthetic" was not always used to distinguish the "refined attention" of the art theater from the "eager interest" of popular halls, a kind of

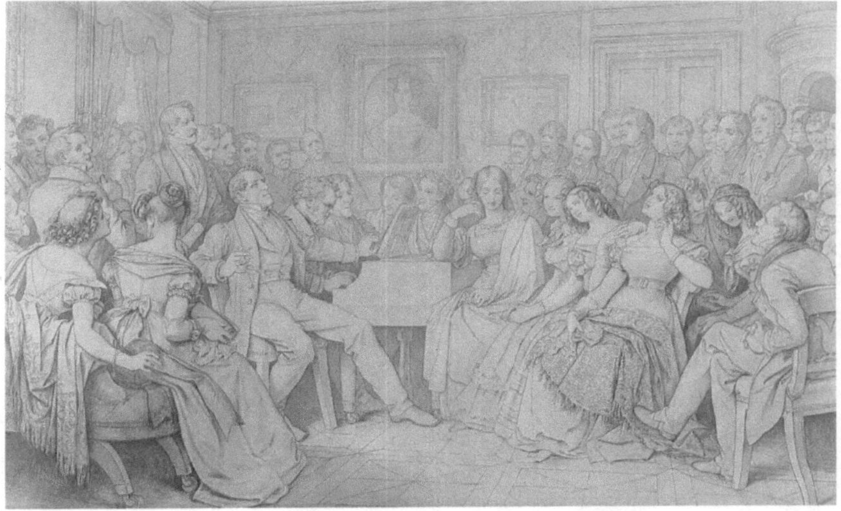

Figure 60. Moritz von Schwind, *An Evening at Baron Spaun's* (1868). Historisches Museum der Stadt Wien, Vienna. Courtesy Erich Lessing/Art Resource, New York. Franz Schubert is at the piano, tenor Johann Michael Vogl is singing.

aesthetic *behavior* was being inculcated and those unwilling to adopt it either were expelled or went elsewhere.

A similar division occurred in music. As William Weber has shown, there was a veritable "concert explosion" in Europe from 1830 to 1848, although in this case led entirely by the upper classes, who were divided in their tastes. One group was especially involved in salon concerts, often organized by women and held in fine homes. They favored the relatively popular music transcribed from opera or the symphonic repertoire adapted for virtuosos such as Liszt. Here was an art world where women—who played the piano themselves and oversaw their children's lessons—were allowed to take the lead (fig. 60). Another part of the upper classes prided themselves on their knowledge of the classical symphony tradition of Haydn, Mozart, and Beethoven and preferred concert hall performances faithful to the composer's text. This group was dominated by men who tended to regard their kind of music as "serious" art and looked down on the salon concerts and popular soloists. Weber suggests that the gradual merger of these two upper-class groups under the dominance of the male-led classical tendency marked the emergence of the modern "serious" music system in Europe. As a result, a patriarchal upper class controlled the emerging concert institutions in a way that subordinated the role of women and excluded the lower social ranks both programmatically and economically (Weber 1975).[1]

At the same time that this little world of fine art music was drawing into itself, other concerts, aimed at a broader spectrum of the middle and lower classes, were developing out of the eighteenth-century choral societies and promenade concerts, the latter providing an attractive setting where people could drink, smoke, talk, and walk about. Although a few people of the lower ranks might save up to attend a "classical" concert and the upper classes might drop in on choral performances or promenades, the social and cultural divisions were becoming well marked as the century wore on. There were also new kinds of commercial musical institutions that flourished in the rapidly growing urban centers, such as the café concert in Paris (fig. 61). Although people commented on the socially mixed audiences who frequented the café concerts in the 1870s and 1880s, these establishments seem to have been predominantly lower-middle-class venues, where singers expressed an idealized version of the life of "the people" in a music that both fascinated and alarmed the cultural elite who also frequented the symphony and opera (Clark 1984). In America, the gradual segregation of higher and lower forms of instrumental music took slightly different forms. The omnipresent community "band" played not only marches and polkas but also excerpts from operas and symphonic selections from

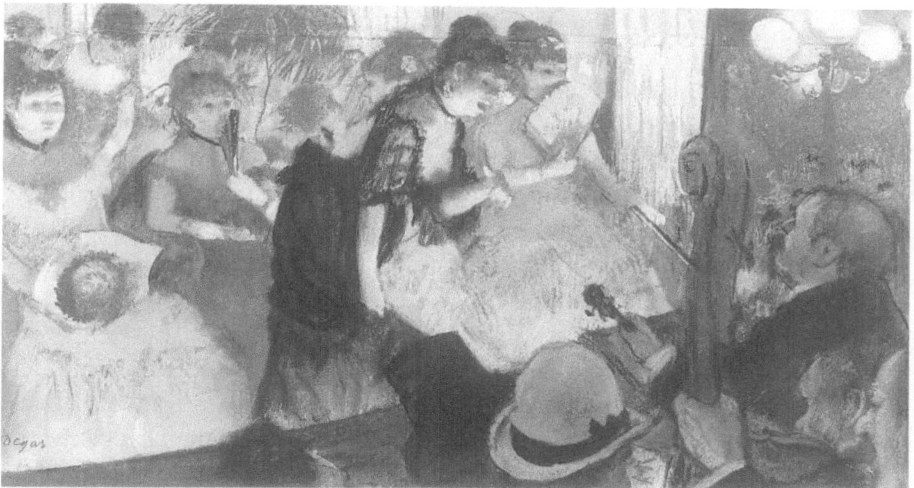


Figure 61. Edgar Degas, *Cabaret* (1882); 9¼ × 17 inches, pastel over monotype. Courtesy Corcoran Gallery of Art, Washington, D.C., William A. Clark Collection. (26.72.)

Haydn. As late as 1873, a Boston critic lamented the absence of a permanent symphony in his city to keep alive "acquaintance with the great unquestioned masterworks" (Levine 1988, 120). The symphony orchestras that were founded in city after city across America in the latter half of the nineteenth century were in fact dedicated to becoming just such "museums of musical works."

If the promenade concert in Europe or popular band music in America mixed genres and allowed freer behavior in a relaxed setting, the concerts of the cultured classes were clearly Art rituals in which a special attitude and silent decorum was expected. Yet even the nineteenth-century upper-class audience had to be "trained in the art of listening" (Gay 1995, 19). In 1803, Goethe, who oversaw the court theater in Weimar, demanded that shouting or hissing stop and that audiences limit themselves to applause at the end of the performance.[2] Complaints about talking and moving about during concerts continued throughout the century, but critics, symphony boards, and conductors kept after the audiences. The American conductor Theodore Thomas was famous for staring down talkers and even stopping the orchestra and raising his hands for silence. Here again, the campaign to quiet audiences was not simply about decorum but about the proper response to fine art. As the music critic Edward Baxter Perry put it, audiences must rise above "mere sensuous pleasure or superficial enjoyment, to a higher . . . spiritual aesthetic gratification" (Levine 1988, 134).

In the realm of literature, questions of public behavior did not arise in the same way as music, although the development of "legitimate" theaters in which Shakespeare's plays were reverently treated as sacred texts offers one parallel. The literary equivalent of the legitimate theater, the concert hall, or the art museum eventually became the college or university literature course and literature anthology. What needed to be "silenced" in the reading of literary works of art was not physical sound or bodily restlessness but the intrusive noise of thrill or amusement or political and moral ideas. People had to learn to attend to the purely aesthetic qualities of the literary work and not simply consume it they way they did popular genres.

Although the ideas and institutions of art, artist, and aesthetic were largely established by the 1830s, it took the rest of the century to separate completely fine art and popular art institutions and to teach the upwardly mobile middle classes the appropriate aesthetic behaviors. What Jacques Attali has said of the evolution of music in the eighteenth and early nineteenth centuries could be applied to all the fine arts: "When the concert hall performance replaced the popular festival and the private concert at court . . . the attitude toward music changed profoundly: in ritual it was one element in the totality of life;

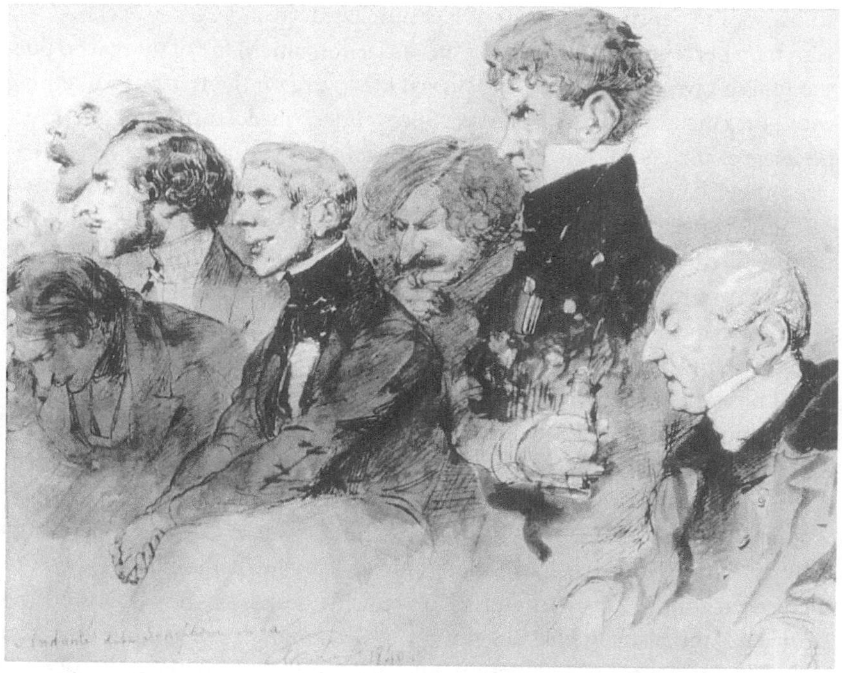

Figure 62. Eugène Lami, *First Hearing of Beethoven's Seventh Symphony* (1840). Courtesy Musée de la Musique, Conservatoire National Supérieur de Musique et de Danse de Paris. Photograph by J.-M. Angles.

in the concerts of the nobility or popular festivals it was still part of a mode of sociality... in the concerts of the bourgeoisie ... the silence greeting the musicians was what created music and gave it an autonomous existence" (Attali 1985, 46) (fig. 62).

## The Rise of the Aesthetic and the Decline of Beauty

If it took a long effort to inculcate a behavior of silent and reverent attention, it also took a long time for the term "aesthetic" to be regularly used for it outside of Germany where it had originated.[3] But more important than the term, was the issue of whether there was, in fact, a special "aesthetic" faculty and what its characteristics were. The general belief in a distinct aesthetic faculty seems to have been widely accepted by the 1850s and even gave rise to a psychological "science" of aesthetics, which has continued its fitful course into our own day. One branch of it was carried on in an empirical vein by Hermann Helmholz's studies of the neurological basis of pleasure in music and Gustav Fechner's research on perceptual preferences in the visual domain. Many of those who pursued these investigations clearly believed they were on the track of something wired into the human brain. Herbert Spencer described a distinct aesthetic experience at the end of his *Principles of Psychology* (1872) and Grant Allen analyzed the differentia of the "aesthetic feelings" from a Darwinian perspective, defining its principle as "Maximum of Stimulation with the Minimum of Fatigue or Waste" (Allen 1877, 39; Spencer [1872] 1881, 2:623–48).

If we turn from the general idea that there is a distinctive aesthetic mode of experience to nineteenth-century beliefs about the *characteristics* of the aesthetic, we find a wide range of views. Some writers stressed sensory or emotional pleasure, while others made central such qualities as imagination, intuition, empathy, or intellectual insight. Although the term "disinterestedness" has never been part of everyday talk about the fine arts, the general idea of an unprejudiced, contemplative attitude toward art continued to make its way among both the public and those who wrote about art. Many nineteenth-century writers who used "disinterestedness" intended the weaker sense of merely excluding crassly utilitarian or selfish interests. Others followed the stronger Kantian or Schillerian notion of a contemplative attitude that sets aside any direct theoretical or moral interests. Naturally, both the moderate and strong versions of disinterestedness admitted degrees of exclusion. Victor Cousin and Théodore Jouffroy developed a French version of Schiller's position, arguing that even though Art indirectly inculcates morality and puts us in touch with the absolute, "it does not try to do so, it does not pose that as its aim.... There must be religion for religion, morality for morality, as art for art" (Bénichou 1973, 258). Of course, there were others who denied even Matthew Arnold's belief in a "subtle and indirect effect" on morals (1962, 270). By 1868 Algernon Swinburne, paraphrasing Scripture, could declare: "Art for Art's sake first of all, and afterward the rest shall be added to her... but from the man who falls to artistic work with a moral purpose shall be taken away even that which he has" (Warner and Hough 1983, 237). By the end of the century small groups of intellectuals and artists had transformed the idea of the aesthetic from the notion of a disinterested faculty for experiencing fine art into an ideal of existence. In a way, the "aestheticization" of life proposed by many of the aestheticists, such as Oscar Wilde, was simply an extension of the superiority of the artist's sensibility into every sphere—although this rejection of mundane instrumentality could take many forms, from the languorous sensuality of Pater to the Promethean overflow of Nietzsche.

We cannot leave the topic of the nature of aesthetic experience without noting one of the most striking differences between nineteenth- and twentieth-century discussions: the near disappearance of beauty as a central concept of aesthetics since the 1950s. The roots of beauty's decline go back to the end of the eighteenth century and the emergence of the idea of the aesthetic itself. As we have seen, eighteenth-century theorists of taste not only were interested in beauty but developed concepts of the sublime, the picturesque, and the novel as well. Beauty, once the sole epithet for highest attainment in the arts, now had several rivals, and one of them, the sublime, was believed by many writers of the eighteenth and nineteenth centuries to be a deeper and more powerful experience. Various nineteenth-century artists and critics added still other values and experiences, such as the grotesque (Hugo), the strange (Baudelaire), the real (Flaubert), and the true (Zola), which they sometimes took to be more forceful than beauty. But there were also problems inherent in the concept of beauty itself. On the one hand, it was too closely associated with academicism and traditional criteria of ideal imitation, harmony, proportion, and unity. On the other hand, it was too mixed up with everyday notions of prettiness and praise—a beautiful horse, a beautiful shot, a beautiful investment. Although Schiller spoke of beauty along with fine art as humanity's salvation in the *Aesthetic Letters* of 1793, a few years later he was writing to Goethe that "beauty" had become so problematic that it should perhaps be "dismissed from circulation" (Beardsley 1975, 228). In England, Richard Payne Knight lamented that "the word Beauty is . . . applied indiscriminately to almost anything that is pleasing" (1808, 9). Nevertheless, most nineteenth- and early twentieth-century critics and philosophers from Hegel to George Santayana continued to use "beauty" as the overarching term for the highest aesthetic value, and aesthetics itself was often defined simply as the theory of beauty. The history and prestige of "beauty" was such that, like "Art," it remained the name for whatever writers found most precious and transcendent in felt experience. Not until the full implications of modernism and the early twentieth-century anti-art movements had made themselves felt was "beauty" relegated to a minor role in critical and philosophical discourse on the arts.

## The Problem of Art and Society

When historians of aesthetics or literary theory come to the nineteenth century, they often reserve a section of their works for the problem of "art and society." This issue is typically described in terms of a battle between those who believed in "art for art's sake" (Gautier, Baudelaire, Whistler, Wilde) and those who believed in the "social responsibility of art" (Courbet, Proudhon, Ruskin, Tolstoy). Some historians have found it necessary to explain why it was that a "theme that had not been given such serious attention between Plato and Schiller" should suddenly become so urgent (Beardsley 1975, 299). The reader who has followed my argument up to this point will have no difficulty understanding one reason why the art and society problem in this broad sense did not receive "serious attention" up to Schiller. It did not because it could not. No one between Plato and Schiller wrestled with the problem of Art and society in this generalized form because they had no concept of Art as a distinct realm or social subsystem whose relation to society needed to be conceptualized. Only *after* fine art was constructed as a set of canonical disciplines and specialized institutions that were then reified as an autonomous domain could one ask what function the realm of Art should play within the larger society.

During the first half of the nineteenth century, there was only occasional talk of "Art for Art's sake" (Gautier), whereas almost everyone still believed that serious works of art should embody a significant moral content, even if some people thought of artworks as having only an indirect moral effect. The full implications of the idea of art as an autonomous realm did not become apparent until near the end of the century. Even so, we can trace the development of a tendency to avoid direct engagement with political and moral issues. This retreat appeared in different countries at different times and was often related to the violent class conflicts of the period. Although there were always writers, painters, and composers who spoke to moral and political questions, the deeper problem was that the relative autonomy of the fine art institutions tended to neutralize social and political content by confining art works within the "world" of art.

The turn from social and political concerns seems to have occurred in the Germanies earlier than elsewhere. Although Schiller and Goethe never completely abandoned the hope that art might improve society, by the late 1790s, both had given up the eighteenth-century view of art as a means of public enlightenment. Schiller could even write in 1803 that Art should "totally shut itself off from the real world" (Berghahn 1988, 96). Many saw art as fundamentally alien to a society propelled by commerce and industry. Moreover, following the collapse of the Napoleonic empire, the various absolute monarchies of Central and Eastern Europe vigilantly exiled or imprisoned most social and political dissenters, including those who championed a politically engaged art, such as Heine. This made it easier for the idea of a completely autonomous art to gain early acceptance. The rest of society might be dominated by the police power and by middle-class materialism, but Art could be a refuge where the human spirit might roam freely (Schulte-Sasse 1988).

In France, in contrast, many romantic poets, painters, and composers remained politically engaged (whether as royalists or republicans) and saw art as a social instrument right up through the Revolution of 1848, when the poet Alphonse de Lamartine's role as head of the failed provisional government symbolized Art's failure in politics. The collapse of the idealism of 1848 and the political repression under Napoleon III blunted many artists' political involvement (with brilliant exceptions, such as Victor Hugo and Gustave Courbet) and led them to a preoccupation with issues within the world of art. Another reason for the decline of political concern was the concurrent growth of the art world itself. After 1848 there was a steady expansion of specialized art institutions, such as the dealer-critic-curator-collector complex for painting and similar support complexes for music and literature. Now success as a writer, composer, or painter meant recognition by one of these art, music, or literary worlds, which were increasingly apolitical as a locus of upper-middle-class leisure activity. Although the deep cleavages in French society (e.g., the Dreyfus Affair) could still draw artists and writers such as Zola into its conflicts as individuals, the worlds of art, music, and literature had taken on a life of their own.

In Britain, as in France, many of the early romantics expressed their social and political engagement through their work, and later, the Victorians, led by Carlyle, Ruskin, and George Eliot, never doubted the high moral and social purpose of Art in reforming and beautifying a crassly utilitarian and materialistic society. One can even find a strain of "aesthetic democracy" in people associated with the aestheticst movement like Walter Pater and Oscar Wilde (Dowling 1996). But once the modern discourse of fine art, artist, and aesthetic was firmly established in Britain around mid-century, the inherent tension between Art as a distinct institution and its role as moral or social educator began to be increasingly acknowledged. The subsequent emergence of a belief in the absolute autonomy of art in some circles went hand in hand with the rise in status of the artist and the growth and privatization of the various art worlds. Late in the century when aestheticists such as Wilde or formalist critics such as Roger Fry attacked Victorian moralism in art, they often argued that artworks should be seen strictly in terms of their relation to the art world.

To follow out the arguments between the proponents of Art for Art's sake and those who believed in the social responsibility of art would take us beyond our main subject and into the details of the history of aesthetics and art or literary theory. What is relevant to our theme is that both sides in these debates were often prisoners of the same regulative polarities of art. The declarations of a Gautier, Wilde, or Bell that Art has nothing to do with morality, politics, or "worldly" life but exists only for itself are a sort of reverse image of the declarations of a Proudhon, Tolstoy, and some marxists that Art exists primarily to serve humanity, morality, or the revolution. The extreme expressions of both positions assumed that Art is in fact an independent realm that has an external relation to the rest of society. For the one side, Art became a spiritual world of its own into which the aesthetically sensitive might retreat from a sordid, materialistic society; for the other Art was seen as a powerful instrument of communication for changing that society. Few nineteenth-century writers attacked the problem at its root: the regulative polarities of the modern system of art. Eventually, artists and critics who shared John Ruskin's or George Eliot's belief in a more intimate connection between works of art and the social good would have to challenge the underlying polarities of the fine art system.

PART V

# Beyond Fine Art and Craft

## Overview

My alternative story of the great division that produced the modern system of the fine arts is largely complete. Obviously, there was no fixed point at which all the main elements of the system were generally accepted. Just as there were anticipations of modern ideals of the artistic vocation from the Renaissance on, so remnants of the old art/craft system have endured. But the period from roughly 1800 to 1830 seems to have been the moment of final consolidation and elevation. Certainly, by the mid-nineteenth century, the term "art" had not only come to designate a category of fine arts (poetry, painting, music, etc.) but also an autonomous realm of works and performances, values and institutions. Art could now be spoken of as a kind of metaphysical essence, whether conceived in the technical terms of idealist or vitalist philosophies or in the more general way that Comte or Tolstoy wrote of it. In either case a reified Art was now something one could live and die for and talk about endlessly, the art Marcel Proust later invoked with such pathos in *Time Regained.* Correspondingly, the ideal of the artist as creator was viewed as a kind of religious calling, sometimes raised to the status of prophet and priest but also allowing for the poses of dandy or bohemian alongside martyr and rebel. Finally, "works of art," as the fixed creations of inspired imagination, were to be reverently attended to aesthetically, "for themselves," a state of mind and behavior steadily inculcated in concert audiences and museum visitors. The shadow side of the nineteenth-century elevation of art was the further demotion of the crafts and popular arts, the reduction of many artisans to industrial operatives and an increased separation of the audiences for fine and popular arts. By the end of the nineteenth century, the great division of the eighteenth century had become a gulf.

Although the main assumptions and institutions of the modern fine art system were largely in place by the 1830s and have endured down to the present, many aspects of the system have continued to be refined and elaborated. This is not the place to follow the evolution of competing theories of art, artist, and the aesthetic or the development of new directions in art institutions; they are the proper subjects for special histories. The developments we do need to follow in order to bring our story of art divided down to the present are two broader processes affecting the fine art system as a whole. I call them simply "assimilation" and "resistance."

By "assimilation" I mean the steady expansion of the domain of fine art from its original core of poetry, music, painting, sculpture, and architecture (plus dance, oratory, etc.) to include new or once-excluded arts, such as photography in the late nineteenth century, film, jazz, and "primitive art" in the early twentieth, arts in "craft" media since the 1950s, electronic music and the new journalism since the 1960s, and since the 1970s, almost anything. The true counter process to these assimilations has not been conservative opposition to expanding the boundaries of art but a more radical resistance to the deeper divisions of the art system, sometimes on behalf of craft in the sense of functional or popular arts, sometimes on behalf of the older union of art and craft in the sense trying to reintegrate art and society or art and life. Thus, the kinds of resistance to the fine art system that I want to explore have not rejected one or two concepts or practices, such as the fetish of "originality" or the self-contained "work," but have attacked the root polarities of the system itself. But just as the emergence of the modern fine art system was not simply the result of changes in theories and ideals but included the creation of separate institutions as well, so assimilation and resistance have been deeply involved with art institutions. This is most obvious in the case of assimilation, which is not only a matter of a few critics or philosophers arguing for the inclusion of new arts or art forms in the category of art but of art museums, symphony organizations, and literature departments actually incorporating them. Similarly, resistance to the underlying polarities of the fine art system is a matter not only of some people verbally attacking the narrowness of the dominant ideals of fine art, artist, and the aesthetic but also of artists and curators working against or outside of established art institutions. Yet assimilation and resistance turn out to be dialectically related. Art institutions seek to perpetuate themselves by incorporating the ideas and works of those who resist them, and those who resist are constantly tempted to be satisfied with merely expanding the categories and institutions of art. "Anti-art" movements such as dada and Russian constructivism or the authors of anti-art gestures such as Marcel Duchamp or John Cage, for example, were often ambivalent toward the category of art and the art institutions they attacked, and those institutions in turn were quick to recuperate anti-art works and actions. Each of the remaining chapters looks at examples of both assimilation and resistance in three overlapping periods: 1830–1914 (chap. 13), 1890–1960 (chap. 14), and 1950 to the present (chap. 15).

In his 1884 essay "The Art of Fiction," Henry James was still discussing the issue of whether the novel is not only "*an* art" but also "one of the *fine* arts" (James 1986, 167). As interesting as it would be to tell the story of the acceptance of the contemporary novel as fine art through its integration into the literary curriculum, I have chosen instead to follow the assimilation of photography, which was invented in 1839 soon after the modern system of fine arts was consolidated. As in the case of the novel, the assimilation of photography was not complete until the early twentieth century when photography began to enter the art museums. In the case of resistance, the earlier tradition exemplified by Hogarth, Rousseau, and Wollstonecraft began to take on a new form with the completion of the system of fine arts in the 1830s. By 1841, Emerson's essay "Art" challenged not only the demotion of the useful arts and ordinary pleasures but also called for overcoming "art's separate and contrasted existence." Other critiques of the categories of the fine art system soon followed from people as diverse in outlook as Kierkegaard, Marx, and Tolstoy. But the most thoroughly worked out challenge to the fine art–versus-craft split was that of Ruskin and

Morris, whose ideas found an institutional embodiment in the Arts and Crafts movement that spread from Britain to the Continent and to America in the last decades of the nineteenth century (chap. 13).

Yet from the 1890s on, the turn toward what we call modernism in the fine arts reaffirmed the divisions of the fine art system and the process of assimilating new styles. At the same time, the modernist rejection of traditional ideas of imitation and beauty demanded new forms of theoretical justification, such as formalism (Roger Fry) and expressionism (Benedetto Croce). But the combined effects of modernist experimentation and the shock of World War I also produced vigorous acts of resistance to the separation of art and society. Three exemplary movements of resistance just after the war were dada/surrealism, Russian constructivism, and the Bauhaus. By the 1930s there were also major critical and philosophical attempts to rethink the fine art–versus-craft and art-versus-life separations by R. G. Collingwood, John Dewey, and Walter Benjamin, but World War II cut them short and the postwar world of the 1950s returned to a preoccupation with formalist and expressionist issues surrounding modernism (chap. 14).

Since the 1960s, the process of assimilation has accelerated until the boundaries of what can count as art have expanded to embrace almost anything—although the fine art system has usually been able to extend the fine art–versus-craft division into each new territory it colonizes. But resistance to the polarities of the modern system of art has also flourished, not only among writers and composers who cross the boundaries between the high and the popular but also among artists identified with conceptual, environmental, and performance approaches. My final chapter explores examples of both assimilation and resistance from the second half of the twentieth century, two processes that work in opposite directions, yet each in its own way undermining the fine art system and raising the question of whether we are moving beyond art divided (chap. 15).

CHAPTER 13

# Assimilation and Resistance

On January 7, 1839, the astronomer François Arago presented Louis Daguerre's discovery of photography to a special session of the French Academy of Sciences. Over the next months, Daguerre demonstrated and publicized his invention around Paris, and the French government finally agreed to purchase the patent rights and make them public property. As the excitement over the new process spread, the painter Paul Delaroche is supposed to have exclaimed, "From this day painting is dead" (Schwarz 1987, 90). As it turned out, painting still had a long career ahead of it, including a remarkable phase of realism. Initially, the French and English press had been in no doubt that a marvelous new fine art medium had been discovered. Yet the limitations of photography as an art medium soon became apparent: not only the lack of color but also the troubling fact that a "machine" did most of the work. Painters such as Delaroche and Eugène Delacroix soon saw that photography would hardly replace painting but could become a useful aid for such things as recording difficult poses of live models (Scharf 1986; Sagne 1982).

## The Assimilation of Photography

Although photography did not kill off painting in the years following 1839, some kinds of functional painting did decline and virtually disappear, such as the affordable miniature portrait, whose makers either quit or became photographers or tinters in photographic shops. Over the next four decades (1840–80) professionals and amateurs around the world experimented with the rapidly improving papers, lenses, and mechanisms, producing millions of images. Amid this enthusiasm for recording the visible, a few photographers sought to make pictures that could claim fine art status. In the ensuing debate over photography as art, both sides worked within the same polarities of the modern discourse of art: fine art versus craft became intellect versus mechanism, artist versus artisan became imagination versus technical skill, aesthetic versus instrumental became the single work viewed for itself versus multiple copies for use or diversion.

The fullest case *against* photography as a fine art was worked out in detail by Lady Eastlake as early as 1857, and the same kind of arguments were recycled from Baudelaire in the 1859 to Santayana and Croce in the early twentieth century. Lady Eastlake was quite willing to grant photography the obvious virtue of accurate reproduction; she even suggested that photography might ultimately liberate painting from slavish imitation. But this did not make photography a fine art. The artist exercises "free-will of the intelligent being," the photographer merely obeys "the machine" (Eastlake [1857] 1981, 98). A second reason photography cannot be a fine art, according to Lady Eastlake, is that it serves practical ends, whereas art "ought to be" pursued "mainly for its own sake." Finally, the artist creates single works, whereas the photographer makes multiple prints, a sure sign that photography is a commodity not a fine art. Photography, Lady Eastlake concluded, is especially appropriate to "the present age, in which the desire for Art resides in a small minority, but the craving for cheap, prompt and correct facts in the public at large" (96–98). Across the channel, Baudelaire was content to snarl that the "squalid public," believing Art to be "the exact imitation of nature" and "photography to be the absolute Art," has "rushed like a single Narcissus, to contemplate its trivial image on a scrap of metal" (Baudelaire [1859] 1986, 289). Honoré Daumier caricatured the mania for photography in his drawing of Nadar photographing Paris from a balloon (fig. 63).

The photographers and critics who set out to answer these objections over the next seventy years seldom attacked the underlying polarity of fine art versus craft; they simply claimed that certain kinds of photographs belonged to the "art" side of it. Applying the art-versus-craft polarity within photography, they used the very criticisms of a Lady Eastlake against the "merely technical" practitioners. As Alfred Stieglitz put it, photography is "a plastic and not a mechanical process," although it can be "made mechanical by the craftsman, just as the brush becomes a mechanical agent in the hands of a mere copyist" (Stieglitz [1899] 1980, 164).

Of course, the champions of art photography didn't just argue their case but, in addition, produced prints whose unusual qualities set them apart from ordinary photographs. Julia Margaret Cameron is among the best known of those who aspired to "ennoble Photography and secure for it the character and uses of High Art" by deliberately idealizing her portrait subjects through costume, lighting, and an ethereal blur (Newhall 1982, 78). Oskar Rejlander and Henry Peach Robinson, in contrast, used multiple negatives of carefully arranged sym-

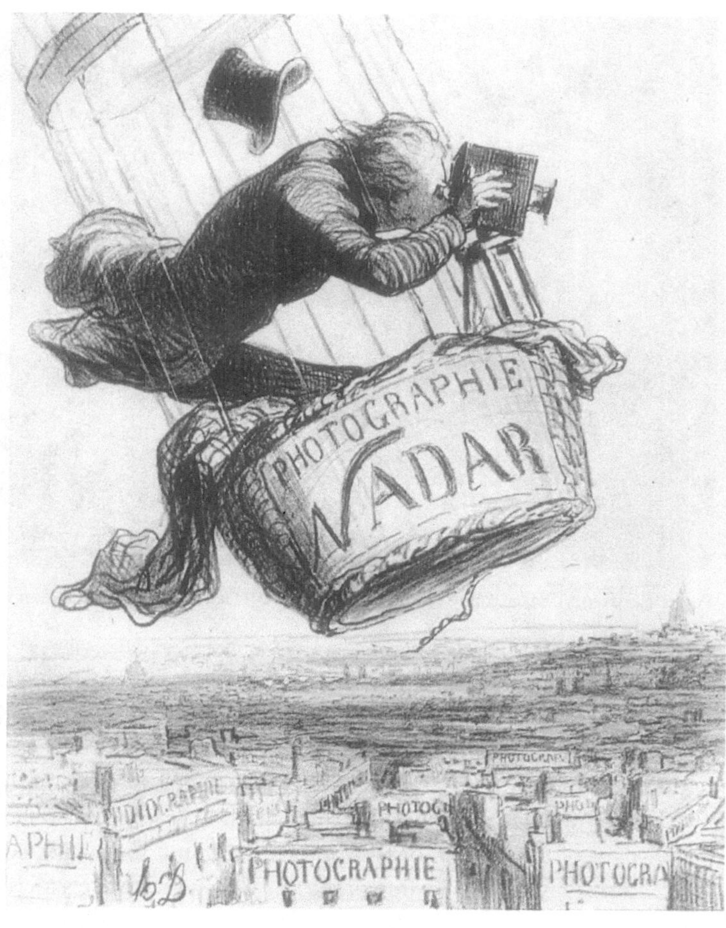


Figure 63. Honoré Daumier, *Nadar Raising Photography to the Height of Art* (1862). Courtesy Bibliothèque Nationale, Paris.

bolic or narrative scenes to produce photographs that looked like contemporary pre-Raphaelite paintings (fig. 64). But it was the pictorialist movement at the end of the century, with its impressionistic soft focus and aestheticized poses, that was most successful in gaining respect for photography's claim to be a fine art medium and for the photographer as an artist (fig. 65).

Key arguments used by many of the late nineteenth-century proponents were expression and originality. It is perhaps no accident that pictorialism and the emphasis on personal expression and the single art print emerged at the same time the cheap hand camera and film were turning photography into a public pastime. "The point is," Stieglitz wrote, "*what you have to say and how to*

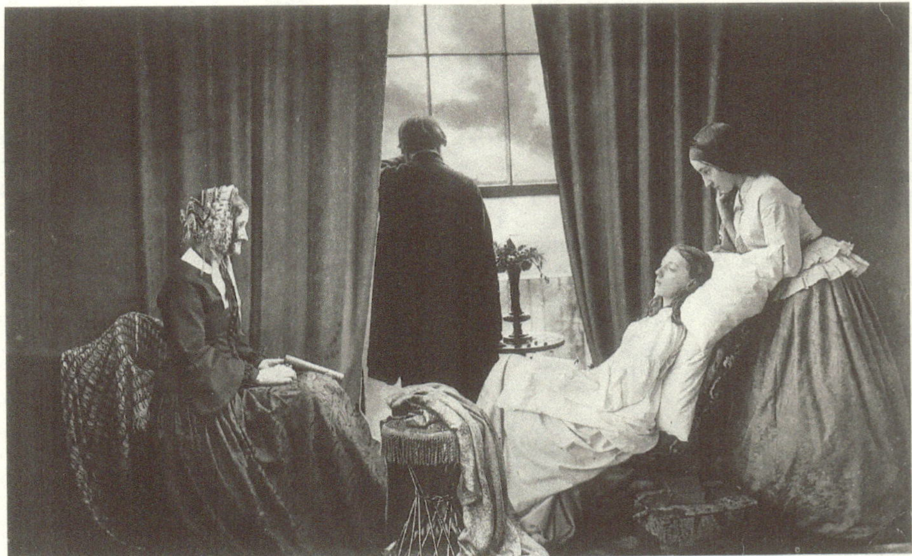

Figure 64. Henry Peach Robinson, *Fading Away* (1858). Courtesy George Eastman House, Rochester, N.Y.

*say it.* The originality of a work of art refers to the originality of the thing expressed and the way it is expressed, whether it be in poetry, photography, or painting" (Stieglitz [1899] 1980, 164).

Ironically, the application of the art-versus-craft polarity to photography may have had a rebound effect on painting, leading to a renewed importance of signs of the hand in brushwork. Richard Shiff has suggested that photography contributed to a rejection of the finished surface of a classicism that now looked too photographic (1988, 28). Whereas once the difference between artist and artisan was defined in terms of mental work versus handwork in order to elevate the artist into the company of gentlemen, now that the artist's place in the world of spirit was secure, signs of the hand could return from impressionism on. The art photographers, of course, were not fighting a prejudice against handwork but the accusation of mindless mechanism. Some of the pictorialists—Edward Steichen, for instance—even left brush marks on their hand-tinted prints in an attempt to show their equality with painters.

Yet the ultimate consecration of photography as part of the fine arts required more than the simulation of handwork or the intellectual conversion of a few art critics; photography also had to be accepted by the art institutions. Pictorialism led the way with a series of well-received exhibitions in the 1890s, one of them, the first ever in an art museum, at the Hamburg *Kunsthalle* in 1893, whose

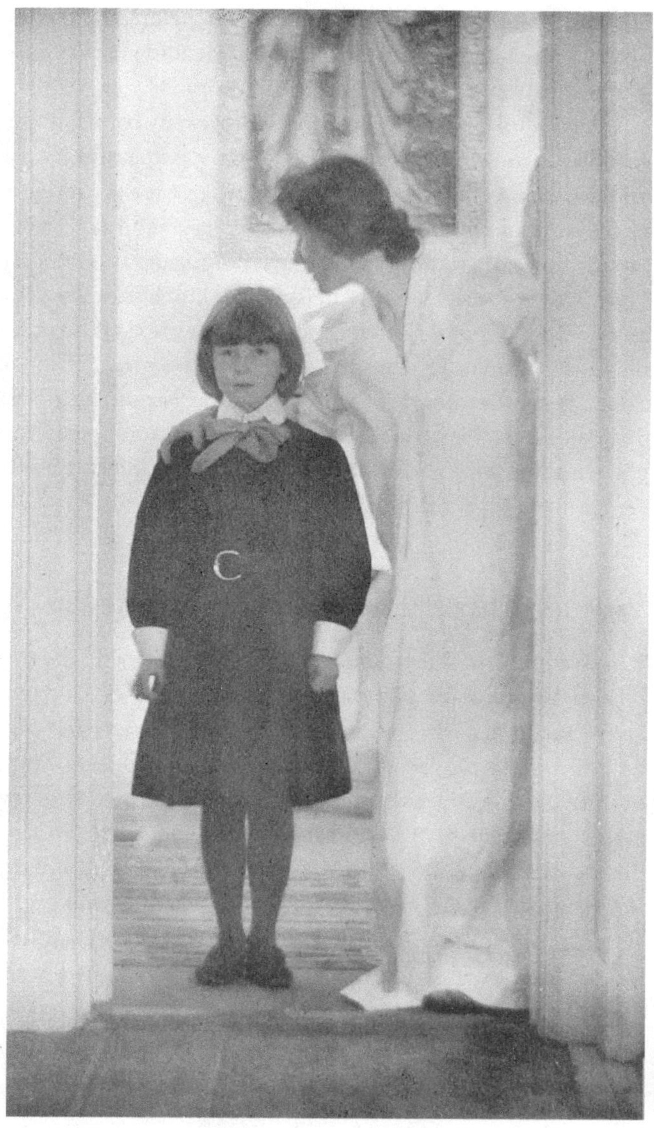

Figure 65. Gertrude Käsebier, *Blessed Art Thou among Women* (1899). Photogravure, 23.6 × 14 centimeters. Gift of Daniel, Richard, and Jonathan Logan, 1984.1638. Photograph © 2000, Art Institute of Chicago. All Rights Reserved.

daring director wrote of the public's astonishment at seeing photographs hung in painting galleries: "To them it seemed like holding a natural history congress in a church" (Newhall 1982, 146). In 1910 the Albright Art Gallery in Buffalo hosted an international exhibition of pictorial photography organized by Stieglitz and even bought twelve prints for permanent display in the museum.

Stieglitz wrote ecstatically to a friend that "the dream I had in 1885 in Berlin has become a reality—the complete acknowledgment of photography by an important institution" (Newhall 1980, 189).

Although the full acceptance of photography by most museums and fine art schools took several more decades, the basic pattern for its assimilation into fine art had been set. The key to this long struggle for the recognition of photography was the application of the art-versus-craft and artist-versus-artisan polarities within photography, plus the sanctioning of art photography by art institutions like the museum, art criticism, and, much later, university schools of fine art. The expressionist and formalist arguments that came in the later stages of the assimilation process were themselves refinements of the regulative assumptions about the nature of fine art, the artist, and the aesthetic established decades earlier. New versions of expressionist and formalist arguments would play an important role in the acceptance of modernism after the turn of the century (see chap. 14).

## Varieties of Resistance: Emerson, Marx, Ruskin, Morris

It is striking that at the same time Stieglitz was using the fine art–versus-craft dichotomy to divide photography, people such as Morris were attacking the art-versus-craft division as ruinous for both the arts and society. Although the Arts and Crafts movement of the end of the nineteenth century focused on reuniting the fine arts and crafts and restoring the dignity of the craftsperson, the earlier resistance of William Wordsworth and Ralph Waldo Emerson focused on the larger separation of art from life. George Leonard has argued that Wordsworth's vision of a "blissful hour" when we will find "Paradise" in "the simple produce of the common day" was a dream of eventually dispensing with the separate work of art. Leonard reads the famous lines from "The Tables Turned" of the *Lyrical Ballads* in this sense:

> We murder to dissect
> Enough of Science and of Art;
> Close up those barren leaves.

Readers have often noticed the dissections of science but overlooked the barrenness of Art (Leonard 1994, 74–79). Yet many of Wordsworth's other writings show he was hardly immune to the ideals of fine art and the artist, and in calling Art barren, he may have been aiming at the artificial diction of established poetic language. We have seen him intoning the artist's "high calling" to "creative Art," or celebrating the imagination's "absolute power," and later in his career he argued for the doubling of the copyright period because it would encourage writing lasting works of art for posterity rather than pleasing readers in the present (Woodmansee 1994).

Emerson's resistance to fine art's separation from life was also ambivalent, but his attack on the separateness of fine art was more direct than Wordsworth's was. Emerson's journals and essays of the 1830s and 1840s are strewn with dismissals of painting and sculpture as "cripples and monsters," "toys and trumpery," "abortive births," "hypocritical rubbish" (1950, 312; 1903, 2:358; 1969, 7:143). Yet in another essay of the same period he spoke of poetry as the summit of the hierarchies and called poets nothing less than "liberating gods." Even so, the true poet for Emerson is not the artist-writer striving to create a self-contained work for our admiration but the person who is open to the life of the universe and allows the ethereal tides to run through him, turning "the world to glass" (1950, 329; 1903, 3:30). Emerson's ambivalence toward the fine arts was deeply rooted in his transcendentalist conviction that the universal mind flows through each of us as through all things: "We are children of the fire" (1950, 320; 1903, 1:10; 1903, 3:30). Reappraising every institution in the light of this conviction, Emerson defined art as creative expression responding to the inflowing of the spirit (1969, 541). As a result, not only individual works but entire arts as well, such as painting or sculpture, become less important than Art, itself, the divine urge to create.

This is the root of Emerson's paradoxical rethinking of the modern idea of art: he talks of the essence of art in tones as exalted as any of the German romantics and idealists, yet he subordinates individual arts and art works in a strikingly new way. Returning from a walk in the woods with Thoreau, he recorded in his journal: "Why should we build a St. Peter's if we had the seeing Eye which beheld all the radiance of beauty & majesty in the matted grass & the overarching boughs? Why should a man spend years carving an Apollo who looked Apollos into the landscape with every glance he threw?" (1969, 7:143). Emerson does grant the fine arts two functions: to help us see the divine in nature and humanity and to remind us of the universal urge for expression in us all. Yet any object in nature—a squirrel jumping from branch to branch or a litter of pigs—might serve to reveal the spirit just as well as poetry or painting. "True art is never fixed, but always flowing. The sweetest music is not in the oratorio, but in the human voice when it speaks from its instant of life tones of tenderness, truth or courage" (1950, 313; 1903, 2:363).

One of Emerson's most persistent criticisms of the fine arts was that they had lost contact with their social functions and become "mere flourishes to please the eye of persons who have associations with books and galleries" (1964–72, 2,

54; 1969, 5:210–11). To counter this trivialization we need to "carry art up into the kingdom of nature, and destroy its separate and contrasted existence" (1950, 313). Despite his subordination of the individual work of Art to the creative spirit and his call for a reunion of the fine and useful arts, even for the disappearance of art as a "separate and contrasted" realm, Emerson still clung to the use of Art as the name for the highest of human spiritual powers and to the ideal of the poet as the bearer of a redemptive revelation, calling poets "liberating gods" (1950, 334). Yet even in the midst of his most ecstatic celebration of the poet, Emerson did not completely forget this vision of overcoming art's separate existence: "We are all poets at last . . . each of us is part of eternity and immensity, a god walking in the flesh." The great poets' superiority is only that they "saw and celebrated this marvel whilst we slept" (1964–72, 3:365). Emerson famously condemned a "foolish consistency" as the "hobgoblin of little minds"; his was a capacious mind indeed, and we have more to learn by allowing him his inconsistencies than in trying to reconcile the tensions. Meanwhile, Karl Marx, John Ruskin, and William Morris were developing more specific, although similarly ambivalent, challenges to the dichotomies of the modern fine art system.

For the young Marx of the 1840s, industrial capitalism not only had divided humanity into capitalist and worker and distorted the human experience of production but it had also perverted the senses themselves. The working classes had been reduced to mechanical activity, whereas the capitalist class no longer made and participated in art but spent their time acquiring money to buy things: "Your money can eat, drink, go dancing, go to the theater, appropriate art" (1975, 361). The combination of private property and the division of labor had resulted in an exaggerated polarity of a use-value reduced to mere utility and an exchange-value that turned all the products of human making into commodities. Marx was convinced that society could only overcome these divisions and restore the unity of use and enjoyment through the abolition of private property. After that happened, both need and enjoyment would have "lost their *egoistic* nature" and use would no longer be "mere *utility*" but, combined with enjoyment, would "become *human* use" (1975, 351). This would be possible because the abolition of private property would enable a mode of production in which making art was not different in kind from other making. In such a society, the artist would no longer stand apart as the only free creator; everyone would be free to develop his or her powers to the fullest. There will be "no painters but, at most, people who engage in painting among other activities" (Marx and Engels 1970, 109). Art will no longer be divided into fine art versus craft and the artist set above the artisan; there will be only human arts and human creating. Of course, the later Marx turned away from such utopian speculations to build a theory of "scientific socialism" and inevitable revolution, but his fragmentary reflections on art still inspire those who seek a reintegration of art and everyday life in a context of social justice (Rose 1984).

Not long after the young Marx formulated his critique of the alienating effects of capitalism on the arts, the socially conservative moralist and art critic John Ruskin began to attack the separation of the fine and applied arts. In his early writings, Ruskin passionately celebrated beauty in nature and art as leading us to love the creator of nature, and Ruskin also celebrated the artist in the usual terms of genius and vision. Although he never wavered in his belief in beauty and creativity, a change came over Ruskin in the 1850s as he turned his attention from painting to architecture. Like many others in the early Victorian era, he became a passionate advocate of Gothic as exemplifying an idealized medieval way of life in which Art was not separated from craft or artist from artisan. Ruskin's chapter on "The Nature of Gothic" in *The Stones of Venice* (1854) was the single most influential document for the Arts and Crafts movement. Today it is especially remembered for its stirring condemnation of the division of labor: "It is not the labour that is divided, but the men," whose individuality and creativity are destroyed (1985, 87). For Ruskin the division of labor meant a radical separation of the artist-designer from the artisan, often turning the craftsperson into little more than a machine operative. Moreover, industrial production had resulted in objects of an ugly uniformity compared to the beauty of craftworks, such as Venetian glass, which bear the variable marks of the human hand. His reappraisal of the importance of craftspeople and their fate under industrialism also led him to criticize the British government's segregation of the fine and applied arts in separate museums and schools. By the 1870s he was describing the totality of arts as a continuum reaching from painting on china to painting on canvas, from the plowshare to the cathedral buttress, with no place to set a logical division. Moreover, he had become convinced that genuine art could have only two functions: "either *to state a true thing*, or *to adorn a serviceable one*" (1996, 140).

William Morris, on whom "The Nature of Gothic" worked a kind of conversion as an Oxford student, was not only a respected poet and painter but also, once committed to restoring the dignity of the crafts, taught himself weaving, dying, stained-glass making, wallpaper and textile design, tile glazing, and bookbinding—all with such energy and success as startled his contemporaries and made him the acknowledged leader of the Arts and Crafts movement

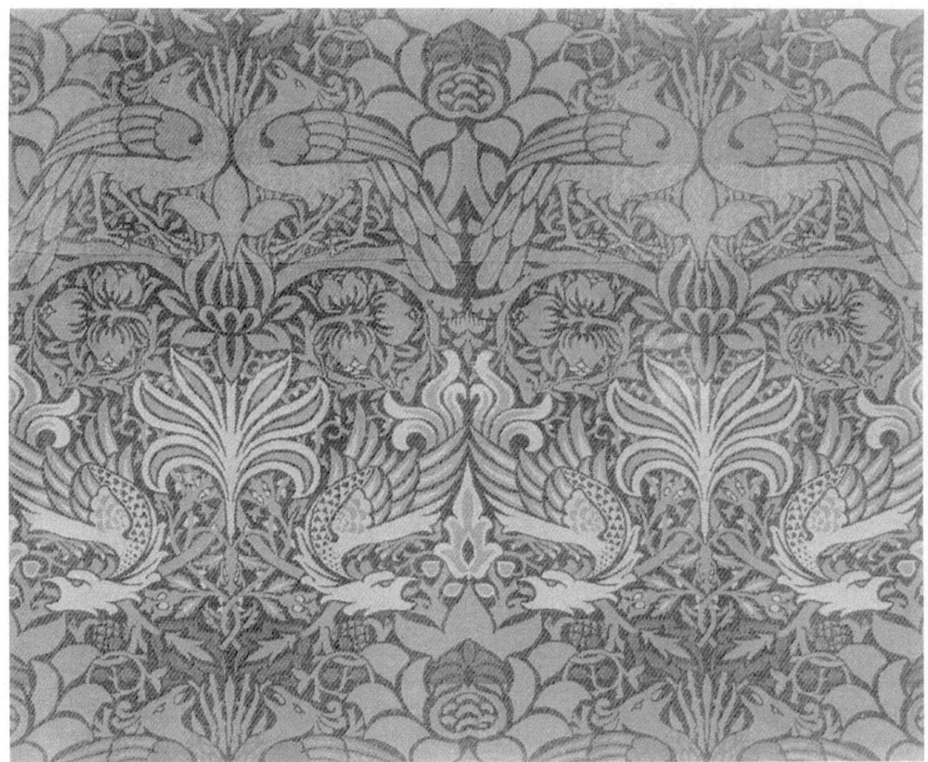

Figure 66. William Morris, "Peacock and Dragon," panel design produced by Morris & Co. (1875–1940). Wool, three-colored complementary weft, twill weave; lined with linen, plain weave, 217.5 × 171.7 centimeters. Restricted gift of Natalie Henry, 1985.74. © 2000, Art Institute of Chicago. All Rights Reserved.

(fig. 66). Like Ruskin, Morris attacked the separation of fine art from craft and the artist from the artisan, arguing that their historical separation had been ruinous to both, leading to a contemptuous attitude on the part of artists and to carelessness on the part of artisans (1948, 499). From the time of his lecture on "The Lesser Arts" in 1877 to his last socialist speeches of the 1890s Morris tirelessly demanded respect for those who labor with their hands. "There is another kind of workman . . . we call by various names, which I am ashamed to say do in most people's minds imply inferiority: artisan, for instance, or operative. . . . I shall use a word . . . to all reasonable people implying honour and not reproach . . . handicraftsman" (1969, 44–49). If art were as it should be, every mason and carpenter would make things of beauty as well as use, and the arts would form a pyramid with the many handicrafts at the base and middle, seamlessly tapering into painting, sculpture, poetry, and music at the apex. Even more than Ruskin, Morris emphasized the class implications of reuniting fine art and craft: "Art made by the people and for the people, a joy to the maker and the user" (1948, 564).

## The Arts and Crafts Movement

In Britain the Arts and Crafts movement had three facets: the many craft production workshops, the London design associations of the 1880s, and a social philanthropy effort aimed at using the craft revival to moralize the working class. Although one of the stated aims of the Arts and Crafts design societies was to restore the "unity of the Arts," there was no intention of diminishing the designers' claim to be gentlemen artists. The Arts and Crafts Exhibition Society, for example, stipulated that no sales were to be made on the premises in order to avoid any appearance that the designers were "tradesmen" (Stansky 1985). Yet some of Morris's spirit remained in the permission for designers to include the name of the actual maker of the work, although Morris remarked caustically that "it is not by printing lists of names in a catalogue that the status of the workman could be raised or the capitalist system altered" (Naylor 1990, 123).

But Morris's own firm hardly matched his ideal since there was often a division of labor between designer and executant, and he paid the prevailing wage while charging premium prices, once blurting out that he had to spend his time "ministering to the swinish luxury of the rich" (Naylor 1990, 108). This was a general problem for most of the Arts and Crafts firms, even the ones that took up a kind of romantic socialism. Many of these reformers went off to a small village and set up a community of workers under the name of such and such "Guild" and scrupulously did their work with hand tools, allowed anyone of talent to be designers, and even shared the profits. But when these craft communities came to sell their products, like Morris & Co., it was mostly the well-to-do who could afford to buy.

Moreover, the Arts and Crafts movement at large often remained captive to gender prejudices. The London design guilds simply excluded women. And even when talented women designers became a majority in firms, such as in the Vienna Werkstätte, they were liable to be dismissed by critics such as Adolf Loos as "painting, embroidering, potting, precious-material-wasting daughters of senior civil servants, or other Fräuleins who regard handicrafts as something whereby one may earn pin-money or while away one's spare time" (Schweiger

1984, 118). The communal craft workshops, by contrast, had many women members and several, such as Compton Pottery, were set up as women's enterprises. But in the movement as a whole, women tended to be directed to "women's" work, such as china painting or needle arts. Encouraging women to do needlework was especially marked in the philanthropic craft revival, which was aimed at keeping the working classes from drinking, gambling, and prostitution and also at providing "suitable employment" for unmarried middle-class women (Callen 1979; Anscombe 1984; Cumming and Kaplan 1991).

The irony of an Arts and Crafts movement aiming to create an "art by the people and for the people," only to end up serving the rich and discriminating against women has led to plenty of dismissive remarks. But no later commentators have been harder on it than one of its own leaders, C. R. Ashbee: "We have made of a great social movement, a narrow and tiresome little aristocracy working with great skill for the very rich" (Naylor 1990, 9). Although communities such as Ashbee's Guild of Handicraft, with its spirit of mutuality, its leisurely pace of work, its profit sharing, and its excursions and plays put on by the members, may not have transformed industrial society, they left a fertile example for reflection (Crawford 1985). Even so, the failure of the Arts and Crafts movement stemmed from its antimachine bias and nostalgia for a workshop form of production impossible to restore on a large scale. Morris, to his credit, gradually realized that the cause of the degradation of the artisan or craftsperson was not just the machine but also the organization of industrial production. Later in his career, he joined the socialist movement, although his commitments to handicraft and social revolution remained in some tension (Thompson 1976).

Two overlapping artistic tendencies emerged from the Arts and Crafts movement by the beginning of the twentieth century (though each had other sources as well): one was the idea of total design, closely linking the decorative arts to architecture and industry; the other was the studio craft movement, with its small production potteries, weaving workshops, and furniture studios. Although many architects considered total design to mean they designed everything, including furnishings, and craftspeople simply carried out orders, architects such as Philip Webb and W. R. Lethaby in England or Gottfried Semper and Peter Behrens in Germany envisaged a more cooperative relationship between architects, artists, and craftspeople. Frank Lloyd Wright rejected Ruskin's condemnation of the machine, but his prairie houses of 1893–1910 owed much to the Arts and Crafts idea of the integration of architecture and the crafts. Wright assembled a team that included the engineer Paul Mueller, the landscape architect Wilhelm Miller, the sculptor Richard Bock, the cabinet-maker George Niedecken, the mosaic designer Catherine Ostertag, the textile and stained-glass maker Orlando Giannini, and the delineator Marion L. Mahony (Frampton 1992). The charismatic Wright believed deeply in architecture as fine art, and he so successfully cultivated his image as genial artist-creator that the extent of his collaborators' contributions often went unnoticed. But recent scholars have reminded us of the important role of his associates, for example, the presentation drawings and designs of Marion L. Mahony or the furniture designed and made by George Niedecken and company (Upton 1998; Robertson 1999) (fig. 67).

The other legacy of the Arts and Crafts movement, the studio craft workshops, continued Ruskin's and Morris' social utopianism and antimachine ethos, sometimes taking the form of a middle-class return to the simple life (Lucie-Smith 1984; Cumming and Kaplan 1991). In Britain and America, the studio craft movement offered a wider opportunity for women to establish independent careers, especially in ceramics where they made important contributions to both glaze technology and artistic form (fig. 68). Some women ran "production" potteries that created both functional and decorative ware (the Overbeck sisters), others maintained studios that specialized in the one-of-a-kind decorative pieces known as "art pottery" (e.g., Adelaide Robineau) (Postle 1978; Clark 1979). But pottery existed on the margins of the fine art world, its products classified as part of the "decorative" or "minor" arts. On the European continent, studio practice merged into the existing "art and industry" drive to inject good design into mass production. In 1896, the Prussian government sent Hermann Muthesius to England as a kind of cultural spy, and when he returned six years later, workshops were introduced into the arts and crafts schools and artists appointed as teachers. During the same period, small workshops producing furniture, pottery, and utensils came into being all over Germany. These workshops not only embraced machinery but newer design styles as well, such as the curvilinear *Jugenstil* (German art nouveau) or the minimalist, geometric forms we typically identify with modernism (fig. 69). In 1907, a Belgian exponent of art nouveau, Henry van de Velde, became head of the Grand-Ducal School of the Arts and Crafts in Weimar and in that same year joined several other artists, architects, and heads of craft firms—Bruno Paul and Peter Behrens, for example—to form the German *Werkbund,* the purpose of which was to promote the cooperation of "art, industry, and crafts" in order to assure "high quality" (Droste 1998, 12). But the tension between the fine art and the craft emphases among the members became apparent in their 1914 meeting

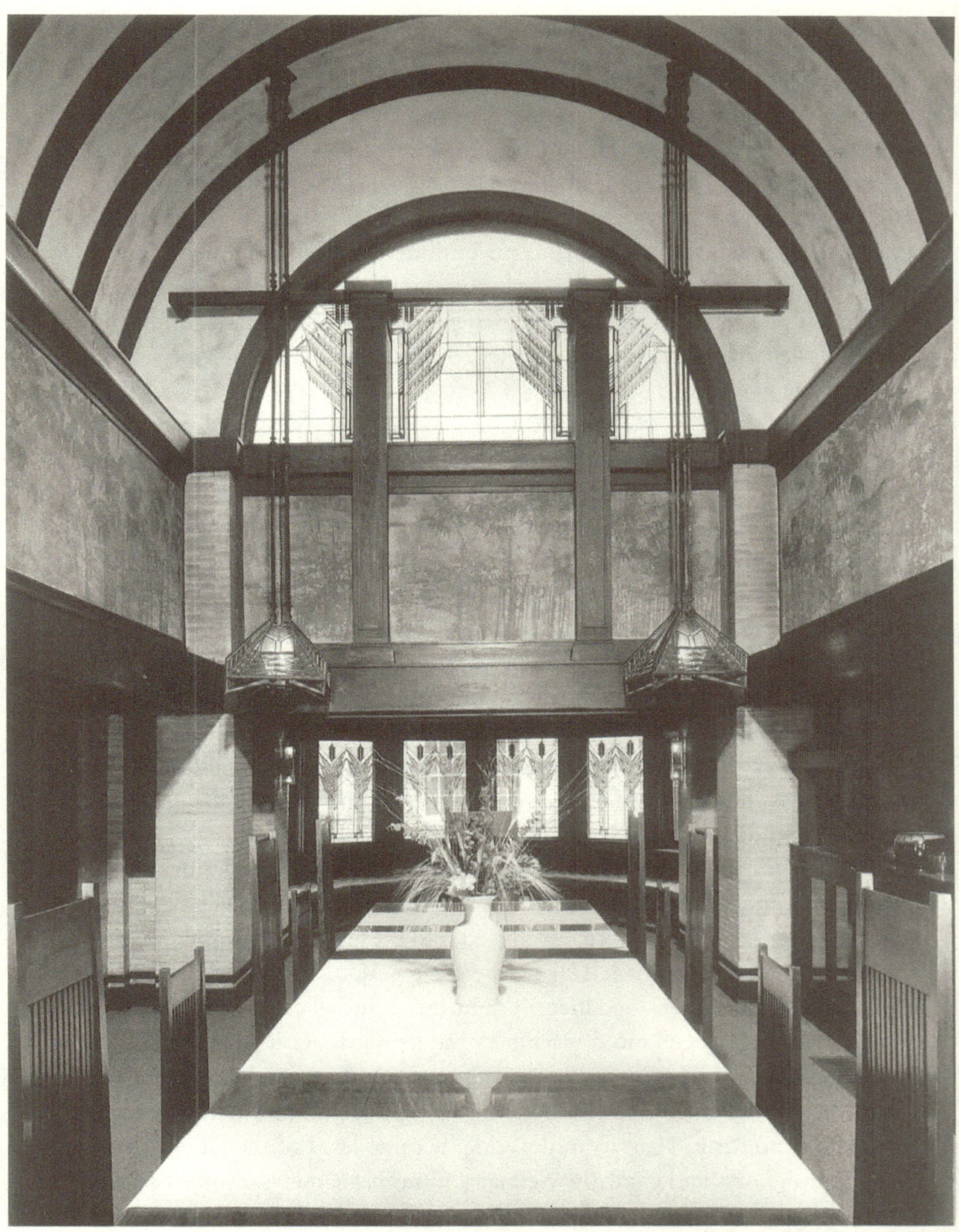

Figure 67. Frank Lloyd Wright, dining room, Susan Lawrence Dana House, Springfield, Illinois (1902–4). Courtesy Illinois Historic Preservation Agency, Dana-Thomas House Collection, Springfield, Ill. Photograph by Douglas Carr. Although Wright was responsible for the overall design—with its flowing spaces and furnishings, including the fanciful "butterfly lamps"—other members of the team were involved in many parts of the house; George Niedecken designed the mural around the upper walls of the dining room, Walter Burley Griffin designed the sconce lamps, Marion Mahony designed the base of the fountain just outside the dining room, and Richard Bock did the fountain's relief as well as the statue that is part of the front entry.

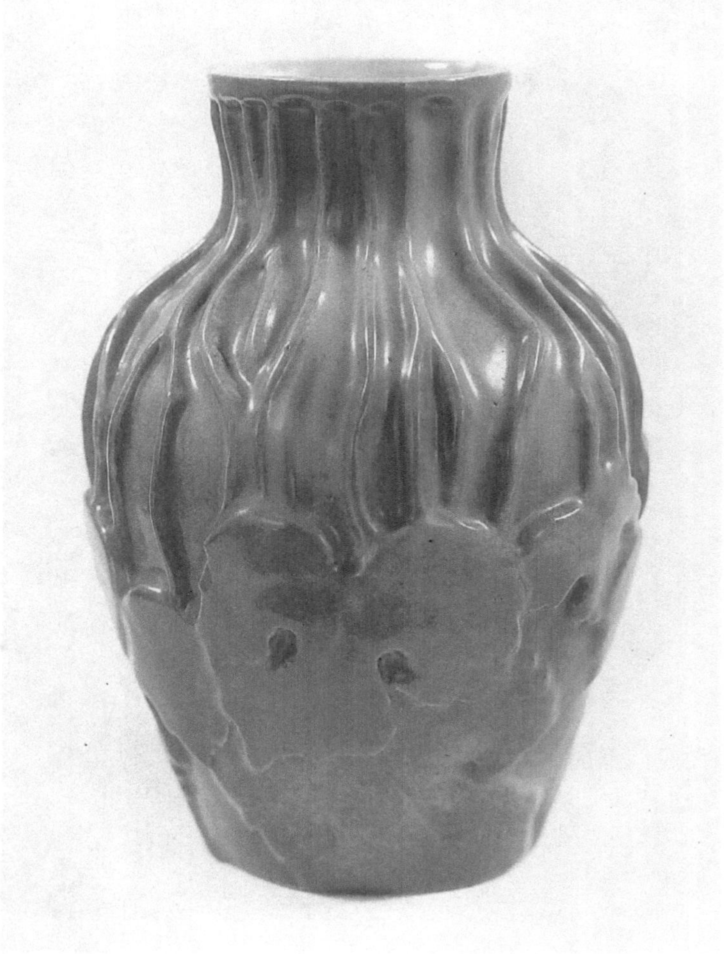

Figure 68. Mary Louise McLaughlin, *Vase* (1902); porcelain. Courtesy Cincinnati Art Museum, gift of the Porcelain League of Cincinnati. McLaughlin was a pioneer in developing glazing techniques and clay bodies, producing her porcelain "Losantiware" between 1899 and 1906.

when Muthesius called for architecture and the applied arts to move toward industrial standardization and Henry Van de Velde riposted: "The artist is essentially a passionate individualist, a spontaneous creator [and] . . . never will submit to a norm" (Conrads 1970, 29).

In the first decades of the twentieth century, despite the new respect for good design and the aesthetic appreciation given the best furniture, textiles, and utensils, the deeper art-versus-craft polarity continued to regulate thought and practice. There were still separate applied art museums (Europe) or separate departments for crafts in fine art museums (America) for what were called

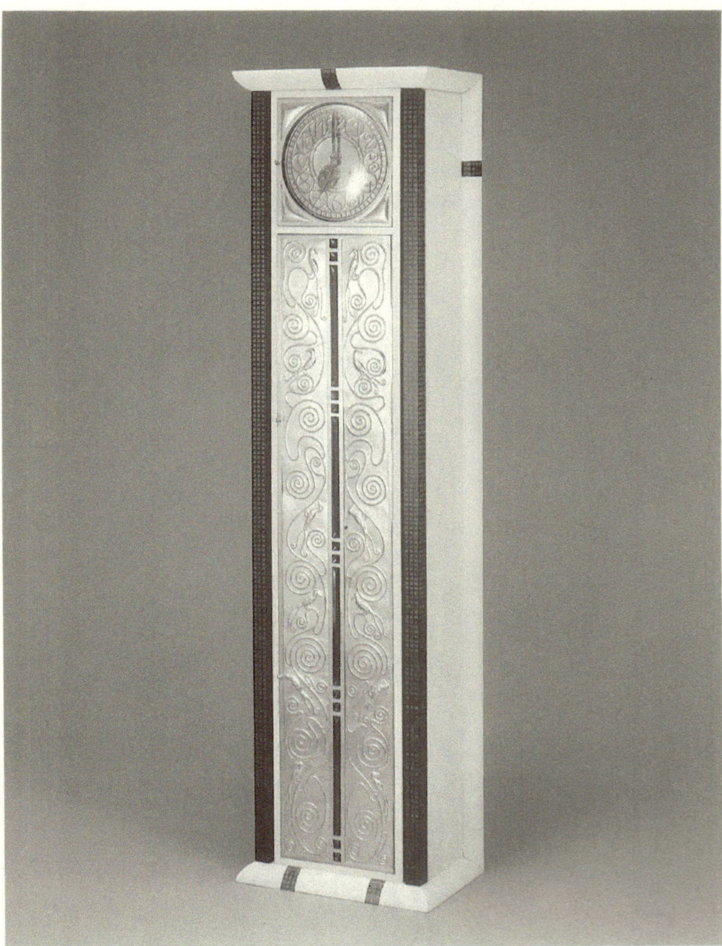

Figure 69. Josef Hoffmann and Carl Otto Czeschka, designers, tall-case clock, Wiener Werkstätte, Vienna (1906). Painted maple, ebony, mahogany, gilded brass, glass, silver-plated copper, clockworks, 179.5 × 46.5 × 30.5 centimeters. Courtesy Laura Matthews and Mary Waller Langhorne funds, 1983.37. Photograph by Robert Hashimoto. © 2000, Art Institute of Chicago. All Rights Reserved.

"decorative," "applied," or "minor" arts. The inclusion of costly decorative arts in American fine art museums was partly the result of a constant stream of gifts from "millionaire collectors in search of aristocratic identities" (Duncan 1995, 65). The term "craft," although used for the studio-made item of clay, wood, glass, or metal, had an ambiguous status owing to its associations with such things as sewing, carpentry, or bricklaying.

Yet, as happened with photography, both formalist and expressionist arguments were already being used to assimilate exceptional instances of craft or applied art into fine art—but at a price. The Viennese historian Alois Riegl (1858–1905), for example, began his career as curator of textiles at the Austrian

Museum of Art and Industry but used the collection to develop a revolutionary theory of ornament, according to which, style in art is not dependent on craft skills, materials, or function but on a universal "art impulse," or "artistic will" *(Kunstwollen).* According to Riegl, the art drive develops progressively over time from tactile, or closely viewed, patterns toward the increasingly optical pleasures of a "redemptive" kind (Iversen 1993; Olin 1993, 149). Paradoxically, Riegl believed that the applied arts sometimes reveal the "art will" of an epoch better than fine arts like painting, since representational content may obscure formal developments that are more obvious in ornamental patterns. Whereas Riegl's older contemporary, the architect Gottfried Semper, made the crafts central to the history of architecture and tried to hold skill, function, and creativity together, Riegl's approach ended up reinforcing their separation. In formalist theories similar to Riegl's, the crafts or applied arts do have a place in art history or the museum but at the price of reducing skill, materials, and function to obstacles overcome by a universal "art impulse" (Riegl 1985, 9). Craft or applied art in the full sense of the purposeful work meant for the satisfactions of ordinary use and enjoyment remained the "other" of fine art.

Varied as they were, the resistance strategies of Emerson, Marx, Ruskin, Morris, the Arts and Crafts movement, and the German *Werkbund* were not the only challenges to the polarities of the fine art system in this period. Some of the other approaches to resistance against the division of art took a more traditional religious form, such as Søren Kierkegaard's critique of the aesthetic mode of existence in the 1840s or Leo Tolstoy's combined religious and social critique in the 1890s. But Kierkegaard's writings remained relatively unknown outside Denmark and Tolstoy's were greeted as the extremist outpourings of a crank—especially when he rejected his own novel *War and Peace* or Beethoven's *Ninth Symphony* in favor of religiously edifying stories and wholesome folk music. But by the time Tolstoy's *What Is Art?* ([1896] 1996) appeared, the worlds of music, literature, and visual arts were preoccupied with an internal issue that seemed far more important than overcoming fine art's "separate and contrasted existence": modernism.

CHAPTER 14

# Modernism, Anti-Art, and the Bauhaus

## Modernism and Purity

ALTHOUGH NOTORIOUSLY hard to define and date, the establishment of modernism is often identified with the period 1890–1930, which witnessed a profound stylistic disruption of representational modes in painting (Picasso), traditional narrative techniques in the novel (Woolf), the standard tonal system in music (Schoenberg), classical balletic movements in the dance (Duncan), and traditional architectural forms (Le Corbusier) (fig. 70).[1] If the characteristics and timing of modernism are hard to pin down, so are the larger social and cultural forces that fed into it. Many historians have seen modernism as an artistic response to the rapid industrialization and urbanization of the late nineteenth century, a profound social disruption that led to the paradoxical extremes of a belief in limitless progress and a growing sense of anomie. The horrors of World War I soon exploded the belief in progress but did not slow the pace of technological and social change or their disorienting effects. The poet T. S. Eliot caught the darkened mood of the postwar era in one of the defining works of modernist literature, *The Waste Land:* "Son of man . . . you know only / A heap of broken images" ([1922] 1952, 38).

Among the many other catalysts of modernism was the discovery of the arts of cultures that had no idea of fine art as an autonomous realm. The assimilation of African ritual masks and fetish figures by Picasso (*Les demoiselles d'Avignon,* 1907), for example, has long been part of the legend of modernism, as has the earlier impact of Japanese prints on the postimpressionists. In music, an equally important moment was the discovery of exotic African and Asian rhythms at the Paris Exposition of 1889 (which also inaugurated the Eiffel Tower). Claude Debussy was excited by the sounds of the Javanese gamelan players and found their rhythmic counterpoint far more complex and subtle than anything in Western music up to then: "If we listen, forgetting our European prejudices . . . we are forced to admit that ours sounds like the barbaric noise of a traveling circus" (Chanan 1994, 227). Three years later, Debussy wrote one of the pioneer works of the transition to modern music, *Prelude to the Afternoon of a Faun.*

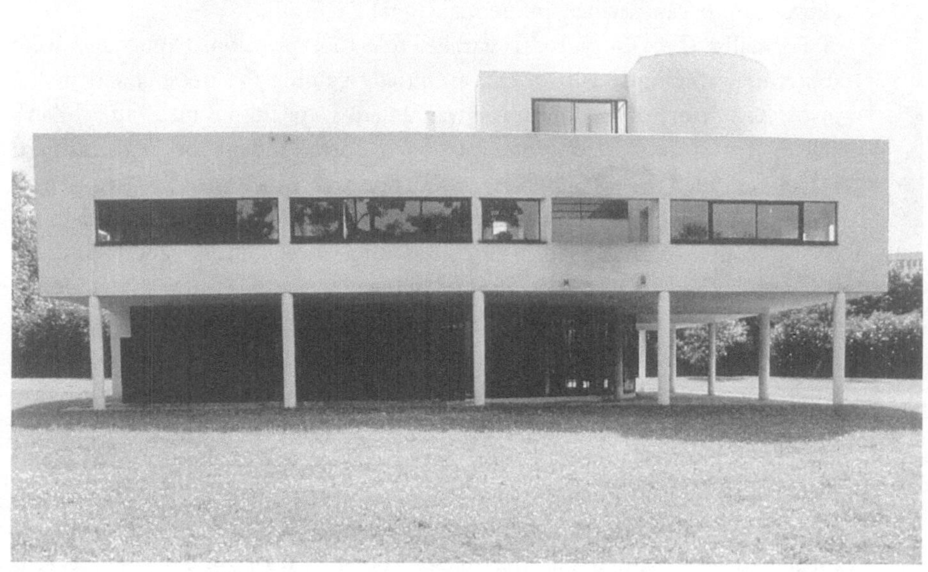

Figure 70. Le Corbusier, Villa Savoye, exterior, Poissy, France (1929–31). Courtesy Anthony Scibilia/Art Resource, New York. © 2000 Artists Rights Society (ARS), New York/ADAGP, Paris/FLC

Yet modernism and its theorists did not radically alter the basic beliefs of the fine art system so much as encourage a shift of emphasis within them. Modernist experiments with abstraction, multiple points of view, and atonality helped finish off such secondary criteria for defining fine art as imitation and beauty, opening the way to their replacement by more complex versions of expressionist and formalist theories. To call something beautiful was coming to seem a weak compliment compared with descriptions such as "significant," "complex," and "challenging." Now the ideal of creative vision was explicitly opposed to representation, function, and beauty.

There were innumerable varieties of expressionist theory, ranging from the naively causal notions of Tolstoy to the subtler idealist theories of Croce or Collingwood, who saw expression as the artist's giving creative form to previously inchoate experiences. Expressionist theories of art obviously fit the early twentieth-century expressionist movement in music, painting, and architecture, but expressionist theories themselves were meant to explain all styles of art and in fact proved useful in describing a wide range of experimental works, as well as the newly discovered "primitive art." In the early decades of the century, Croce's expressionist philosophy of art, captured in the phrase "intuition equals expression" became widely influential (1992).

Formalist theories played a parallel role to expressionist ones and were sometimes combined with them, eventually gaining the upper hand in the 1950s. As a theory of art, formalism was already implicit in Kant's and Schiller's call for the disinterested contemplation of form, and in the 1850s, Eduard Hanslick argued that what makes music a fine art are its formal patterns of harmony and melodic structure. Music is something "self-contained and in no need of content from outside itself," consisting "solely of tones and their artistic combination" (1986, 28). By the end of the nineteenth century, art historians such Riegl and Heinrich Wölfflin had developed a complex formalist approach to the visual arts, and critics such as Roger Fry and Clive Bell were soon defending postimpressionist and cubist painting, as well as "primitive" carvings, by arguing that what makes something art is the formal exploration of line, color, and composition, not representational content or beauty (Bell [1913] 1958). At about the same time that Bell was dismissing imitation and beauty in favor of "significant form," the literary theorists and critics known as Russian formalists were arguing that what makes a poem or novel "literary" are its self-referential features of pattern, image, trope, and rhythm.

Although modernists produced a bewildering variety of manifestos and programs, one recurring motif was the special importance many ascribed to "purity" of medium, an exigency that "postmodernist" artists of our time have taken particular delight in violating. "Purity," for early modernists, meant a drive to cleanse painting, music, or literature of everything extraneous to their essence. Yet purity did not necessarily mean an absolute formalism or a belief in art for art's sake but could be combined with the established notion that Art reveals deeper truths inaccessible to science or discursive thought. Thus, Joyce's *Ulysses,* Woolf's *To the Lighthouse,* and Proust's *Remembrance of Things Past* used experimental techniques to embody the texture of everyday experience and explore the deeper spiritual conflicts of modern life. The painters Kasimir Malevich and Wassily Kandinsky believed that abstraction could express the spiritual realm more aptly than representational styles, and the composer Arnold Schoenberg held onto the romantic conviction that pure music with no external reference reveals "a higher form of life towards which mankind evolves" (Schoenberg [1947] 1975, 136; Kandinsky [1911] 1977) (fig. 71).

The purity-of-medium ideal was soon interpreted to mean that abstraction in painting, atonality in music, and experimentalism in literature were not just contingent stylistic possibilities but also the destiny of each of the fine arts.

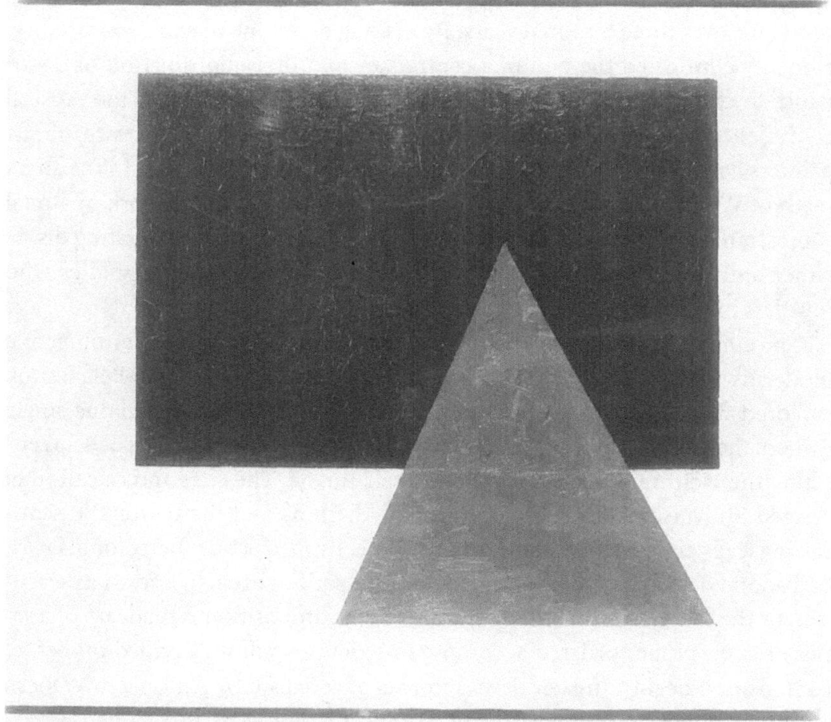

Figure 71. Kasimir Malevich, *Black Rectangle, Blue Triangle* (1915). Stedelijk Museum, Amsterdam. Foto Marburg/Art Resource, New York.

Schoenberg remarked in 1912 that when Kandinsky or Kokoschka painted pictures that seem to be "hardly more than an excuse to improvise in colors and forms" they expressed themselves "as only the musician expressed himself until now" and were part of a new movement that had discovered "the true nature of art" ([1947] 1975, 144). Piet Mondrian caught this aspect of the modernist ethos with particular acuity in an essay of 1920: "At present each art strives to express itself more directly through its *plastic means* and seeks to *free* its means as much as possible. *Music* tends toward the liberation of *sound, literature,* toward the liberation of *word* . . . painting . . . *expresses pure relationship*" ([1920] 1986, 138). Henceforth, "true art" for most of the modernists was to be the "pure" art of abstraction or experimentalism; even so, not all artists interpreted it as art for art's sake, but, like Mondrian, believed abstraction would unite all the fine and applied arts and lead to a better world.

Schoenberg's own contribution to the purist and experimentalist trends was a systematic assault on the traditional tonal system that had ruled European music for over three hundred years. By making each tone of equal importance, atonality eliminated the pull of a central key and the subordination of dissonance to consonance. This freeing of dissonance could be seen as the musical equivalent of the garish colors and distorted shapes by which expressionist painters conveyed the turmoil and anguish of modern experience. In the aftermath of World War I, Alban Berg produced the quintessential work of atonal expressionism with his opera *Wozzeck* (1917–20), which used ear-grating dissonance and unresolved tonalities to tell the story of a distraught soldier who murders his mistress and commits suicide.

The embrace of atonality and dissonance was only one among innumerable modernist innovations in music, as composers from Charles Ives to Béla Bartók explored new chromatics, structures, and rhythms. The most famous single work of the new music became Igor Stravinsky's 1913 *Rite of Spring,* a ballet reenacting the sacrifice of maidens in prehistoric Russia. The cries and catcalls that greeted Stravinsky's deafening "primitive" rhythms and the dancers' disconcerting leaps almost stopped the performance. By 1920 Schoenberg, for his part, had adopted an even more abstract and systematic approach, known as serialism, or the twelve-tone method, in which each composition is made up of a series of twelve tones ordered according to strict procedures decided on before composition begins. In later developments of serialism by Anton von Webern and others, duration, intensity, timbre, and texture were also treated as elements for which order could be predetermined, affording the composer a sense of "total control." To listeners brought up on the major-minor tonal system, the music produced by these highly rational techniques actually sounded random and meaningless. Serialism, more than other modernist experiments with tonality, timbres, and rhythms, was a pure, abstract music, which lent itself especially well to formalist justifications. Although Schoenberg himself continued to see abstract music as a revelation of the infinite, other modernist composers and critics took up more finite versions of formalist theory. In 1939, Stravinsky spoke of music very much as Hanslick had, calling it "a form of speculation in terms of sound and time" and denying such goals as expressing feelings or representing actions (1947, 19, 79).

Although some critics and historians have trotted out the old chestnut of a heroic avant-garde rejected by the ignorant middle class, the reception of modern music has been much more complex. Stravinsky's *Rite of Spring,* for example, had defenders not only in its first audience but was also generally well received by the critics and soon entered the classical repertory. The serialists had a harder time getting their music performed by established orchestras, and a deep split developed between the most abstract and experimental of the new composers and traditional audiences. Yet serialism was always considered part of "art music," even by those who didn't like it. Its problem was less one of assimilation into the category of fine art than of acceptance by the existing classical music audience. Even so, conductors began to insert "modern" pieces among the traditional baroque and romantic favorites, and people learned to take their modernist medicine with stoic silence and polite applause.

## The Case of Photography

If assimilation was a foregone conclusion in the case of abstract or experimental forms in music, painting, and literature, the assimilation of new arts such as photography, film, or jazz involved a constant fight against the perception that they were not fine arts at all but mere crafts or popular entertainments. As a result, the new versions of expressionist and formalist theories of art played an important role in the final stages of the assimilation of art photography, art film, and art jazz into high art. A good place to observe this process is to trace the drive for purity of medium and the shift from expressionist to formalist arguments in art photography between 1915 and 1940.

As we saw in the previous chapter, expressionist arguments had already played a key role in late nineteenth-century justifications for applying the fine art–versus-craft dichotomy within photography, and by the turn of the century a couple of museums had held exhibitions of pictorialist work. But early in the twentieth century, many art photographers turned against the pictorialist's attempt to make photographs look like paintings and began to champion what they called pure or "straight photography," rejecting both the arranged tableaux of Robinson and the manipulated prints of Steichen. The crisply focused and unaltered print was now claimed to be more artistic than posed, soft-focused, or retouched prints precisely because it was more purely "photographic" (Newhall, 1980, 188). The arguments of many leading straight photographers were now emphatically formalist. In a 1923 lecture Paul Strand said the artist-photographer should respect the "instruments of form, texture and line possible and inherent in strictly photographic processes" (1981, 283) (fig. 72). That same year Edward Weston was photographing his glossy white enamel toilet and writing in his daybooks of his "excitement . . . about absolute aesthetic response to form" (1981, 305).

Although European photographic modernists tended to emphasize experimental techniques such as the photomontage, they shared the Americans' confidence in photography as art, a confidence many art photographers on

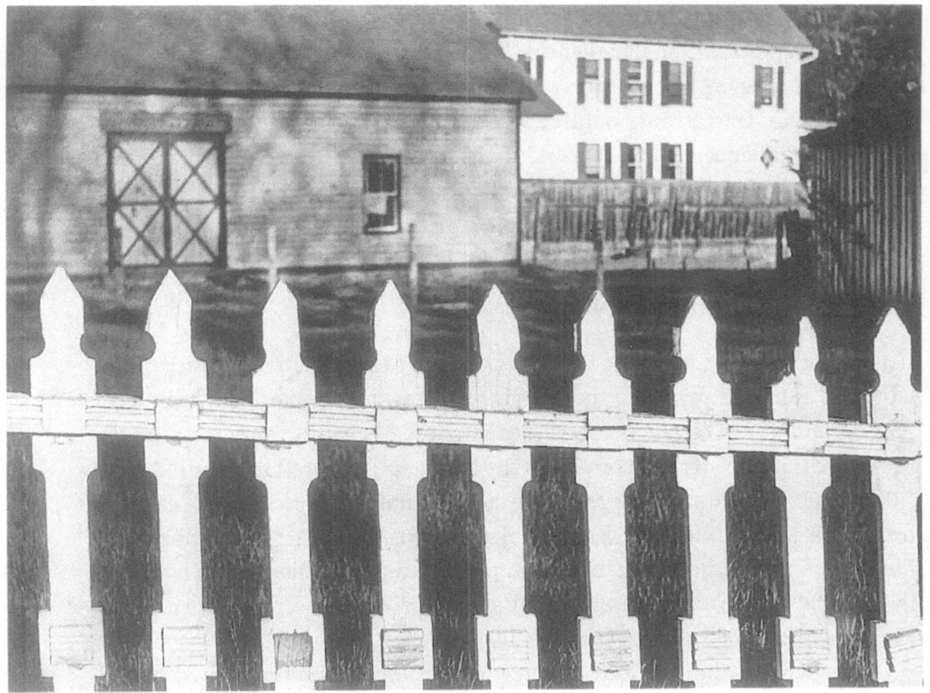

Figure 72. Paul Strand, *The White Fence, Port Kent, New York* (1916). Silver gelatin print, 24.7 × 32.7 centimeters. Gift of the Paul Strand Foundation, 1983.954a. © 2000, Art Institute of Chicago. All Rights Reserved. Also © 1971, Aperture Foundation, Inc./Paul Strand Archive, Millerton, N.Y.

both sides of the Atlantic expressed by proudly dismissing the fine art issue as irrelevant. Yet, as the European avant-garde increasingly turned its attention to social and political issues, many of them began to view formalism as elitist and politically retrograde. Karel Teige declared in a 1931 essay that "unpretentious documentation" has "a far superior cultural and social value than mere 'art'" (Teige 1989, 321). But these outright refusals to be concerned with art status remained marginal compared to the fine art claims of the modernist majority, especially in the United States. Yet, the crisis of the Depression led many American art photographers, such as Walker Evans, for example, into documentary work for the government.

By the 1930s even the staid Metropolitan Museum of Art in New York had begun to accept photographs for its permanent collection. In 1937, the Museum of Modern Art mounted a big retrospective in anticipation of the hundredth anniversary of photography and, in 1940, named Beaumont Newhall curator of the first department of photography in a major American art museum. Newhall adopted three practices that were to dominate the American art museums' assimilation of photography. First, he included in the collection many images originally made for scientific, journalistic, or governmental purposes, such as Charles Marville's 1860s documentation of Paris streets, William Henry Jackson's topographical views of the American West for the U.S. Survey, or the Civil War photographs taken by Mathew Brady's studio. Second, each photograph, whatever its original intention or use, was treated as a single aesthetic object, matted, framed, and hung at eye level. Finally, Newhall adopted the art historian's notion of a canon of masterpieces and geniuses, deftly combining expressionist, formalist, and purist arguments to justify the assimilation of utilitarian images: "From the prodigious output of the last hundred years relatively few great pictures have survived—pictures which are personal expressions of their maker's emotions, pictures which have made full use of the inherent characteristics of the medium of photography. These living photographs are, in the fullest sense of the word, works of art" (Phillips 1989, 20).[2]

## Anti-Art

During the same 1936–38 period in which the Museum of Modern Art put on its photography retrospective, it also devoted exhibitions to cubism, abstraction, dada/surrealism, and the Bauhaus. Championing cubism and abstraction reflected the core of the museum's original mission, as did its formalist embrace of photography and industrial design. But in reaching out to assimilate movements such as dada, surrealism, and the Bauhaus, which were deeply critical of, if not hostile to, established fine art assumptions, the museum also offered an exemplary case of the fine art system's ability to appropriate the works of those who oppose it. Formalist art historians did their part by treating these movements as if they were simply particular styles or tendencies of modernist art, whereas many representatives of dada/surrealism and Russian constructivism had consciously attacked the institution of art as such (Bürger 1984). Even granting that some adherents of dada or constructivism were still more or less under the spell of fine art ideals, the anti-art ethos had been a defining feature of both movements.

Dada began in Zurich in 1917 and soon spread to Berlin, Paris, and other cities as a protest against a war in which each side claimed to be defending their nation's highest cultural values (Richter 1965). Dada borrowed many of its ideas and techniques from the Italian futurists' wild pronouncements and activities of 1911–14, especially their poems of nonsense syllables, their "noise intoners" for music, and their provocative performance evenings, which assaulted all established values. But the futurists were not anti-art; they simply wanted an "art of the future," as did some dadas. Among those in the anti-art wing of dada, Tristan Tzara was perhaps cleverest at provocation: "ART—a parrot word—replaced by DADA, PLESIOSAURUS, or handkerchief" (Motherwell 1989, 82). George Grosz, like other Berlin dadas, was more political in his hostility to art and remembers aiming his blow at "so-called sacred art which reflected upon cubes and gothic structures while the marshals were painting in blood" (Erickson 1984, 43).

The brutal caricatures of George Grosz and the derisive photomontages of Hannah Höch and John Heartfield were brilliant attacks on oppressive industrialists, militarists, and the rising fascist movement. Grosz's 1921 drawing *At 5 O'Clock in the Morning* shows, in its lower segment, some rich industrialists still out puking and whoring at the very hour a throng of workers, shown in the upper segment, trudge toward their factories. In a less political vein Marcel Duchamp's "readymades"—ordinary objects to which he affixed a title such as the snow shovel called *In Advance of the Broken Arm*—parodied the sacrosanct "work of art." Man Ray came up with some memorable "assisted" readymades such as *Gift,* an ordinary flat iron with a row of tacks glued down the middle, their sharp points rendering it wittily useless and dreamily menacing (fig. 73). Yet most dadas, whether in Zurich, Paris, or New York, did not want to abolish art but to integrate it with life. "Art," Tzara declared, "is not the most precious manifestation of life. Art does not have the celestial and universal value people like to attribute to it. . . . Dada introduces it into daily life, and vice versa" (Motherwell 1989, 248). Here again, the Berlin dadas were more radical, believing that the only way to reintegrate art and life was to place both at the service of the socialist revolution. In Paris, the surrealist successors of dada sometimes claimed theirs was not merely an art movement but a philosophy and a social revolt. They used the dream and unconscious not only as an art technique, as in André Breton's "automatic writing," but as an instrument of social negation as well, calling the new journal they founded in 1930, *La révolution surrealist.*

But even as dada and surrealism challenged the modern system of fine art, they succumbed to its pervasive force (something realized by Marcel Duchamp, whose most famous readymade, *Fountain,* we will look at in the next chapter). Much of the normative view of the artist's superior freedom and genius remained intact in both dadaistic and surrealist practice. With the exception of Sophie Taeuber-Arp and a few women surrealists who reached into the craft realm, the main effect of the turn to modernist experiments with chance, assemblage, and readymade images was to further separate the poet and artist as

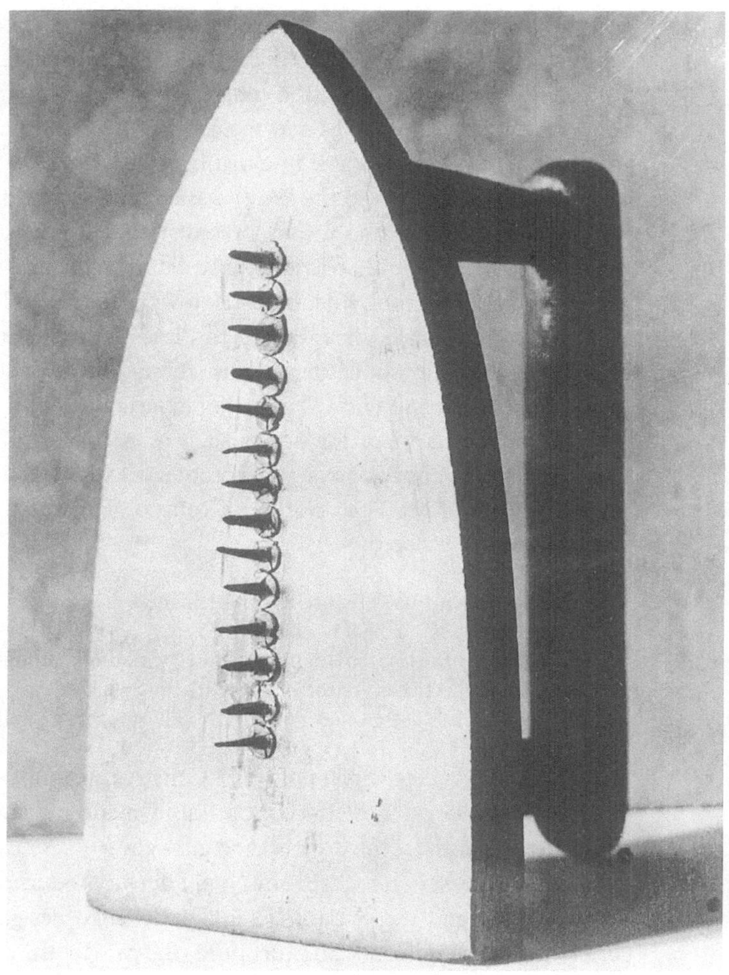

Figure 73. Man Ray, *Gift* (1921). ©2001, Man Ray Trust/Artists Rights Society (ARS), New York/ADAGP, Paris.

seer of the unconscious from the ordinary writer and craftsperson. Many of the surrealists, in particular, "proved incapable . . . of relinquishing the modern ideal of art as an absolute value" (Wolin 1994, 137). In fact, the later recapture of dada and surrealism by art and literary history and by the art museum was already foreshadowed by its first audiences. As the critic Albert Gliezes wrote of Paris dada in 1920, the audience was "composed of curiosity seekers and of highly Parisian boulevardiers, the arbiters of artistic fashion for snobbish circles. These elements are in quest of the 'modern direction'" (Motherwell 1989, 302).

If the provocations of Tzara seem merely naughty and those of Breton overly esoteric, the anti-art declarations of the Russian constructivists were potentially of greater social importance, given constructivism's roots in marxist theory and its opportunity to help build a new society. Russian constructivism of the revolutionary period (which should be distinguished from the stylistic constructivism Naum Gabo took to the West) was a combination of the pre-1917 idea that the artwork should be a nonrepresentational construction and the post-1917 idea that artists should become constructors of the new socialist society. In 1913, Vladimir Tatlin took a decisive step toward the general constructivist position when he returned from a trip to Picasso's studio and began to make painterly reliefs that soon turned into three-dimensional constructions of wood, metal, glass, and wire. The spell of painting was broken and "construction" had taken its place for artists such as Aleksandr Rodchenko, Vavara Stepanova, and Lyubov Popova, who combined it with socialist commitment to become leaders of the First Working Group of Constructivists. One of their early manifestos declared:

> 1. Down with art, long live technical science.
> 2. Religion is a lie. Art is a lie.
> 3. Destroy the last remaining attachment of human thought to art. . . .
> 6. The collective art of today is constructive life.
>
> (Elliot 1979, 130; Lodder 1983, 94–99)

And what should take the place of "art"? Construction. One should simply participate in producing a useful object. Tatlin made his famous architectural model for a gigantic, revolving steel and glass government complex, *Monument to the Third International,* Stepanova and Popova produced extraordinary abstract clothing and textile designs, and Rodchenko designed photomontage posters, worker's uniforms, and furniture (fig. 74). Yet the early constructivists also firmly distinguished what they were doing from both handicraft and applied art—from handicraft since virtuosity with brush or chisel was to be replaced by precision design and machine tools, from applied art since construction was a matter of total design not the decoration of an existing object (Elliott 1979, 130).

Outside Russia, the Berlin dadas—Grosz and Heartfield, for example—immediately understood the constructivist's intentions and put up a sign at the 1920 Berlin Dada Fair that said "ART IS DEAD: THE MACHINE ART OF TATLIN LIVES." But already in 1922 the Van Diemen Gallery in Berlin presented a First Russian Art Exhibition in which Russian constructivism was treated as just another modernist art style. A member of the Moscow group attacked this kind of

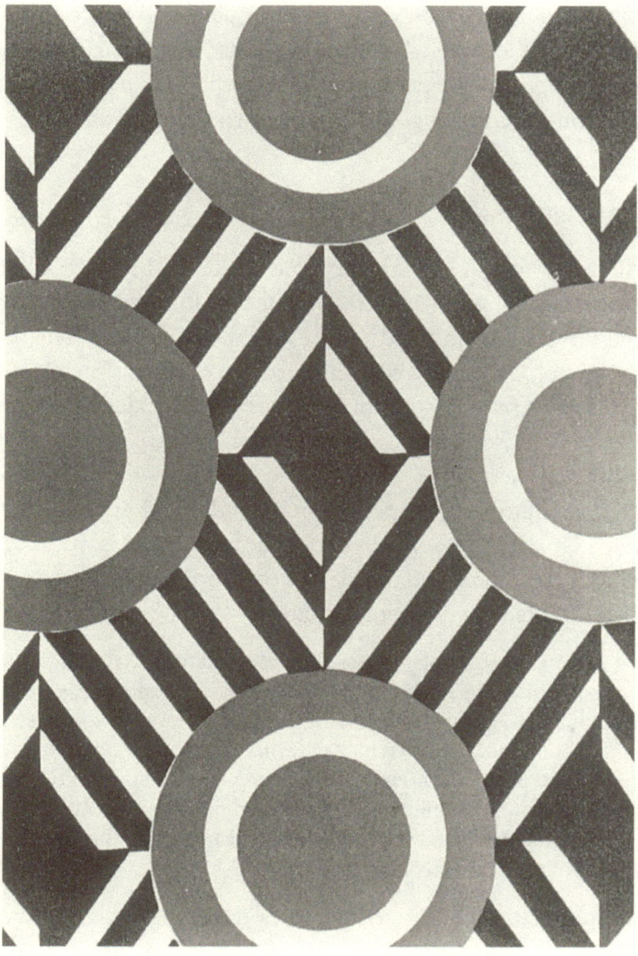

Figure 74. Lyubov Popova, textile design (1924). As reproduced in *Left Front of the Arts,* vol. 2, no. 2 (1924).

appropriation, lamenting the failure of even some Russians to "tear themselves away from art" (Lodder 1983, 238). Unfortunately for the constructivists, neither their modernist experimentalism nor their antiromantic attacks on Art survived the triumph of Stalin. Although Lenin had no understanding or sympathy for modernism and avant-garde experimentalism, his minister of education and culture, Anatoly Lunacharsky, let all styles flourish in the early 1920s. But by the time Stalin had consolidated his power in 1934, the theory of "socialist realism" (socialist in content, realist in style) had been worked out and was imposed by the Communist Party. Party leaders were even suspicious of experiments in "proletarian art" and felt safer supporting conformist versions of high art genres, such as oil painting, opera, and ballet. In such an atmosphere, neither modernist styles (denounced as "formalism") nor talk of anti-art had much appeal to the party bureaucrats who took over the art and music schools and controlled what got shown, performed, and published.

## The Bauhaus

Although not an anti-art movement, the Bauhaus school of architecture, art, and crafts (1919–32) also resisted the established fine art system by trying to reunite art and craft and restore art's social purpose. The Bauhaus was created by Walter Gropius, who combined the Weimar School of Fine Arts with its School of Arts and Crafts in 1919, the new name deriving from the *Bauhütte*, the medieval mason's guilds. Founded during the political and economic turmoil following Germany's defeat in World War I, the ideas and practices of the Bauhaus remained suspect to both traditional artists and political conservatives. Gropius's 1919 manifesto for the new school is worth citing at length since it not only announced the ideal of overcoming the art-versus-craft division but also reflected the inherent difficulty of the task:

> Architects, sculptors, painters, we must all turn to the crafts. . . . There is no essential difference between the artist and the craftsman. The artist is an exalted craftsman. In rare moments of inspiration, moments beyond the control of his will, the grace of heaven may cause his work to blossom into art. *But proficiency in his craft is essential to every artist.* Therein lies a source of creative imagination. Let us create a new guild of craftsmen, without the class distinctions, which raise an arrogant barrier between craftsman and artist. Together let us create a new building of the future. (Naylor 1968, 50)

Gropius's statement nicely captures the existing division between the ideal of the artist's superiority as imaginative genius, creating self-contained works, and the craftsperson's skill and knowledge of materials in the service of functional demands. By italicizing "proficiency in craft is essential to every artist," Gropius showed he knew how difficult it would be to get aspiring artists to accept the humble role of learning craft skills and working cooperatively on functional design and construction (Forgács 1991). Even the school's organization reflected this tension since the workshops were presided over by two instructors, the form teacher, who taught design, and the practice teacher, who taught materials and craft skills. Thus, in the first weaving workshop a young painter, Georg Muche, was made form teacher whereas weaving techniques were taught by Helene Börner, retained along with her looms from the previous arts and crafts school.

Yet Gropius's primary aim was not to turn out skilled craftspeople but to draw art, craft, and technology together in the training of designers and architects. After a few years, each workshop had only a single artist-designer as teacher, usually drawn from Bauhaus graduates who had imbibed the original ideal of the artist-craftsman-designer (Gropius 1965). Gropius managed to attract such already well-known artists as Lyonel Feininger, Wassily Kandinsky, Paul Klee, and Theo van Doesburg, as well as younger people, such as Josef and Anni Albers, Herbert Bayer, Marcel Breuer, and Lázló Moholoy-Nagy, who would become well known. Some of the artists never gave up a sense of their superiority and autonomy, but others—Breuer and Moholy-Nagy, for instance—became dedicated exponents of Gropius's aim of uniting art, craft, and technology in the service of society. Thanks to Gropius's combination of diplomacy and firmness, students not only imbibed modernist artistic theory from van Doesburg, Kandinsky, and Klee, but they also learned practical skills and the nature of materials in the textile, pottery, metalworking, and furniture shops prior to the final courses in architecture. When the Bauhaus was forced to move to Dessau in 1926, Gropius designed the main building in a severe modernist style and furnished it with chairs, tables, and light fixtures designed and made in Bauhaus workshops (fig. 75). Eventually, more and more modernist Bauhaus designs, such as Breuer's famous tubular chairs, Marianne Brandt's lamps, and Gunta Stölzl's textiles, won praise in international competition and were adopted for industrial production. The long-term result, if not exactly Morris's "art of the people for the people," was furniture, utensils, and fixtures that were of exceptional modern design and sold at more affordable prices than the handmade productions of arts and crafts guilds (Whitford 1984) (fig. 76).

By the time Gropius resigned as director in 1928 to pursue his own architectural work, the Bauhaus was the leading center for modernism in design and was poised to become a leader in architectural education as well. To understand what happened next at the Bauhaus, we need to look at the general debate among architectural modernists over the implications of such new materials as steel, aluminum, glass, and reinforced concrete. Some modernists viewed the new industrial materials primarily as providing the architect with opportunities for artistic expression, whereas others saw the new materials as an opportunity to design badly needed affordable housing and healthier factories and schools. Thus, both the art and function aims of architecture now took on a special coloring from their association with the new technologies. When Louis Sullivan, coined the famous phrase "form follows function" in the 1890s, he meant the shaping of new materials and techniques to serve human needs. But when Le Corbusier celebrated function in 1923, he understood it in a more technological

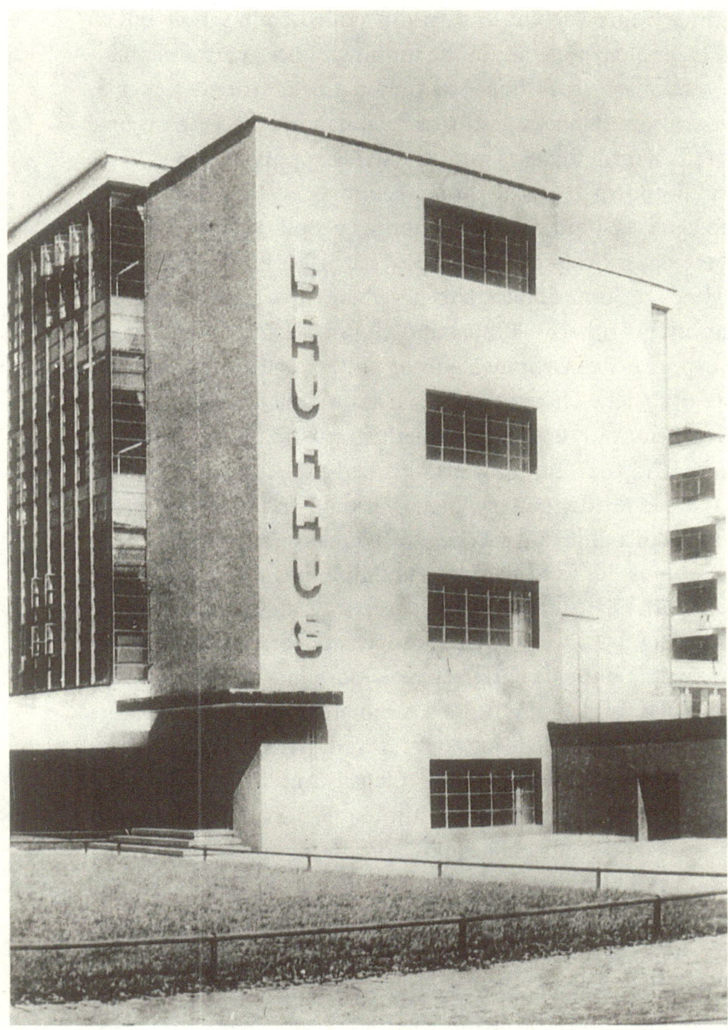


Figure 75. Walter Gropius, Bauhaus, Dessau, Germany (1925–26). Detail of exterior. Courtesy Foto Marburg/Art Resource, New York.

sense and combined it with a "pure" art of geometric abstraction, turning the house into a "machine to live in" (Le Corbusier [1923] 1986) (fig. 70). This in no way diminished Le Corbusier's elevated notion of architecture as a fine art or of the architect as the heroic artist-redeemer of society. Although there were some architects who argued for the complete autonomy of the formal aspects of architecture, most, including Le Corbusier, tried to hold the aesthetic, functional, and technological in some sort of balance.[3]

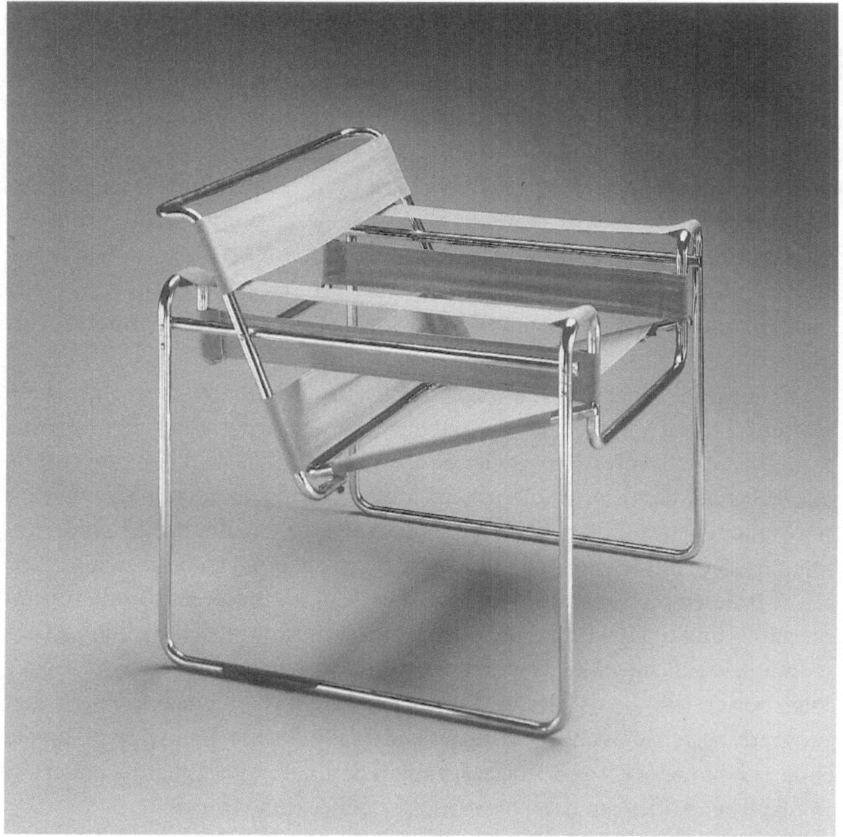

Figure 76. Marcel Breuer, chair, model B32 (ca. 1931). Courtesy Victoria and Albert Museum, London/Art Resource, New York.

If Gropius's educational and design work at the Bauhaus up to 1928 was guided by a vision of keeping art and function in equilibrium, his successor, Hannes Meyer, went to the functionalist and technological extreme: "Building is a technical, not an aesthetic process, and time and again the artistic composition of a house has contradicted its practical function" (Kruft 1994, 386). Meyer's architectural views combined an austere modernist style with a commitment to teaching students to design in a "functional-collectivist-constructive" manner (Droste 1998, 166). By 1930 Meyer was fired for his socialist views and replaced by the apolitical Ludwig Mies van der Rohe, who shifted the Bauhaus curriculum toward pure architectural theory and design, eliminating the craft workshop requirement and turning the shops into design studios. Although Mies emphasized the technological determinants of architecture and the need for unornamented designs, he had a refined sense of form and a preference for fine materials that always gave his buildings a subtle aesthetic dimension. While Meyer called architecture simply Building *(Bauen)*, Mies called it Art-Building *(Baukunst)*, and whereas Meyer gave students design problems defined by specific social needs, Mies's problems were pure design tasks with few specifications. In Mies's Bauhaus teaching "architecture was art, confrontation with space, proportion and material" (Droste 1998, 212–14). And so the Bauhaus itself, founded to unite art and craft, the aesthetic and the functional, spent its last four years swinging wildly between the poles of art divided.

Meanwhile, Hitler and the Nazis had begun their march to power by exploiting the resentments and discontents of a defeated nation now suffering from the Great Depression. As German writers, painters, and composers soon discovered, Hitler hated modernist art in all its forms. The Nazis later staged a now infamous exhibition of "Degenerate Art" (1937) and attacked modernist literature and music, favoring the "German" music of Wagner. In architecture, Hitler ordered monumental neoclassical works with hundreds of columns for his public buildings, whereas in housing the Nazis supported a traditional German folk look. One of the Nazi's first political conquests on the way to seizing total power was a 1931 electoral victory in the city of Dessau, where they promptly began harassing the Bauhaus and finally closed it in 1932. Mies van der Rohe tried to revive it as a private school in Berlin, but it was hardly underway in 1933 when Hitler came to power and the police shut it down.

Many Bauhaus teachers, including Gropius, Moholy-Nagy, and Mies Van der Rohe eventually emigrated to the United States, where they had a great influence (Gropius 1965). Despite Gropius's pronouncements and the example of the Bauhaus experiments in reuniting art and craft in the 1920s, the later modernist design and architecture movements in America and Europe could not overcome the separation of the designer (artist) and the maker (artisan). As serially produced functional items for commercial distribution, design products remained part of the lesser arts even when taken into places like the Museum of Modern Art. The textiles, chairs, and lamps in these museums are seldom exhibited as the work of those who actually produced them or because they successfully fulfilled their function but as examples of formal stylistic development or the expressive genius of the artist-designer. Like the very different movements of dada/surrealism and Russian constructivism, the Bauhaus ideal and practice had combined modernism with a drive to overcome the separation of art from everyday life. By ensuring the triumph of modernism and functionalism in the design of everyday objects, the Bauhaus came closer to its goals of reuniting art and everyday life than did dada or Russian constructivism. Yet all three movements were eventually assimilated by formalist art history and the art museum as styles and theories of art in ways that neutralized their protest against the isolation of art.

## Three Philospher-Critics on the Division of Art

I want to conclude these remarks on the processes of assimilation and resistance in the early years of modernism by looking briefly at three philosopher-critics who went beyond the internal problems generated by modernism to address directly the underlying art-versus-craft division in the 1930s: the British idealist R. G. Collingwood, who sought to reinforce the division, the American pragmatist John Dewey, who sought to dissolve it, and the German-Jewish mystic and marxist Walter Benjamin, who sought to transcend it. Their thought can only be adequately understood, however, if we keep in mind that European culture, traumatized by the slaughter of World War I and the revolutionary aftermath that brought fascism to Italy and communism to Russia, was again deeply shaken in the 1930s by the Great Depression and the rise of Hitler and Stalin. In such a climate, many artists and critics in both Europe and the Americas turned away from modernist abstraction and experimentalism toward representational styles they thought would be better able to carry a political message.

Collingwood's defense of the fine art–versus-craft division in his writings of the 1920s and 1930s is particularly interesting for our purposes since he explicitly recognized that the modern fine art–versus-craft polarity only goes back to the eighteenth century, prior to which the word "art" meant something closer to "craft" and artists thought "of themselves as craftsmen" (1938, 6). Collingwood's task was complicated because he wanted not only to support modernism's struggle against representation but also to expose the error of thinking that genuine art could serve a political purpose (he complained of "our young writers" pursuing "the propaganda . . . of communism") (1938, 71). Collingwood was convinced that most people mistakenly took representational or utilitarian craftworks, such as portraits or hymns, to be art rather than understanding art in its "proper" aesthetic meaning. Craft, according to Collingwood, is any work that deliberately uses a technique (such as representation) to achieve a specific effect on its audience. Representational arts, whether patriotic songs, landscapes, or moralistic poetry such as Kipling's, aim at generating specific emotions that will be useful in practical life. In addition to these "magically" useful crafts, Collingwood also excluded from art such "amusement" crafts as detective stories, dance music, radio shows, and films—which aim at arousing emotions simply for diversion. In contrast to both the useful and amusement crafts, true art is an act of imaginative expression requiring interpretive understanding. Unlike the craft maker who aims at a preconceived result, the true artist does not know in advance the outcome of the process of discovery and creation (1930). Despite appearances, Collingwood's restatement of the regulative assumptions of fine art does not really consign entire media or genres to the realm of craft; what makes something either craft or art is the *way* artists engage the medium. Although Collingwood seemed to regard most films as amusement or propaganda crafts since they employ techniques to achieve a specific effect, his theory would allow the possibility that a true artist might use the medium of film for imaginative self-discovery and creation. Yet the price Collingwood's expressionist theory pays for this openness to selective assimilation into "art proper" is of the same kind as formalist theories: the demotion of specific function and the depreciation of technique.

At the same time that Collingwood was exposing what he took to be the error of mistaking craft for art proper, John Dewey was vigorously attacking the separation of the fine and useful arts and the separation of art and life generally: "To institute a difference of *kind* between useful and fine arts is . . . absurd . . . the only *basic* distinction is that between bad art and good art, and this . . . applies equally to things of use and of beauty" ([1925] 1988, 282–83). Like Collingwood, Dewey defended modernism, and he specifically rejected the idea of a "proletarian art" then coming out of the Soviet Union (1934, 344). But unlike Collingwood, he wanted not only to include in art the conventional applied and popular arts but to identify an "art" dimension in everyday activities from sewing and singing to gardening and sports. The key to Dewey's effort to reunite art and the everyday was his reframing of the idea of the aesthetic to make it a dimension of all human experience rather than a separate kind of experience. The core of any memorable experience for Dewey is a feeling of harmony after disequilibrium and the only thing distinguishing aesthetic experience from other kinds of experience is that the aesthetic is a particularly integrated and consummate moment of such harmony. Although all the arts from cooking to the canvas afford a degree of aesthetic or integrative experience, "the fine arts lay hold of this fact and push it to its maximum of significance" (1934, 26, 195). Dewey emphasizes that utility need not interfere with having an aesthetic experience of harmony after imbalance; the person who uses a tea cup is not prevented from enjoying its aesthetic aspect anymore than the fisherman who eats his catch is prevented from enjoying the aesthetic pleasure of the cast (1934,

13–15, 46–56, 261). True art is "simultaneously instrumental and consummatory," and anytime we divide art into useful and fine we "destroy its intrinsic significance" ([1925] 1988, 271). One practical outcome of Dewey's effort to unite the fine and useful arts was the way his wealthy friend, Albert Barnes, hung his collection of finely shaped barn hinges among the world-class modernist paintings in his private museum in Pennsylvania.

Although Dewey clearly established a continuity between fine art and craft by allowing that any useful object *may* afford an aesthetic experience, there are other passages in *Art as Experience* that downplay both craft skill and specific use. Sometimes he sets up a dichotomy between "mere utility," in which we are "indifferent to the object itself," and aesthetic experience, in which we are indifferent to use. The "work of esthetic art . . . serves life rather than prescribing a defined and limited mode of living" (1934, 135). Dewey's effort to overcome the fine art–versus–useful art polarity falters at this point. Rather than locate the aesthetic dimension of useful objects *in* their use in the normal sense of the word—which means in their specific functions—Dewey, like Emerson, often located aesthetic quality in a metaphoric "use" for "life purposes." Although Dewey grants function, technique, and materiality a more positive role in the arts than either Riegl's formalist or Collingwood's expressionist theories, his position on the useful arts was finally ambiguous. Even so, Dewey remains a key figure for the tradition of resistance, and there has been a revival of interest in his attempt to reconstruct the concepts of art and the aesthetic (Shusterman 2000).

In the late 1920s and early 1930s, Walter Benjamin lived through Germany's devastating inflation, unemployment, and political violence, his only income from writing reviews. After the Nazis seized power, he went to Paris, where he received a small stipend from the German Institute for Social Research, by then in exile in America. Benjamin's early literary studies and speculations had been informed by the Jewish mystical tradition, but by 1930 he had been drawn toward a materialist perspective—although he never gave up his religious utopianism. His often cited and anthologized essay of 1936, "The Work of Art in an Age of Mechanical Reproduction," argues that until the age of mass media, the work of art possessed an "aura." In the Middle Ages and Renaissance, its aura was a religious one, derived primarily from what it represented; in the early modern period, the work of art was gradually secularized, its ritual aura becoming the aesthetic aura of the unique self-contained work, a kind of religion of Art. But in the twentieth century, the aura of the singular work of art had in turn been diminished by the new mass media of photography, film, and the audio recording, which produced cheap, multiple copies. Benjamin goes on to suggest that these new media are the crucial art forms of the twentieth century because they free art from its aesthetic isolation and allow art to perform a political and informational function in daily life (1969, 217–52).

Benjamin's enthusiastic embrace of the mass media and his rejection of the autonomous artwork have been widely criticized, starting with Theodor Adorno.[4] But many of Benjamin's other writings are more open ended than the occasionally heavy-handed marxism of his most famous essay. In "The Storyteller," for example, he claims that storytelling by peasants, artisans, and merchants in preindustrial society was a craft growing out of personal experience and carrying the traditional wisdom of proverbs. But the coming of print gradually diminished the role of personal storytelling so that genres such as the novel, with its lone artist-writer and solitary readers, began to take the place of storytelling. Benjamin describes the craft of the storyteller with an evident nostalgia, and Bernd Witte has suggested we connect it to Benjamin's admiration for the "worker-correspondents" who flourished in the Soviet Union before they were eliminated under Stalin (Witte 1991). According to Benjamin's essay "The Author as Producer," in the figure of the worker-correspondent "the distinction between author and public" begins to disappear and "the reader is always ready to become a writer." Writing ceases to be a specialist art and becomes an everyday practice (1986, 225). In 1940 Benjamin fled the advancing German armies to the Spanish border; when his group was detained, he feared he would be captured and committed suicide. Although Benjamin never had a chance to reconcile the mystical and materialist sides of his thinking about art in the age of mechanical reproduction, many have found his essays among the most suggestive twentieth-century texts for reflecting on art divided.

## Modernism and Formalism Triumphant

After World War II, the art worlds of music, literature, and painting returned to the internal struggles of modernism. Although existentialism in France provided a focus for a socially concerned literature of an intensely individual type, in the United States, the preoccupation with social issues and the use of representational styles fell quickly into disfavor in both literature and painting as modernist experimentation revived and triumphed, thanks partly to lessons learned during the 1940s from the many European exiles. Paralleling this shift in the arts themselves, formalist theories gained ascendance among critics of literature (Cleanth Brooks), the visual arts (Clement Greenberg), and aestheticians (Monroe Beardsley). Fundamental explorations of the underlying fine art–versus-craft and art-versus-society divisions of the kind raised by Collingwood, Dewey, and Benjamin faded into the background along with the socially conscious art, literature, and music of the 1930s and the war years. In the visual arts, some critical supporters of the abstract expressionism of Jackson Pollock and Willem de Kooning were prepared to deny that realist works were really art at all. In literary criticism and literature departments, the formalist movement called the New Criticism now became dominant, and students were encouraged to focus on detailed internal analysis of poems or novels rather than biographical origins or political implications. Leaders of the musical avant-garde, such as Pierre Boulez, were ready to dismiss tonal composers as useless, and Milton Babbitt made a virtue of modernist music's tiny audience in a famous essay of 1958, "Who Cares If You Listen?" (Schwartz and Childs 1998).

In the 1950s, modernism and formalism got an unexpected boost from the Cold War. With the memory of Hitler and the Nazis still fresh and with Stalin's culture minister Andrei Zhdanov once again publicly condemning "formalism" as a sign of capitalist "decadence," modernism and formalism now carried the cachet of antitotalitarianism. Acting as surrogate for the U.S. government, the Museum of Modern Art supported traveling exhibitions of abstract expressionist painting as a sign of America's creative freedom and artistic leadership in contrast to the communist bloc's censorship and stagnation. In West Germany, the annual *Documenta* exhibition of contemporary art, inaugurated in Cassel in 1956, declared on its posters: "Abstract Art is the idiom of the free world." Meanwhile, in Darmstadt a series of now legendary "summer courses for new music" had been going on since 1946, which drew an international following among avant-garde composers, including Pierre Boulez, Luciano Berio, and Karlheinz Stockhausen. The early Darmstadt participants could not help but be conscious of the Soviet condemnation of formalism in music since it was reiterated by the Central Committee of the Communist Party in 1948, the year of the Berlin blockade and Allied airlift. It is no surprise, then, that one of the leading philosophers to write on musical aesthetics, Theodor Adorno, would champion serialism against both Western popular music ("the capitalist entertainment industry") and the tonal music favored by both American symphony audiences and the "vulgar marxists" of Eastern Europe. Yet, as Karol Berger has pointed out, when Stalin died in 1955, the ruling parties of Communist countries such as Poland realized that modernist abstraction in music was politically harmless. At the same time, the West European musical avant-garde was settling "into the comfortable role of . . . combining official support with the flattering self-image of antibourgeois subversiveness," whereas the American musical avant-garde was "settling into tenured positions in the universities" (Berger 2000, 147).

By the mid-1950s, New York had become the world mecca for the arts, and American composers, writers, and artists were on the way to becoming international celebrities. At the same time, programs in university departments of literature, music, and theater and schools of fine art expanded and enrollments soared. In the visual arts, there were new majors in media like ceramics, weaving, photography, and film, which most people had previously learned by apprenticeship or in commercial schools. The more general process of assimilating new genres and new arts into fine art institutions now operated in an expansive and optimistic social/economic environment. In 1964, art in the United States received a major public consecration with the creation of the National Endowment for the Arts, followed by an unprecedented expansion in the number of galleries, museums, symphonies, dance and theater companies, arts festivals, literary journals and prizes, and local and state arts councils. Art had finally been publicly recognized in a country that had never placed investment in culture among its highest priorities. In fact, the rhetoric of art's elevated place in life was such that a reaction came from within the art world itself in the form of pop art, especially Andy Warhol's send-up of hallowed notions like "originality" with his silkscreen images derived from publicity or news photos and calling his studio—where assistants often did much of the work—"The Factory." Of course, with the exception of a few diehard formalists such as Clement Greenberg, all this only made Warhol's reputation as an artist that much bigger. Yet the underlying fine art–versus-craft polarity continued to distort the production and reception of the arts, now complicated by the processes of assimilation and resistance. My concluding chapter will look at a few examples from the past half-century.

CHAPTER 15

# Beyond Art and Craft?

INVITED TO THE Telluride Film Festival in 1977 to show her film *Kitch's Last Meal,* Carolee Schneemann was provoked to "step out of frame" and confront her audience directly. Taking off her clothes and applying stripes of mud to her body, she slowly began to unravel a scroll from her vagina, reading as she went. It described a confrontation with a filmmaker who complains of her film's "personal clutter . . . hand-touch sensibility . . . diaristic indulgence." Known as *Interior Scroll,* Schneemann's performance raised issues on several levels—of women's identity as creators and procreators, the place of personal experience in making art, and the locus of wisdom in the body. Like much performance art of the 1970s, *Interior Scroll* was also intended to overcome what Schneemann called "the distancing of audience perception," the passive looking, listening, or reading that so often occurs with film, music, or literature (Sayre 1989, 90).

Although the arts since 1970 have been characterized by a pluralism that de fies generalization, it is fair to say that one major trend of the past thirty years has tried to reintegrate art with life, from the intimately personal to the broadly political. Yet, like a compulsive who must repeat the same actions over and over, Western culture has seemed unable to stop repeating the kind of division by which it originally split art into fine art versus craft and segregated art from the rest of society. But this continued division has also been entangled with the processes of assimilation and resistance, which, in their different ways, have tended to undermine it. In this chapter, I will examine some of the paradoxes and distortions resulting from this interplay between the art-versus-craft division and the processes of assimilation and resistance. I will look at these effects in relation to "primitive" or "tribal" art, the "crafts-as-art" movement, the tension between "art" and "function" in architecture, the photography-as-art boom, the fear of a "death of literature," the debate over mass music and film, the varied art-world gestures toward getting art and life back together, and some controversial works of public art.

## "Primitive" Art

At the beginning of the twentieth century, European artists from Paris to Moscow became fascinated with everything "uncivilized": the arts of children, naive amateurs, the mentally ill, peasant folk, "primitive" peoples.[1] Although "primitive art" was securely assimilated into fine art institutions by mid-century, in the 1980s attacks on the patronizing implications of the term "primitive" were so successful that it has almost disappeared from museum facades and book covers (Fabian 1983; Clifford 1988; Torgovnick 1990). In 1983, when I first visited Phoenix's Heard Museum devoted to Southwest Indian arts, the words "Anthropology * Primitive Art" were still affixed to the front wall; by 1991 not only had they been taken down but, in addition, the museum itself presented an exhibition called *Exotic Illusion: Art, Romance, and the Market Place* that raised questions about the appropriation of native artifacts as art.

Yet abolishing politically incorrect terminology may only create the illusion that we have changed our thinking by substituting one word for another.[2] Some well-meaning critics believe they can simply drop the term "primitive" as invidiously ethnocentric but keep "art" as complimentary and universal and still talk of ethnographic objects being "elevated to the status of a work of art" (Price 1989, 68). Yet this elevation has usually tended to promote only those things that fit European ideas of fine art, while relegating the rest to the status of craft, even though no such division existed within the cultures of origin. A State Arts Council representative in Alaska, for example, had to explain constantly to Alaskan Inuits in the 1980s that ivory carving and beadwork could be supported "as art" but not kayak or harpoon making (Jones 1986). What seems a natural division between art and craft to us appears merely arbitrary to those not fully acculturated to the Euro-American system of art. The art-versus-craft polarity appears to impose the following alternative: either we force the arts of these societies into an alien mold of (fine) art or we appear to denigrate them as mere crafts. To avoid the negative ethnocentrism of relegating the music, dance, or carvings we admire to the status of craft, we embrace the positive ethnocentrism of assimilating them into fine art. But to take African or Polynesian masks out of their ritual context, cut them from their costumes, and enshrine them in Plexiglas cases for our Sunday contemplation will only seem an inevitable "elevation" to those who place "art for itself" at the apex of values (figs. 77, 78).

Nowhere is the failure to rethink the "art" in the phrase "primitive art" or "tribal art" more revealing than in the alarm over "primitive fakes" and the contempt for "tourist art." Almost as soon as Europeans and Americans began collecting the artifacts and recording the music and dances of small-scale soci-

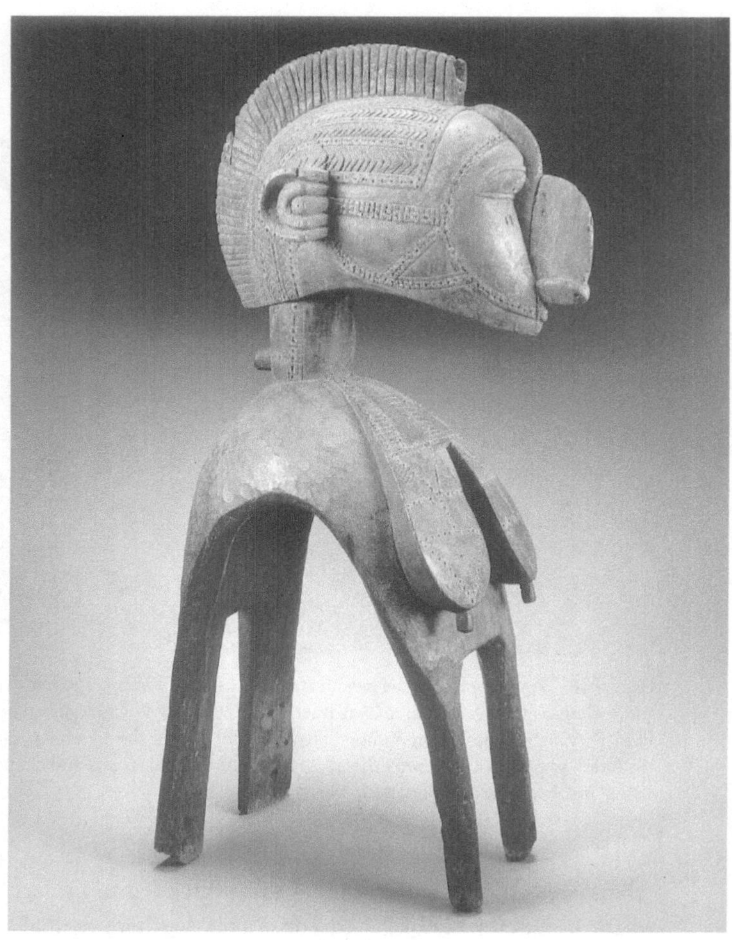

Figure 77. Baga people, headdress (Nimba), mid-nineteenth to early twentieth century; wood, residue from metal tacks, 119.4 × 33 × 61 centimeters. W. G. Field Fund, Inc., and E. E. Ayer Endowment in memory of Charles L. Hutchinson, 1957.160. Photograph © 2000, Art Institute of Chicago. All Rights Reserved. To see a similar headdress worn with a costume in its original context, compare figure 78 on the following page.

eties as Art, people in those societies adapted to the new opportunities. Today, the performance of ritual dances and music or the production of carvings, weavings, and pottery for outsiders has become a major source of income for many communities (Jules-Rosette 1984). But because of the fine art prejudice against trade, Europeans and Americans are disdainful of anything performed or made for money, wanting only what they define as authentic. "Authentic" usually means only those things that have been made in an inherited style to serve a traditional purpose, whereas things made to be sold to outsiders are scorned as fakes, tourist art, or craft kitsch. In African art galleries one sometimes finds penciled onto the price tag of a mask not only a designation of "tribe" but also the phrase "has been danced." What is conceptually interesting

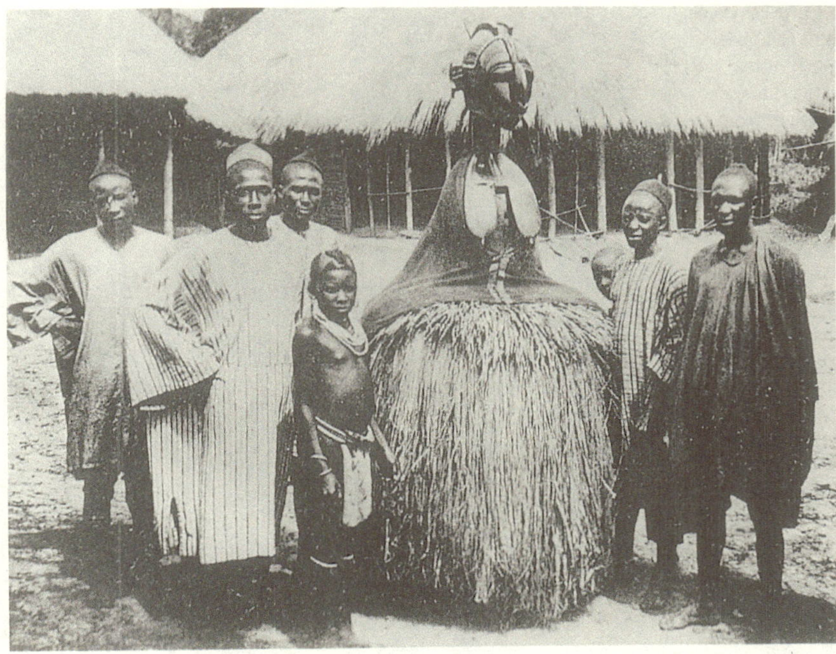

Figure 78. Baga people, Nimba headdress with costume. Photograph from André Arcin, *Histoire de la Guinée française* (Paris: A Challamel, 1911). This posed picture, taken before the days of widely available stop-action photography, does not convey the dynamism of the costumed figure in action as part of a ceremony that included drumming, dancing, and chanting in a dramatic ritual involving a crowd of participants.

about this attitude is that carvings not intended to be "art" in our sense but made as functional objects are considered "authentic tribal art," whereas carvings intended to be "art" in our sense—that is, made to be appreciated and acquired primarily for their appearance—are reduced to the status of craft. In the context of the "tribal art" market, the traditional European fine art–versus-craft distinction undergoes a paradoxical reversal. The utilitarian artifacts are elevated to the status of art and the nonutilitarian artifacts are relegated to the category of craft.

Of course, there *is* an important difference between a mask or power figure carved for sale to outsiders and the rich associations of pieces used in ceremonies. But it is not the difference between art and craft. The spiritual meanings of carvings made for specific ritual uses are not the same as the spirituality we ascribe to fine art. A Baule carver produces a fearsome helmet mask to be worn in dances to protect his village, but once the mask is isolated in the art museum case, photographed for the coffee-table book, or wrapped in the modern discourse of art, it enters a different system of meanings. Tales of its rich associations may provide a shiver of excitement for the jaded art viewer, but the mask has become, as Quatremère said of altarpieces wrenched from Italian churches for the Louvre, only art.[3]

There are signs that the distorting effects of the art-versus-craft division are becoming more widely recognized. Although some museums continue their jewelry case displays, others such as the Heard Museum, in the 1991 exhibition mentioned above, have more directly addressed the differences between the European fine art system and the socially integrated art/craft traditions of other cultures. Susan Vogel's exemplary 1997 exhibition *Baule: African Art Western Eyes* was so effective in contextualizing objects and raising the issue of difference that some critics complained it felt like an anthropology exhibit (Vogel 1997). Native peoples themselves have sometimes overcome outsiders' attempts at "elevation," such as the Zuni, who forced the Denver Art Museum to return their Ahauuta (war gods), or the Kwagiulth of the northwest coast, who have gathered their artifacts into cultural museums organized on different principles than the typical Euro-American art museum (Clifford 1988, 1997). Even within more traditional art museums Native American voices are making themselves heard. The following statement by Michael Lacapa, who is of mixed Apache, Hopi, and Tewa heritage, accompanied an exhibit at the Museum of Indian Arts and Culture in Santa Fe—a new kind of museum where Native Americans help shape the research, education, and exhibition activities.

> What do we call a piece of work created by the hands of my family? In my home we call it pottery painted with designs to tell us a story. In my mother's house, we call it a wedding basket to hold blue corn meal for the groom's family. In my grandma's place we call it a Kachina doll, a carved image of a life force that holds the Hopi world in place. We make pieces of life to see, touch, and feel. Shall we call it "Art?" I hope not. It may lose its soul. Its life. Its people.[4]

In Africa and the Pacific, many of the small-scale societies in which traditional arts are still produced have for decades been part of new nation-states, the rapid modernization of which has steadily undermined the social and religious context of traditional arts. Some African nations fund art schools and museums patterned on European models even as they try to prevent their cultural heritage from disappearing into an insatiable world-art market. Traditional masks and carved figures have become collectors' items for the African upper class, and some governments now seek traditional carvers to reproduce ritual pieces for national museums. But at the same time that traditional carving, music, and ritual are disappearing or being transformed into hybrid genres, many urbanized African painters, sculptors, musicians, and writers successfully compete in the international market using the latest genres and styles. Like many Native American artists who resent the tendency of whites to stereotype them as "Indian artists," African painters and sculptors see themselves simply as artists working within the global fine art or popular art systems (Oguibe and Enzwezor 1999). Meanwhile, many dealers, galleries, and museums in Europe and America not only have continued to show a preference for traditional ritual carvings but have also begun to assimilate pieces of contemporary African functional and folk art—from coffins in the shape of automobiles, to slingshots and barbershop signs (Vogel 1991; Steiner 1994).[5]

## Crafts-as-Art

It is not surprising to see the fine art–versus-craft division used to appropriate the arts of other cultures; it *is* surprising to see it used to divide the very crafts that Morris hoped would overcome it. Although the proponents of what has been called the "crafts-as-art movement" claim to have overthrown the barrier between fine art and craft, the actual effect of the movement has been to divide the studio crafts themselves into art and craft approaches. The assimilation of craft media into fine art began in the late 1950s from two directions: from the side of artists, who began to take up craft-identified materials, and from the side of craftspeople who began to take up the styles and nonfunctional aims of fine art. After World War II, many university fine art departments began to offer programs in the studio crafts, which meant that ceramics, weaving, and woodworking students, who might otherwise have gone through an apprenticeship or vocational school, imbibed the same kind of art history and art-world ideas as their fellow students in painting, sculpture, or graphics. Then, in the late 1950s, as neodada and pop artists began to experiment with wood, clay, fibers, resins, and plastics, some ceramists, such as Peter Voulkos, began to borrow from abstract expressionist styles in their glazes and to put multiple spouts and strange bulges on vessel forms or cut holes in them so as to make them useless as "pots" (fig. 79). Voulkos and his followers were soon called "ceramic sculptors" rather than "potters" or "craftsmen" (Slivka 1978). Similar transformations were occurring in other craft media. What had once been "weaving" became "fiber art" through the abstract, three-dimensional work of Lenore Tawney, Sheila Hicks, and Claire Zeisler. Handcrafted furniture was turned into "art furniture" by people as varied in outlook as Sam Maloof, Wendell

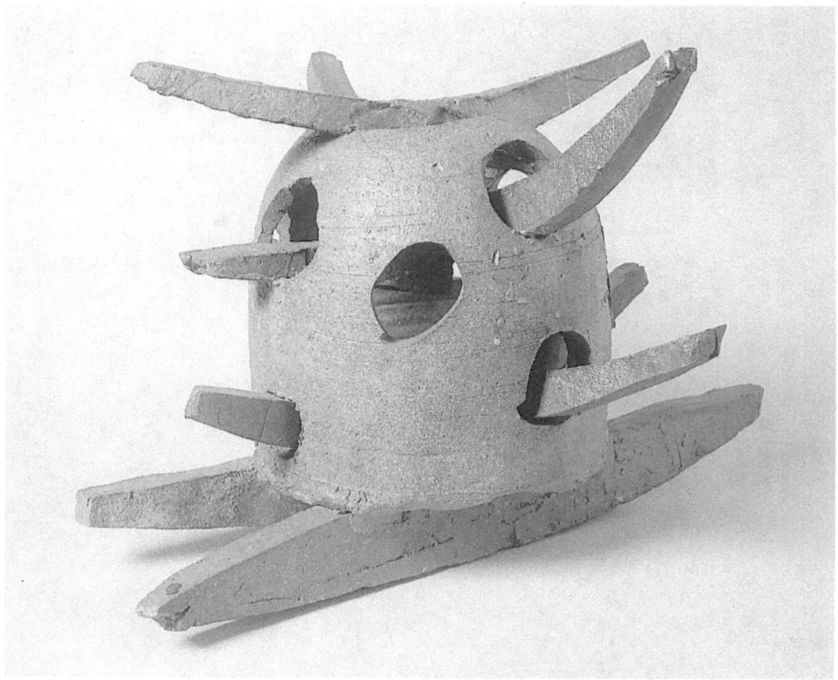

Figure 79. Peter Voulkos, *Rocking Pot* (1956). Wheel-thrown and slab-constructed stoneware. Courtesy National Museum of American Art, Smithsonian Institution, Washington, D.C./Art Resource, New York.

Castle, and Richard Artschwager, whose approaches form a continuum from the always functional to the seldom usable. In glass, the great turn is dated from 1962 when Harry Littleton introduced a studio-size kiln and "glass art" emerged, later achieving a kind of apotheosis of pure form in the work of Dale Chihuly.

With an extra boost from feminists, quilt making also became part of the crafts-as-art movement; the Whitney museum consecrated the American quilt in a 1971 exhibition, and other major museums soon followed (fig. 80). In the rush to collect older quilts as art, Amish quilts were especially favored by some curators and collectors because their simple geometric patterns reminded them of abstract paintings. But what began as an experimental craft revival was soon invaded by professional artists and led to exhibitions such as *The Art Quilt* or *The Artist and the Quilt* (McMorris and Kile 1986). Many women artists influenced by feminism were attracted to quilt making as a way of connecting

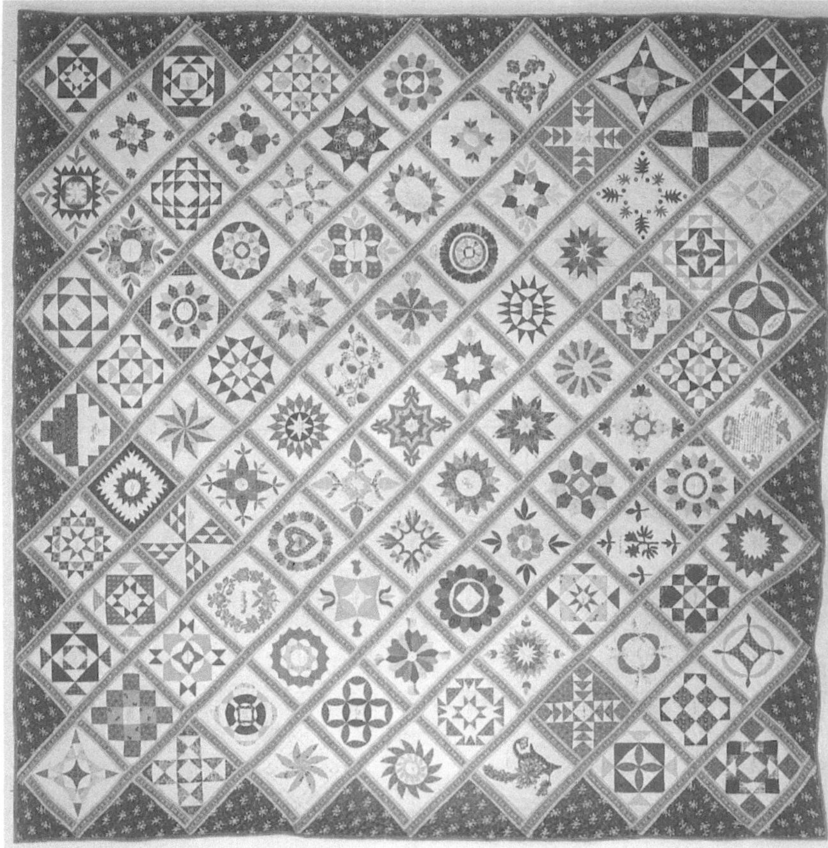

Figure 80. American quilt (1842), Mount Holly, New Jersey: bedcover made for Ella Marie Deacon; cotton, plain weaves; pieced and appliquéd with cotton, plain weaves, some printed in a variety of techniques, some glazed; quilted; inscriptions in ink; edged with woven tape; backed with cotton, plain weave; printed; 264.7 × 272.6 centimeters. Gift of Betsey Leeds Tait Puth, 1978.923. Photograph by Nancy Finn, © 2000, Art Institute of Chicago. All Rights Reserved. In the past, quilts were used as bedcovers until worn out, and then they found their way to the barn or machine shed; many of the finer quilts, such as this one, which were preserved and handed down in memory of their makers, began to enter fine art collections in large numbers in the 1970s as prices soared.

with creative women of the past, although occasionally professional artists merely designed original patterns and paid others to make them into quilts. Yet there were also artists who already knew or learned the necessary sewing techniques and began to focus their careers on creating quilted wall hangings in contemporary art styles, variable sizes, and unusual materials. Although these wall hangings were a species of fiber art, calling them "quilts" was a way of connecting them to the warm associations of an older rural way of life with its communal-support activities, especially the quilting bee. Intended only as works of art rather than as bed or furniture covers, art quilts sometimes ran into a double resistance. The prejudice against needlework was still strong enough that some museum curators resisted quilted wall hangings, even as some traditional quilters and quilting groups rejected them for not following inherited patterns and using hand stitchery (Huitt 1998).

Despite numerous holdouts in both the fine art and craft worlds, the new crafts-as-art approach soon came to dominate the leading craft organizations and journals, as well as craft departments in university art schools. By the 1970s, as the critic John Perreault has remarked, the dividing line between art and craft had become "a dotted line" (Manhart and Manhart 1987, 190). When I attended a national symposium titled "Criticism in the Craft Arts" in 1992, what struck me most was the audience response. Declarations that "craft is art" were greeted with cheers and applause, but suggestions that the term "craft" had a dignity and honor of its own, or Perrault's provocative comment, "I made the mistake once of saying craft was art; no, it is better than art," were met with silence and a shuffling of feet. Even the Smithsonian's Renwick Gallery of American Crafts in Washington, D.C., has fervently embraced the crafts-as-art ideal. A wall panel at a 1997 exhibition declared that "aesthetics [and] not function or design" is the "essential criteria" for its collection, and when the Renwick's permanent collection was reinstalled in 1999, new panels relentlessly drummed into viewers the message that works in so-called craft media were really "art" and that function was incidental.

And yet the larger craft world has been far from unanimous about crafts-as-art; hardly a month went by in the 1980s and 1990s without reference to the issue in one of the craft journals (Andrews 1999). The pro-art party has tended to dismiss traditional craftspeople as mere technicians—when Richard Meyer, for instance, once introduced himself as a "potter," a well-known craft artist sneered, "You make bricks or toilets?" (Meyer 1987, 21). The pro-craft party, on its side, charges the art crowd with selling out workmanship and service for the sake of a trendy and superficial art world (Barnard 1992). Although nearly all the pro-art people are consummate technicians, they downplay the importance of skill, generally reject traditional forms, and treat function as dispensable. Pots with holes in them, cups you can't drink out of, chairs you can't sit on, books you can't open have become the popular hallmark of crafts-as-art. The philosopher Arthur Danto has argued more subtly that what transforms a craftwork into art is not the rejection of function per se but a self-consciousness that lifts it from the plane of the merely well made and useful to the plane of significance. The cabinetmaker Garry Knox Bennett understood this, Danto says, when he drove a sixteen-penny nail into the front of his beautiful rosewood cabinet, bent it over and added a halo of hammer marks. Bennett "hammered home . . . the truth that art . . . is a matter of meaning . . . and furniture can be an art when it is about its own processes" (1994, 78). From the pro-craft perspective, however, the meanings and pleasures derived from a piece of furniture or a quilt are not merely self-referential but deeply tied to human associations (Ruff 1983). As quilt maker Sandi Fox said of her collection, "I like to know that the quilt was used to keep bodies warm, that it was passed from one generation to another" (Diamonstein 1983, 70).

Ironically, the cutting-edge artists and critics of the 1980s and 1990s art world were largely indifferent to crafts-as-art works, which they often found still too well made and beautiful. So low had the value of craft skill sunk in some quarters by the early 1990s that when Martin Puryear, the much admired wood sculptor, was complimented by an interviewer on his superb craftsmanship, he quickly changed the subject as if sensing that his status as an artist was in danger (Danto 1994). I find it equally symptomatic that "America's Museum of Craft," as the Renwick calls itself, keeps denying that the works it shows are craft. But even if all crafts-as-art works were to be enthusiastically accepted as art and all the museums of craft and applied arts in the world changed their names to something like "Museum of Fine Arts in Formerly Craft-Identified Media," the fine art–versus-craft dualism would not be overcome. As we have seen, the polarities of art/craft, mind/body, male/female, white/black have been historically interrelated in their subordination of the second term to first. One does not transcend such polarities by assimilating a few "worthy" representatives of the subordinate term, and leaving the "superior" side unchanged—in this case by merely absorbing some craft works "into fine art on fine art's terms" (Guthrie 1988, 29).

## Architecture as Art

The clash between aesthetics and function that has divided the studio crafts has also continued to trouble architecture. The ideal place for showing off crafts-as-art furniture, ceramics, or textiles in the 1960s and 1970s was within the white walls of the architect-designed modernist house or apartment, itself meant to be a "work of art." By then the ideal image of the architect had become that of the autonomous artist as "exalted purveyor of form" who imposed "his" individual vision on a passive consumer (Ghirardo 1998, 10). Frank Lloyd Wright, like H. H. Richardson before him, had already set the tone in the 1920s and 1930s, with his capes and quips, reinforcing his "artistic persona with a self-conscious rhetoric of integrity, embattlement, and singularity" (Upton 1998, 265). Of course, few architects or art critics of the postwar period would have denied that a house or office building should be functional as well as visually compelling. On the contrary, the modern movement had embraced Sullivan's phrase "form follows function," although, as we have seen, interpreting it to mean the union of new materials and technologies with unornamented, geometric forms. Not all architects went to the extreme of the Bauhaus's Hannes Meyer in opposing "function" to "art," but the spare, rectilinear profiles that dominated skylines in the 1960s came to be associated with "functionalism" even if many of the buildings themselves were not very functional in a human sense. Whatever resistance modernism met early on after World War II, its rectangular steel and glass envelopes, minimalist facades, and acres of open floors were quite popular with corporate executives and real-estate developers who appreciated the modernist style's relatively low cost, quick construction, monumental scale, and cachet as abstract art.

Signs of discontent with modernism already began to surface in the 1960s as books such as Jane Jacobs's *The Death and Life of Great American Cities* (1961) revealed the bankruptcy of an urban renewal policy that bulldozed whole neighborhoods and replaced them with antiseptic high-rises, and Robert Venturi's *Complexity and Contradiction in Modern Architecture* (1966) criticized the boring reductivism of the modernist style. By the 1970s, the postmodern movement was underway with the return of exterior decoration, columns, peaked roofs, cupolas, bas-reliefs, and color. Like many stylistic movements, postmodernism produced some distinguished buildings, and it should be credited with restoring the idea that buildings can also be fun—for example, Michael Graves's hotel for Walt Disney World, with the giant swans and scallop shells on top. But a lot of postmodernism was primarily a stylistic shift, a matter of surface aesthetics and in-jokes for the art historical crowd, rather than a deep reformation of either architecture or the image of the architect as sovereign artist. By now postmodernism has given way to an exuberant pluralism in architecture as in the other arts, so that buildings can look like anything, from geometric cubes to exploding sculptural fantasies.

The swing from the modernist ideology of function back to the pole of fine art in postmodernism reveals how stultifying the art-versus-craft/aesthetic-versus-function split can become. Some critics of modernism have overreacted

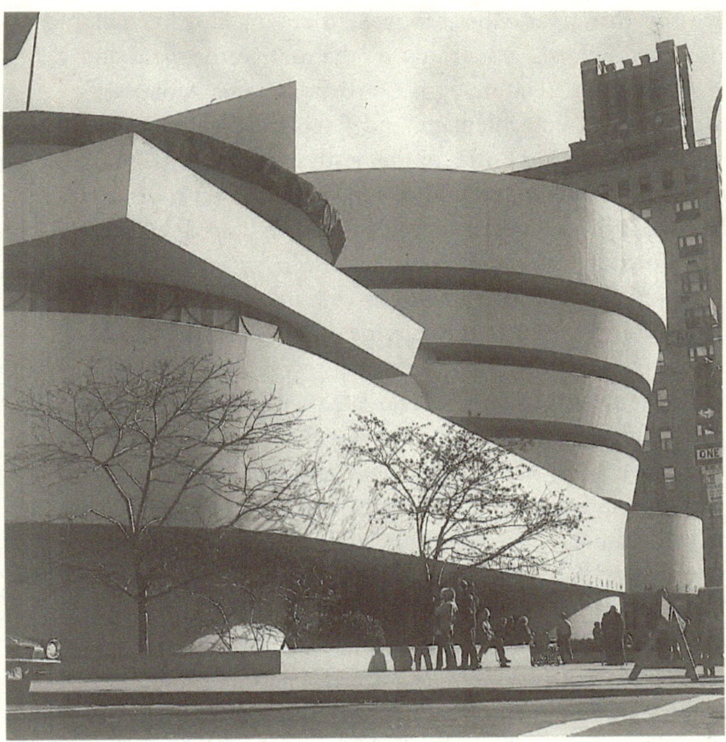

Figure 81. Frank Lloyd Wright, Solomon R. Guggenheim Museum, New York (1959). Exterior seen from Fifth Avenue, New York. Courtesy Art Resource, New York. Wright's spiral ramp design was meant to enhance the viewer's experience of consecutive exposure; the visitor was supposed to take the elevator to the top and walk down the ramp. It works well for some types of works or series but does not allow one to stand back from larger works.

and made "functionalism" a dirty word. But we need to distinguish two kinds of functionalism: the technological and the humanistic. Some modernist buildings seemed to follow a philosophy of form follows technology rather than shaping humane environments for work, leisure, or living. The technological functionalism and rectilinear sameness of many modernist buildings, especially as copied by a host of lesser talents, drew the postmodern reaction that was its welcome, if all too formalist, footnote. Restoring a central role to human functioning in architecture would not mean the triumph of some crudely conceived utility over art, but the integration of functional spaces with a sense of place, a satisfying experience of volume, light, and form, and appropriate attention to symbolic meanings.

Certainly, one of the functions of architecture is to afford pleasure for the eye and the mind, but too often this has been at the expense of the body, as we move through buildings and use their spaces for the activities of life. As in the case of crafts-as-art works, the danger of focusing on architecture as "art" is that primacy is given to visual appearance—especially as it strikes the visiting critic or art tourist—to the exclusion of the experience of those who live and work in buildings day after day. As Witold Rybczynski has remarked, in the past it would have been unimaginable that "a building with absolutely no social, civic, or cultural significance could be considered an important piece of architecture. It is only in the modern period that a building's aesthetic achievement has been divorced from its actual function" (Rybczynski 1994, 3). And Dell Upton has suggested that the ideal of the artist-architect imposing a personal vision on clients has turned "Art-architecture" into the "quintessential gesture of consumer culture, a commodity made for a passive consumer" (Upton 1998, 283).

Because the art museum has been so important to the construction of the modern system of fine art, we should briefly consider the special challenge of relating art and function in the design of museums. In the second half of the twentieth century, the art museum has been a special temptation for architect-artists to make a "work of art" that upstages its contents, from Wright's Guggenheim in New York (1956) to Frank Gehry's Guggenheim in Bilbao (1998) (figs. 81 and 82). Yet art museums, like churches and civic buildings, are also symbolic monuments—in this case, to art itself—and so we are somewhat more forgiving of slights to function. Naturally, one would like to have the best of both worlds: a museum that was itself an exciting building but also served

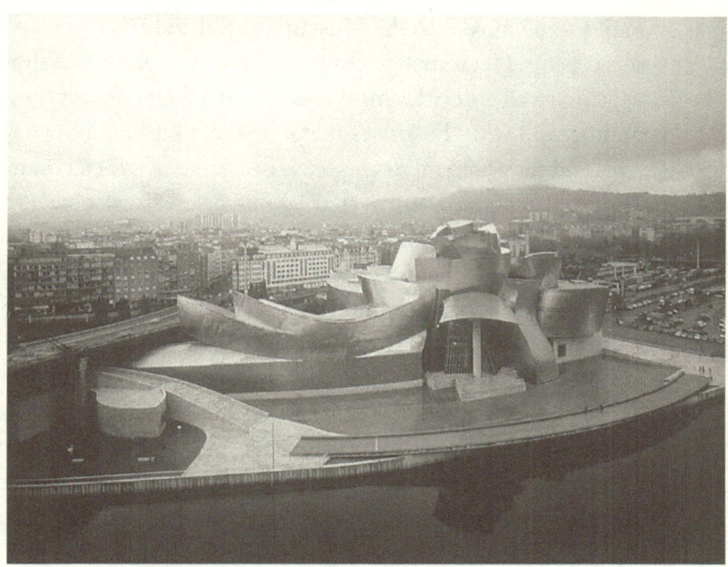

Figure 82. Frank Gehry, Guggenheim Museum, Bilbao, Spain (1998). Photography by David Heald.  Computer-aided design makes possible both the drawing and the structural calculations for the striking sculptural curves of Gehry's signature style. The equally curvilinear interior of the Bilbao museum is intended for a few large permanent works with the majority of the space going to temporary exhibits.

the art works that it contained. But that content has itself radically changed over the past forty years. At a time when many contemporary artists no longer focus on producing self-contained objects for contemplation, some recent museums have been designed less as neutral containers for permanent works than as sites for an interactive experience among the architecture, the temporary exhibits and installations, and a public that seeks high-level cultural diversion (Newhouse 1998).

## The Photography-as-Art Boom

As we saw in the previous chapter, art photography was accepted into the major art museums by 1940, and curators such as Beaumont Newhall used a combination of expressionist and formalist arguments to justify assimilating large bodies of functional photography. These arguments and practices took a revealing turn in the postwar period. In 1955 what was perhaps the single most successful photographic exhibition in history—*The Family of Man*—opened at the Museum of Modern Art. Three thousand people a day stood in line in New York, and when the exhibition had finished traveling to thirty-seven countries, some nine million people had seen it. The *Family of Man* was a romantic celebration of the oneness of humanity, its 503 images grouped around the themes of love, birth, childhood, work, death, and so forth. The show's curator, Edward Steichen, was praised by the public but vilified by many art critics and art photographers, one of whom said the exhibition was "not art at all" and ought to be moved to the Museum of Natural History (Jay 1989, 6). Although some people legitimately complained of the show's shallow sentimentalism, what angered art critics most was that Steichen had not framed and hung each photograph with the artist's name beside it but had blown them up to various sizes and mounted them on panels in a series of eye catching montages (fig. 83). The photographs were treated less as discreet art objects than as parts of a didactic and inspirational experience. The depth of the hostility toward the *Family of Man*—which can still be felt in snide references to it forty-five years later—reflects the angry intervention of the keepers of the discourse of fine art whenever its norms of the sovereign artist and sacred work are violated.

After the art world's stinging rebuke of *The Family of Man,* the next curator of photography at the Museum of Modern Art, John Szarkowski, returned to the practice of exhibiting single prints as autonomous works of art. But Szarkowski also made a play for the growing photography audience of the 1960s and 1970s by expanding the appropriation of utilitarian photography to include

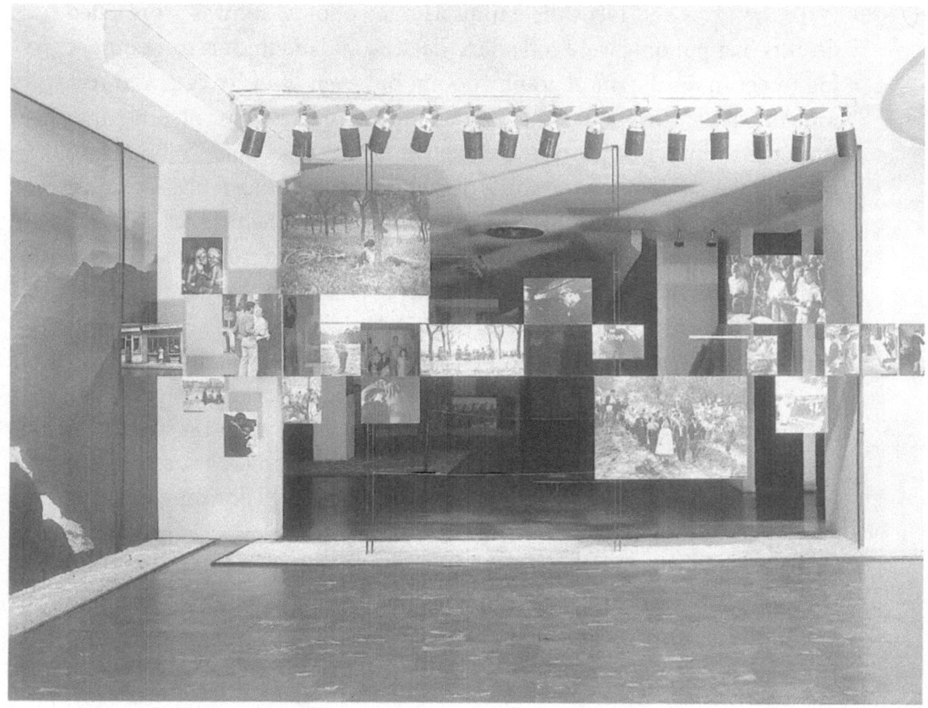

Figure 83. Installation view of the *Family of Man* exhibition at the Museum of Modern Art, New York, January 24–May 8, 1955. Photograph © 2000 Museum of Modern Art, New York.

even the most crassly commercial or opportunistic pictures. In the exhibition *From the Picture Press* he presented news photos of crime scenes and human-interest stories, shorn of their original captions, calling them a series of "short poems" (1973, 5). But more significant in enlarging the scope of art photography was the use of photography by people who considered themselves artists who happened to employ photography (Andy Warhol, Cindy Sherman, Sherrie Levine, Andreas Serrano), rather than photographers who made art photographs. Now photography entered the museum in two ways: on the one hand as photography, a medium with its own purely "photographic" uniqueness and canon of masterpieces (whether made as art or appropriated later), and on the other hand as part of postmodern multimedia experiments by artists who did not hesitate to violate the rules of "straight" photography by using posed scenes, darkroom manipulation, collage, and, more recently, digital imaging and computer enhancement.

In the 1970s and 1980s the enthusiasm for photography as art reached such heights that not only were collectors, dealers, and old line art museums scurrying to get in on the photography boom, but even libraries began to reclassify nineteenth-century books that contained photographic prints, moving them from the science, history, or travel shelves to the art section. In this assimilative activity, the subject matter and original purpose of older photographs, even when known, were neutralized in order to reprocess them as Art (Crimp 1993). Of course, art museums and art historians have not appropriated every photograph for fine art any more than they take in all medieval or all Yoruba artifacts but, instead, only those that fit certain aesthetic agendas. The fine art–versus-craft division has continued to be applied within photography to determine which of thousands of nearly indistinguishable historical images "shall pass into the temple of Art" (Solomon-Godeau 1991, 22). As in the case of "primitive" art or folk quilts, reclassification and assimilation are usually regarded as merely a benign promotion to higher status. But in transforming many of these photographs into art we also neutralize their power as witness. In the context of the art museum and the art history text, a photograph of concentration camp survivors at Bergen-Belsen becomes testimony not of the Holocaust but of Art and of the artist, Margaret Bourke-White.

## The "Death of Literature"?

The literary version of the art-versus-craft polarity is the division between an autonomous "literature" appreciated for itself and "mere writing" aimed at ordinary pleasure or utility. In the broader culture this division is often used by book reviewers to contrast literature to mere fiction, an opposition given palpable form by one bookstore chain that sets up an entire wall designated "fiction" and a few shelves nearby called "literature," where one finds Austen and Tolstoy. Of course, the most powerful institutional expression of the Literature-versus-literature division has been the traditional canon taught in schools and universities. From around 1940 to 1970, the separation of literature from the rest of writing was often justified by the principles of the "New Criticism." In this formalist view, a novel, play, or poem was a self-contained object to be carefully examined for its internal unity. Of course, that didn't prevent my college English teachers in the 1950s from claiming that literature offered the deepest of spiritual nourishments, and I remember the warmth and zeal with which many played out their role as secular clerics.

This lovely world was rudely broken in upon during the 1960s not only by such conflicts as the Civil Rights and antiwar movements but also by new theories emanating from France, such as structuralism and deconstruction. Although the new theories were themselves rather formalist and clashed with each other, they shared an indifference to the sacrosanct notions of "literature" and the "great writer." The titles of two of the most accessible of the new theoretical writings drove home the point, Roland Barthes's "From Work to Text" and "The Death of the Author." Using the same semiotic techniques on great works of literature that they used on marriage customs, clothing styles, or news stories, the structuralists treated literary works as "texts," as tissues of social and linguistic codes. The "death of the author" was a strict corollary of the shift from work to text since authorial genius was now less important than the general circulation of signs. Deconstructionists only made things worse for the idea of Literature when they argued that language never quite reaches its object but constantly displaces reference in an infinite chain of signifiers, leaving even the structuralists' "text" a field of hopelessly deferred meanings. As if structuralism and deconstruction were not enough, fresh theoretical approaches such as reader response theory and New Historicism plunged canonical works and authors ever deeper into the web of social determination as feminist, marxist, Afrocentric, gay/lesbian, and postcolonial theorists condemned the traditional literary canon as narrowly male, middle-class, heterosexual, white, and Eurocentric.

Traditionalists were deeply wounded by these successive assaults on the great works and great artists of Literature, and by the time the new theoretical approaches began to dominate the graduate schools and literary journals in the 1980s, a movement of reaction had set in. A lot of the theory bashing of the 1990s alternated between ill-humored carping and nostalgia for the good old days when people were content to "love literature." Many "theorists," on their part, continued to parade a pompous jargon and the smug tone of those who believe they alone hold the moral high ground. Are we threatened with *The Death of Literature,* as the title of one of the better surveys of the predicament of literature puts it? (Kernan 1990). If what is threatened is the idea of an eternal Literature of self-contained works forming an "ideal order" for the spiritual solace of a cultured elite, perhaps it deserves to die. That does not mean we should swing to the opposite pole and treat all texts as equal. Yet the Literature-versus-literature polarity, like the underlying fine art–versus-craft dichotomy, is so deeply embedded in our thinking and practice it will not be easy to reunite the sundered halves. Although hard to hear above the noise of the theory/antitheory debate, quieter voices have for some time been trying to redefine the specifically "literary" and create a multicultural canon without falling back into the essentialist and elitist trap of the modern idea of Literature (Bérubé 1998; Scholes 1998; Widdowson 1999).

## Mass Art

A more long-standing worry for the survival of "serious" literature, music, and drama has been competition from popular fiction, recordings, radio, television, and film. Although the guardians of high culture have tended to dismiss ordinary pleasures and diversions as "mere entertainment," the practitioners of the lesser arts have unabashedly claimed the titles of "art" and "artist." In a 1991 interview, Barry Manilow showed all the angst appropriate to the modern ideals of art and the artist: "It had gotten to the point where it wasn't art, and it wasn't music—it was business. . . . I had made it so big and so fast I lost my balance, and a lot of artists to whom that happens never find their way back home. . . . The art takes a beating" (Holden 1991). Although the nineteenth-century separation of works, audiences, and institutions remained largely in place during the first half of the twentieth century, the expansion and improvement of film, radio, sound recording, and printed photography gradually transformed the relation of the fine and popular arts. Walter Benjamin's marxist embrace of the new mass arts was as complex and nuanced as the American critic Gilbert Seldes's was simple: for Seldes it was enough that popular arts like the cartoon strip or film had already produced masters such as George Herriman and Charlie Chaplin (Seldes [1924] 1957). Yet the majority of philosophers and critics during the first half of the century, from Collingwood and Dwight MacDonald to Theodor Adorno and Clement Greenberg, vehemently reiterated their belief in a deep opposition between serious art and popular art. And even though the new media permitted the mass distribution of accessible versions of high-art works, critics like Greenberg sneered at such "middle-brow" culture, challenging intellectuals with an apocalyptic choice: avant-garde or kitsch (Greenberg 1961; Kulka 1996).

Many critics sympathetic to new media followed the pattern used earlier for the novel and photography, applying the fine art–versus-craft distinction *within* film and jazz. Just as there was the "art novel" or "art photography," in which complexity, experimental forms, or daring subject matter set it off from more accessible novels and pictures, so an "art film" tradition has developed. In the realm of music, jazz was also split. Thanks to the early efforts of Charlie Parker, Dizzy Gillespie, and Thelonius Monk, one part of jazz was transformed from danceable pieces for noisy clubs into a recognized art form for pure listening, whereas the rest evolved into swing and other popular genres. By now, art jazz is not only taught in conservatories alongside classical music but has also achieved "museum" status, with the Lincoln Center touring band playing the jazz classics of Ellington and others for polite middle-class audiences around the country. Yet the fine art model, especially the image of the artist as heroic loner, ill suits arts such as jazz and film, whose finest productions are so often collaborative. In studies of film as fine art, for example, the ideal of the lone artist-genius led to a focus on the director as auteur, which dominated film criticism for many years, a practice still reflected in our habit of referring to films as "by" their director. But if a film like *Citizen Kane* is rightly considered one of the greatest films of the century, it is as much thanks to Herman Mankiewicz's script and Greg Toland's cinematography as to Orson Welles's directing (fig. 84).

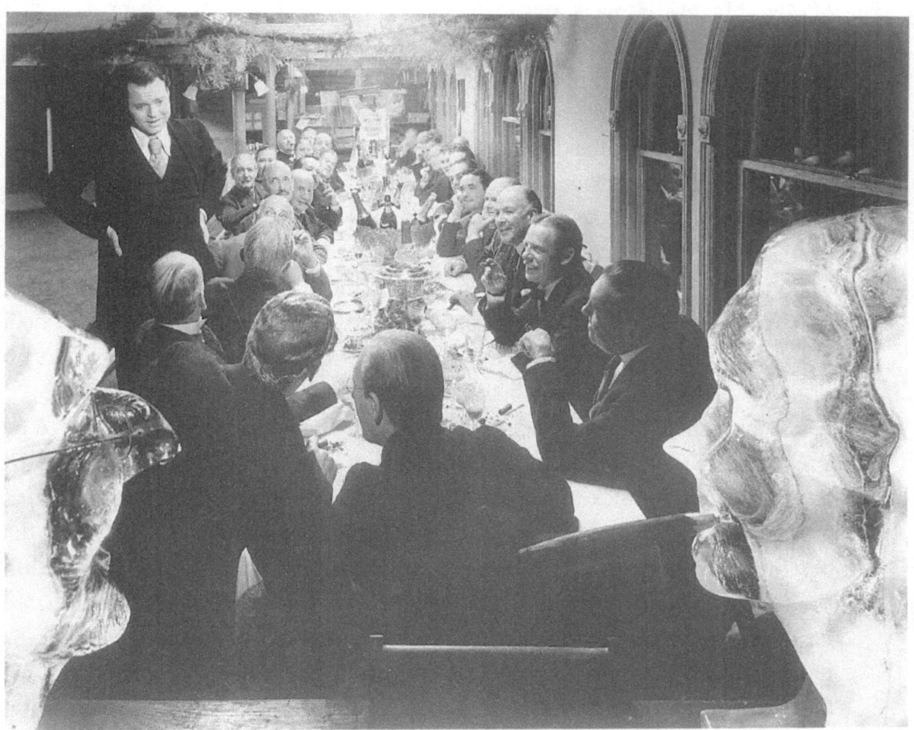

Figure 84. *Citizen Kane* (1941), Orson Welles, director; Herman Mankiewicz, screenplay, Greg Toland, cinematography. Film still. Courtesy Museum of Modern Art/ Film Stills Archive, New York. Turner Entertainment Company.

Yet the boundary between art music or the art film and popular works has become more permeable than ever, less a boundary than a continuum. In music, the traffic between classical and popular, folk, or ethnic music—already engaged in by Bartók, Ives, and Stravinsky at the beginning of the century—has remained brisk, and popular music on its side has continued to borrow from the classics. In defending his fusion of classical and jazz idioms, the composer Gunther Schuller remarked, "It is a way of making music which holds that *all musics are created equal*" (Schwartz and Childs 1998, 413). In film, the finest filmmakers of the twentieth century—Chaplin, Eisenstein, and Renoir, early on, and, later, Hitchcock, Truffaut, and Kurosawa—made works that were artistically innovative and challenging yet accessible and popular. The same is true of the novel. Although some academic critics treat only the most difficult and esoteric of experimental novels as "art," the writings of Marguerite Duras, John Updike, Toni Morrison, or Milan Kundera have achieved interesting artistic effects while remaining accessible to a broad audience. Meanwhile, Norman Mailer, Maxine Hong Kingston, Joan Didion, and others have bridged the gap between fiction and fact, the purely literary and the social-political in what is now taught in literature departments as the "new journalism" or "creative nonfiction."

One reason the status of popular art is so hard to pin down is that it has historically been the intersection of various political and cultural agendas, sometimes with surprising results. Thus, both conservative and radical critics in the past have often agreed that popular art is exploitive, commercial kitsch. Theodor Adorno's left-wing attacks on jazz and popular music were as savage as Allan Bloom's conservative blasts at rock, if a good deal more sophisticated. Many of those who have taken a negative view of popular art, such as Adorno or Dwight MacDonald, have insisted that we ought to call it "mass culture" or "mass art" since it is not the culture of the people but something concocted by a manipulative "culture industry." Such critics have typically contrasted fine art to mass art as complex to simple, original to formulaic, critical to conformist, challenging to escapist. Those more sympathetic to popular art reply that the best works of popular art are often complex, original, and challenging within the limits of accessibility and that the "masses" are not an undifferentiated lump of passive consumers but are capable of skepticism and independent interpretation. Such arguments were reinforced in the 1960s and 1970s by pop art and crossover experiments in music and literature that encouraged critics in both the art and academic worlds to offer serious aesthetic analyses of popular culture. Progressive literature professors began to teach courses on detective fiction, Hollywood films, and television sitcoms alongside Eliot, Woolf, and

Faulkner, and some art galleries began to exhibit framed Disney panels along with Roy Lichtenstein's high-art takeoffs on them.

Today, instead of jeremiads, many critics and philosophers are trying to reconcile fine and popular art by seeking a purely classificatory definition of art that will allow a noninvidious distinction between fine and popular (Dickie 1997). Ted Cohen suggests that the fine arts create small communities of appreciators who are intensely linked by a knowledge of tradition, whereas the popular arts link us less intensely to larger communities of interest (1999). Arthur Danto is willing to take in a great deal of what has traditionally been classified as commercial or mass art so long as it uses its medium to make a statement about its medium (Danto 1997). Noël Carroll has developed an extensive case for distinguishing avant-garde or high art from mass art in a way that allows for an appreciation of the positive features of both (1998).

Despite the attempt of some philosophers to get us to treat art as a neutral category, for most people who care about whether something is art or not, it is the evaluative sense that counts—the "aura" of lofty connotations that still surround "art" and "artist" (Shusterman 2000). Walter Benjamin's claim about the decline of the aura in an age of mechanical reproduction is often quoted as a truism, yet it is not clear that the mass media have eliminated either the aura of the original work or the aura surrounding the ideal of art itself. For it was not only nineteenth-century office clerks who wanted to devote their lives to "divine Art" but a host of twentieth-century artists of every type as well, from Proust to Madonna. That is why it is so important to some critics that we "elevate" the music, dances, and masks of traditional African or Native American societies to the status of art, or why some artists working in clay or wood are ready to put holes in pots or drive sixteen-penny nails into fine finishes. The aura clings—even if it has dimmed.

## Art and Life

If the fine art–versus-craft division hangs on in faded glory despite a century and a half of trying to overcome it, attempts to transcend the related but more general separation of art and life might appear to have fared better (Kaprow 1993). Some dadas, as we have seen, already made reuniting art and life part of their attack on Art in 1917, and the Russian constructivists made even more sweeping pronouncements and backed them up by working for industry and the state. Efforts to get art and life back together over the next fifty years careened wildly from the "Bureau of Surrealist Research" in Paris in the 1920s to social realist films, novels, and paintings of the 1930s, to the New York "happenings" of the 1950s, to the Situationist International's political gestures and the Fluxus movement's art pranks of the 1960s. Yet few twentieth-century gestures have achieved the notoriety of Marcel Duchamp's *Fountain,* the men's urinal to which he affixed the signature "R. Mutt" before attempting to exhibit it at the Society of Independent Artists show in New York in 1917 (fig. 85). Although it physically belongs to the beginning of the twentieth century, its influence—and Duchamp's interpretation of its implications—have been most important since the 1950s. By turning things such as snow shovels, bottle racks,

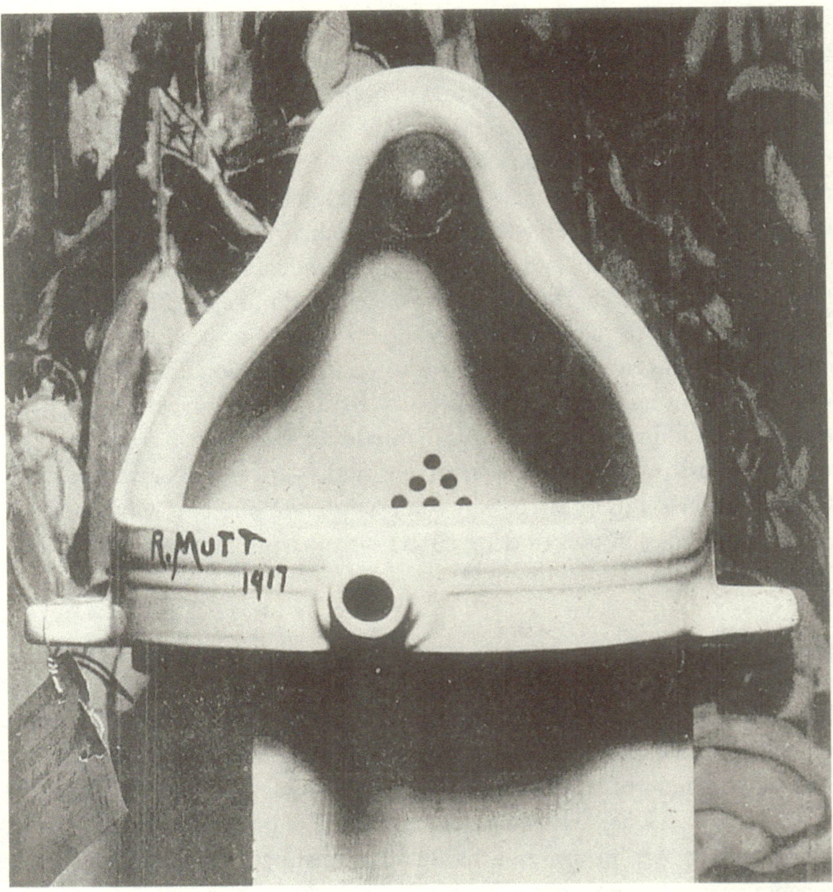


Figure 85. Marcel Duchamp, *Fountain* (1917). Photography by Alfred Stieglitz; reproduced in *The Blind Man,* no. 2 (May 1917). Courtesy Philadelphia Museum of Art, the Louise and Walter Arensberg Archives. © 2001 Artists Rights Society (ARS), New York/ADAGP, Paris/Estate of Marcel Duchamp.

pocket combs, and urinals into fine art by fiat, it is said, Duchamp knocked fine art off its pedestal and erased the distinction between art and life. Yet Duchamp himself was too shrewd simply to adopt an outright negative position, as becomes apparent when one looks more closely at the context of *Fountain* and Duchamp's later comments on his readymades.

Duchamp was a member of the board of the Society of Independent Artists, which had declared that "any artist" might enter its 1917 exhibition since there would be "no jury, no prizes" (de Duve 1991, 191). Duchamp decided to test whether his artist-colleagues meant what they said. Signing the urinal "R. Mutt" assured anonymity, and the board took the bait, refusing to exhibit *Fountain* on the grounds that it was obscene, was not art, and would bring ridicule on the society. Duchamp not only resigned in protest (still not revealing it was he who presented *Fountain*) but also joined with two friends to produce a little magazine called *The Blind Man,* which ridiculed the act of rejecting *Fountain,* claiming that it was art since Mr. Mutt "CHOSE it. He took an ordinary article of life, placed it so that its useful significance disappeared under the new title and point of view—created a new thought for that object" (de Duve 1991, 198).

Was *Fountain* a work of art or anti-art? As a strategy vis-à-vis the Society of Independent Artists, *Fountain* staked a claim to be art just as much as the paintings they exhibited, although Duchamp always insisted it was not for any "aesthetic" qualities (Sanouillet and Peterson 1973, 141). But at the same time *Fountain* was anti-art in the sense that it radically challenged what the art world took to be the limits of art. In the latter case, *Fountain* would seem once again to be art, since its aim was not so much to overthrow the system of art as to open it up. Duchamp's dialectic of art and anti-art infected his response to most of the central components of the modern system of art. He attacked the idea of art as a separate realm and entity: "We created it for our sole and unique use; it's a little like masturbation. I don't believe in the essential aspect of art" (Cabanne 1971, 100). Yet the same Duchamp could also say: "Only in art is [man] capable of going beyond the animal state, because art is an outlet toward regions which are not ruled by time and space" (Sanouillet and Peterson 1973, 137).

Duchamp's relation to the art-versus-craft dichotomy was equally ambiguous. At first glance his readymades might seem to break down the barrier between art and craft, but they actually reinforce it since the readymade is not a piece of handicraft but an industrial product removed from its function and transformed into art by the artist's mind. Duchamp also rejected the "attitude of reverence" for the artist: "Art, etymologically speaking, means 'to make.' Everybody is making, not only artists, and maybe in coming centuries there will be the making without the noticing" (Duchamp 1968, 47, 62). Yet Duchamp himself was far from "making and not noticing," since he helped Walter Arensberg gather Duchamp's works and negotiate the most favorable deal for their long-term exhibition (the Philadelphia Art Museum won out by guaranteeing twenty-five years to the Art Institute of Chicago's ten and the New York Metropolitan Museum's five) (Cabanne 1971,87; Kuenzli and Naumann 1990, 4).

Duchamp's ambivalence about the major facets of the modern system of art were not the result of some puckish desire to befuddle but reflected a deep awareness of the power of art as a social institution. In a note to himself jotted down back in 1913, he asked, "Can one make a work that is not a work of art?" (Sanouillet and Peterson 1973, 137). The long series of readymades that began shortly after could be seen as a strategy for exploring that question. Yet these early anti-art gestures of Duchamp, like those of dada/surrealism and Russian constructivism, have long since been recaptured by the art world in ways that blunt their critique of the fine art system. "The fact that they are regarded with the same reverence as objects of art," Duchamp remarked in the 1960s, "probably means that I have failed to solve the problem of trying to do away entirely with art" (Duchamp 1968, 62; Cabanne 1971, 71).

George Leonard has argued that whereas Duchamp failed to do away with art, the composer, John Cage succeeded, bringing Western society to Wordsworth's hoped-for "blissful hour" when the art object can be dispensed with, and we may emerge "into the light of things" (Leonard 1994). During a period when the atonal and serial experiments of the musical avant-garde were becoming ever more self-reflexive and inaccessible to the ordinary musical public, Cage and others deeply challenged the fine art ideal of the self-contained musical work. Certainly, his *4′ 33″* will stand alongside Duchamp's *Fountain* as one of the most important art/anti-art moments of the twentieth century. In *4′ 33″* as first performed in 1952, the pianist David Tudor came on the stage, sat down at the piano and held his hands above the keys for four minutes, thirty-three seconds, making gestures to indicate three movements. The music consisted not only of the four minutes and thirty-three seconds of silence but of the sounds of coughing, rustling programs, and other noises that penetrated the concert area. Cage's piece showed more than any previous composition that the ordinary sounds around us can be just as much a part of music as the sounds of traditional instruments playing formal compositions. Although Cage had already been experimenting in the 1930s and 1940s with indeterminacy and unusual sounds by combining multiple recordings or writing works for the "prepared piano" (a piano with bolts and other items lying on the strings), in *4′ 33″* indeterminacy is so great that there is no way to predict what sounds will emerge. Both art and artist seem reduced to the task of pointing us toward the "music" of the world around us (Kostelanetz 1996).

In subsequent works—Cage sometimes took to calling them "art pieces" in an effort to defeat the work concept—he increased indeterminacy by multiplying the sources of sounds and by further randomizing procedures, including having the performance end when the last auditor got up to leave. In some ways Cage did go beyond Duchamp, who had minimized the role of the artist as one of selection, whereas Cage made the artist's role merely one of setting up the conditions of indeterminacy. Yet, by emphasizing the composer's intellectual capacity rather than facility for rhythm, melody, or harmony, Cage also raised the composer as thinker even higher above composers devoted to the craft of producing musical works. Like Duchamp before him and the conceptualists later, getting art and life together did not mean placing a higher value on craft skills or function but, instead, teasing the mind into seeing art and the surrounding world in a new way. Moreover, just as *Fountain* has both been hailed as a liberation from the fetishism of the art work and been appropriated as an art work itself, so has *4′ 33″*. Cage's *4′ 33″* along with his other compositions, performance pieces, and prose poems have been easily assimilated by the art world and are performed in concert halls or art galleries and discussed primarily in music, art, and literature classrooms and journals.

The possibilities for musical experimentation since Cage's *4′ 33″* were enormously expanded with the development of the synthesizer, which gave both the high serialism of the academic composers and the high jinks of the experimentalists an almost unlimited range of sounds (Nyman 1974). Experimental composers associated with the loosely defined Fluxus movement took up a direction Cage had not developed, engaging in a kind of theater or performance art parodying traditional concert procedures. In the Fluxorchestra concerts of 1964–65, programs were sailed from the balcony as folded airplanes, the musicians fell off their chairs at a signal, scores made of flash paper ignited, and Ben Vautier's *Secret Room* ended by leading the audience to the "secret room," which was actually the back exit into the street (Kahn 1993). A more traditional way of connecting with audiences came from experiments using electronic resources to create musical environments of pulsating sounds and rhythms, many of them drawn from non-Western musical traditions. Philip Glass has integrated India's rhythmically organized music with Western melody, consonance, and harmonic progression to create operas and instrumental pieces that have appealed to a varied audience, including rock enthusiasts. Although some music critics have charged Glass and other "minimalist" composers with exploiting tonality and pulsing rhythms in an unseemly quest for audience approval, Glass sees himself as reconnecting "serious" music with the world outside the academic enclaves into which so many modernist composers had retreated. For years, Glass supported himself by odd jobs and by touring with his own ensemble, and it was playing for live audiences that led him back to the old idea of the composer/performer: "We became real people again to audiences. We learned to talk to people again. As a group we lost our exclusivity, the kind that had been built up through years of academic life. . . . We saw the role of the artist in a much more traditional way—the artist being part of the culture that he lives in" (Duckworth 1995, 337). If Glass and other process composers are known beyond the small middle-class concert audience, however, it is due to the most important factor of all in the development of music since the 1950s: the exponential transformation and spread of recording and playback devices, which have gone from the transistor radio through the cassette to the portable CD player and now the computer. Music in the largest sense is already electronically integrated into everyday life, and younger people respond to musical sounds they like without asking their artistic pedigree.

In the visual arts since the 1960s, a great deal of pop, conceptual, performance, installation, and environmental art has also resisted the polarities of the fine art system and tried to bring art and life closer, sometimes charmingly, as in Jenny Holzer's marquee banalities, such as her 1985 electronic sign "Protect me From What I Want," and sometimes more threateningly, as in Hans Haake's highly charged political installations, such as his 1971 exposé of Manhanttan slum lord holdings. Environmental artists such as Michael Heizer and Robert Smithson shunned galleries in the 1970s to make huge earth pieces in the Western deserts. Warhol and other pop artists continued to make fun of the sacrosanct aura of the artist and the work of art, and conceptual artists often produced no "work" at all. Vito Acconci's pieces often consisted of prescriptions for repetitive actions, such as stepping up and down off a chair, whereas Bruce Nauman spewed water out of his mouth and called it *Fountain*, thereby going Duchamp one better. Performances like Carolee Schneemann's *Interior Scroll* or many of Joseph Beuys's political and environmental "actions" often took place outside of or in conflict with the usual art venues. Beuys even founded a political party and an independent university in Germany as part of his art activities, claiming that anything one does freely and creatively is art, whether teaching or peeling a potato. Feminist artists such as Barbara Kruger used conventional advertising techniques to drive home her message, whereas Judy Chicago's *Dinner Party* was collaborative, unashamedly didactic, and celebrated the low-ranked crafts of ceramics and embroidery. Other feminist artists have used perfor-

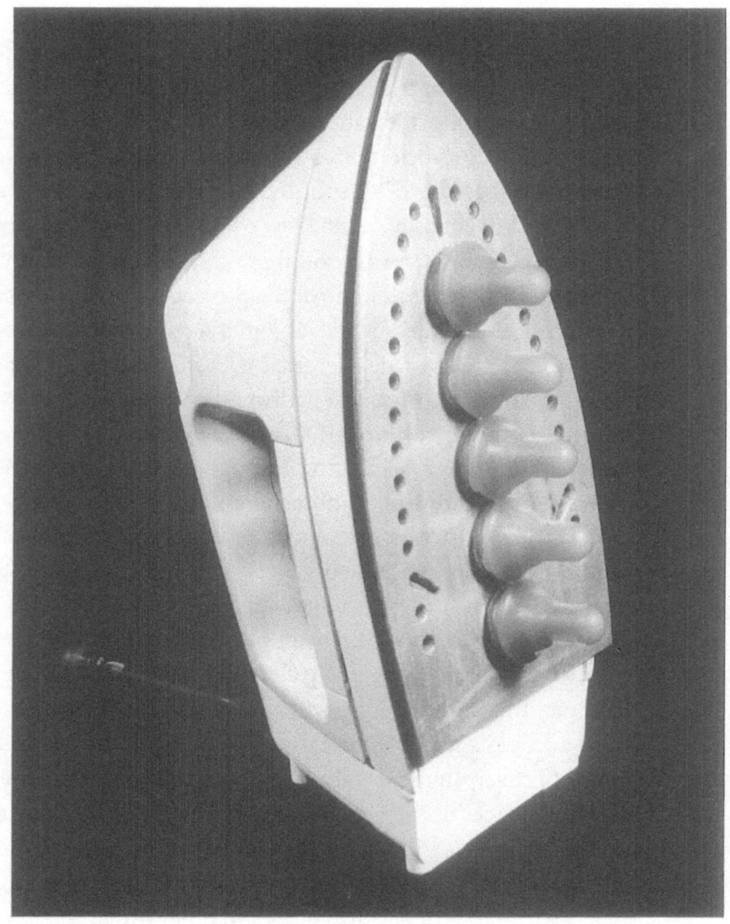

Figure 86. Christine Nelson, *Man Ray's Irony* (1997); household iron, latex. Courtesy the artist. This feminist parody of Man Ray's *Gift* (fig. 73) puts baby bottle nipples in the place of sharp tacks and is part of Nelson's "redress" series in which small household appliances are dressed up in spandex, tassels, fake furs, and so forth, making them at once playfully erotic and critical of consumerism and mass-marketing ploys.

mance, installation, transformations of "readymade" consumer goods, and parodies of canonical "male" works to reconnect their work with everyday concerns (fig. 86). Among the artists most successful at integrating art and society is Christo, whose wrapped building projects often require months or even years of negotiations with governments, community groups, and individual property owners, their completion drawing on collaborative teams of engineers, technicians, manufacturers, construction workers, and volunteers. The wrapping of the Berlin Reichstag for two weeks in 1995 took place after twenty years of intermittent negotiations, climaxing in an intense debate in the German parliament. The entire process engaged thousands of people in discussions on the nature of art and its relation to society (Christo 1996).

But there have been experiments in bringing art into daily life even more intimately collaborative than Christo's, such as the neighborhood mural movement in which artists design and paint side by side with local people or various quilt projects such as the nationwide Names Project AIDS Memorial Quilt. Activities of this kind belong to a diffuse movement that has come to be called "community-based art." One of the best examples is the 1993 "Culture in Action" project in Chicago, curated by Mary Jane Jacob, which involved a dozen artists working with a variety of interest groups, organizations, and neighborhoods on eight projects. Some of the projects were a candy bar called "We Got It!" which was designed, made, and marketed by members of the candy workers union; a series of videos created by Latino youth and shown on monitors around their neighborhood; a hydroponic vegetable garden whose growth site and produce was tied into AIDS service agencies; and three parades through ethnic communities celebrating immigrant labor. Scattered around the city among people who would not feel comfortable in places like the Museum of Contemporary Art, these activities reversed cultural power relations so that members of the museum and gallery world, for a change, were the outsiders who wondered why these strange activities were called "art" (Jacob 1995). "Culture in Action," Michael Brenson has written, had "as much to do with the essence of art as anything in a gallery or museum." As Brenson sees it, "Modernist painting and sculpture will always offer an aesthetic experience of a profound and indispensable kind, but it is one that can now do very little to respond effectively to the social and political challenges and traumas of American life. Its dialogues and reconciliations are essentially private and metaphorical, and they now have limited potential to speak to those citizens of multicultural America whose artistic traditions approach objects not as worlds in themselves but as instruments of performances and other rituals that take place outside institutions" (Jacob 1995, 29).

"Culture in Action" raised questions about the nature of art that were even more difficult than those posed by many individual conceptual and performance pieces, which the art world has often comfortably ingested. Some of individual projects in "Culture in Action" were almost indistinguishable from the sorts of things done by imaginative grassroots political activists who would not think of calling what they do "art." To that extent, parts of "Culture in Action" could be seen as the true heir of Russian constructivism. Art is not simply integrated into life but disappears as a distinctive activity. It remains an open question whether we want to go that far in dissolving art into life.

## Public Art

Community-based art projects such as "Culture in Action" draw on a variety of funding sources: mainline foundations, corporate sponsors, individual givers, business donations in kind, and, of course, the National Endowment for the Arts, along with state and local arts councils. The conception, location, and funding of community-based projects makes them "public art" in a special sense (Lacy 1995). But some of their intense dedication to bringing art and life together can also be found in many art works that are "public" in a more traditional way, that is, works directly commissioned by government bodies. Thanks in part to the many "percent for art programs" (which set aside half of one percent of public constructions costs to be used for artwork), enormous numbers of sculptures, paintings, and mixed media pieces have been created for public buildings and plazas over the past thirty years. Many public art works have been self-contained abstract sculptures meant for aesthetic contemplation, and some have graced their locations, such as the big Picasso in Chicago's downtown or the Serra piece in Pittsburg. But if the age of the bronze general on a horse is long past, the dominance of the self-contained work for aesthetic encounter is also being challenged, not only by colorful mixed-media pieces that directly address the viewer but also by designs for public spaces by such artists as Mary Miss or Scott Burton, who join art and craft by seeking visual engagement and providing places to sit, gather, or play (Senie 1992).

We can get a better sense of the issues at stake in the older and newer kinds of public art by comparing two particularly controversial American works from the 1980s: Richard Serra's *Tilted Arc* in New York and Maya Lin's *Vietnam Veterans Memorial* in Washington, D.C. The intense debate surrounding Serra's *Tilted Arc* (1981) rehearsed all the established values of the modern system of art with its exalted ideal of the artist as creative genius and the artwork as sacred object. The controversy began when office workers objected that Serra's twelve-foot-high steel wall bisecting the plaza in front of their building destroyed the plaza's potential usefulness (fig. 87). When hearings opened over the work's removal, Serra claimed that his work was "site specific" and would be destroyed if moved, but it is clear that Serra's idea of site specific did not include how people might use the plaza other than how they would respond to *Tilted Arc* as an autonomous artwork (Weyergraf-Serra and Buskirk 1991). Serra was not being a bad actor in taking this stand; he was simply expressing the regulative norms of the modern system of fine art and carrying out the wishes of a selection committee that also shared them. The art-world critics who rushed to Serra's defense often dismissed the complaining workers as ignorant philistines, and one

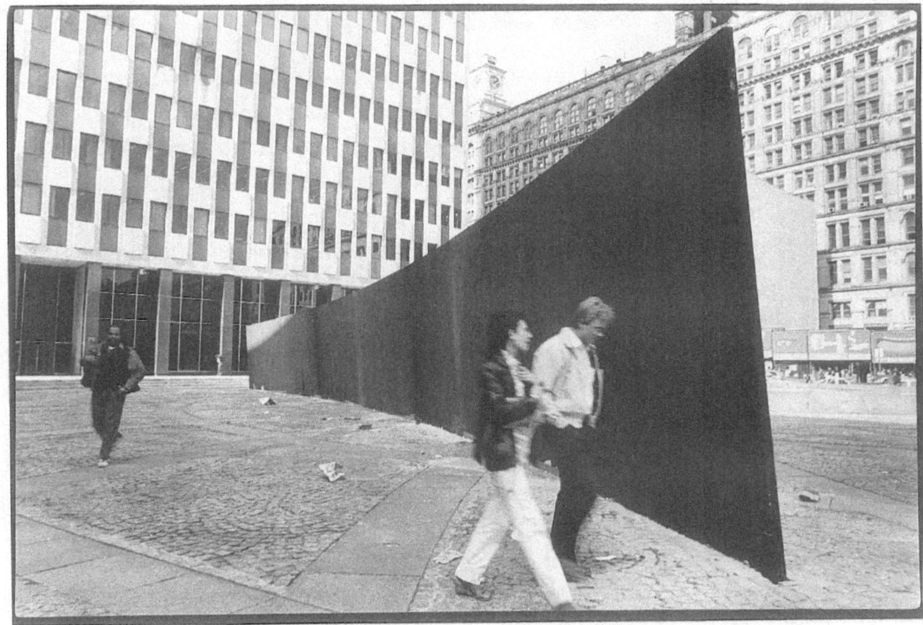

Figure 87. Richard Serra, *Tilted Arc*, New York (1981). Photograph courtesy of Robin Holland.

even compared the hearings to Nazi tribunals. Most of those who defended *Tilted Arc* clearly believed that an artwork's formal and expressive achievements should take precedence over the functions and pleasures of everyday life and that the opinions of art-world experts should be the final court of appeal. *Tilted Arc* was eventually removed in 1989 to cries of outrage in the art-world press.

The other controversial work of public art, Maya Lin's *Vietnam Veterans Memorial* (1982), generated heated objections to the unconventional appearance of its long, low wall with the names of those killed in the war, with the result that a figural monument by Frederick Hartt was also erected nearby. But the "wall," as it is known, has become one of the most visited places in Washington, D.C., a deeply affecting memorial where the names of those who died and the feelings and questions of those who remember take precedence over Art (fig. 88). Here, art and craft, beauty and function, creative imagination and public service join in a new way, offering a democratic version of what once happened under the old system of art. Serra's "wall" and the controversy over it played out the exalted claims for art, artist, and the aesthetic of the modern system of art, while Maya Lin's wall points us beyond art and craft.[6]

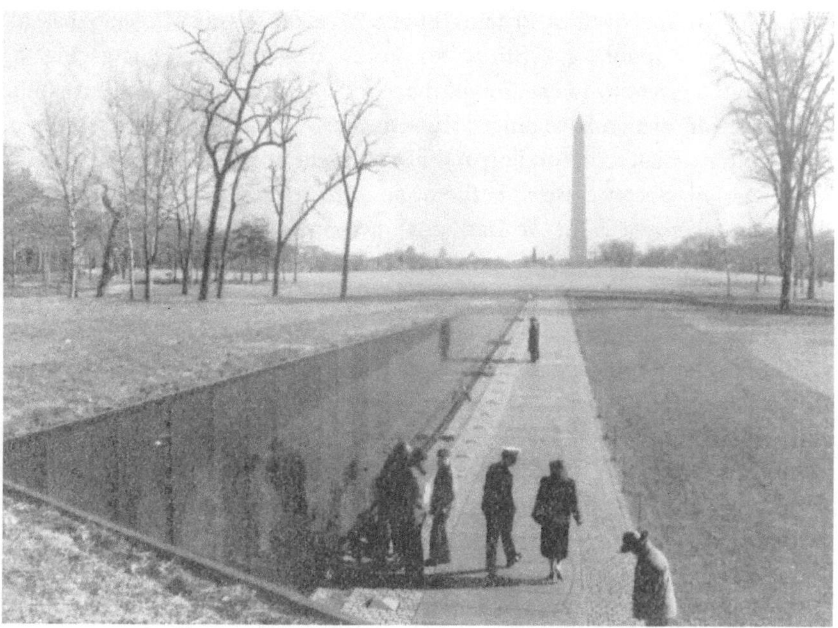

Figure 88. Maya Lin, *Vietnam Veterans Memorial,* Washington, D.C. (1982). Photograph courtesy Stephen Griswold.

One positive outcome of the Serra and Lin cases has been a new way of approaching public art in recent years. Instead of a panel of art-world insiders choosing an artist to drop a self-contained work into the public square, selection committees now attempt to represent the broader community, and artists often talk with the people who will have to live with the work. In St. Louis, where another Serra "wall" has rankled some residents for over a decade, the artist Mary Miss received a commission in 1999 for a nearby public project and began meeting with civic groups, not just to fend off potential complaints but actually to listen. In the same Federal Plaza in lower Manhattan where Serra's *Tilted Arc* once stood, the artist Martha Schwartz created a new work in 1996. Schwartz decided to "shape the space for the way people actually use it" and created continuous curves of brightly colored benches surrounding a half-dozen conical grass mounds topped with mist fountains. Instead of an aggressive wall or a barren void, Federal Plaza workers now have a more inviting space that combines function and aesthetic interest (Beardsley 1998, 151).

In Europe, public art has undergone a shift similar to that in the United

States. As Vivien Lovell of Britain's Public Art Commissions Agency has remarked, today's public art "prioritizes process over product by engaging the public in the genesis and creation of the work" (Gooding 1999). Recent public art projects in Britain have ranged from the abstract simplicity of the town of Shrewsbury's small sculptural memorial to the war poet Wilfred Owen, featuring lines of his poetry chiseled in the stone at the request of the community, to the comprehensive "Out of Darkness" project in Wolverhampton, where twelve artists have made creative use of lighting to bring nighttime excitement and enhance the sense of security by outlining buildings, highlighting architectural features, and illuminating open spaces. And in France, in a concrete courtyard just behind the eighteenth-century Palais Royale in the center of Paris, Daniel Buren has erected a series of cut-off columns of varied height, decorated with his signature stripe pattern. Although not designed through public consultation and highly controversial at first, Buren's *Columns* not only echoes the neoclassical architecture of its surroundings but has become a place of relaxation and play, where adults sit or stand on the lowest columns and children run and skate among them (fig. 89). Buren envisaged his piece not only as a "monumental sculpture" that would relate to the surrounding colonnades and reveal the presence of the lower level of the courtyard but also as a pedestrian environment in which the columns were available to be sat or climbed on, turning visitors into "living sculptures" (Nuridsany 1993, 5).

When the German artist Jochen Gerz received a commission to redesign the crumbling war memorial in the French village of Biron (pop. 500), he could have leveled the eighty-year-old stone cube with its typical stubby obelisk on top. Instead he asked over a hundred of the inhabitants of the village to respond to a confidential question having to do with the meaning of sacrifice in life and war and engraved each person's statement on an enamel plaque. The plaques were then affixed to the old monument. A typical one said: "Life is incredible. Wars haven't gotten us anything. For me, what we have lived through in this century is abominable. My brother was arrested. He went to prison Monday, he was shot on Tuesday. Certain things have been taken care of since then. But I feel sorry for the young. They have to vandalize, try to grab some cash here or there. To say what is worth the effort is difficult, I don't know the future. We live in a hard time" (Aboudrar 2000, 273). The artist and his "work" are almost invisible at the *Living Monument of Biron;* the creativity is not only in Gerz's conception but also in the life of the community expressed by its citizens. Gerz has remarked, "I like the idea that the author of the work is not just the artist . . . what pleases me is that the people of Biron are making their own monument" (Aboudrar 2000, 273–74). Gerz hopes that one of the villagers will now take

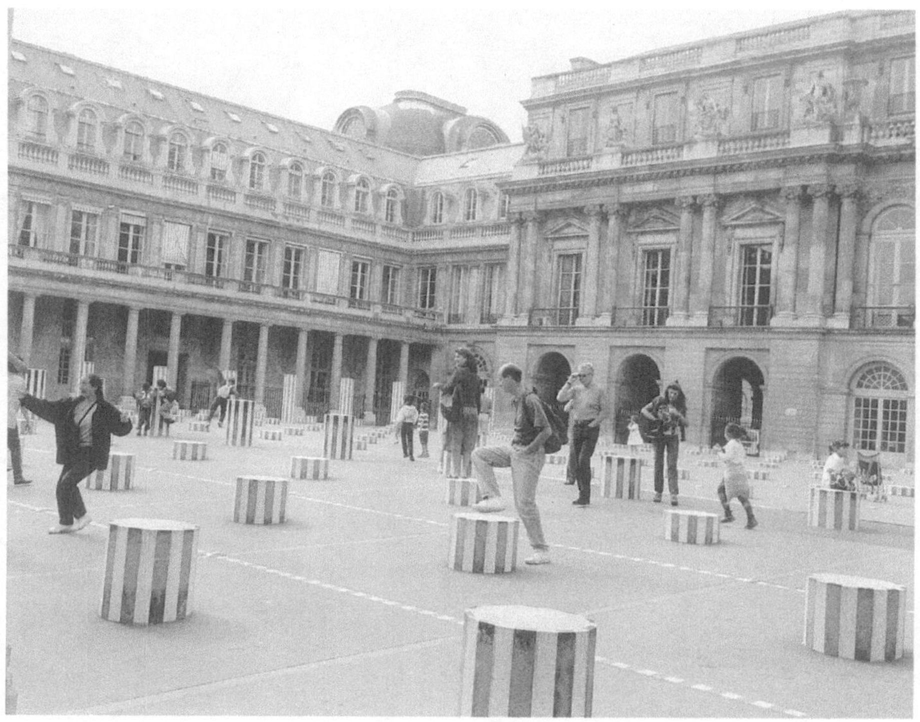

Figure 89. Daniel Buren, *Les deux plateaux,* known as *The Columns* (1986). Photograph courtesy Suzanna Williams.

over and continue to gather testimonies so that *Living Monument* will remain just that. Gerz's monument reminds me of Rousseau's idea of the festival as an alternative to the exclusivity of the fine art theater. As in the festival, where the people are the actors and show themselves to one another, so in the Biron monument the people are themselves the artists and speak to one another. Like Maya Lin's *Vietnam Veterans Memorial,* Gerz's *Living Monument of Biron* resolutely turns away from the modern ideals of the autonomous artist and the self-referential work to embrace a democratic vision of collaboration, service, and social function.

# Conclusion

As recently as fifty years ago there were influential artists and critics ready to deny the name "art" to any work of literature, painting, or music that did not participate in the modernist quest for purity. Since then, two forms of assimilation have converged to explode the category of art: on the one hand, movements within the fine arts have been able to turn almost any conceivable material, sound, or activity into art and get it accepted by art institutions; on the other hand, fine art institutions themselves have used the art-versus-craft polarity to divide and appropriate everything from so-called primitive art to jazz and the new journalism. Yet even as assimilation has been gaining momentum, the tradition of resistance has also flourished, offering challenges to the underlying polarities of the fine art system as varied as those of John Cage, Roland Barthes, Maya Lin, and Mary Jane Jacob.

Although traditional fine art institutions have tried in the past to recuperate or neutralize many of these challenges to Art, some of those same institutions have begun to change under the combined effects of economic necessity, social criticism, and new editors, music directors, and curators. The movement called "the new museology," for example, has been rewriting the history of museums and reappraising collection and exhibition practices, the place of the museum in society, and even the museum's effect of "making art" by assimilation. In response, museums have revised exhibition policies, expanded educational and outreach programs, and even gone outside their walls with participatory community projects. The proliferation of gift shops, bookstores, cafés, special events, blockbuster exhibitions, explanatory wall panels, background videos, and headsets has gone so far that some critics now complain of museums pandering to commercialism and popular taste rather than focusing on art. Some symphony, dance, and theater companies have also increased efforts at audience education, expanded crossover programming, and taken performances into everyday contexts that break the traditional "art" illusion of the concert hall or proscenium stage. Festival organizations and community arts councils have been even quicker to embark on experimental programming and new venues in the quest for larger and more diverse audiences and have funded storefront art centers and community-based projects such as "Culture in Action."[1]

The disciplines devoted to the teaching, criticism, and history of the fine arts have also been changing. Literature departments have expanded the canon and the scope of what counts as "literature," and literary scholars have begun exploring the implications of the late emergence of literature as a discipline. Art history, dominated in the mid-twentieth century by a formalism that virtually ignored women and minority artists and sometimes wrote off entire areas of art as retrograde (e.g., the Mexican muralists), long ago recovered an interest in social and political context and new methods of analysis. Historians of music have also begun to question the traditional preoccupation with analyzing a limited canon of masterpieces by great (male) composers and have sought to broaden the scope and methods of musicology. Philosophers have been exploring the historicity of the idea of art, and feminists in all disciplines have shown that we can no longer do aesthetics and the history and criticism of the arts while ignoring issues of gender. Finally, the most radical disciplinary revisionists would dissolve literature into cultural studies, art history into a history of images, and the history of Western classical music into an enlarged ethnomusicology. Yet most of these new interdisciplinary proposals seem destined to supplement rather than supplant existing disciplines.[2]

But to move beyond the modern system of art would mean not only reshaping the institutions and disciplines of the fine art system but also overcoming its ambivalence toward skill, beauty, function, and sensual pleasure. Although facility has never been wholly eliminated from the ideal of fine art, the dream of reuniting fine art and craft at the level of the body has now been further complicated by the digital revolution. The advent of hypertext, cyberart, virtual architectural models, synthesized sound, and automatic transcription has made traditional forms of writing, drawing, or composing "by hand" seem ever more problematic in many arts. Of course, traditional storytelling, music making, dance, and handicraft still go on in the villages of so-called Third World countries—although these activities sometimes become part of exploitative marketing systems serving tourists and folk art consumers. In advanced industrial economies, handcrafts—such as woodworking, sewing, gardening, and even weaving and pottery—that were once necessities or occupations have long been part-time or leisure options for the middle classes. When it comes to music, literature, and drama, there is still the family piano (or electronic keyboard) in some homes; and community choral ensembles, poetry circles, and theater groups still develop skills and provide the opportunities for expression and participation without which we would all be reduced to nothing but consumers of art.

Of equal importance to a revival of respect for craft skills are the linked values of function and sensual pleasure—often depreciated in the past as "mere utility" and "mere entertainment." As the "mere" indicates, the fine art tradition has seldom rejected function and sensory pleasure outright but has made them incidental to the autonomy of the artwork and the refined sensibility of the aesthetic. It is here that the highest price has been paid for the autonomy of art, an elevation and spiritualization that often isolated the fine arts in a cultural enclave and generated the drive to reintegrate art and society or art and life. Yet just as the term "art" carries within it not only the exclusive notion of "fine art" but also the older sense of "an art," so "aesthetic" can be either restricted to a detached contemplation aimed at fine art or reconceived to include ordinary sensuality and purpose. This reconstruction of the aesthetic is most prominently associated with John Dewey but has roots in some aspects of Baumgarten and Kant and, more particularly, in the tradition exemplified by Hogarth's "line of beauty," Rousseau's "temperate sensuality," and Wollstonecraft's joining of pleasure and political justice.

Many contemporary critics and philosophers have been exploring approaches to art and the aesthetic that do give a prominent place to ordinary pleasures and everyday functions (Berleant 1991; Leddy 1995; Sartwell 1995; Shusterman 2000). Carolyn Korsmeyer's discussion of the symbolic meanings of the sensual pleasures of the palate is an important corrective to the traditional emphasis on distanced viewing and listening (1999). Yuriko Saito suggests that we have a good deal to learn about an "aesthetics of the everyday" from certain traditional practices of Japan. Unlike the Western fine art system that has often taught people to direct a disinterested gaze on self-contained works, traditional Japanese culture valued sensory experiences of transient aspects of life: the pleasure of a bath, the sound of rain on a roof, the conversation and sounds of drinking at a tea ceremony. Similarly, the Japanese tradition gave equal value to formal beauty, craftsmanship, and function in such everyday things as the wrapping of packages or the design and use of utensils. Whereas mainstream Western aesthetics can treat a kitchen knife as if it were a work of art so long as function is subordinated to form, an aesthetic of the everyday would attend not only to the knife's visual appearance but also to its "feeling in the hand . . . its weight, and balance, but most importantly . . . how smoothly and effortlessly" it cuts (Saito 1999, 9). Saito's insights also suggest that true multiculturalism is not a matter of including a few Japanese or African examples in our art, music, or literature anthologies but an issue of learning from other cultures the limitations of our traditional categories.

But the arts have always had multiple functions, and among them, education has been central (Horace's "please and instruct"). Arthur Danto's rethinking of the cognitive role of art as "embodied meaning" has proved especially useful for illuminating some of the maddest and murkiest corners of the fine art world of the last half-century (Danto 1997, 2000). Whereas Danto's philosophy still wrestles primarily with how to define art in the light of changes in the visual arts, Karol Berger focuses directly on the issue of function, refreshingly approaching it from the perspective of music and literature. For Berger, the highest function of the arts is to represent fictional worlds in ways that give us a new understanding of ourselves and our surroundings. Although versions of this view can be traced from Aristotle to Schiller and Hegel, Berger's theory does not make edification a characteristic of the fine arts alone but recognizes a continuum between the everyday arts and high arts. Moreover, he deftly meets the greatest challenge for any contemporary mimetic view of the arts—the modernist drive toward abstraction, experimentation, and lack of closure—arguing that modernism itself mirrors the exhilarating and terrible freedom of the modern self to define its own identity (Berger 2000).

Here we touch on the nettlesome issue of art as a surrogate religion. Berger confronts the issue unflinchingly, arguing that the fine arts offer our secular and individualistic society more varied spiritual insights than do the historical religions, with their demand for conformity and claims of exclusivity. It is a complex and delicate issue. For a small segment of the cultured elite, the fine arts have indeed been invested with the kinds of feeling and commitment once reserved for traditional religions. Yet the anti-art movements of the early twentieth century and many of the parodic gestures of recent decades, have often aimed their sharpest barbs at just such lofty claims for art. As sources of spiritual insight and consolation, art and religion can be mutually enriching. Yet we need to unite this legitimate concern for finding spiritual significance in the fine arts with those uses and pleasures of the more ordinary arts that, as thinkers from Rousseau to Saito have reminded us, are also bearers of meaning.

Although the dichotomies of the fine art system have been severely weakened, they still have the capacity to distort many areas of experience, as we have seen. A third system of art transcending the divisions of the modern fine art system has yet to establish itself. But even if it were possible in some wild anti-art dream to dismantle existing institutions and replace the one-sided ideals of fine art with the norms of craft and popular art, we would simply be reversing an invidious polarity rather than healing a fracture that occurred long ago. The answer to art divided is obviously not to reject such ideals as freedom, imagination, and creativity but to unite them with facility, service, and function. Yet there is no magic formula for the correct balance. It would be silly to demand that every piece of music, literature, or visual art manifest an equal dose of imagination and skill, form and function, spiritual and sensual pleasure. And, rightly understood, there is a time and place for disinterested attention and formal analysis as well as for the renewed interest in beauty (Brand 2000; Scarry 2000). In pluralistic democracies there will probably always be multiple art worlds, including small coteries who will consider only the most daunting and esoteric or the most socially and politically shocking works to be "real art." But most people will participate in several kinds of art worlds, moving across the old divisions and hierarchies and juggling more or less successfully the relationships among art, religion, politics, and everyday life.

In this book I have tried to show that (fine) art, as we have generally understood it, is neither eternal nor ancient but a historical construction of the eighteenth century, and I have traced a parallel tradition of resistance extending down to the present. I am also aware that "you can't go home again." We cannot resurrect the old system of art. Nor can we simply wish away the break that split apart the old system of art, arrogating intellect, imagination, and grace to fine art and disparaging craft and popular culture as the realm of mere technique, utility, entertainment, and profit. Like other dualisms that have plagued our culture, the divisions of the fine art system can only be transcended through a continuing struggle. I believe we do transcend them in practice from time to time; what is harder is naming and articulating what we have done.

# Notes

## Introduction

1. Although Kristeller was aware of the need to consider both institutional and socioeconomic factors, his phrase "modern system of the arts" refers to a system of classification, whereas I use it to emphasize the inseparability of concepts from practices, institutions, and social structures.

2. I am using "regulative" to mean a concept that underlies thinking and practice in particular areas of life. For a more technical discussion of regulative concepts and their difference from constitutive ones, see Goehr (1992, 102–6). John Searle makes a similar distinction, viewing the regulative concepts as guiding a preexisting activity and constitutive ones as creating an activity (1995). In the case of art, we have a preexisting practice that undergoes a radical transformation in the eighteenth century. My distinction between "ideas" and "ideals" is also a more general one than Goehr's (97–101). I usually refer to the idea of art but the ideal of the artist, that is, the normative image about what an artist ought to be like. But I make no attempt to develop either term into a technical concept.

3. Such a working description is the best we can do for a historical account of something as expansive and malleable as the idea of art. See Berys Gaut's paper "'Art' as a Cluster Concept" (2000).

4. For example, in a remarkable study tracing the Aristotelian and medieval roots of Renaissance naturalism, David Summers brilliantly demonstrates the continuity of the idea of the *sensus communis* from Leonardo to Kant. But this continuity is perfectly compatible with the idea of a decisive break in the concept of art in the eighteenth century. The deeper continuity across the break is with the older idea of art and the gradual development of a higher estimation of sense experience (Summers 1987, 8–9, 17, 319).

5. As Hayden White has argued, any narrative history tends toward a certain tone or tropism. In White's terms, I am opposing an ironic story to synecdochic narratives that see the modern ideas of art and the artist as an inevitable emergence (1987).

6. These brief remarks on Danto's work hardly do justice to the philosophical and historical sophistication of his argument, which offers us an enormous gain in understanding all kinds of contemporary art. This becomes especially apparent in Danto's incisive art criticism of the past fifteen years (1992, 1994, 2000).

## 1. The Greeks Had No Word for It

1. Havelock and Pollitt mean not only that there was no "word" like "fine art" but also that there was no concept or practice either. Unfortunately, students are likely to be

misled by anachronizing translations. For example, *mimetes* is literally "imitator" but many translations use "artist" with its modern connotations. Some of the best discussions of these and related problems are to be found in the volume on classical criticism edited by George A. Kennedy (1989).

2. See Detienne and Vernant (1978) and Dunne (1993). Aristotle himself can sometimes use *techne* in a more supple fashion, though usually for performative as opposed to productive arts.

3. Only in the Hellenistic period do we find discussions of imagination and then primarily among theorists of rhetoric, who talked of vivid visualization in oratory, but that is a long way from Kant and the Romantics (Pollitt 1974; Barasch 1985; Vernant 1991).

4. An example of conflicting views on whether modern ideas of art were present in ancient Greece are the articles in the new Grove *Dictionary of Art* (Turner 1996), by Paolo Moreno and Martha Nussbaum. Moreno finds the modern distinction between fine art and craft already in the Classical period (Moreno 1996, 13:548, 549, 553); Nussbaum says that one "must begin by stressing how different Greek conceptions were" from our own (Nussbaum 1996, 1:175).

5. Proportion in physical beauty was an idea connected to the notion of measure and order in the cosmos and human society and not something restricted to the arts (Pollitt 1974, 14–22).

6. Barasch has made the case for Plotinus espousing creativity (1985, 34–42). But see Tatarkiewicz (1970, 322).

7. Alsop (1982) emphasizes collecting, but Gombrich believes collecting is an ambiguous indicator and that copying is the crucial sign of the presence of something like the modern idea of art for itself (1960, 111; 1987). On the question of aesthetic versus other motives for collecting statuary, see Gruen (1992).

## 2. Aquinas's Saw

1. Architecture was a subdivision of *armatura* or "constructed coverings" and "theatrics" embraced entertainment of any kind, including wrestling, racing, and dances.

2. There is some evidence that in the thirteenth century, due to more complex building techniques, a few master masons began to design in greater detail and leave the actual day-to-day construction management to intermediaries. At least one sermon compares lazy prelates to architects who only visit the scaffolds, cane and gloves in hand, never doing any real work but drawing big salaries. For a general discussion of the medieval artisan/artist, see Castelnuovo (1990) and Kristeller (1990). For the architect, see Goldthwaite (1980) and Kimpel (1986).

3. An example of the lengths to which modernizers will go is E. H. Kantorowicz's argument for the "origin" of the "sovereignty of the Artist" in medieval notions of the Pope as able to create ex nihilo, which were then picked up by Dante and through him passed on to the Renaissance. Apart from the fact that the argument is strained and the similarities contestable, the normative concepts of "art" and "artificer" in this period were deeply different from our own (Kantorowicz 1961).

4. Edgar de Bruyne, offers a passage from John Scotus Erigena in which two men react with pleasure to a gold chalice; one desires to possess it, but the other, "simply refers its natural beauty to the glory of God alone." This is not "disinterested aesthetic

pleasure," as Bruyne calls it, but a Christian use of the Neoplatonic idea of rising through the sensible to the One, or seeing the Creator in the creation (Bruyne 1969, 117–18). Another way to find "the modern concept of fine art" in the Middle Ages is to emphasize the pleasures taken in gargoyles and Romanesque capitals; but these were not the disinterested, intellectualized pleasure of the post-Kantian "aesthetic" (Shapiro 1977, 1–27).

## 3. Michelangelo and Shakespeare: Art on the Rise

1. The importance of the carpenter-carvers declined in the late fifteenth century as the rectangular panel became popular, but even then frames and frameworks remained elaborate.

2. This consensus stands despite attempts to rehabilitate the idea of a Renaissance "discovery of the individual" (Martin 1997).

3. I follow Lydia Goehr's argument that the modern idea of a work of art involves a complex set of notions that did not come together until the late eighteenth century, e.g., autonomy, repeatability, permanence, perfect compliance, exact notation, and the rejection of borrowing and recycling. Many of these concepts appeared piecemeal from the Renaissance on, but they did not coalesce to establish a new norm until the period 1750–1800.

4. Fortunately, surveys and textbooks since 1997 have begun to turn away from the traditional story of stylistic progression based on a small elite and their masterpieces (Brown 1997; Welch 1997; Paoletti and Radke 1997; Turner 1997).

5. Perhaps one reason Vasari did not use *artista* is that it normally referred to either liberal arts students or alchemists. The recent Oxford translation by Julia Conaway Bondanella and Peter Bondanella at least calls attention to the terminological problems (Vasari 1991b). Misleading translations of *artifice* also occur in the case of Marsilio Ficino (Tigerstedt 1968, 474, 487). Michelangelo did use *artista* for the sculptor in his famous sonnet, "The best artist has no concepts that one single marble does not contain" *(Non has l'ottimo artista alcun concetti)* (Summers 1981, 206).

6. On collaboration and the workshop, see Cole (1983), Burke (1986), and Welch (1997). On the status of the architect, see Wilkinson (1977), Ettlinger (1977), and Wilton-Ely 1977, and Ackerman 1991.

7. I use "talent" rather than "genius" since *ingegno* and *genio* had different meanings, the first being natural ability, the second a tutelary spirit. The translation "innate brilliance" is Martin Kemp's (1977, 384–91). Because the notion of natural talent *(ingenium)* and divine male force *(genio)* became conflated in the seventeenth century, it has been easier to project modern ideas of creative genius onto *ingenium.* The difficulty/facility/grace trio had a different origin since it paralleled an ideal of *sprezzatura* or nonchalance in aristocratic society (Summers 1981). "Imagination," or *fantasia,* was often used in the sense of "invention" but did not yet have its modern sense of "creative imagination" outside the bounds of reason. See Kemp (1997).

8. Shakespeare wrote slapstick antics for William Kempe as Dogberry in *Much Ado about Nothing* but shifted to characters like Touchstone in *As You Like It* or the gravedigger in *Hamlet* when a subtler player, Robert Arnim, took Kempe's place (Bradbrook 1969).

## 4. Artemisia's Allegory: Art in Transition

1. The 1694 dictionary of the Académie Française also gives alchemist as a primary meaning of "artist."

2. Although there was a theosophical and mystical tradition with a more positive view of the imagination, it played only a marginal role in seventeenth-century writing on the arts (Becq 1994a).

3. François Blondel, an architect writing in 1675, twice linked architecture, painting, and sculpture to poetry, eloquence, theater, and ballet on the basis of harmony and pleasure but did not elaborate his remarks into a category (Tatarkiewicz 1964).

4. David Summers believes that the late seventeenth-century interest in "taste" was really a continuation of the older idea of a "practical intellect" or *sensus communis*. Both Summers and Robert Klein make much of the use of *gusto* as the equivalent of judgment in some Renaissance writers who were still read in the seventeenth century (Klein 1979; Summers 1987).

5. Many writers struggled over whether please or instruct takes precedence. Dryden's 1668 defense of the "Essay of Dramatic Poesy" claims that "delight is the chief, if not the only, end of poesy; instruction can be admitted but in the second place" (1961, 1:113). But his 1679 essay dealing with "the grounds of criticism in tragedy" says, "to instruct delightfully is the general end of all poetry" (142). The 1671 "Preface to an Evening's Love" cuts the difference, making instruction tragedy's chief aim and pleasure the means, whereas in comedy, pleasure is the first aim and instruction the means (142–43).

## 5. Polite Arts for the Polite Classes

1. For J. Schlegel and Mendelssohn, see (Kristeller 1990, 213, 217). See also Robertson ([1784] 1971, 14–17). Marmontel actually uses the term "liberal-arts" yet gives roughly the same list as others do for "beaux-arts" ([1787] 1846, 177–79). In addition, see Lacombe (1752); Estève (1753, 9); Kames (1762, 6); and Kant (1987, 190–94). Of course, several of the above writers included more than one additional art in their fine art list: Batteux included both oratory and dance, Kant included oratory and landscape gardening, and Robertson incorporated oratory, gardening, dance, and even history.

2. The word "canon" previously referred to the authoritative books of the Bible or to a "rule" (as in canon law), but its gradual extension in both senses to the secular realm occurs in the eighteenth century.

3. Pomian estimates that in France the number of collectors increased from around 150 in 1700–1720 to at least five hundred between 1750 and 1790. This influx of new buyers was accompanied by a rapid increase in the number of auctions held each year (1987, 147–58).

4. This audience was part of what has been called the "public sphere" created by the spread of newspapers, coffeehouses, and reading clubs for the free exchange of ideas. The classic discussion of the public sphere is by Habermas ([1962] 1989). An enormous scholarly literature on the meaning and usefulness of the concept has appeared since 1962; see Chartier (1988, 20–37).

## 6. The Artist, the Work, and the Market

1. Among the English dictionaries, Baily (1770), Ash (1775), and Webster (1807) all use the term "artist" to define "artisan." The terms "craftsman" and "handicraftsman" seem more specifically associated with mechanical arts, yet there is no suggestion that "artist," "artisan," or "artificer" were radically different in meaning from "craftsman." All of these terms are defined with notions like trade, manufacture, and workman. The 1726 dictionary of the Spanish Academia defines "artifice" (artificer) as a worker in the manual or mechanical arts but gives as examples "sculpture and architecture." Rather than encumber this note with the bibliographical detail on every dictionary consulted I suggest the reader look at the published bibliography of the Cordell collection. See Cunningham Memorial Library (1975).

2. Nathalie Heinich has suggested that three models of the painter's career overlapped in the eighteenth century: the older workshop model, the academy model, and the new market-driven reputation model (Heinich 1993).

3. References to Joseph Addison and the *Spectator* will be given by year and number throughout, rather than the usual author-date system, since there are innumerable editions and it might be difficult for the reader to locate the various editions I have used over the years. One edition, though, is Addison and Steele (1907).

4. Addison and Johnson are cited in the text above; for André, see Becq (1994a, 417); and see Kant (1987, 182).

5. As Mary Astell wrote in 1696, men "have endeavored to train us up altogether to Ease and Ignorance. . . . About the Age of six or seven the sexes begin to be separated, and the boys are sent to the Grammar School and the Girls to Boarding Schools, and other Places, to learn Needlework, Dancing, Singing, Music, Drawing, Painting and other Accomplishments" (Pears 1988, 186).

6. Goehr's thesis has drawn the fire of some musicologists but has been supported by others (White 1997; Erauw 1998).

## 7. From Taste to the Aesthetic

1. As the stages were cleared, another change in behavior developed that was connected to later aesthetic theories: the majority of listeners no longer looked to the nobles and connoisseurs on stage or in the boxes for cues to the proper response but increasingly relied on personal judgment (Johnson 1995, 92).

2. The story of how the problem of taste in British theory led to Kant is the hinge of most English language histories of aesthetics. Among several recent attempts to rewrite the traditional story are De Bolla (1989), McCormick (1990), Barnouw (1993), Gadamer (1993), Becq (1994a), Bohls (1995), and Paulson (1996).

3. In the early nineteenth century, Alexis de Tocqueville, looking back nostalgically to the time before the Revolution, emphasized the quality of disinterestedness in the aristocratic ideal, something he found lacking in the ambitious and grasping middle class then in ascendancy. See Shiner (1988).

4. The enormous outpouring of recent analyses of Kant's third *Critique* testify to its importance as a founding document for modern theories of art and the aesthetic. With formalist theories out of favor at the moment, recent interpreters are rediscovering a

moral and political dimension in the *Critique,* whereas others point out that the connection of the first half on aesthetics to the second half on teleology in nature has been neglected (Cohen and Guyer 1982; Derrida 1987; Caygill 1989; McCormick 1990; Lyotard 1991; Guyer 1997).

5. Terry Eagleton (1990) believes it is no accident that this exalted view of the aesthetic was formulated by writers living in small absolutist states and argues that Schiller's view of the political effects of the aesthetic seems to situate obedience to established authority in the very feelings of the political subject.

## 8. Hogarth, Rousseau, Wollstonecraft

1. The most important and balanced treatment of Rousseau's views on the arts is Robinson (1984). Michael O'Dea, studying Rousseau on music, agrees with Robinson that the tensions in Rousseau's attitude toward the fine arts were never resolved (1995). All serious students of Rousseau now have an extraordinary aid in Trousson and Eigeldinger (1996).

2. Where double citations are given, the first reference is to the French text, which I am translating; the second to a readily available English edition.

3. As Rousseau imagined them, these first gatherings for group song and dance soon led to envy and inequality in the form of quarrels over who was the best singer and dancer, and it was downhill from there. From now on, instead of the positive drive of self-preservation or self-love *(amour de soi)* characteristic of the isolated state of nature, a new motive for human action developed, pride or selfish-love *(amour propre),* a negative drive fueled by comparison. Rousseau's imagined transitional period of "nascent society" is idealized as a time when the seeds of comparison and *amour propre* were planted but had not yet come to produce their poisonous flowers.

4. Wollstonecraft not only touched on aesthetic issues in many of her well-known political writings, but she also wrote a novel and reviewed novels and poetry for the radical *Analytical Review.* For a brief discussion of her aesthetic ideas, see Jump (1994). The best overall treatment of her thought is Shapiro (1992).

5. The first chapter of *A Vindication of the Rights of Woman,* for example, takes vigorous exception to the condemnation of the fine arts in Rousseau's *First Discourse.* Her discussions of poetry speak of genius in the conventional terms of enthusiasm and imagination and describe taste as spontaneous, showing refined feeling, and so on. See the essay "On Poetry" in the collected works (1989, vol. 7). She also writes in the *Letters* that those whose judgment is not "formed by the cultivation of the arts and sciences" lack "that delicacy of feeling and thinking . . . characterized by the word sentiment" (1989, 6:250–51). Bohls believes this passage is an exception to Wollstonecraft's usual "attribution of aesthetic capacities to everyone," but it does reflect a tension in her thinking (Bohls 1995, 168).

## 9. Revolution: Music, Festival, Museum

1. Several years after the "kings" were chiseled off Notre Dame, the debris came into the hands of a lawyer who, on discovering he had purchased consecrated statuary, buried

the heads in accord with canon law. In 1977, when the French government bought the lawyer's former house and opened a wall during remodeling, they found the buried remains; after almost two hundred years, the vigorously sculptured heads of the kings, a few pieces missing, finally entered a museum! (E. Kennedy 1989, 204–6). In addition to Kennedy's book on the culture of the Revolution, a number of works since the 1970s have revised the image of the arts in the Revolution. See Ehrard and Viallaneix (1977); Julien and Klein (1989); Julien and Mongrédien (1991); and Boyd (1992).

2. A new musical society founded in 1792, the Lycée des Arts, made one of its aims to banish the barriers between the *arts agréable* and the *arts utile.* Kant and mainstream aesthetics were looking for a way of transcending both in a higher kind of experience (Julien 1989, 72–73).

3. Actually, the provisions of the decree were contradictory; the first article called for removal and conservation, the second for melting down all bronze works, the third for "destruction without delay," and the fourth for the conservation of objects that might "interest the arts" (Pommier 1991, 101–2).

4. McClellan points out that Pope Pius VII apparently did not agree with Quatremère's notion that paintings should be seen in the setting for which they were intended since he intercepted several works the French were sending back to churches and made them part of the Vatican Museum of Painting, which opened in 1817 (1994, 200–201).

## 10. Art as Redemptive Revelation

1. Of course, a few older works of nonfiction such as Gibbon's *Decline and Fall* or Bossuet's sermons have reentered the literature curriculum to be studied for their style. Books on the topic "history of literature" written in English, French, and German during the first decades of the nineteenth century still included works on philosophy, natural science, and politics as well as poetry and epic (Gossman 1990, 32). For the process by which history ceased to be "literature" and became "science," see White (1973). There is still a great deal of research to be done in tracing the emergence of the modern idea of literature. See Becq (1994b, 293–301).

2. An Italian writer changed the title of his *Idea della poesia alemanna* of 1779 to *Idea della bella letteratura alemanna* when he published a second edition in 1784 (Wellek 1982, 16).

3. Jean-Marie Schaeffer places the break that established the modern idea of fine art between Kant and the romantics (1992, 16–24).

## 12. Silences: Triumph of the Aesthetic

1. As Weber (1975) shows, ticket prices were set at a level effectively excluding most of the lower social ranks, and innovations such as reserved seats further limited social range. As with most general trends, there were variations and exceptions; opera in Italy retained, and retains to this day, a broader audience than in northern Europe and America.

2. Peter Gay mentions a middle-class cultural society in Frankfurt that adopted the

following guidelines in 1808: "During literary or musical performances everyone is asked to refrain from speaking. . . . Signs of disapproval are not to be expected. . . . Dogs are not tolerated" (1995, 18–19).

3. Most writers in the first half of the century continued to use the term "taste" despite the disadvantages Wordsworth noted in his preface to the *Lyrical Ballads* of 1802, e.g., that the word "taste" seems to reduce the experience of fine art to the same level as rope dancing or sherry. Coleridge still regretted in 1821 that there was not "a more familiar word than aesthetics for works of taste and criticism" (Williams 1976, 21). And the *Encyclopedia of Architecture* in 1842 could complain that "there has lately grown into use in the arts a silly pedantic term under the name of Aesthetics" (Steegman 1970, 18). In France, the term "aesthetic" played little role in Victor Cousin's influential lecture course *Du vrai, du beau, du bien* (the true, the beautiful and the good) of 1818, but in 1826 Théodore Jouffroy called his lecture series *Cours d'esthétique* (Jouffroy 1883). The Académie Française finally accepted the term in 1838, and Comte and Baudelaire both used it in the 1850s (Comte [1851] 1968; Baudelaire [1859] 1986).

## 14. Modernism, Anti-Art, and the Bauhaus

1. The roots of modernism go far back into the nineteenth century, varying from art to art and varying also according to which characteristics of modernism are emphasized. The bibliography on the definition and development of modernism is enormous. A good place to start is William Everdell's *The First Moderns*, which is also a delightful discussion of the beginnings of modernism between the 1880s and World War I (1997, 1–12, 363–64).

2. For years the perspective enunciated by Newhall dominated the history of photography to which he made signal contributions (1980, 1982), but other source books (Goldberg 1981; Phillips 1989) and essay collections (Bolton 1989; Solomon-Godeau 1991) have suggested a more complex story.

3. The art historian Geoffrey Scott, e.g., claimed that "optical effect and structural requirements" were distinct, and the Czech architect Pavel Janak gave primacy to artistic expression over both function and technology. The career of the talented Bruno Taut shows how hard it was to hold both sides together as he swung from an early dream that "architecture has no other purpose than to be beautiful" to his socialist agitation within the Worker's Council for Art after the war, only to return to a view that function and construction were subordinate to "the art of proportion"(Kruft 1994, 367–74).

4. Adorno argued that the most difficult avant-garde art, such as that of Schoenberg or Kafka, did not simply encourage apolitical aesthetic contemplation and that the mass media by contrast were retrograde tools of a capitalist "culture industry" that turned workers into passive consumers. Others since have found the whole concept of the "aura" to be somewhat confused and questionable.

## 15. Beyond Art and Craft?

1. One of the popular myths of modernism is that Picasso "discovered" primitive art; the real story of how African, Oceanic, and Native American objects migrated from

ethnography collections to art museums is far more complex and involves many factors, from eighteenth-century ideas of the unspoiled primitive through the nineteenth-century quest for the "origins" of Art and Gauguin's and Conrad's projection of sexual license and dark spirituality onto native peoples, to early twentieth-century expressionist and formalist theorists like Roger Fry who patronizingly praised the "complete plastic freedom" of "these nameless savages" ([1920] 1956, 100).

2. "Tribal" has many of the same problems as "primitive," but finding a satisfactory general term for the enormous variety of societies that have produced these works is difficult. I have adopted "small scale" as the least objectionable even though it is not a perfect sorter. See Anderson (1989) and Graburn (1976). In France, where the Louvre only got around to opening a gallery of "arts primitifs" in the spring of 2000, some people prefer the term "arts premiers."

3. Many of the same carving workshops that make reproductions (or "fakes," according to curators and dealers) also make pieces for ritual use and tend to view their profession "matter-of-factly as aiming to satisfy the requirements set down by patrons" (Kasfir 1992, 45). Among the best discussions of an actual reproduction workshop is Ross and Reichert (1983). On the complex symbolic interchange involved in "tourist art," see Jules-Rosette (1984); for the African art market, see Steiner (1994). For a defense of assimilation, see Danto (1994), Davies (2000), and Dutton (2000), and for a critique, see Shiner (1994).

4. I saw this statement on a visit in 1997. The museum's web site, as of July 2000, defines the museum mission as one of "pioneering a new approach to the interpretation of Native American arts and culture, one in which Native and non-Native people are active partners in research, scholarship, exhibitions and education" (http://www.miaclab.org).

5. Some of the same problems with the appropriation of tribal art occur in the eagerness to assimilate folk art into fine art. The folklorist John Michael Vlach, e.g., insists that folk quilts, pottery, and furniture should be seen "as the equal of fine art, not its weak and imperfect echo" (1991). And Henry Glassie, although admitting that most folk pieces are judged by those who make and use them in terms of craft skill and function, says we should call them not craft but art since "art is such an exalted term among us" (1989, 50). Although I sympathize with Vlach's and Glassie's desire to raise the status of folk art, it is striking that neither of them questions a category of fine art that leads to these distortions; they just want to get folk art into it. The distortions are even worse in the appropriation of what is called "outsider" art, for which the deep psychic and religious struggles and visions of its makers are either ignored or exploited to enhance the interest of art audiences. See the articles by Ames, Cubbs, Lippard, and Metcalf in Hall and Metcalf (1994).

6. It should be noted, in Serra's defense, that the hearings on *Tilted Arc* were run by a conservative bureaucrat, that many of the people who objected to Serra's piece were indeed ignorant of modern art, and that the plaza was hardly user friendly to begin with. Serra and his wife have published their own account with documents relating to the hearings (Weyergraf-Serra and Buskirk 1991). For a subtle political-aesthetic defense of *Tilted Arc*, see Crimp (1993, 150–98). One of the best discussions of the Serra/Lin comparison is by Michael Kelly (1996). A sensitive discussion of the *Vietnam Veterans*

*Memorial* in relation to its setting can be found in Charles L. Griswold (1992). Among the more helpful books that include discussion of the general issues raised by the Serra and Lin controversies are Raven (1989), Mitchell (1992), Senie (1992), and Gooding (1999).

## Conclusion

1. There is an enormous and ever-growing literature just on the history and purpose of art museums and their need to diversify programming and audiences. See Vergo (1989); Karp and Lavine (1991); Hooper-Greenhill (1992); Bennett (1995); and Duncan (1995). There are also a number of useful collections dealing with general cultural policy, such as Smith and Berman (1992) or Bradford, Gary, and Wallach (2000).

2. On literary and cultural studies, see Smithson and Ruff (1994); Scholes (1998); and Bérubé (1999). For new ways of thinking about art history, see Preziosi (1989); Moxey (1994); and Melville and Readings (1995). For some current issues within musicology, see Bergeron and Bohlman (1992). Goehr (1992), Mattick (1993), Woodmansee (1994), and Mortensen (1997) are among those who have most forcefully made the case for the relevance of the eighteenth-century revolution in the meaning of "art" for doing philosophy of art. For attempts at a historical definition of art in philosophy, see Carroll (1993, 2000); Levinson (1993); and Danto (1997). Kivy (1993) and Margolis (1993) have each argued on different grounds that defining "Art" may be less useful than cultural and historical explorations of the various "arts." For a feminist perspective on aesthetics and its history, see Hein and Korsmeyer (1993); and Brand and Korsmeyer (1995). I will not even begin to list the enormous number of works on the recovery of long-ignored women writers, artists, and composers or the many theoretical discussions of gender that have been written by literary, art, and music historians and critics over the past thirty years.

# References


Aboudrar, Bruno-Assim. 2000. *Nous n'irons plus au musée.* Paris: Aubier.

Abrams, M. H. 1958. *The Mirror and the Lamp: Romantic Theory and the Critical Tradition.* New York: W. W. Norton.

———. 1989. *Doing Things with Texts: Essays in Criticism and Critical Theory.* New York: W. W. Norton.

Ackerman, James S. 1991. *Distance Points: Essays in Theory and Renaissance Art and Architecture.* Cambridge, Mass.: MIT Press.

Adams, John. 1963. *Adams Family Correspondence.* 4 vols. Cambridge, Mass.: Harvard University Press.

Addison, Joseph, and Richard Steele. 1907. *The Spectator.* 4 vols. London: J. M. Dent & Sons, Ltd.

Allen, Grant. 1877. *Physiological Aesthetics.* London: Henry S. King.

Alpers, Svetlana. 1983. *The Art of Describing: Dutch Art in the Seventeenth Century.* Chicago: University of Chicago Press.

———. 1988. *Rembrandt's Enterprise: The Studio and the Market.* Chicago: University of Chicago Press.

Alsop, Joseph. 1982. *The Rare Art Traditions: The History of Art Collecting and Its Linked Phenomena Wherever These Have Appeared.* Princeton, N.J.: Princeton University Press.

Anderson, Richard L. 1989. *Art in Small-Scale Societies.* Englewood Cliffs, N.J.: Prentice-Hall.

Andrews, Malcolm. 1989. *The Search for the Picturesque: Landscape Aesthetics and Tourism in Britain, 1760–1800.* London: Scholar Press.

Andrews, Marilyn. 1999. "Crossing Categories." *Ceramics Monthly* 47 (October): 44–47.

Anscombe, Isabelle. 1984. *A Woman's Touch: Women in Design from 1860 to the Present Day.* New York: Viking.

Arcin, André. 1911. *Histoire de la Guinée française.* Paris: A. Challamel.

Arnold, Matthew. 1962. *Lectures and Essays in Criticism.* Vol. 3 of *The Complete Prose Works of Matthew Arnold,* edited by R. H. Super. Ann Arbor: University of Michigan Press.

———. 1966. *Essays in Criticism: Second Series.* New York: St. Martin's Press.

Ashfield, Andrew, and Peter de Bolla, eds. 1996. *The Sublime: A Reader in British Eighteenth-Century Aesthetic Theory.* Cambridge: Cambridge University Press.

Attali, Jacques. 1985. *Noise: The Political Economy of Music.* Minneapolis: University of Minnesota.

Auberlen, Eckhard. 1984. *The Commonwealth of Wit: The Writer's Self-Representation in Elizabethan Literature.* Tübingen: Gunther Narr.

Auerbach, Erich. 1993. *Literary Language and Its Public in Late Latin Antiquity and in the Middle Ages.* Princeton, N.J.: Princeton University Press.

Austen, Jane. 1995. *Northanger Abbey.* London: Penguin.

Baldick, Chris. 1983. *The Social Mission of English Criticism, 1848–1932.* Oxford: Clarendon Press.

Barasch, Moshe. 1985. *Theories of Art from Plato to Winckelmann.* New York: New York University Press.

Barber, Robin. 1990. "The Greeks and Their Sculpture." In *"Owls to Athens": Essays on Classical Subjects Presented to Sir Kenneth Dover,* edited by E. M. Craik. Oxford: Clarendon Press.

Barker, Emma, Nick Webb, and Kim Woods. 1999. *The Changing Status of the Artist.* New Haven, Conn.: Yale University Press.

Barnard, Rob. 1992. "Speakeasy." *New Art Examiner* 19 (January): 13.

Barnouw, Jeffrey. 1993. "The Beginnings of 'Aesthetics' and the Leibnizian Conception of Sensation." In Mattick 1993.

Barrell, John. 1986. *The Political Theory of Painting from Reynolds to Hazlitt.* New Haven, Conn.: Yale University Press.

Bartlet, M. Elizabeth C. 1991. "Gossec, l'offrande à la liberté et l'histoire de la *Marseillaise.*" In Julien and Mongrédien 1991.

Battersby, Christine. 1989. *Gender and Genius: Towards a Feminist Aesthetics.* Bloomington: Indiana University Press.

Batteux, Charles. (1746) 1989. *Les beaux arts réduits à un même principe.* Paris: Aux Amateurs de Livres.

Baudelaire, Charles. 1968. *L'art romantique: Littérature et musique.* Paris: Flammarion.

———. (1859) 1986. *Écrits esthétiques.* Paris: Union Générale d'Édition.

Baumgarten, Alexander. 1954. *Reflections on Poetry.* Berkeley: University of California Press.

Baxandall, Michael. 1988. *Painting and Experience in Fifteenth-Century Italy.* Oxford: Oxford University Press.

Beardsley, John. 1998. *Earthworks and Beyond: Contemporary Art in the Landscape.* New York: Abbeville Press.

Beardsley, Monroe C. 1975. *Aesthetics from Classical Greece to the Present.* Tuscaloosa: University of Alabama Press.

Becq, Annie. 1994a. *Genèse de l'esthétique française moderne: De la raison classique à l'imagination créatrice.* Paris: Albin Michel.

———. 1994b. *Lumières et modernité: De Malebranche à Baudelaire.* Orleans: Paradigme.

Beethoven, Ludwig van. 1951. *Beethoven: Letters, Journals and Conversation,* edited by Michael Hamburger. New York: Thames & Hudson.

Bell, Clive. (1913) 1958. *Art.* New York: G. P. Putnam's Sons.

Bénichou, Paul. 1973. *Le sacré de l'écrvain, 1750–1830: Essai sur l'avènement d'un pouvoir spirituel laïque dans la France moderne.* Paris: José Corti.

Benjamin, Walter. 1969. *Illuminations.* New York: Schoken Books.

———. 1986. *Reflections: Essays, Aphorisms, Autobiographical Writings.* New York: Schocken Books.

Bennett, Tony. 1995. *The Birth of the Museum: History, Theory, Politics.* London: Routledge.

Bentley, Gerald Eades. 1971. *The Profession of Dramatist in Shakespeare's Time, 1590–1642.* Princeton, N.J.: Princeton University Press.

Berger, Karol. 2000. *A Theory of Art.* New York: Oxford University Press.

Bergeron, Katherine, and Philip V. Bohlman, eds. 1992. *Disciplining Music: Musicology and Its Canons.* Chicago: University of Chicago Press.

Berghahn, Klaus L. 1988. "From Classicist to Classical Literary Criticism, 1730–1806." In Hohendahl 1988.

Berleant, Arnold. 1991. *Art and Engagement.* Philadelphia: Temple University Press.

Bermingham, Ann. 1992. "The Origin of Painting and the Ends of Art: Wright of Derby's *Corinthian Maid.*" In *Painting and the Politics of Culture: New Essays on British Art, 1700–1800,* edited by John Barrell. Oxford: Oxford University Press.

Bérubé, Michael. 1998. *The Employment of English: Theory, Jobs and the Future of Literary Study.* New York: New York University Press.

Boardman, John. 1996. *Greek Art.* London: Thames & Hudson.

Bohls, Elizabeth A. 1995. *Women Travel Writers and the Language of Aesthetics, 1716–1818.* Cambridge: Cambridge University Press.

Boileau, Nicolas. 1972. *L'art poétique.* Paris: Bordas.

Bolton, Richard, ed. 1989. *The Contest of Meaning: Critical Histories of Photography.* Cambridge, Mass.: MIT Press.

Bouhours, Dominique. 1920. *Entretiens d'ariste et d'Eugène.* Paris: Bossard.

Boyd, Malcolm. 1992. *Music and the French Revolution.* Cambridge: Cambridge University Press.

Bradbrook, M. C. 1969. *Shakespeare the Craftsman.* New York: Barnes & Noble.

Bradford, Gigi, Michael Gary, and Glenn Wallach, eds. 2000. *The Politics of Culture: Policy Perspectives for Individuals, Institutions and Communities.* New York: The New Press.

Brand, Peggy Zeglin, ed. 2000. *Beauty Matters.* Bloomington: Indiana University Press.

Brand, Peggy Zeglin, and Carolyn Korsmeyer, eds. 1995. *Feminism and Tradition in Aesthetics.* University Park: Pennsylvania State University Press.

Bredekamp, Horst. 1995. *The Lure of Antiquity and the Cult of the Machine: The Kunstkammer and the Evolution of Nature, Art and Technology.* Princeton, N.J.: Markus Wiener.

Brevan, Bruno. 1989. "Paris: Cris, sons, bruits: L'environnement sonore des années prérévolutionnaires d'après 'Le Tableau de Paris,' de Sébastien Mercier." In Julien and Klein 1989.

Briggs, Robin. 1991. "The Académie Royale des Science and the Pursuit of Utility." *Past and Present,* no. 131:38–88.

Brown, Jonathan. 1986. *Velázquez: Painter and Courtier.* New Haven, Conn.: Yale University Press.

Brown, Patricia Fortini. 1997. *Art and Life in Renaissance Venice.* New York: Harry N. Abrams.

Brunhammer, Yvonne. 1992. *Le beau dans l'utile: Un musée pour les arts décoratifs.* Paris: Gallimard.

Brunot, Ferdinand. 1966. *Histoire de la langue Française des origins à nos jours.* Vol. 6, pt. 1. Paris: Armand Colin.

Bruyne, Edgar de. 1969. *The Aesthetics of the Middle Ages.* New York: Friedrich Ungar.

Burford, Alison. 1972. *Craftsmen in Greek and Roman Society.* Ithaca, N.Y.: Cornell University Press.

Bürger, Peter. 1984. *Theory of the Avant-Garde.* Minneapolis: University of Minnesota Press.

Burke, Edmund. (1790) 1955. *Reflections on the Revolution in France.* Indianapolis: Bobbs-Merrill.

———. (1757) 1968. *A Philosophical Enquiry into the Origin of Our Ideas of the Sublime and Beautiful.* Notre Dame, Ind.: University of Notre Dame.

Burke, Peter. 1978. *Popular Culture in Early Modern Europe.* New York: Harper & Row.

———. 1986. *The Italian Renaissance: Culture and Society in Italy.* Princeton, N.J.: Princeton University Press.

———. 1993. "Popular Culture in Early Modern Europe: A Concept Revisited." *Intellectual History Newsletter* 15:3–13.

———. 1997. *Varieties of Cultural History.* Ithaca, N.Y.: Cornell University Press.

Burton, Anthony. 1976. *Josiah Wedgwood: A Biography.* London: Andre Deutsch.

Cabanne, Pierre. 1971. *Dialogues with Marcel Duchamp.* New York: Viking.

Cahn, Walter. 1979. *Masterpieces: Chapters in the History of an Idea.* Princeton, N.J.: Princeton University Press.

Callen, Anthea. 1979. *Women Artists of the Arts and Crafts Movement, 1870–1914.* New York: Pantheon Books.

Caplan, Jay L. 1989. "Clearing the Stage." In *A New History of French Literature,* edited by Denis Hollier. Minneapolis: University of Minnesota Press.

Carroll, Noël. 1993. "Historical Narratives and the Philosophy of Art." *Journal of Aesthetics and Art Criticism* 51:313–27.

———. 1998. *A Philosophy of Mass Art.* Oxford: Clarendon Press.

———, ed. 2000. *Theories of Art Today.* Madison: University of Wisconsin Press.

Cassirer, Ernst. 1951. *The Philosophy of the Enlightenment.* Boston: Beacon Press.

Castelnuovo, Enrico. 1990. "The Artist." In *Medieval Callings,* edited by Jacques Le Goff. Chicago: University of Chicago Press.

Castiglione, Baldesare. 1959. *The Book of the Courtier.* New York: Doubleday.

Caygill, Howard. 1989. *The Art of Judgment.* Oxford: Basil Blackwell.

Chadwick, Whitney. 1996. *Women, Art and Society.* London: Thames & Hudson.

Chambers, Ephraim. 1728. *Cyclopedia: An Universal Dictionary of the Arts and Sciences.* 2 vols. London: J. & J. Knapton.

Chanan, Michael. 1994. *Musica Practica: The Social Practice of Western Music from Gregorian Chant to Postmodernism.* London: Verso.

Charlton, D. G. 1963. *Secular Religions in France, 1815–1870.* London: Oxford University Press.

Charlton, David. 1992. "Introduction: Exploring the Revolution." In Boyd 1992.

Chartier, Roger. 1988. *Cultural History: Between Practices and Representations.* Ithaca, N.Y.: Cornell University Press.

———. 1991. *The Cultural Origins of the French Revolution.* Durham, N.C.: Duke University Press.

Chatelus, Jean. 1991. *Peindre à Paris au xviiie siècle.* Paris: Jacqueline Chambon.

Christo. 1996. *Wrapped Reichstag, Berlin, 1971–95.* Köln: Taschen.

Clark, Garth. 1979. *A Century of Ceramics in the United States, 1878–1978: A Study of Its Development.* New York: E. P. Dutton.

Clark, Priscilla Parkhurst. 1987. *Literary France: The Making of a Culture.* Berkeley: University of California Press.

Clark, T. J. 1984. *The Painting of Modern Life: Paris in the Art of Manet and His Followers.* Princeton, N.J.: Princeton University Press.

Clifford, James. 1988. *The Predicament of Culture: Twentieth-Century Ethnography, Literature, and Art.* Cambridge, Mass.: Harvard University Press.

———. 1997. *Routes: Travel and Translation in the Late Twentieth Century.* Cambridge, Mass.: Harvard University Press.

Clunas, Craig. 1997. *Art in China.* Oxford: Oxford University Press.

Cohen, Ted. 1999. "High and Low Art, and High and Low Audiences." *Journal of Aesthetics and Art Criticism* 57:137–43.

Cohen, Ted, and Paul Guyer. 1982. *Essays in Kant's Aesthetics.* Chicago: University of Chicago Press.

Cole, Bruce. 1983. *The Renaissance Artist at Work: From Pisano to Titian.* New York: Harper & Row.

Coleridge, Samuel Taylor. 1983. *Biographia Literaria.* Princeton, N.J.: Princeton University Press.

Collingwood, R. G. 1938. *The Principles of Art.* Oxford: Oxford University Press.

Comte, Auguste. (1851) 1968. *System of Positive Polity.* 4 vols. New York: Burt Franklin.

Conrads, Ulrich. 1970. *Programs and Manifestoes on Twentieth-Century Architecture.* Cambridge, Mass.: MIT Press.

Court, Franklin E. 1992. *Institutionalizing English Literature: The Culture and Politics of Literary Study, 1750–1900.* Stanford, Calif.: Stanford University Press.

Cranston, Maurice. 1991a. *Jean-Jacques: The Early Life and Work of Jean-Jacques Rousseau, 1712–1754.* Chicago: University of Chicago Press.

———. 1991b. *The Noble Savage: Jean-Jacques Rousseau, 1754–1762.* Chicago: University of Chicago Press.

Crawford, Alan. 1985. *C. R. Ashbee: Architect, Designer and Romantic Socialist.* New Haven, Conn.: Yale University Press.

Crimp, Douglas. 1993. *On the Museum's Ruins.* Cambridge, Mass.: MIT Press.

Croce, Benedetto. 1992. *The Aesthetic as the Science of Expression of the Linguistic in General.* Cambridge: Cambridge University Press.

Crow, Thomas E. 1985. *Painters and Public Life in Eighteenth-Century France.* New Haven, Conn.: Yale University Press.

Cumming, Elizabeth, and Wendy Kaplan. 1991. *The Arts and Crafts Movement.* London: Thames & Hudson.

Cunningham Memorial Library. 1975. *A Short-Title Catalogue of the Warren N. and Suzanna B. Cornell Collection of Dictionaries, 1475–1900.* Terre Haute: Indiana State University Press.

Curtius, E. R. 1953. *European Literature and the Latin Middle Ages.* Princeton, N.J.: Princeton University Press.

Da Costa, Feliz. (1696) 1967. *The Antiquity of the Art of Painting.* New Haven, Conn.: Yale University Press.

Dahlhaus, Carl. 1989. *The Idea of Absolute Music.* Chicago: University of Chicago Press.

D'Alembert, Jean. 1986. *Encyclopédie, ou dictionnaire raisonné des sciences des arts et des métiers, articles choisie.* Vol. 1. Paris: Flammarion.

Danto, Arthur. 1992. *Beyond the Brillo Box.* New York: Farrar, Straus, & Giroux.

———. 1994. *Embodied Meanings: Critical Essays and Aesthetic Meditations.* New York: Farrar, Straus & Giroux.

———. 1997. *After the End of Art: Contemporary Art and the Pale of History.* Princeton, N.J.: Princeton University Press.

———. 2000. *The Madonna of the Future: Essays in a Pluralistic Art World.* New York: Farrar, Straus & Giroux.

Darnton, Robert. 1979. *The Business of Enlightenment: A Publishing History of the Encyclopédie.* Cambridge, Mass.: Harvard University Press.

———. 1982. *The Literary Underground of the Old Regime.* Cambridge, Mass.: Harvard University Press.

David, Hans T., and Arthur Mendel. 1966. *The Bach Reader: A Life of Johann Sebastian Bach in Letters and Documents.* New York: W. W. Norton.

Davies, Stephen. 2000. "Non-Western Art and Art's Definition." In Carroll 2000.

De Bolla, Peter. 1989. *The Discourse of the Sublime.* Oxford: Basil Blackwell.

de Duve, Thierry, ed. 1991. *The Definitively Unfinished Marcel Duchamp.* Cambridge, Mass.: MIT Press.

DeJean, Joan. 1988. "Classical Reeducation: Decanonizing the Feminine." *Yale French Studies* 25:26–39.

———. 1997. *Ancients against Moderns: Culture Wars and the Making of a Fin de Siècle.* Chicago: University of Chicago Press.

Derrida, Jacques. 1987. *The Truth in Painting.* Chicago: University of Chicago Press.

Detienne, Marcel, and Jean-Pierre Vernant. 1978. *Cunning Intelligence in Greek Culture and Society.* Atlantic Highlands, N.J.: Humanities Press.

Dewey, John. 1934. *Art as Experience.* New York: G. P. Putnam's Sons.

———. (1925) 1988. *John Dewey: The Later Works, 1925–1953.* Vol. 1, *1925, Experience and Nature.* Carbondale: Southern Illinois University Press.

Diamonstein, Barbaralee, ed. 1983. *Handmade in America: Conversations with Fourteen Craftmasters.* New York: Harry N. Abrams.

Dickie, George. 1997. *The Art Circle: A Theory of Art.* Evanston, Ill.: Chicago Spectrum Press.

Diderot, Denis. 1968. *Oeuvres esthétiques.* Paris: Garnier.

———. (1767) 1995. *Diderot on Art.* Vol. 2, *The Salon of 1767.* New Haven, Conn.: Yale University Press.

Diderot, Denis, and Jean Le Rond d'Alembert. 1751–72. *Encyclopédie, ou dictionnaire raissoné des sciences, des arts et des métiers.* 17 vols. Paris: Briasson.

Dieckmann, Herbert. 1940. "Diderot's Conception of Genius." *Journal of the History of Ideas* 2:151–79.

Dowling, Linda. 1996. *The Vulgarization of Art: The Victorians and Aesthetic Democracy.* Charlottesville: University of Virginia Press.

Droste, Magdalena. 1998. *Bauhaus, 1919–1933.* Berlin: Bauhaus Archiv.

Dryden, John. 1961. *Essays of John Dryden.* 2 vols. New York: Russell & Russell.

Dubos, Abbé. (1719) 1993. *Réflexions critiques sur la poésie et sur la peinture.* Paris: École Nationale Supérieur des Beaux-Arts.

Duchamp, Marcel. 1968. "I Propose to Strain the Laws of Physics." *ARTnews* 34 (December): 47–62.

Duckworth, William. 1995. *Talking Music: Conversations with John Cage, Philip Glass, Laurie Anderson, and Five Generations of American Experimental Composers.* New York: Schirmer Books.

Duff, William. 1767. *Essay on Original Genius . . . in Philosophy and the Fine Arts.* London: Edward & Charles Dilly.

Duncan, Carol. 1995. *Civilizing Rituals: Inside Public Art Museums.* London: Routledge.

Dunne, Joseph. 1993. *Back to the Rough Ground: "Phronesis" and "Techne" in Modern Philosophy and in Aristotle.* Notre Dame, Ind.: University of Notre Dame Press.

Dutton, Denis. 2000. "'But They Don't Have Our Concept of Art.'" In Carroll 2000.

Eagleton, Terry. 1990. *The Ideology of the Aesthetic.* Oxford: Basil Blackwell.

Eastlake, Lady Elizabeth. (1857) 1981. "A Review in the *London Quarterly Review.*" In Goldberg 1981.

Eco, Umberto. 1986. *Art and Beauty in the Middle Ages.* New Haven, Conn.: Yale University Press.

———. 1988. *The Aesthetics of Thomas Aquinas.* Cambridge, Mass.: Harvard University Press.

Edwards, Philip. 1968. *Shakespeare and the Confines of Art.* London: Methuen.

Ehrard, Jean, and Paul Viallaneix. 1977. *Les fêtes de la révolution: Colloque de Clermont-Ferrand (Juin, 1974).* Paris: Société des Études Robespierristes.

Eitner, Lorenz. 1970. *Neoclassicism and Romanticism, 1750–1850: Sources and Documents.* Vol. 2. Englewood Cliffs, N.J.: Prentice-Hall.

Elias, Norbert. 1994. *Mozart, Portrait of a Genius.* Berkeley: University of California.

Eliot, T. S. 1952. *The Complete Poems and Plays, 1909–1950.* New York: Harcourt Brace & Co.

———. 1989. "Tradition and Individual Talent." In *The Critical Tradition,* edited by David H. Richter. New York: St. Martins Press.

Elliot, David, ed. 1979. *Rodchenko and the Arts of Revolutionary Russia.* New York: Pantheon Books.

Elsner, Jas. 1995. *Art and the Roman Viewer: The Transformation of Art from the Pagan World to Christianity.* Cambridge: Cambridge University Press.

Emerson, Ralph Waldo. 1903. *The Complete Works of Ralph Waldo Emerson.* 12 vols. Boston: Houghton, Mifflin.

———. 1950. *The Complete Essays and Other Writings of Ralph Waldo Emerson.* New York: Modern Library.

———. 1966–72. *The Early Lectures of Ralph Waldo Emerson.* 3 vols. Cambridge, Mass.: Harvard University Press.

———. 1969. *The Journals and Miscellaneous Notebooks of Ralph Waldo Emerson.* 16 vols. Cambridge, Mass.: Harvard University Press.

Engell, James. 1981. *The Creative Imagination: Enlightenment to Romanticism.* Cambridge, Mass.: Harvard University Press.

Erauw, William. 1998. "Canon Formation: Some More Reflections on Lydia Goehr's Imaginary Museum of Musical Works." *Acta Musicologia* 70:109–15.

Erickson, John D. 1984. *Dada: Performance, Poetry, Art.* Boston: Twayne Publishers.

Erlich, Victor. 1981. *Russian Formalism: History-Doctrine.* New Haven, Conn.: Yale University Press.

Estève, Pierre. 1753. *L'esprit des beaux-arts.* Vol. 1. Paris: J. Baptiste Bauche.

Ettlinger, Leopold D. 1977. "The Emergence of the Italian Architect during the Renaissance." In Kostof 1977.

Everdell, William R. 1997. *The First Moderns: Profiles in the Origins of Twentieth-Century Thought.* Chicago: University of Chicago Press.

Eze, Emmanuel Chukwudi, ed. 1997. *Race and the Enlightenment: A Reader.* Oxford: Blackwell.

Fabian, Johannes. 1983. *Time and the Other: How Anthropology Makes Its Object.* New York: Columbia University Press.

Fantham, Elaine. 1996. *Roman Literary Culture: From Cicero to Apuleius.* Baltimore: Johns Hopkins University Press.

Farago, Claire J. 1991. "The Classification of the Visual Arts in the Renaissance." In *The Shapes of Knowledge from the Renaissance to the Eighteenth Century,* edited by Donald R. Kelley and Richard H. Popkin. Dordrecht: Kluwer Academic.

Ferry, Luc. 1990. *Homoa aestheticus: L'invention du goût à l'age démocratique.* Paris: Bernard Grasset.

Fielding, Henry. (1742) 1961. *Joseph Andrews.* New York: Signet Classics.

Flaubert, Gustave. 1980. *The Letters of Gustave Flaubert, 1830–1857.* Cambridge, Mass.: Harvard University Press.

Forgács, Éva. 1991. *The Bauhaus Idea and Bauhaus Politics.* Budapest: Central European University Press.

Frampton, Kenneth. 1992. *Modern Architecture: A Critical History.* London: Thames & Hudson.

Franz, Pierre. 1988. "Pas d'entreacte pour la Révolution." In *La Carmagnole des muses: L'homme de lettres et l'artiste dans la Révolution,* edited by Jean-Claude Bonnet. Paris: Armand Colin.

Freedberg, David. 1989. *The Power of Images: Studies in the History and Theory of Response.* Chicago: University of Chicago Press.

Fry, Roger. (1924) 1956. *Vision and Design.* New York: Meridian Books.

Fumaroli, Marc. 1980. *L'age de l'éloquence: Rhétorique et "res literaria" de la Renaissance au seuil de l'époque classique.* Geneva: Librairie Droz.

Furetière, Antoine. (1690) 1968. *Essai d'un dictionnaire universel.* Geneva: Slatkine Reprints.

Gadamer, Hans Georg. 1993. *Truth and Method.* New York: Continuum Publishing Co.

Garrad, Mary D. 1989. *Artemisia Gentileschi: The Image of the Female Hero in Italian Baroque Art.* Princeton, N.J.: Princeton University Press.

Gaut, Berys. "'Art' as a Cluster Concept." In Carroll 2000.

Gay, Peter. 1995. *The Bourgeois Experience: Victoria to Freud.* Vol. 4, *The Naked Heart.* New York: W. W. Norton.

Geiringer, Karl. 1946. *Haydn: A Creative Life in Music.* New York: W. W. Norton.

Gentili, Bruno. 1988. *Poetry and Its Public in Ancient Greece: From Homer to the Fifth Century.* Baltimore: Johns Hopkins University Press.

Gerard, Alexander. (1774) 1966. *An Essay on Genius.* Munich: Wilhelm Fink.

Gessele, Cynthia M. 1992. "The Conservatoire de Musique and National Music Education in France, 1795–1801." In Boyd 1992.

Ghirardo, Diane. 1996. *Architecture after Modernism.* London: Thames & Hudson.

Gillett, Paula. 1990. *Worlds of Art: Painters in Victorian Society.* New Brunswick, N.J.: Rutgers University Press.

Gilpin, William. 1782. *Observations on the River Wye.* London: Blamire.

Glasser, Hannelore. 1977. *Artists' Contracts of the Early Renaissance.* New York: Garland.

Glassie, Henry. 1989. *The Spirit of Folk Art: The Girard Collection at the Museum of International Folk Art.* New York: Harry N. Abrams.

Goehr, Lydia. 1992. *The Imaginary Museum of Musical Works: An Essay in the Philosophy of Music.* Oxford: Oxford University Press.

Goethe, Johann Wolfgang von. (1774) 1989. *The Sorrows of Young Werther.* Harmondsworth: Penguin.

Gold, Barbara, ed. 1982. *Literary and Artistic Patronage in Ancient Rome.* Austin: University of Texas Press.

Goldberg, Vicki, ed. 1981. *Photography in Print.* Albuquerque: University of New Mexico Press.

Goldstein, Carl. 1996. *Teaching Art: Academies and Schools from Vasari to Albers.* Cambridge: Cambridge University Press.

Goldthwaite, Richard A. 1980. *The Building of Renaissance Florence.* Baltimore: Johns Hopkins University Press.

Gombrich, E. H. 1960. *Art and Illusion: A Study in the Psychology of Pictorial Representation.* Princeton, N.J.: Princeton University Press.

———. 1984. *The Story of Art.* Englewood Cliffs, N.J.: Prentice-Hall.

———. 1987. *Reflections on the History of Art: Views and Reviews.* Berkeley: University of California.

Gooding, Mel. 1999. *Public, Art, Space: A Decade of Public Art Commissions Agency.* London: Merrill Halberton.

Goodman, Deana. 1994. *The Republic of Letters: A Cultural History of the French Enlightenment.* Ithaca, N.Y.: Cornell University Press.

Gossman, Lionel. 1990. *Between History and Literature.* Cambridge, Mass.: Harvard University Press.

Goubert, Pierre, and Daniel Roche. 1991. *Les Français de l'ancient régime.* Vol. 2, *Culture et société.* Paris: Armand Colin.

Goulemot, Jean M., and Daniel Oster. 1992. *Gens de lettres, écrivains et bohèmes: L'imaginaire littéraire, 1630–1900.* Paris: Minerve.

Graburn, Nelson H. H. 1976. *Ethnic and Tourist Arts: Cultural Expressions from the Fourth World.* Berkeley: University of California Press.

Graff, Gerald. 1987. *Professing Literature: An Institutional History.* Chicago: University of Chicago Press.

Grana, Cesar. 1964. *Bohemian versus Bourgeois: French Society and the French Man of Letters in the Nineteenth Century.* New York: Basic Books.

Greenberg, Clement. 1961. *Art and Culture: Critical Essays.* Boston: Beacon Press.

Gribenski, Jean. 1991. "Un métier difficile: Éditeur de musique à Paris sous la révolution." In *Le tambour et la harpe.* In Julien and Mongrédien 1991.

Griswold, Charles L. 1992. "The Vietnam Veterans Memorial and the Washington Mall: Philosophical Thoughts on Political Iconography." In *Art and the Public Sphere,* edited by W. J. T. Mitchell. Chicago: University of Chicago Press.

Grivel, Charles. 1989. "Le provocateur: L'écrivain chez les modernes." In *Écrire en France au XIXme siècle,* edited by Graziella Pagliano and Antonio Gomez-Moriana. Montreal: Le Préambule.

Gropius, Walter. 1965. *The New Architecture and the Bauhaus.* Cambridge, Mass.: MIT Press.

Gruen, Eric S. 1992. *Culture and National Identity in Republican Rome.* Ithaca, N.Y.: Cornell University Press.

Guillory, John. 1993. *Cultural Capital: The Problem of Literary Canon Formation.* Chicago: University of Chicago Press.

Guthrie, Derek. 1988. "The 'Eloquent Object' Gagged by Kitsch." *New Art Examiner* 15 (September): 29.

Guyer, Paul. 1997. *Kant and the Claims of Taste.* Cambridge: Cambridge University Press.

Habermas, Jürgen. (1962) 1989. *The Structural Transformation of the Public Sphere: An Inquiry into a Category of Bourgeois Society.* Cambridge, Mass.: MIT Press.

Hahn, Roger. 1981. "Science and the Arts in France: The Limitations of an Encyclopedic Ideology." In *Studies in Eighteenth-Century Culture.* Vol. 10. Madison: University of Wisconsin Press.

Hall, Michael D., and Eugene W. Metcalf, Jr., eds. 1994. *The Artist Outsider: Creativity and the Boundaries of Culture.* Washington, D.C.: Smithsonian Institution Press.

Halliwell, Stephen. 1989. "Aristotle's Poetics." In G. A. Kennedy 1989.

Hanslick, Eduard. 1986. *On the Musically Beautiful: A Contribution towards the Revision of the Aesthetics of Music.* Indianapolis: Hackett Publishing.

Harth, Erica. 1983. *Ideology and Culture in Seventeenth-Century France.* Ithaca, N.Y.: Cornell University Press.

Haskell, Francis. 1976. *Rediscoveries in Art: Some Aspects of Taste, Fashion and Collecting in England and France.* Ithaca, N.Y.: Cornell University Press.

———. 1980. *Patrons and Painters: Art and Society in Baroque Italy.* New Haven, Conn.: Yale University Press.

Havelock, Eric A. 1963. *Preface to Plato.* Cambridge, Mass.: Harvard University Press.

Hegel, G. W. F. (1823–29) 1975. *Aesthetics: Lectures on Fine Art.* Oxford: Clarendon Press.

Hein, Hilde, and Carolyn Korsmeyer. 1993. *Aesthetics in Feminist Perspective.* Bloomington: Indiana University Press.

Heine, Heinrich. (1830) 1985. *The Romantic School and Other Essays.* New York: Continuum Publishing Co.

Heinich, Nathalie. 1993. *Du peintre à l artiste.* Paris: Minuit.

Helgerson, Richard. 1983. *Self-Crowned Laureates: Spenser, Jonson, Milton and the Literary System.* Berkeley: University of California Press.

Herder, Johann Gottfried. 1955. *Kalligone.* Weimar: Hermann Böhlaus Nachfolger.

Hobbes, Thomas. (1651) 1955. *Leviathan.* Oxford: Basil Blackwell.

Hogarth, William. (1753) 1997. *The Analysis of Beauty,* edited by Ronald Paulson. New Haven, Conn.: Yale University Press.

Hohendahl, Peter Uwe. 1982. *The Institution of Criticism.* Ithaca, N.Y.: Cornell University Press.

———, ed. 1988. *A History of German Literary Criticism, 1730–1980.* Lincoln: University of Nebraska Press.

———. 1989. *Building a National Literature: The Case of Germany 1830–1870.* Ithaca, N.Y.: Cornell University Press.

Holden, Stephen. 1991. "Barry Manilow: Yes, He Still Writes the Songs." *New York Times* October 13, H27.

Honour, Hugh. 1979. *Romanticism.* New York: Harper & Row.

Hooper-Greenhill, Eileen. 1992. *Museums and the Shaping of Knowledge.* London: Routledge.

Huitt, Sue. 1998. "The Art Quilt and Art Museum Exhibits." M.S. thesis, University of Illinois at Springfield.

Hume, David. 1993. *Selected Essays.* Oxford: Oxford University Press.

Hunt, Lynn. 1984. *Politics, Culture, and Class in the French Revolution.* Berkeley: University of California Press.

Iversen, Margaret. 1993. *Alois Riegl: Art History and Theory.* Cambridge, Mass.: MIT Press.

Jacob, Mary Jane, ed. 1995. *Culture in Action: A Public Art Program of Sculpture Chicago Curated by Mary Jane Jacob.* Seattle: Bay Press.

Jacobs, Jane. 1961. *The Death and Life of Great American Cities.* New York: Vintage.

Jaffe, Kineret S. 1992. "The Concept of Genius: Its Changing Role in Eighteenth-Century French Aesthetics." In *Essays on the History of Aesthetics,* edited by Peter Kivy. Rochester, N.Y.: University of Rochester Press.

Jam, Jean-Louis. 1989. "Le clarion de l'avenir." In Julien and Klein 1989.

———. 1991. "Pédagogie musicale et idéologie: Un plan d éducation musicale durant la révolution." In Julien and Mongrédien 1991.

James, Henry. 1986. *The Art of Criticism: Henry James on the Theory and the Practice of Fiction.* Chicago: University of Chicago Press.

Jay, Bill. 1989. "The Family of Man: A Reappraisal of the 'Greatest Exhibition of All Time.'" *INsight* 2:5.

Johnson, James H. 1995. *Listening in Paris: A Cultural History.* Berkeley: University of California Press.

Johnson, Samuel. (1781) 1961. *Lives of the English Poets.* London: Oxford University Press.

———. (1750–52) 1969. *The Rambler.* 3 vols. New Haven, Conn.: Yale University Press.

Jones, Suzi. 1986. "Art by Fiat: Dilemmas of Cross-Cultural Collecting." In *Folk Art and Artworlds,* edited by John Michael Vlach and Simon J. Bronner. Ann Arbor, Mich.: UMI Research Press.

Jonson, Ben. 1616. *The Workes of Benjamin Jonson.* London: William Stansby.

———. (1605) 1978. *Volpone; Or, The Fox,* edited by John W. Creaser. New York: New York University Press.

Jouffroy, Theodore. 1883. *Course d'esthétique.* Paris: Hachette.

Jules-Rosette, Benetta. 1984. *Messages of Tourist Art: An African Semiotic System in Comparative Perspective.* New York: St. Martin's Press.

Julien, Jean-Rémy. 1989. "La Révolution et ses publics." In Julien and Klein 1989.

Julien, Jean-Rémy, and Jean-Claude Klein. 1989. *Orphée phrygien: Les musiques de la Révolution.* Paris: Éditions du May.

Julien, Jean-Rémy, and Jean Mongrédien. 1991. *Le tambour et la harpe: Oeuvres pratiques et manifestations musicales sous la Révolution, 1788–1800.* Paris: Éditions du May.

Jump, Harriet Devine. 1994. *Mary Wollstonecraft: Writer.* New York: Harvester/Wheatsheaf.

Kahn, Douglas. 1993. "The Latest: Fluxus and Music." In *In the Spirit of Fluxus,* edited by Janet Jenkins. Minneapolis: Walker Art Center.

Kames, Henry Home, Lord. 1762. *Elements of Criticism.* London: A. Millar.

Kandinsky, Wassily. (1911) 1977. *Concerning the Spiritual in Art.* New York: Dover Publications.

Kant, Immanuel. 1960. *Observations on the Feeling of the Beautiful and Sublime.* Berkeley: University of California Press.

———. 1987. *Critique of Judgment.* Indianapolis: Hackett.

Kantorowicz, Ernst H. 1961. "The Sovereignty of the Artist: A Note on Legal Maxims and Renaissance Theories of Art." In *Essays in Honor of Erwin Panofsky,* edited by Millard Meiss. New York: New York University Press.

Kaprow, Allan. 1993. *Essays on the Blurring of Art and Life.* Berkeley: University of California Press.

Karp, Ivan, and Steven D. Lavine, eds. 1991. *Exhibiting Cultures: The Poetics and Politics of Museum Display.* Washington, D.C.: Smithsonian Institution Press.

Kasfir, Sidney. 1992. "African Art and Authenticity: A Text with a Shadow." *African Arts* 25:45.

Kelly, Michael. 1996. "Public Art Controversy: The Serra and Lin Cases." *Journal of Aesthetics and Art Criticism* 54:15–22.

Kemp, Martin. 1977. From "'Mimesis' to 'Fantasia': The Quattrocento Vocabulary of Creation, Inspiration and Genius in the Visual Arts." *Viator* 8:383–97.

———. 1997. *Behind the Picture: Art and Evidence in the Italian Renaissance.* New Haven, Conn.: Yale University Press.

Kempers, Bram. 1992. *Painting, Power and Patronage: The Rise of the Professional Artist in the Italian Renaissance.* London: Penguin.

Kennedy, Emmet. 1989. *A Cultural History of the French Revolution.* New Haven, Conn.: Yale University Press.

Kennedy, George A., ed. 1989. *The Cambridge History of Literary Criticism.* Vol. 1, *Classical Criticism.* Cambridge: Cambridge University Press.

Kernan, Alvin B. 1982. *The Imaginary Library: An Essay on Literature and Society.* Princeton, N.J.: Princeton University Press.

———. 1989. *Samuel Johnson and the Impact of Print.* Princeton, N.J.: Princeton University Press.

———. 1990. *The Death of Literature.* New Haven, Conn.: Yale University Press.

———. 1995. *Shakespeare, the King's Playwright: Theater in the Stuart Court, 1603–1613.* New Haven, Conn.: Yale University Press.

Kimpel, Dieter. 1986. "La sociogenèse de l'architecte moderne." In *Artistes, artisans et production artistique au moyen age,* edited by Xavier Barral i Altet. Paris: Picard.

Kivy, Peter. 1993. "Differences." *Journal of Aesthetics and Art Criticism* 51:2123–32.

Klein, Lawrence E. 1994. *Shaftesbury and the Culture of Politeness: Moral Discourse and Cultural Politics in Early Eighteenth-Century England.* Cambridge: Cambridge University Press.

Klein, Robert. 1979. *Form and Meaning: Essays on the Renaissance and Modern Art.* New York: Viking.

Knight, Richard Payne. 1808. *An Analytical Inquiry into the Principles of Taste.* London: T. Payne & J. White.

Koerner, Joseph Leo. 1993. *The Moment of Self-Portraiture in German Renaissance Art.* Chicago: University of Chicago Press.

Korsmeyer, Carolyn. 1999. *Making Sense of Taste.* Ithaca, N.Y.: Cornell University Press.

Kostelanetz, Richard. 1996. *John Cage (Ex)plain(ed).* New York: Schirmer Books.

Kostof, Spiro, ed. 1977. *The Architect: Chapters in the History of the Profession.* Oxford: Oxford University Press.

Kristeller, Paul Oskar. (1950) 1990. *Renaissance Thought and the Arts.* Princeton, N.J.: Princeton University Press.

Kruft, Hanno-Walter. 1994. *A History of Architectural Theory: From Vitruvius to the Present.* Princeton, N.J.: Princeton University Press.

Kuenzli, Rudolf E., and Francis M. Naumann. 1990. *Marcel Duchamp: Artist of the Century.* Cambridge, Mass.: MIT Press.

Kulka, Tomas. 1996. *Kitsch and Art.* University Park: Pennsylvania State University Press.

Lacombe, Jacques. 1752. *Dictionnaire portatif des beaux-arts, ou abrégé de ce qui concern l'architecture, la sculpture, la peinture, la graveur, la poésie et la musique.* Paris: Estienne & Fils.

Lacy, Suzanne, ed. 1995. *Mapping the Terrain: New Genre Public Art.* Seattle: Bay Press.

Lambert, Anne-Thérèse de. (1747) 1990. *Oeuvres,* edited by Robert Granderoute. Paris: Librairie Honoré Champion.

Laurie, Bruce. 1989. *Artisans into Workers: Labor in Nineteenth-Century America.* New York: Farrar, Straus & Giroux.

Le Corbusier. (1923) 1986. *Towards a New Architecture.* New York: Dover Publications.

Leddy, Thomas. 1995. "Everyday Surface Aesthetic Qualities: 'Neat,' 'Messy,' 'Clean,' 'Dirty.'" *Journal of Aesthetics and Art Criticism* 53:259–68.

Lee, Renselaer. 1967. *Ut Pictura Poesis: The Humanistic Theory of Painting.* New York: W. W. Norton.

Le Huray, Peter, and James Day, eds. 1988. *Music and Aesthetics in the Eighteenth and Early-Nineteenth Centuries.* Cambridge: Cambridge University Press.

Leibniz, Gottfried Wilhelm. 1951. *Selections.* New York: Charles Scribner's Sons.

———. 1969. *Philosophical Papers and Letters.* Dordrecht: D. Reidel.

Lentricchia, Frank. 1996. "Last Will and Testament of an Ex–Literary Critic." *Lingua Franca* 6:59–67.

Leonard, George J. 1994. *Into the Light of Things: The Art of the Commonplace from Wordsworth to John Cage.* Chicago: University of Chicago Press.

Lessing, Gotthold Ephraim. 1987. *Laokoon: Oder über die grenzen der malerei und poesie.* Stuttgart: Philipp Reclam.

Levine, Lawrence W. 1988. *Highbrow/Lowbrow: The Emergence of Cultural Hierarchy in America.* Cambridge, Mass.: Harvard University Press.

Levinson, Jerrold. 1993. "Extending Art Historically." *Journal of Aesthetics and Art Criticism* 51:411–24.

Link, Anne-Marie. 1992. "The Social Practice of Taste in Late Eighteenth-Century Germany: A Case Study." *Oxford Art Journal* 15, no.2: 3–14.

Lippman, Edward. 1992. *A History of Western Musical Aesthetics.* Lincoln: University of Nebraska Press.

Lodder, Christina. 1983. *Russian Constructivism.* New Haven, Conn.: Yale University Press.

Loewenstein, Joseph. 1985. "The Script in the Marketplace." *Representations* 12 (Fall): 106.

Lough, John. 1957. *Paris Theatre Audiences in the Seventeenth and Eighteenth Centuries.* London: Oxford University Press.

———. 1978. *Writer and Public in France: From the Middle Ages to the Present Day.* Oxford: Clarendon Press.

Lucie-Smith, Edward. 1984. *The Story of Craft: The Craftsman's Role in Society.* New York: Van Nostrand Reinhold.

Lyotard, Jean-François. 1991. *Leçons sur l'analytique du sublime.* Paris: Galilée.

Malebranche, Nicolas. 1970. *Oeuvres complètes.* Paris: J. Vrin.

Mandeville, Bernard. 1729. *The Fable of the Bees; Or, Private Vices, Publick Benefits.* Vol. 2. London: J. Roberts.

Manhart, Marcia, and Tom Manhart, eds. 1987. *The Eloquent Object: The Evolution of American Art in Craft Media since 1945.* Tulsa, Okla.: Philbrook Museum of Art.

Mantion, Jean-Rémy. 1988. "Déroutes de l'art: La destination de l'oeuvre d'art et le débat sur le musée." In *La Carmagnole des Muses,* edited by Jean-Claude Bonnet. Paris: Armand Colin.

Margolis, Joseph. 1993. "Exorcising the Dreariness of Aesthetics." *Journal of Aesthetics and Art Criticism* 51:133–40.

Marino, Adrian. 1996. *The Biography of the "Idea of Literature": From Antiquity to the Baroque.* Albany: State University of New York Press.

Marmontel, Jean-François. (1787) 1846. *Élements de littérature.* Paris: Firmin-Didot.

Marotti, Arthur P. 1986. *John Donne: Coterie Poet.* Madison: University of Wisconsin Press.

———. 1991. "The Transmission of Lyric Poetry and the Institutionalizing of Literature in the English Renaissance." In Logan and Rudnytsky 1991.

Marshall, David. 1988. *The Surprising Effects of Sympathy.* Chicago: University of Chicago Press.

Martin, John. 1997. "Inventing Sincerity, Refashioning Prudence: The Discovery of the Individual in Renaissance Europe." *American Historical Review* 102:1309–42.

Marx, Karl. 1975. *Karl Marx: Early Writings.* Introduction by Lucio Colletti. Harmondsworth: Penguin.

Marx, Karl, and Frederick Engels. 1970. *The German Ideology: Part One,* edited by C. J. Arthur. New York: International Publishers.

Mattick, Paul, Jr., ed. 1993. *Eighteenth-Century Aesthetics and the Reconstruction of Art.* Cambridge: Cambridge University Press.

McClellan, Andrew. 1994. *Inventing the Louvre: Art, Politics, and the Origins of the Modern Museum in Eighteenth-Century Paris.* Cambridge: Cambridge University Press.

McCormick, Peter J. 1990. *Modernity, Aesthetics, and the Bounds of Art.* Ithaca, N.Y.: Cornell University Press.

McKendrick, Neil. 1961. "Josiah Wedgwood and Factory Discipline." *Historical Journal* 4, no. 1:30–55.

McKendrick, Neil, John Brewer, and J. H. Plumb. 1982. *The Birth of a Consumer Society: The Commercialization of Eighteenth-Century England.* Bloomington: Indiana University Press.

McMorris, Penny, and Michael Kile. 1986. *The Art Quilt.* San Francisco: Quilt Digest Press.

Melville, Stephen, and Bill Readings, eds. 1995. *Vision and Textuality.* Durham, N.C.: Duke University Press.

Meyer, Richard. 1987. "The Common Cause." *Ceramics Monthly* 35:21.

Mill, John Stuart. 1965. *Mill's Essays on Literature and Society,* edited by J. B. Schneewind. New York: Collier Books.

Miller, Edwin Haviland. 1959. *The Professional Writer in Elizabethan England.* Cambridge, Mass.: Harvard University Press.

Miller, Naomi J., and Gary Waller. 1991. *Reading Mary Wroth: Representing Alternatives in Early Modern England.* Knoxville: University of Tennessee Press.

Mitchell, W. J. T. 1992. *Art and the Public Sphere.* Chicago: University of Chicago Press.

Mondrian, Piet. (1920) 1986. *The New Art—the New Life: The Collected Writings of Piet Mondrian,* edited by Harry Holtzman and Martin James. Boston: G. K. Hall.

Mongrédien, Jean. 1986. *La musique en France des lumières au romantisme (1789–1830).* Paris: Flammarion.

Montias, John Michael. 1982. *Artists and Artisans in Delft.* Princeton, N.J.: Princeton University Press.

Moreno, Paolo. 1996. "Painters and Society." In Turner 1996.

Moritz, Karl Philipp. 1962. *Schriften zur Äesthetik und Poetik.* Tübingen: Max Niemeyer.

Morris, William. 1948. *William Morris: Stories in Prose, Stories in Verse, Shorter Poems, Lectures and Essays,* edited by G. D. H. Cole. London: Nonesuch Press.

———. 1969. *Unpublished Lectures of William Morris,* edited by Eugene D. LeMire. Detroit: Wayne State University Press.

Mortensen, Prebend. 1997. *Art in the Social Order: The Making of the Modern Conception of Art.* Albany: State University of New York Press.

Mortier, Roland. 1982. *L'orgininalité: Une nouvelle catégorie esthétique au siècle des limières.* Geneva: Droz.

Motherwell, Robert. 1989. *The Dada Painters and Poets: An Anthology.* Cambridge, Mass.: Harvard University Press.

Moxey, Keith. 1994 *The Practice of Theory: Poststructuralism, Cultural Politics, and Art History.* Ithaca, N.Y.: Cornell University Press.

Muir, Kenneth. 1960. *Shakespeare as Collaborator.* London: Methuen.

Murray, Timothy. 1987. *Theatrical Legitimation: Allegories of Genius in Seventeenth-Century England and France.* New York: Oxford University Press.

Nagy, Gregory. 1989. "Early Greek Views of Poets and Poetry." In G. A. Kennedy 1989.

Nakov, Andrei B. 1983. *The First Russian Show: A Commemoration of the Van Diemen Exhibition, Berlin, 1922.* London: Annely Juda Fine Art.

Naylor, Gillian. 1968. *The Bauhaus.* London: Studio Vista.

———. 1990. *The Arts and Crafts Movement: A Study of Its Sources, Ideals and Influence on Design Theory.* London: Trefoil Publications.

Neils, Jenifer, ed. 1992. *Goddess and Polis: The Panathenaic Festival in Ancient Athens.* Princeton, N.J.: Princeton University Press.

Newhall, Beaumont, ed. 1980. *Photography: Essays and Images.* New York: Museum of Modern Art.

———. 1982. *History of Photography.* New York: Museum of Modern Art.

Newhouse, Victoria. 1998. *Towards a New Museum.* New York: Monacelli Press.

Nietzsche, Friedrich. 1967. *The Will to Power.* New York: Random House.

Norton, Robert E. 1991. *Herder's Aesthetics and the European Enlightenment.* Ithaca, N.Y.: Cornell University Press.

Nuridsany, Michel, ed. 1993. *Daniel Buren au Palais-Royal: "Les deux plateaux."* Villeurbanne: Art Edition, Nouveau Musée/Institut.

Nussbaum, Martha C. 1986. *The Fragility of Goodness: Luck and Ethics in Greek Tragedy and Philosophy.* Cambridge: Cambridge University Press.

———. 1996. "Greek Aesthetics." In Turner 1996, vol. 1.

Nyman, Michael. 1974. *Experimental Music: Cage and Beyond.* New York: Schirmer Books.

O'Dea, Michael. 1995. *Jean-Jacques Rousseau: Music, Illusion and Desire.* New York: St. Martin's Press.

Oguibe, Olu, and Okwui Enzwezor, eds. 1999. *Reading the Contemporary: African Art from Theory to the Marketplace.* Cambridge, Mass.: MIT Press.

Olin, Margaret. 1993. *Forms of Representation in Alois Riegl's Theory of Art.* University Park: Pennsylvania State University Press.

Ozouf, Mona. 1988. *Festivals and the French Revolution.* Cambridge, Mass.: Harvard University Press.

Panofsky, Erwin. 1968. *Idea: A Concept in Art Theory.* Columbia: University of South Carolina.

Paoletti, John T., and Gary M. Radke. 1997. *Art in Renaissance Italy.* New York: Harry N. Abrams.

Parker, Roziska. 1984. *The Subversive Stitch: Embroidery and the Making of the Feminine.* London: Women's Press.

Parker, Roziska, and Griselda Pollock. 1981. *Old Mistresses: Women, Art and Ideology.* New York: Pantheon.

Pascal, Blaise. 1958. *Pensées.* Paris: Garnier.

Pater, Walter. (1873) 1912. *The Renaissance: Studies in Art and Poetry.* London: Macmillan & Co.

Patey, Douglas Lane. 1988. "The Eighteenth Century Invents the Canon." In *Modern Language Studies* 18:17–37.

Patterson, Annabel. 1989. *Shakespeare and the Popular Voice.* Oxford: Basil Blackwell.

Paulson, Ronald. 1991–93. *Hogarth.* Vol. 1, *The "Modern Moral Subject," 1697–1732;* vol. 2, *High Art and Low, 1732–1750;* vol. 3, *Art and Politics* . New Brunswick, N.J.: Rutgers University Press.

——— 1996. *The Beautiful, Novel, and Strange: Aesthetics and Heterodoxy.* Baltimore: Johns Hopkins University Press.

Pears, Iain. 1988. *The Discovery of Painting: The Growth of Interest in the Arts in England, 1680–1768.* New Haven, Conn.: Yale University Press.

Pelles, Geraldine. 1963. *Art, Artists and Society: Origins of a Modern Dilemma, Painting in England and France, 1750–1850.* Englewood Cliffs, N.J.: Prentice-Hall.

Perrault, Charles. 1971. *Parallèl des anciens et des modèrnes.* Geneva: Slatkine Reprints.

Pevsner, Nikolas. 1940. *Academies of Art, Past and Present.* Cambridge: Cambridge University Press.

Phillips, Christopher. 1989. "The Judgment Seat of Photography." In Bolton 1989.

———, ed. 1991. *Photography in the Modern Era: European Documents and Critical Writings, 1913–1940.* New York: Metropolitan Museum of Art and Aperture.

Piles, Roger de. (1708) 1969. *Cours de peinture par principes.* Paris: Jacques Estienne.

Plumb, J. H. 1972. "The Public, Literature and the Arts in the Eighteenth Century." In *The Triumph of Culture: Eighteenth-Century Perspectives,* edited by Paul Fritz and David Williams. Toronto: A. M. Hakkert.

Pollitt, J. J. 1974. *The Ancient View of Greek Art.* New Haven, Conn.: YaleUniversity Press.

Pomian, Krystoff. 1987. *Collectors and Curiosities: Paris and Venice, 1500–1800.* Oxford: Polity Press.

Pommier, Edouard. 1988. "Idéologie et musée à l'époque révolutionnaire." In *Les images de la Révolution,* edited by Michel Vovelle. Paris: Publications de la Sorbonne.

———. 1991. *L'art de la liberté: Doctrines et débats de la Révolution française.* Paris: Gallimard.

Porter, Roy. 1990. *English Society in the Eighteenth Century.* Harmondsworth: Penguin.

Postle, Kathleen R. 1978. *The Chronicle of the Overbeck Pottery.* Indianapolis: Indiana Historical Society.

Preziosi, Donald. 1989. *Rethinking Art History: Meditations on a Coy Science.* New Haven, Conn.: Yale University Press.

Price, Sally. 1989. *Primitive Art in Civilized Places.* Chicago: University of Chicago Press.

Quatremère de Quincy, Antoine-Chrysostome. (1815) 1989a. *Considérations morales sur la destination des ouvrages de l'art.* Paris: Fayard.

———. (1796) 1989b. *Lettres à Miranda sur les déplacements des monuments de l'art de l'Italie,* edited by Edouard Pommier. Paris: Macula.

Raczymow, Henri. 1994. *La mort du grand écrivan: Essai sur la fin de la littérature.* Paris: Stock.

Raven, Arlene. 1989. *Art in the Public Interest.* Ann Arbor, Mich.: UMI Research Press.

Raynor, Henry. 1978. *A Social History of Music: From the Middle Ages to Beethoven.* New York: Taplinger.

Reiss, Timothy J. 1992. *The Meaning of Literature.* Ithaca, N.Y.: Cornell University Press.

Reynolds, Joshua. (1770) 1975. *Discourses on Art.* New Haven, Conn.: Yale University Press.

Richards, Charles R. 1927. *Industrial Art and the Museum.* New York: Macmillan Co.

Richter, Hans. 1965. *Dada: Art and Anti-Art.* New York: Oxford University Press.

Riegl, Alois. 1985. *Late Roman Art Industry.* Rome: Giorgio Bretschneider.

Robertson, Cheryl. 1999. *Frank Lloyd Wright and George Mann Niedecken: Prairie School Collaborators.* Milwaukee, Wis.: Milwaukee Art Museum.

Robertson, Claire. 1992. *"Il Grande Cardinale," Alessandro Farnese, Patron of the Arts.* New Haven, Conn.: Yale University Press.

Robertson, Thomas. (1784) 1971. *An Inquiry into the Fine Arts.* New York: Garland Publishing.

Robinet, Jean-Baptiste. 1776. *Supplément à l'"Encyclopédie.* 4 vols. Amsterdam: M. M. Rey.

Robinson, Philip E. J. 1984. *Jean-Jacques Rousseau's Doctrine of the Arts.* Berne: Peter Lang.

Roochnik, David. 1996. *Of Art and Wisdom: Plato's Understanding of Techne.* University Park: Pennsylvania State University Press.

Rose, Margaret A. 1984. *Marx's Lost Aesthetic: Karl Marx and the Visual Arts.* Cambridge: Cambridge University Press.

Rosenau, Helen. 1974. *Boullée and Visionary Architecture.* London: Academy Editions.

Rosenfeld, Myra Nan. 1977. "The Royal Building Administration in France from Charles V to Louis XIV." In Kostof 1977.

Ross, Doran H., and Raphael X. Reichert. 1983. "Modern Antiquities: A Study of a Kumase Workshop." In *Akan Transformations: Problems in Ghanian Art History,* edited by Doran H. Ross and Timothy F. Garrard. Los Angeles: Museum of Cultural History, University of California, Los Angeles.

Rougemont, Martine de. 1988. *La vie théâtrale en France au xviiie siècle.* Paris: Champion-Slatkine.

Rossi, Paolo. 1970. *Philosophy, Technology and the Arts in the Early Modern Era.* New York: Harper & Row.

Rousseau, Jean-Jacques. 1954. *Du contrat social.* Paris: Garnier.

———. (1762) 1957. *Émile, ou de l éducation.* Paris: Garnier.

———. 1960. *Politics and the Arts: Letter to d'Alembert on the Theater.* Glencoe, Ill.: Free Press.

———. (1768) 1969. *Dictionnaire de musique.* New York: Johnson Reprints. ().

———. 1979. *Emile; Or, On Education.* New York: Basic Books.

———. (1761) 1997. *Julie, or the New Heloise.* Hanover, N.H.: University Press of New England.

———. 1992. *Discourse on the Origins of Inequality.* Hanover, N.H.: University Press of New England.

Rudnytsky, Peter L. 1991. "More's History of King Richard II as an Uncanny Text." In *Contending Kingdoms: Historical, Psychological, and Feminist Approaches to the Literature of Sixteenth-Century England and France,* edited by Marie-Rose Logan and Peter L. Rudnytsky. Detroit: Wayne State University Press.

Ruff, Dale. 1983. "Towards a Postmodern Pottery." *Ceramics Monthly* 31:48.

Ruskin, John. 1985. *Unto This Last, and Other Writings.* Harmondsworth: Penguin.

———. 1996. *Lectures on Art.* New York: Allworth Press.

Rybczynski, Witold. 1994. "A Truly Important Place: The Abundant Public Architecture of Robert Mills." *Times Literary Supplement* (November 11), 3.

Sagne, Jean. 1982. *Delacroix et la photographie.* Paris: Herscher.

Saisselin, Remy G. 1970. *The Rule of Reason and the Ruses of the Heart.* Cleveland: Case Western Reserve University Press.

———. 1992. *The Enlightenment against the Baroque: Economics and Aesthetics in the Eighteenth Century.* Berkeley: University of California Press.

Saito, Yuriko. 1998. "Japanese Aesthetics." In *Encyclopedia of Aesthetics,* edited by Michael Kelly. New York: Oxford University Press, 1998.

———. 1999. "Art-Based Aesthetics vs. Everyday Aesthetics." Paper presented at the annual meeting of the American Society for Aesthetics, Washington, D.C., October 30.
Salmen, Walter. 1983. *The Social Status of the Professional Musician from the Middle Ages to the Nineteenth Century.* New York: Pendragon Press.
Sanouillet, Michel, and Elmer Peterson. 1973. *The Writings of Marcel Duchamp.* New York: Da Capo Press.
Sartwell, Crispin. 1995. *The Art of Living: Aesthetics of the Ordinary in World Spiritual Traditions.* Albany: State University of New York Press.
Sayre, Henry M. 1989. *The Object of Performance: The American Avant-Garde since 1970.* Chicago: University of Chicago Press.
Scarry, Elaine. 2000. *On Beauty and Being Just.* Princeton, N.J.: Princeton University Press.
Schaeffer, Jean-Marie. 1992. *L'art de l'âge moderne.* Paris: Gallimard.
———. 1996. *Les célibataires de l'art: Pour une esthétique sans mythes.* Paris: Gallimard.
Schapiro, Meyer. 1977. *Romanesque Art.* New York: George Braziller.
Scharf, Aaron. 1986. *Art and Photography.* New York: Viking Penguin.
Schelling, F. W. J. (1800) 1978. *System of Transcendental Idealism.* Charlottesville: Univerity Press of Virginia.
Schiller, Friedrich. 1967. *On the Aesthetic Education of Man: In a Series of Letters.* Oxford: Clarendon Press.
Schlanger, Judith E. 1977. "Le peuple au front grave." In Ehrard and Viallaneix 1977.
Schmidgall, Gary. 1990. *Shakespeare and the Poet's Life.* Lexington: University Press of Kentucky.
Schmiechen, James A. 1995. "Reconsidering the Factory, Art-Labor, and the Schools of Design in Nineteenth-Century Britain." In *Design History: An Anthology,* edited by Dennis P. Doordan. Cambridge, Mass.: MIT Press.
Schoenberg, Arnold. (1947) 1975. *Style and Idea: Selected Writings of Arnold Schoenberg.* New York: St. Martin's Press.
Scholes, Robert. 1998. *The Rise and Fall of English: Reconstructing English as a Discipline.* New Haven, Conn.: Yale University Press.
Schopenhauer, Arthur. 1969. *The World as Will and Representation.* 2 vols. New York: Dover Publications.
Schueller, Herbert M. 1988. *The Idea of Music: An Introduction to Musical Aesthetics in Antiquity and the Middle Ages.* Kalamazoo, Mich.: Medieval Institute Publications.
Schulte-Sasse, Jochen. 1988. "The Concept of Literary Criticism in German Romanticism, 1795–1810." In Hohendahl 1988.
Schwartz, Elliott, and Barney Childs. 1998. *Contemporary Composers on Contemporary Music.* New York: Da Capo Press.
Schwarz, Heinrich. 1987. *Art and Photography: Forerunners and Influences.* Chicago: University of Chicago Press.
Schweiger, Werner J. 1984. *Wiener Werkstaette: Design in Vienna, 1903–1932.* New York: Abbeville Press.
Scott, Joan Wallach. 1974. *The Glassworkers of Carmaux.* Cambridge, Mass.: Harvard University Press.
Searle, John R. 1995. *The Construction of Social Reality.* New York: Free Press.
Seldes, Gilbert. (1924) 1957. *The Seven Lively Arts.* New York: Sagamore Press.

Semper, Gottfried. 1989. *The Four Elements of Architecture and Other Writings.* Cambridge: Cambridge University Press.

Senie, Harriet F. 1992. *Contemporary Public Sculpture: Tradition, Transformation and Controversy.* New York: Oxford University Press.

Shaftesbury, Anthony, Earl of. (1711) 1963. *Characteristics of Men, Manners, Opinions, Times, etc.* Gloucester, Mass.: Peter Smith.

Shapin, Steven. 1996. *The Scientific Revolution.* Chicago: University of Chicago Press.

Shapiro, H. A. 1992. "Mousikoi Agones: Music and Poetry at the Panathenaia." In Neils 1988.

Shapiro, Meyer. 1977. *Romanesque Art.* New York: George Braziller.

Shelley, Percy Bysshe. 1930. *The Complete Works.* 10 vols. New York: Charles Scribner's Sons.

Shiff, Richard. 1988. "Phototropism (Figuring the Proper)." *INsight* 1:2–3, 19–34.

Shiner, Larry. 1988. *The Secret Mirror: Literary Form and History in Tocqueville's "Recollections."* Ithaca, N.Y.: Cornell University Press.

———. 1994. "'Primitive Fakes,' 'Tourist Art,' and the Ideology of Authenticity." *Journal of Aesthetics and Art Criticism* 52:225–34.

Shroder, Maurice A. 1961. *Icarus: The Image of the Artist in French Romanticism.* Cambridge, Mass.: Harvard University Press.

Shusterman, Richard. 1993. "Of the Scandal of Taste: Social Privilege as Nature in the Aesthetic Theories of Hume and Kant." In Mattick 1993.

———. 2000. *Pragmatist Aesthetics: Living Beauty, Rethinking Art.* Lanham, Md.: Rowman & Littlefield.

Slivka, Rose. 1978. *Peter Voulkos: A Dialogue with Clay.* New York: Little, Brown.

Smith, Ralph A., and Ronald Berman, eds. 1992. *Public Policy and the Aesthetic Interest.* Urbana: University of Illinois Press.

Smithson, Isaiah, and Nancy Ruff. 1994. *English Studies/Culture Studies: Institutionalizing Dissent.* Urbana: University of Illinois Press.

Soboul, Albert. 1977. "Préambule." In Ehrard and Viallaneix 1977.

Solkin, David. 1992. *Painting for Money: The Visual Arts and the Public Sphere in Eighteenth-Century England.* New Haven, Conn.: Yale University Press.

Solomon-Godeau, Abigail. 1991. *Photography at the Dock: Essays on Photographic History, Institutions and Practices.* Minneapolis: University of Minnesota Press.

Sommer, Hubert. 1950. "A propos du mot 'Génie.'" In *ZeItschrift fürRomanische Philologie* 66:1.

Sonneck, Oscar. 1954. *Beethoven: Impressions by His Contemporaries.* New York: Dover.

Soussloff, Catherine. 1997. *The Absolute Artist: The Historiography of a Concept.* Minneapolis: University of Minnesota Press.

Spencer, Herbert. (1872) 1881. *Principles of Psychology.* 2 vols. London: Williams & Norgate

Spingarn, J. E., ed. 1968. *Critical Essays of the Seventeenth Century.* 3 vols. Bloomington: Indiana University Press.

Spivey, Nigel. 1996. *Understanding Greek Sculpture: Ancient Meanings, Modern Readings.* London: Thames & Hudson.

Staël, Germaine de. (1807) 1987. *Corrine, or Italy.* New Brunswick N.J.: Rutgers University Press.

Stansky, Peter. 1985. *Redesigning the World: William Morris, the 1880s and the Arts and Crafts Movement.* Princeton, N.J.: Princeton University Press.

Steegman, John. 1970. *Victorian Taste: A Study of the Arts and Architecture from 1830–1870.* London: Nelson.

Steiner, Christopher B. 1994. *African Art in Transit.* Cambridge: Cambridge University Press.

Stieglitz, Alfred. (1899) 1980. "Pictorial Photography." In Newhall 1980.

Strand, Paul. 1981. "The Art Motive in Photography." In Goldberg 1981.

Stravinsky, Igor. 1947. *Poetics of Music in the Form of Six Lessons.* New York: Vintage Books.

Strunk, Oliver, ed. 1950. *Source Readings in Music History: From Classical Antiquity through the Romantic Era.* New York: W. W. Norton.

Summers, David. 1987. *The Judgment of Sense: Renaissance Naturalism and the Rise of Aesthetics.* Cambridge: Cambridge University Press.

———. 1981. *Michelangelo and the Language of Art.* Princeton, N.J.: Princeton University Press.

Sweeney, Kevin. 1998. "Alexander Gerard." In *Encyclopedia of Aesthetics,* edited by Michael Kelly. New York: Oxford University Press.

Szarkowski, John. 1973. *From the Picture Press.* New York: Museum of Modern Art.

Tatarkiewicz, Wladyslaw. 1964. "The Historian's Concern with the Future." In *British Journal of Aesthetics* 4:246–47.

———. 1970. *History of Aesthetics.* Vol. 1, *Ancient Aesthetics.* The Hague: Mouton.

Teige, Karel. 1989. "The Tasks of Modern Photography." In Phillips 1989.

Thompson, E. P. 1976. *William Morris: Romantic to Revolutionary.* New York: Pantheon Books.

Tigerstedt, E. N. 1968. "The Poet as Creator: Origins of a Metaphor." *Comparative Literature Studies* 5:474–87.

Tolstoy, Leo. 1996. *What Is Art?* Indianapolis: Hackett Publishing.

Tomkins, Calvin. 1989. *Merchants and Masterpieces: The Story of the Metropolitan Museum.* New York: Henry Holt.

Tompkins, Jane P. 1980. *Reader-Response Criticism: From Formalism to Post-Structuralism.* Baltimore: Johns Hopkins University Press.

Torgovnick, Marianna. 1990. *Gone Primitive: Savage Intellects, Modern Lives.* Chicago: University of Chicago Press.

Townsend, Dabney. 1988. "Archibald Alison: Aesthetic Experience and Emotion." *British Journal of Aesthetics* 28:132–44.

Trousson, Raymond, and Frédéric S. Eigeldinger, eds. 1996. *Dictionnaire de Jean-Jacques Rousseau.* Paris: Honoré Champion.

Turner, Jane, ed. 1996. *The Dictionary of Art.* 34 vols. New York: Grove's Dictionaries.

Turner, A. Richard. 1997. *Renaissance Florence: The Invention of a New Art.* New York: Harry N. Abrams.

Upton, Dell. 1998. *Architecture in the United States.* Oxford: Oxford University Press.

Vasari, Giorgio. 1965. *Lives of the Artists.* Vol. 1. London: Penguin.

———. 1991a. *Le vite dei piu eccellenti pittori, scultori e architetti.* Rome: Newton Compton.

———. 1991b. *Lives of the Artists,* translated by Julia Conaway Bondanella and Peter Bondanella. Oxford: Oxford University Press.

Vergo, Peter. 1989. *The New Museology.* London: Reaktion Books.

Venturi, Robert. 1966. *Complexity and Contradiction in Modern Architecture.* New York: Museum of Modern Art.

Vernant, Jean Pierre. 1991. *Mortals and Immortals: Collected Essays.* Princeton, N.J.: Princeton University Press.

Viala, Alain. 1985. *Naissance de l'écrivain: Sociologie de la littérature à l'age classique.* Paris: Minuit.

Vlach, John Michael. 1991. "The Wrong Stuff." *New Art Examiner* 18 (September): 22–24.

Vogel, Susan. 1991. *Africa Explores: Twentieth-Century African Art.* New York: Prestel.

———. 1997. *African Art Western Eyes.* New Haven, Conn.: Yale University Press.

Wall, Wendy. 1993. *The Imprint of Gender: Authorship and Publication in the English Renaissance.* Ithaca, N.Y.: Cornell University Press.

Warner, Eric, and Graham Hough. 1983. *Strangeness and Beauty: An Anthology of Aesthetic Criticism, 1840–1910.* Cambridge: Cambridge University Press.

Warnke, Martin. 1980. *Peter Paul Rubens: Life and Work.* Woodbury, N.Y.: Barron's Educational Series.

———. 1993. *The Court Artist: On the Ancestry of the Modern Artist.* Cambridge: Cambridge University Press.

Watelet, Claude-Henri. 1788. *Encyclopédie méthodique.* Paris: Panckoucke.

Weber, William. 1975. *Music and the Middle Class: The Social Structure of Concert Life in London, Paris and Vienna.* New York: Holmes & Meier.

Welch, Evelyn. 1997. *Art and Society in Italy, 1350–1500.* Oxford: Oxford University Press.

Wellek, Rene. 1982. *The Attack on Literature and Other Essays.* Charlottesville: University of North Carolina Press.

Weston, Edward. 1981. "Daybooks." In Goldberg 1981.

Weyergraf-Serra, Clara, and Martha Buskirk, eds. 1991. *The Destruction of "Tilted Arc": Documents.* Cambridge, Mass.: MIT Press.

White, Harrison C., and Cynthia A. White. 1965. *Canvases and Careers: Institutional Change in the French Painting World.* New York: John Wiley.

White, Harry. 1997. "If It's Baroque Don't Fix It: Reflections on Lydia Goehr's 'Work Concept' and the Historical Integrity of Musical Composition." *Acta Musicologia* 69:94–105.

White, Hayden. 1987. *The Content of the Form: Narrative Discourse and Historical Representation.* Baltimore: Johns Hopkins University Press.

Whitehill, Walter Muir. 1970. *Museum of Fine Arts, Boston: A Centennial History.* Vol. 1. Cambridge, Mass.: Harvard University Press.

Whitford, Frank. 1984. *Bauhaus.* London: Thames & Hudson.

Whitney, Elspeth. 1990. *Paradise Restored: The Mechanical Arts from Antiquity through the Thirteenth Century.* Philadelphia: American Philosophical Society.

Widdowson, Peter. 1999. *Literature.* London: Routledge.

Wilkinson, Catherine. 1977. "The New Professionalism in the Renaissance." In Kostof 1977.

Williams, Raymond. 1976. *Keywords: A Vocabulary of Culture and Society.* New York: Oxford University Press.

Wilton-Ely, John. 1977. "The Rise of the Professional Architect in England." In Kostoff 1977.

Winckelman, Johann Joachim. (1764) 1880. *The History of Ancient Art.* Boston: J. R. Osgood.

Winkler, John J., and Froma I. Zeitlin, eds. 1990. *Nothing to Do with Dionysus?* Princeton, N.J.: Princeton University Press.

Witte, Bernd. 1991. *Walter Benjamin: An Intellectual Biography.* Detroit: Wayne State University Press.

Wolin, Richard. 1994. *Walter Benjamin: An Aesthetic of Redemption.* Berkeley: University of California Press.

Wollstonecraft, Mary. 1989. *The Works of Mary Wollstonecraft.* 7 vols. New York: New York University Press.

Woodmansee, Martha. 1994. *The Author, Art, and the Market: Rereading the History of Aesthetics.* New York: Columbia University Press.

Woods-Marsden, Joanna. 1998. *Renaissance Self-Portraiture: The Visual Construction of Identity and the Social Status of the Artist.* New Haven, Conn.: Yale University Press.

Wordsworth, William. (1850) 1959. *The Prelude or Growth of a Poet's Mind.* Oxford: Clarendon Press.

———. 1977. *The Poems.* 2 vols. New Haven, Conn.: Yale University Press.

Wotton, William. (1694) 1968. *Reflections upon Ancient and Modern Learning.* Hildesheim: Georg Olms Reprint.

Young, Edward. 1759. *Conjectures on Original Composition.* London: Millar & Dodsley.

Zilsel, Edgar. 1993. *Le génie: Histoire d'une notion de l'antiquité à la Renaissance.* Paris: Minuit.

Zola, Émile. (1877) 1965. *L'assommoir.* Paris: Fasquelle.

———. (1877) 1995. *L'assommoir.* Oxford: Oxford University Press.

# Index

*Italicized page numbers indicate figures.*

www.ingramcontent.com/pod-product-compliance
Lightning Source LLC
LaVergne TN
LVHW041103080826
845145LV00007B/1680

* 9 7 8 0 2 2 6 7 5 3 4 3 0 *